DANTE GABRIEL ROSSETTI

HIS FAMILY-LETTERS

WITH A MEMOIR

BY

WILLIAM MICHAEL ROSSETTI

MANUS ANIMAM PINXIT

VOL. II.

LONDON

ELLIS AND ELVEY

1895

FRANCES M. L. ROSSETTI.

FAMILY-LETTERS.

LIST OF PORTRAITS Etc.
VOL. II.

ERRATA.

Vol. II.

Page 3, line 2. *for* fifteenth *read* fourteenth
,, 34 ,, 14, *after* may have been *add* the most probable is Theodore von Holst
,, 53 ,, 10 from bottom, *after* grave *add* .
,, ,, ,, 8 from bottom, *for* that *read* the
,, 56 ,, last, *after* day *add* .
,, 57 ,, 7, *for* nearly *read* merely
,, 73 ,, last, *after* this *add* —
,, 77 ,, 18, *after* strong *add* ;
,, 104 ,, 10 from bottom, *for* then I think already *read* soon afterwards
,, 123, head-line, *for* 1853 *read* 1854
,, 183, line last, *for* I have not any distinct idea *read* it was probably one named
    Husband and Wife
,, 184 ,, 16, *for* ead *read* dead
,, 185 ,, 5, *after* Christina *add* (but there was a crayon-head in September 1866)
,, 188 ,, 17, *after* Beatrice *dele* ;
,, 210 ,, last, *for* phras *read* phrase
,, 272 ,, 8 from bottom, *before* 99 *add* C
,, 274 ,, 9 from bottom, *for* o. *read* of
,, 287 ,, 8, *before* Letter of 27 March 1873 *add* B 63
,, 302 ,, 10, *for* 1892 *read* 1893
,, 352 ,, 5 from bottom, *for* 564 *read* 344
,, 380 ,, 1, *after* language *add* .
,, 391 head-line, *for* 1881 *read* 1882

12 East Parade
Hastings
April 13th 1860 Friday

My dear Mother

I write you this word to say that Lizzy and I are going to be married at last, in as few days as possible. I may be in town again first, but am not certain If so, I shall be sure to see you, but write this as I should be sorry that the news should reach you first from any other quarter

Like all the impor-tant things I ever meant to do, to fulfil duty or secure happiness, this one has been deferred almost beyond possibility. I have hardly deserved that Lizzy should still consent to it, but she has done so, and I trust I may still have time to prove my thankfulness

to her. The constantly
failing state of her
health is a terrible
anxiety indeed, but I
must still hope for
the best, and am
at any rate at this
moment in a better
position to take the
step, as regards money
prospects, than I
have even been before.
I shall either see
you or write again
soon, and meanwhile
and ever am
your most affectionate Sea
D G Rossetti

THE FAMILY-LETTERS

OF

DANTE GABRIEL ROSSETTI.

As in a gravegarth, count to see
The monuments of memory.

FAMILY-LETTERS.

A 1.

My brother, when he wrote this note, was in the fifteenth year of his age. My only object in preserving so boyish an affair is to show that he was then already exercising himself in drawing in a sort of way.

The "Bazaar" must have been patronized (I take it) by the family of the Earl of Wicklow, in which our aunt, Miss Charlotte Lydia Polidori, was then a governess. A "harp" could not now be copied off a "halfpenny"; but Irish halfpence bearing this device were at that time in frequent circulation in London.

Our aunt died in January 1890, at the great age of eighty-seven. She was a person of uncommon equanimity and amenity—none more so within my experience—and was an agreeable talker, though without marked intellectual gift. For unselfish complaisance she might be reckoned a model.

Only one letter from Gabriel earlier than this is in my possession. It is dated 10 January 1836, and is addressed to our Father. It is of course mere childishness. I ought not to thrust it upon the reader, and I shall not.

[50 CHARLOTTE STREET, PORTLAND PLACE, LONDON.]
1 *February* 1842.

MY DEAR AUNT CHARLOTTE,

I send you twelve drawings for the Bazaar, which I hope will not arrive too late for admission. Julian Peveril, the Turk, the Pygmy, the Brigand, Barnaby Rudge, the Butterfly, the Huntsman, the Harp, and the Shamrock, are copies. Quentin Durward, the Highlander, and the Dandy, are originals. The Huntsman and the Highlander are *intended* for Fitzjames and Roderick Dhu, from *The Lady of the Lake*.

I should have drawn some more, for I have remaining three cards and two pieces of cardboard; but I was fearful that they should reach you too late.

I hope that, should you answer this letter, you will favour me with a "full, true, and particular account" of the proceedings, how many and which of my drawings were sold, and the price which they fetched.

Having nothing more to say, I remain,

My dear Aunt Charlotte,

Your affectionate Nephew,

GABRIEL C. ROSSETTI.

P.S.—The Harp (but this is a strict secret) is copied off a halfpenny.

A 2.

In this letter my brother copied out the whole of Walter Scott's poem. I have omitted all except the first stanza. His coloured drawing of *The Cavalier* is still extant.

A music-master (a family friend, Signor Rovedino) was eventually called in for our elder sister Maria, whose destined career was that of a governess or teacher. She had a very fine voice and elocution in speaking, which might have developed into a good contralto voice in singing; but she (like all the family except our Father) had little musical aptitude, and never did anything in that way.

[50 CHARLOTTE STREET.]
Thursday 2 June 1842.

MY DEAR AUNT CHARLOTTE,

Perhaps you remember that, one day when you were admiring the drawings which I sent to the Bazaar, I said that I would draw you one. In fulfilment of this promise I send you the accompanying figure, hoping that it will meet with your approbation. It is pronounced by every one to be the best figure I have ever drawn, and I trust that such will also be your opinion. It is intended as an illustration of the following verses by Sir Walter Scott :—

THE CAVALIER.

"While the dawn on the mountain was misty and grey
My true love has mounted his steed and away:
Over hill, over valley, o'er dale and o'er down,
Heaven shield the brave gallant that fights for the Crown !"

* * * * * *

P.S.—Mamma sends you her love, and wishes me to tell you that she has just been talking to Papa of procuring a music-master for Maria, and that he says he will *see about it* (?).

P.P.S.—The figure is *entirely original.*

B I.

This letter must have been written about the time when my brother, had he returned to King's College School after the summer vacation of 1842, would have been wending thither; but, instead of that, he relinquished ordinary school attendance, and began studying for the profession of painting. He had now just gone to Chalfont-St.-Giles in Buckinghamshire, where our maternal uncle Mr. Henry Francis Polydore, whom he accompanied, had lately settled, to practise as a solicitor. Chalfont was the village or townlet to which Milton retired during the plague of London. "Uncle Henry's Swearing-book" was the volume which some client of his had from time to time to kiss, in taking an oath. Our uncle —who had turned his surname of Polidori into the Anglicized form Polydore for professional convenience—died in January 1885; a very strict devout Roman Catholic, and the most scrupulously conscientious of men—somewhat parsimonious (in proportion to his lifelong restricted means), and more than duly fidgeting to himself and others. He was a fairly diligent book-reader, without either ambition or aptitude towards authorship.

CHALFONT-ST.-GILES.
Thursday 1 September 1842.

MY DEAR MAMMA,

We arrived safely at Chalfont at 12 o'clock yesterday. The village is larger than I expected. The first thing we did on our arrival was to demolish some bread and butter, of which I at least was much in want. We then, with considerable difficulty, opened Uncle Henry's trunks, and, after depositing a part of their contents in a chest of drawers, we sallied forth to reconnoitre. I saw Milton's house, which is unquestionably the ugliest and dirtiest building in the whole village. It is now occupied by a tailor. . . .

Yesterday I commenced reading *The Infidel's Doom*, by Dr. Birch, which valuable work forms part and parcel of Uncle Henry's library. However, I have abandoned the task in despair. I then began *The Castle of Otranto*, which shared the same fate, and am now engaged on Defoe's *History of the Plague*. This morning we deposited Uncle Henry's books (exclusive of the law books, which are in the parlour) in a closet in Uncle Henry's bedroom, which, in common with all the other closets in this house, possesses a lock but no key.

I do not think that I shall go to church on Sunday, for in the first place I do not know where I can sit, and in the second place I find that we are so stared at wherever we go that I do not much relish the idea of sitting for two hours the lodestone of attraction in the very centre of the aborigines, on whose minds curiosity appears to have taken a firm hold.

I have just had some luncheon, of which however Uncle Henry did not partake, asserting that he was unwell, and would take some pills for his luncheon. Milk is an extremely rare article here; so much so that it was with great difficulty that we obtained a pint this morning and half a pint yesterday, and it still remains in doubt whether we shall be able to procure half a pint this evening for tea. I "in longing expectation wait" the appearance of my dinner; for which however I need not yet look, since it is now nearly 3 o'clock, which is the nominal dinner-hour, but, the fire having gone out, Uncle Henry prophesies that it will not come till 4.

I remain, dear Mamma,
Your affectionate Son,
GABRIEL ROSSETTI.

P.S.—I intend to make, for Maria's accommodation, a sketch of the church, which I think pretty, but which Uncle Henry condemns as exceedingly flat and ugly.

P.P.S.—I am sure that by this time you must be tormenting yourself because I forgot to take a Prayer-Book; however, you may set your mind at rest on that subject, since Uncle Henry's Swearing-book combines both Bible and Prayer-Book, out of which I can read the Psalms and Lessons on Sunday in case I stay at home.

C 1.

This letter is, so far as I know, the earliest that I ever received from my brother. I had now, succeeding him, left London to spend a few days with our uncle in Chalfont-St.-Giles. The opening observations, as to my discomforts with my uncle, will be rightly understood as mere "chaff." There was nothing to complain of in his modest (then bachelor) establishment. "A Philippic expression" means an expression of our other uncle Philip Robert Polidori —a rather odd not strong-witted person. My brother and I (for books, prints, etc., were then and for several years afterwards all in common between us) were at that time taking-in a serial edition of the *Waverley Novels*, and buying up prints to illustrate it—even, in some instances, prints which were not really intended for the *Waverley Novels*. About this period of his boyhood my brother's health was not strong, as is the case with so many growing boys. Reynolds was a good-humoured little print-seller on a small and dingy scale, close to St. Giles's Church, whose shop my brother and I haunted with spectral pertinacity for some years—spending pennie and sixpences as opportunity allowed.

[50 CHARLOTTE STREET.]
Wednesday evening. 28 December 1842.

MY DEAR WILLIAM,

I took up my pen, fully intending to commence by *hoping* that you found yourself comfortable at Chalfont-St.-Giles; but I rejected the idea almost as soon as formed, for sad experience has taught me that over the portal of "the lawyer" (to make use of a Philippic expression) might well be inscribed, in the words of the poet, "All hope abandon, ye who enter here."   I make no enquiries as to the particulars of your sufferings and agony both in the $7\frac{1}{2}$ miles' walk to, and in the residence at, said Chalfont.   I do not ask how you relished the "odours of Edom" which emanate (at least according to Uncle Henry) from your downy couch. . . . I do not, I say, ask all this, because I know that I shall have an opportunity of receiving answers to these enquiries, and as many more as I please to make, within a short time after you have perused this precious epistle.   I would not mind staking any sum, if I had any sum to stake (for Heaven knows my Christmas-box has been long since landed safely on the classic shores of pot), that you and our mutual relative have ere this had recourse for amusement to the pages of Horace or Virgil. With the former the above-mentioned relative has disgusted me by constantly showing me that he does understand it, and then telling me that I do not.   Of the latter we have my favourite poet's opinion—

> "That Virgil's songs are good, except that horrid one
> Beginning with *Formosum pastor Corydon*."

So said Byron—so say not I.   The Eclogue which he seems to dislike is the very one by construing which from beginning to end (having learnt it at school in capacity of an imposition) I can defeat the malice of Uncle Henry when he defies me so to do.

I have already told you that my Christmas-box has taken up its residence at pot.   I will now proceed to acquaint you with the means by which it found its way to that "undis- covered country from whose bourne no traveller returns." To you probably this will be interesting news—to Uncle Henry it will be one continued nuisance.   I well know his abhorrence of a long list of purchases.

I will begin, then, with the prints I have bought for my *Waverley Novels*—viz., a proof of *The Pass of Aberfoil— Stand*, which you already know, and for which I gave 9*d.*;

Leslie's *Charles and Lady Bellenden*, and *McIvor and the Grey Spirit* (1s. 6d. the couple); *Sir W. Scott in his Study* (4d.); a splendid engraving of *The Fortress*, which I suppose to be the Fortress of Man in *Peveril* (6d.); Gilbert's *Richard trampling on the Austrian Flag*, which, on a second inspection, I find to be not nearly so good as I expected, but which is nevertheless very good, like everything of Gilbert's (1d.); and lastly, Warren's *Escape*, from the *Protestant Annual*, which I intend to introduce into *The Pirate*, and of which, as well as of *The Widow Maclure's Son*, plenty of copies are to be had at the Publisher's in Oxford Street. I have purchased a proof of *The Shipwreck in Don Juan*, which you already know, and which I got (at Palser's) for 1s., the original price being 1s. 6d.; also (at Reynolds's) a print of *The Widow* by Boxall (2d.); also a scene in the *Merry Wives of Windsor*, which I have put into my Shakespear (3d.). I have likewise procured 4 parts of the *Shakespear* itself. I had almost forgotten to tell you of one more purchase which I have made—viz., *A Shillingsworth of Nonsense*, by the editors of *Punch*, which you have no doubt seen, and which is indeed a shillingsworth of the vilest twaddle that was ever written down. It possesses however one redeeming quality which, in my eyes at least, more than compensates for all its defects—it contains 48 splendid wood-engravings by Phiz.

So much for every one of my purchases, so much for every farthing of my money, and so much for *almost* every syllable of my letter; except that Mamma and all send you their loves, and that Dr. Locock, whom we visited again this morning, says that I must not recommence my studies till after New Year's Day; and so

Believe me,

My dear William,

Yours affectionately,

G. ROSSETTI.

P.S.—I forgot to tell you that, if you want to get splendid prints dirt-cheap, now's your time. Reynolds told me that he would have (to-morrow most probably) a set of Finden's engravings (either the *Tableaux* or the series of *Groups from Different Nations*; I believe the latter) for rather more than *three shillings*! I intended to have bought them myself, only I found after I had bought the *Shakespear* that my pockets were a vacuum.

B 2.

When this letter was written our Mother was at Hastings, along with our Father, in an endeavour—for a long while fruitless—to cure him of a severe attack of bronchitis.

No. 15 Park Village East, Regent's Park (now No. 30), was the residence of our grandfather Gaetano Polidori and his family. Our Uncle Henry had then abandoned Chalfont-St.-Giles, and was pursuing his profession at 15 Park Village East. The phrase about the "press of clients" sounds like and is irony. Mr. Leader is Mr. Charles Temple Leader, a Radical M.P. of those days, afterwards a conspicuous English resident in Florence. He is still alive, I think, at a great age. Sangiovanni had taken, from a natural bent of genius, to the modelling of picturesque clay figures—brigands, contadini, Albanians, etc. "The Cavaliere" was the Cavalier Mortara, an exceedingly frequent visitor at our parents' house—brother of a Conte Mortara, a bibliophile of some name. The "Signora Carlotta" means our aunt Miss Charlotte Polidori.

50 CHARLOTTE STREET.
Sunday 2 June 1843.

MY DEAR MAMMA,

"Better late than never," as the cat said to the kitten when the latter relinquished the Wellington boot in despair. And now, having sent preliminaries to pot in one pithy and well-concocted sentence, I shall proceed forthwith to news.

Yesterday Aunt Margaret, William, and myself, betook ourselves in the afternoon to 15 Park Village East, having been thereunto invited. The first thing I did on my arrival was to enter the office of Uncle Henry. The air therein was however so suffocating, owing to the press of clients, that I effected a hasty retreat, leaving William to the full enjoyment of the black hole of Calcutta.   I then proceeded to the parlour, where I dawdled about till teatime. . . .

I finished yesterday the first volume of *Ten Thousand a Year*, the commencement of which, as Aunt Margaret intends to testify in her next epistle, is very unpromising.   As it proceeds however it becomes splendid ; and, having completed the volume, I laid it down with the impression that it was equal to Dickens.   To-morrow I hope to begin the second volume.   William is also perusing *Charles O'Malley*, which he finds very entertaining.

Dr. Heimann has called several times since your departure, and testifies great interest in Papa's health.   He was here yesterday to give us our lesson.   He intends to take us out with him, and will write a note to fix the day.   He surveyed our libraries, and was glad to see that Maria possessed *Keble*, which he has read, and admires exceedingly (!)   Mr. Leader called to-day ; and, on hearing that Papa was in the country, seemed pleased, and asked us for his address, which we gave him.   The visits of enquiring friends since your disappearance have been so numerous that it would be impossible to remember them.   Suffice it to say that all the "amici" small and great have been here.   Sangiovanni says that he intends to write (!)   The Cavaliere wishes that your correspondence was more voluminous, and says that the Signora Carlotta, having nothing else to do, should write letters *ad infinitum*.

I have nearly finished studying the bones, and my next drawing will most probably be an anatomy-figure.

Everybody at 15 Park Village East and at 50 Charlotte Street sends his or her love to everybody at 9 High Street, Hastings.   And so, having nothing more to say,

> Believe me,
> My dear Mamma,
> Your affectionate Son,
> GABRIEL ROSSETTI.

B 3.

Our Father, still in quest of health, had now gone to Paris with our Mother. The experiment, after a moderate interval of time, proved very satisfactory.

I do not remember much now about "the Sketching Club" of which my brother speaks. It cannot have included any of the artist-students, predestined to renown, with whom he was afterwards closely associated.

50 CHARLOTTE STREET. 7 *July* 1843.

MY DEAR MAMMA,

On Monday last (the first day of opening) I visited the exhibition at Westminster Hall of the cartoons for deco-rating the New Houses of Parliament. When I say cartoons I mean of course the large drawings executed in chalks which are afterwards to be painted in fresco on the walls. It is indeed a splendid sight; by far the most interesting exhibition in fact at which I have ever been, more so even than the Royal Academy. The *tout ensemble* on first entrance is most imposing. The figures are, almost without exception, as large as life, and in many instances considerably larger; added to which Westminster Hall is of itself a most magnificent structure. The subjects are taken chiefly from English history, and a great part of them relate to the times of the ancient Britons and the introduction of Christianity. A full third of the exhibition (not to say more) is occupied by subjects from Milton. There are also a great many from Shakespear and Spenser, a few foreign subjects, and one or two national allegories. Scriptural subjects were I believe excluded; however that may be, not one has made its appearance on the walls. The plan of the exhibition was as follows: Whatever cartoons were sent in (so long as they belonged to the class of subjects specified in the prospectuses—viz., history or some great English author) the Committee promised to exhibit them; and, in proof of the strict manner in which they have kept their word, a quantity of abomina-tions have been hung up which are a disgrace to British Art, and to exclude which it appears to me that the Committee should have deviated from the general rule. There is one especially, representing the signing of Magna Charta, which I am convinced must either be the work of some child of six or seven years old, or else that it must have been sent in by somebody for a joke, to prove to what lengths the Committee would go in keeping their engagement. But to return to the regulations. All the cartoons having been sent in and hung up in Westminster Hall, a day was set apart, previous to the exhibition being opened to the public, in order that the Committee, with Mr. Eastlake at their head, might take a private view, and decide upon those which were to receive the prizes. Accordingly on the day when I went, which was, as I have before stated, the first day of the exhibition, the fortunate competitors were already known. I forgot to say that it was one of the rules that every cartoon should be accompanied on sending in by the artist's name, but that only those of the successful candidates should be published in the printed catalogue. Thus I was only able to recognize a few of the rejected, either by the style being known to me or by the reports of others. The prizes are universally acknowledged to have been most justly awarded. There is only one which appears to me an exception to this rule, and this one is, I am sorry to say, no other than Mr. Severn's. The subject is *Queen Elinor sucking the Poison from her Husband's Arm*. It is almost completely wanting in expression; which can however scarcely be avoided, as the artist has been so injudicious as to choose the moment when Edward becomes insensible. The drawing is generally good, but this also is in some parts sadly defective. Mr. Cary has exhibited one, the subject of which is from Spenser. It possesses considerable merit, but not enough to receive a prize.

I will now mention a few of those which particularly elicited my admiration. The three which are perhaps generally thought the most of are : *The Landing of Julius Cæsar in Britain and his Opposition by the Natives*, by Armitage ; *Caractacus led captive through the Streets of Rome*, by Watts ; and *Boadicea*

addressing her Army before her last Battle with the Romans, by
Selous.   Among these, that which I like the best, and indeed
more than any other in the exhibition, is the *Caractacus*, the
artist of which, a young man by name Watts, has been, ever
since he took to the arts, struggling with the greatest poverty.
He is however as good as he is talented, and has been for
many years, in spite of his miserable circumstances, the sole
support of his mother.   Good fortune has however found him
out at last in the shape of a £300 prize, which will be
followed by much greater remuneration as soon as his picture
(of which, as I said before, the cartoon is but a rough sketch)
shall have been painted.   All this I learnt from one of the
models who sat to him, and with whom he agreed that, if his
cartoon gained a prize, he (Watts) would pay the model three
times the usual sum, but that, if it was rejected, he should not
be considered in any way his debtor, since it was utterly
impossible that he should pay, owing to the wretched state
of his finances.   The model will now reap a rich harvest from
the £300 prize.

I find that I have not room to dilate any further on the
merits of the individual cartoons, as I had intended, and so
I must finish with a few general remarks.   Taken on the
whole, this exhibition may be considered as a proof that High
Art and high talent are not confined to the Continent.   The
common accusation brought against British painters cannot
be brought forward here with any show of reason.   The
accusation to which I allude is that the English clothe their
figures too much ; that they conceal their ignorance of
anatomy by working up satin and jewels and cloth of gold
to the highest state of finish ; and thus, by forcing the
spectator as it were to admire these outside ornaments, cause
him to overlook the want of correct drawing.   Here, however,
such artifices are utterly out of the question.   In the first
place, the absence of colour renders it impossible that such
stratagems should be resorted to ; and in the second place,
the subjects (principally taken from Milton and the early
English history) make the naked figure positively necessary,

and thus cut off effectually any such means of escape. There is also another very gratifying feature in this exhibition. Almost all the successful competitors are young men who now appear for the first time before the public, thus directly giving the lie to the vile snarling assertion that British Art is slowly but surely falling, never more to rise. After the first fortnight (during which the price of admission is one shilling) the exhibition will be opened gratuitously—a step which, it is feared, will prove somewhat rash on the part of the Committee, as they have not an Italian public to deal with but an English one.

I shall now relinquish this topic, fearing that I may perhaps have tired you, although it is so interesting to me that I can scarcely imagine that it is not equally so to everybody else. I will now proceed to what little other news I have in store.

I have, since I wrote last, drawn some more bones, as well as an entire skeleton. I am now engaged on an outline of the Hercules. There have been two meetings of the Sketching Club since your departure, for which I have made three drawings, one of which was the *Death of Marmion*, and the other two were of the same subject—viz., The old Soldier relating his battles to the Parson, from *The Deserted Village*. One of the two which I made for this subject is the most finished and perhaps the best pen-and-ink drawing which I have ever executed. I have given them both to the Cavaliere, who seemed to like them very much. The next subject is to be the Parting of two Lovers, unspecified and indefinite, which I intend to treat in several different manners, and to get up in prime style.

I have just finished *Ten Thousand a Year*, which is indeed one of the most splendid works (not to say *the* most splendid) which I ever read. It is a most interesting story, and evidently written by a religious person. It relates almost entirely to a series of law proceedings (not, however, dry and disgusting ones), in which the author seems so much at home that I am convinced he must belong to the profession which has "proved a step-mother" to Uncle Henry. . . . Will you give my love to Papa with thanks for all his kind messages? After which having no more to say,

> Believe me,
> My dear Mamma,
> Your affectionate Son,
> GABRIEL C. D. ROSSETTI.

B 4.

To discuss the cost of an easel as a somewhat grave matter, and finally to price the article at five shillings, as in the ensuing letter, indicates (the reader may readily infer) that cash was not superfluous in our household at this period.

Pistrucci, from whom my brother adopted a design of the *Death of Virginia*, was Filippo Pistrucci, a painter and teacher of Italian. He was an intimate and peculiarly kind-hearted friend of our family. Another design here mentioned—*Minotti firing the Train*—is the only one of these early drawings of my brother which I remember with particularity. I cannot recall much about the *Illustrated Scrapbook* in which we all appear to have co-operated. But I recollect the *Hodge-podge*, which had been a still more juvenile attempt in the same line. My brother was certainly mistaken in thinking that the poems by Christina (then only twelve years of age)—*Rosalind* and *Corydon's Resolution*—were "very good." *Rosalind* is indisputably bad, and neither of these effusions found favour with our partial grandfather when he produced in 1847 a privately printed volume of Christina's *Verses*. Maria's *Vision of Human Life* seems to be the same thing as *The Rivulets*—a little religious allegory which she published in 1846. *Ulfred the Saxon* was a "Tale of the Conquest" which I began in my school-days. "Every one" must have been singularly weak-minded or mealy-mouthed in acknowledging any part of it to be "excellent."

> 50 CHARLOTTE STREET.
> 14 *August* 1843.

MY DEAR MAMMA,

We received this morning Papa's letter of the 12th, which caused us, as you may well imagine, the greatest pleasure. Dr. Heimann, however, who came to-day to give us our lesson (not having been able to do so on Saturday), was much concerned on hearing of Papa's intention to leave Paris so soon, since he fears that a London winter may be productive of a relapse. He strongly recommended us on this account to prevent, if possible, so early a return. Dr. Heimann has manifested throughout a great interest in Papa's health.

You wish me to inform you of my progress in drawing, and of the time at which I hope to become a student of the Academy. Upon the first point I answer that I have finished the outline of the Hercules, and drawn the anatomy-figure. I am now engaged on a finished drawing of the Antinous, which, supposing it to prove good enough, I may perhaps send in to the Academy. The next opportunity for so doing will be at Christmas, when I may probably try, though certainly not unless I feel sure of success, for a rejection is a thing I should by no means relish. Besides this there are other matters to be attended to ; for, even granted that in the first instance I am admitted, still this is not all. Every successful candidate is required to execute a second drawing, in order to prove that the merit of the first is entirely his own. Added to which he must make drawings of the anatomy-figure and of the skeleton, in any of which if he fail he ceases to be a student ; and very few have the courage to venture on a second trial after the disgrace of a rejection. Having considered these things, I shall certainly decline making the attempt at Christmas unless by that time I shall be fully competent to the ordeal; my knowledge of anatomy, in spite of my efforts at improvement, being at present less than imperfect. I intend to commence drawing at home from those casts which I possess, and thus endeavour to get into the habit of working without assistance of any kind. For this purpose I shall want an easel, since I have lately been so accustomed to use one that I find it impossible now to draw otherwise. It is a thing that I must have sooner or later, and it is not so expensive as I supposed, since I find that a very decent one can be got for five shillings.

The Sketching Club continues, and I derive great improvement from it. The subjects I have drawn since I last wrote to you are : *The Parting of Two (indefinite) Lovers*, for which I made no less than six different drawings, which may perhaps take rank as my best sketches ; *The Death of Virginia*, which, being lazy, I am ashamed to confess I copied from Pistrucci ; and *Orlando and Adam in the Forest*, which I have prepared for the day after to-morrow, being the next club-day. It will then be my turn to propose the new subject, and I have fixed upon *Minotti firing the Train* from the *Siege of Corinth.*

The *Illustrated Scrap-book* continues swimmingly. It improves with every number. Of the number on which William and myself are at present employed I am particularly proud. It contains some of my choicest specimens of sketching. Its pages are likewise adorned with two poetic effusions by Christina, the one entitled *Rosalind* and the other *Corydon's Resolution*, both of which are very good, especially the latter, which elicited the warm admiration of Dr. Heimann. Maria has also authorized me to insert in the victorious *Scrap-book* her *Vision of Human Life*, originally written for the fallen *Hodge-podge*, the "weekly efforts" contained in which have I fear given their last gasp, since not a single perfect number has appeared since your departure.

William has written an enormous quantity of *Ulfred the Saxon*, which increases in interest as it proceeds. His description of the battle of Hastings and death of Harold is acknowledged by every one to be excellent.

I have not written anything new lately except a third chapter of *Sorrentino*; an unfortunate work, the tribulations whereof have been so many and so great that, if the approbation of others were the only encouragement to an author to continue his literary labours, the romance in question would long since have found its way behind the grate. The new chapter has not been more fortunate than its predecessors, since Maria eschews it and obstinately refuses to hear it, under the impression that it is "horrible." No one however pretends to deny that it is my *chef-d'œuvre*, an opinion in which I hope you will coincide after having perused it. The charge of indecency can no longer be laid upon the former portion with any show of reason, since I have purged and purified it most effectually, and burnt up the chaff with unquenchable fire. On the completion of this work I intend offering it to some publisher, for, defying all accusations of vanity and self-esteem, I cannot help considering that it is equal to very many of the senseless productions which daily issue from the press.

I have finished reading *Ernest Maltravers*, which is indeed a splendid work. I also began *Alice, or The Mysteries*, but could get no further than the first two or three chapters, so stupid did I find it. As to the indecent books which you speak of in your last letter to me (and of which report I find that Aunt Margaret was the origin), I am completely in the dark, since I have not read a single volume, except those of which I have spoken to you, from the day of your departure up to the time at which she wrote. I really wish that Aunt Margaret would refrain from circulating such falsehoods.— On enquiry I have succeeded in eliciting that the origin of all this was my having hinted at a vague intention of purchasing at some indefinite period the works of Shelley—which I should peruse solely on account of the splendid versification, and not from any love of his atheistical sentiments.

*   *   *   *   *   *

B 5.

This letter was written from Boulogne. To keep my brother's health in good condition, our parents sent him, on two occasions, to spend a few weeks with some old friends at Boulogne, Signor Maenza and his wife—he an Italian, she an Englishwoman. Maenza was a political refugee, a man of character and honour; an artist in the way of water-colour sketching etc., who taught drawing, and I suppose Italian as well. He died in 1870, his wife towards 1880. My brother's affectionate regard for them found steady practical expression up to the last. Peppino, mentioned in the letter, was the only son of the Maenzas—a student of painting, who never made a professional position, and whose final fate (he is now no doubt dead) was never known to his family or friends. He may have been three or four years my brother's senior.

This letter from my brother follows on the same sheet on which Signor Maenza had written to our father. He describes Gabriel as having "a pleasant smile, and a well-developed and agreeable mind. I have already given a look at his sketches, and assure you that he promises highly."

Although I have spoken of my brother, in the Memoir, as "Dante," I always call him "Gabriel" in these notes attached to his letters, as that was the only name by which he was designated in the family, and generally by his closer intimates.

6 RUE DE LA COUPE, BOULOGNE-SUR-MER.
20 October 1843.

DEAR MAMMA,

I arrived here yesterday a little before six, after having suffered considerably during the voyage. Fortunately for me the weather has suddenly become fine, after having been very rough for a considerable time. I like Boulogne exceedingly, but I am, if possible, yet more pleased with the Maenza family. They are some of the kindest people I ever knew. I find that Peppino's tastes coincide in every respect with mine. He draws splendidly, and is very fond of poetry, especially Byron.

*   *   *   *   *   *

D I.

This is the only letter from Gabriel to my grandfather which I find extant: there can never have been many.

I have no recollection of the "new Romance" which my brother announces: probably it perished abortive. The "Ballad" is clearly *Sir Hugh the Heron*.

6 RUE DE LA COUPE, BOULOGNE.
Thursday 26 October 1843.

MY DEAR GRANDFATHER,

It is now exactly a week since I arrived in Boulogne. I like the place exceedingly. The views are most beautiful, and the sailors and fishermen, with their wives and children, extremely picturesque. . . .

My gigantic literary pursuits . . . have prompted me to write a new Romance, which I have already commenced, and which Peppino has undertaken to illustrate. I have made several purchases here, both of books and prints. Among others I have bought Bulwer's *Leila, or the Siege of Granada, Calderon the Courtier*, and *The Lady of Lyons*, all in one volume—which I purchased, entirely new and uncut, for two shillings; their price in England, exclusive of the last-named work, being fourteen shillings. I shall however be obliged to smuggle it in under my coat, since I hear that they do not allow French editions of English works to enter the latter country. The other day I went out with Peppino for the purpose of taking a view, but the wind was so high that we found it impossible to draw, and were forced to retreat from the scene of action.

Mr. Maenza has been reading Papa's *Beatrice*, which he admires very much. My Ballad has also been read, and received the necessary amount of compliments. I find that Mr. M[aenza] is a great admirer of English literature, and is particularly well-acquainted with Byron. I have been reading here *The Deformed Transformed* by that author, which is a strange drama relative to the Siege of Rome by Bourbon the Constable of France. It is perhaps not equal to many of his works, but nevertheless contains some sublime passages, particularly a quantity of songs and choruses. They have some most splendid books in this house, one of which is a Molière, illustrated by Tony Johannot in a manner so exquisitely comic that it almost made me split my sides with laughing. *Le Bourgeois Gentilhomme* and *Monsieur de Pourceaugnac* are particularly fine.

* 　 * 　 * 　 * 　 * 　 *

Believe me, my dear Grandfather,
　　　　Your affectionate Grandson,
　　　　　　　GABRIEL CHAS. ROSSETTI.

E 1.

6 RUE DE LA COUPE, BOULOGNE-SUR-MER.
1 *November* 1843.

MY DEAR FATHER,

I was much grieved yesterday evening on receiving Mamma's letter, and no less ashamed of myself for my unpardonable neglect in not enquiring after your health. I assure you, and I hope you will believe me, that it seems as unkind to myself, now that I reflect upon it, as it possibly can to you. Nevertheless I cannot imagine that you, who have hitherto enjoyed such excellent sight, are now about to be deprived of it. Had this defect of vision come over you when in a perfect state of health, I should certainly have entertained great fears that you were about to become blind; but, as it is, I cannot but hope, and even trust, that it is merely a temporary consequence of the weakness attendant on your long illness. Did you represent this to Mr. Lawrence, and if so did he not lay some weight upon it?

Mr. Maenza agrees with me on this point. He told me of a woman he knew—and who is still living in Boulogne—who had been given over by the doctors as completely blind, but who, in spite of this, recovered naturally in a short time, and sees now, and has for years, as well as he does.

Nevertheless this belief which I venture to entertain cannot prevent me from feeling great anxiety and uneasiness on your account. You say that William is unhappy; can you believe that I am less so? I assure you that Mamma's letter has made me very dull; it does not contain one single piece of good news. . . . The only good I can gather from the letter is that, as Mamma does not mention the state of your health in other respects, I presume that the illness has entirely left you.

As to my own health, which you so kindly enquire after, I am convinced that you will scarcely recognize me on my return. . . . I now feel better than ever I did in my life. Mrs. Maenza says she should not know me for the same person, and that she is convinced you will find me considerably grown as well as improved in looks! I walk generally for nearly half the day, the views hereabouts being enough to drag out of his bed the greatest sluggard who ever snored. I intend to copy some of Mr. M[aenza]'s landscapes, since I have picked up a little taste that way.

To conclude : the whole family join in affectionate regards and confident hopes for your recovery with

Your affectionate Son,

GABRIEL CHAS. ROSSETTI.

C 2.

This letter (it will be perceived by the date and the altered address) belongs to the *second* visit which my brother paid to Boulogne. The sketch which Peppino made of him in 1843 is still extant—an unsightly and unresembling sketch, with an almost mulatto cast of countenance.

"Byron's mad drama" is (as shown before) *The Deformed Transformed*. Mrs. Wood was a lady of some pretence to fashion living near us in Charlotte Street. "De Bazan"—the drama of *Don Cæsar de Bazan*—is spoken of as "accursed" only because it was then unevadable, as being played all over Europe. "Sue's novel" was the *Juif Errant*; *Barbe-bleue* was also (if I remember right) an early novel of Sue's. "The Voyage" was a *Voyage où il vous plaira*, illustrated by Tony Johannot with woodcut designs of remarkable power of a nightmare kind. "The Barone" was a Sicilian, Calfapietra, a very agreeable companionable man, who had damaged himself by gambling before coming to England.

35 GRANDE RUE [BOULOGNE].
Saturday [1 *December* 1844].

MY DEAR WILLIAM,

I received yesterday evening your unsightly missive containing the two *Chuzzlewits*, which were much admired. They greeted Mr. Maenza and myself on our return from an evening walk, during which we met the postman, who informed us that he had left a "gros paquet" at our house, which proved on inspection to be your epistolary eyesore.

The only passages in Byron's mad drama which have left any impression on my mind are the battle-choruses, which are sublime, and the last scene, which is lively and spirited. It was never finished.

I walk out here a great deal, gloating over all manner of Gavarnis, Johannots, Nanteuils, and other delicacies. I have got a large advertisement of the *Beautés de l'Opéra*, containing a cut by the last-named artist, as fine as anything in the *Tasso*. I begin already to feel better here. The weather is cold, but clear and beautiful. None of the filthy vapours—half-fog, half-smoke—through which you are doubtless endeavouring to decipher my epistle, while a poetical mind might figure forth the sun "taking a sight" at you—his face twisted into that comical expression which Phiz is in the habit of inflicting upon him.

Our house is in a most beautiful situation. The window of what Mrs. Wood would call our "salon" looks out upon the market, which Mamma doubtless remembers, and whose pretty groups of pretty girls are at this moment regaling my eye.

Boulogne is certainly, as Mr. Maenza says, a splendid place for an artist. The evening before last Mr. Maenza and I walked about the principal church of the town during mass or vespers or whatever they call it. What between the fine old Gothic interior, adorned with pictures and images of saints—the music and the chanting—the magnificent groups of old fishwomen, whose intense devotion has in it something sublime—and the "dim religious light" of the lamps placed against the Gothic pillars, which glimmered faintly up and struggled through the gathering darkness—the scene was so solemn and impressive that Maria (whom I wished for much) might have gone a Protestant, but would most certainly have returned a Catholic.

I was talking with Mr. Maenza the other day about Papa's poems, and I mentioned among others *Minaccioso l'Arcangel di Guerra*, which I find he has not seen. Would Papa be so kind (if he does not mind the postage) as to forward me a copy, should any remain?

Franconi is here, with his *manège*, which we intend visiting —perhaps to-night. Conspicuous likewise among the fashionable arrivals stands that wandering Spaniard, that dramatic cholera, the accursed De Bazan.

Do *not* tell me how Sue's novel goes on, since I do not wish to have it stale on my return. Does Papa continue to like it, and was he not pleased with the scene where Gabriel "flayres uppe" so strong?

Is the *Barbe-bleue* finished? If so, not a word about the end.

Tell the Cavaliere (whom I often remember) that I left his parcel at Lady Hartwell's door, and should have delivered it in person but for the best of reasons—that she was not at home.

I am glad that Papa's eyes are no worse. How is Grandpapa, how is Aunt Charlotte, and how are all the family?

I have bought several things here. Among others I picked up yesterday for fifteen sous ($7\frac{1}{2}d$. English) no less than five coloured Gavarnis, being three *Enfants Terribles*, one *Fourberies de Femmes*, and one *Étudiants de Paris*—all splendid specimens, and which usually sell at a franc apiece. I have likewise got six numbers of Johannot's *Don Quixote*, which is actually being re-issued at four sous the number! I have likewise got several of the *Voyage*, and ordered the rest. I have got several other things, but must defer mentioning them for want of space.

Remember me most extra especially to those real friends the Heimanns, and tell the Doctor that I shall write to him as soon as I have the slightest pretence for so doing.

Love to all the family, including the Barone and Cavaliere, and (if you see them) Sangiovanni and Pistrucci.

Mr. and Mrs. Maenza salute you all warmly.

Your affectionate Brother,

GABRIEL CHAS. ROSSETTI.

P.S.—Looking over some of Peppino's sketches to-day, I found one which he made of me last year, and which I begged for Mamma, thinking she might care to have it.

E 2.

The letter from Signor Maenza, which accompanied this one from my brother, speaks of the latter as " much grown " since 1843. "His conversation is lively, and his mind acts like a thunderbolt as soon as anything of high compass is spoken of. He will do, I am certain, all that is to be expected from an elevated spirit." There is another letter from Maenza, written on 25 January 1845, when Gabriel was returning to London, saying, " His imagination promises much, and I am persuaded that he will reach the goal aright." He then recommends that my brother should take—which he never did—to fencing or gymnastics, "to check the sedentary habits to which he is greatly inclined." An account follows, showing that the payment for house and board was £1 per week.

35 GRANDE RUE [BOULOGNE].
Thursday 10 December 1844.

MY DEAR FATHER,

I hope that you will excuse my writing this letter in English, but my Italian is so "stentato" [strained] that, although perhaps, when finished, it may be passably decent, still the labour of composing in a language in which I am so imperfect is an agony that I would willingly avoid.

I was much grieved to hear that your sight had deteriorated, especially as I had hoped that what remained was almost secure. Have you consulted the German you mentioned ? and, if so, would you tell William or somebody to write to me as soon as possible on the subject ? Mr. Maenza, who will contribute his part to this letter, is of opinion that Paris is the best place for the treatment of your malady. I fear you must have thought me very remiss in not writing sooner. I should have done so, had I had anything to say which I thought would interest you. In fact I have not much even now, and only write to avoid the appearance of having forgotten you.

My health continues good, with the exception of the toothache—which however confines itself to meal-times. I go out as much as the cold permits me, which, between wind and frost, is biting in these parts. There are no beastly stifling fogs however, and the sun looks out brightly every day at noon. We are anxiously expecting Peppino, whom we hope to see in about a week. His letters lead us to think that he has become more settled and steady. His last, which Mr. M[aenza] received a few days ago, was very sentimental, and spoke of some most amiable private pupil, "with whom" (to use his own words), "through the kindness of the mother, I am very intimate."

After much racking of the brains I am sorry to find that this first piece of news is likewise the last. I have therefore only to forward you Mrs. Maenza's kind remembrances (letting Mr. M[aenza] speak for himself), and [to beg] that you will deliver that valuable article, my love, to all friends at home, keeping a large portion for yourself and Mamma.

C 3.

"The last *Diables*" means the last numbers of an illustrated serial we were then taking in, *Le Diable à Paris*. The *Canto Marziale* is the same patriotic lyric by our Father previously mentioned as *Minaccioso l'Arcangel di Guerra*. The *Salterio* (Psaltery) is one of his books of religious-humanitarian poetry. The P.S., "Is Maria yet arrived?" must point to the fact that our elder sister, then a governess in the country, was expected home at this time.

[BOULOGNE] *Tuesday 17 December* 1844.

MY DEAR BROTHER,

Following your example, I hasten, as in duty bound, to acquit me of the commission contained in your last. I have enquired at the two principal shops in the town for Ragon's *Cours Philosophique*, and find that neither of them has got it. Ask Cavalier Mortara whether or not he wishes me to order it from Paris.

I am glad to say that the weather has changed since Saturday, and that the cold is no longer so severe. On Sunday I spent a most agreeable day in the country at the house of a friend who lives about five or six miles from Boulogne in a most delightful situation, and close to a village which contains some of the most splendid sketches imaginable.

I have been reading George Sand's *Horace* and Paul de Kock's *Ce Monsieur.* As regards the first, it certainly contains some splendid and even sublime pieces of writing ; but it is full of Saint Simonisme, communism, and sermons of all kinds, which render it both tedious and disgusting. Besides which, there is a great deal of French sentimentalism, and not a single possible character or probable incident. *Ce Monsieur*, as you may imagine, is glorious from title-page to finis. After all, Paul de Kock is unquestionably the most amusing and the most natural of the novelists. The interest of his works never flags for a moment, and even his pathetic scenes are perfectly true and unaffected. To-day or to-morrow I shall get another by the same author. Should you wish to see a more extended critique on these two works, you may look for it in a letter which I wrote yesterday to Dr. Heimann, wherein I have set forth my opinion at greater length.

I will tell you a few of my purchases. Imprimis seven heads in lithography by Gavarni, which I got cheap at the same shop as the others I told you of. Item, *Contes des Fées par Perrault.* This little book contains all our old friends, Blue-beard, Cinderella, etc., which I find were originally written by one Charles Perrault, born in 1633. It is full of most exquisite cuts, by Nanteuil, Devéria, Giraud, and, though last not least, a man of the name of Thomas, who is as fine as anybody I know. The misfortune is that, as they are published very cheap in order I suppose to be within the reach of every child, the cuts are printed on the same paper as a little book called the *Tour de Nesle*, which, as you doubtless remember, I bought last year, and many of the impressions are consequently completely ruined. Nevertheless they will be a capital acquisition for our scrap-book. Item, twelve more numbers of *Don Quixote.* Item, some numbers of the *Musée Philipon*, full of first-rate Chams, Grandvilles, and Daumiers, and containing even a few most sublime Gavarnis.

There are a few other things, to see which you must, in the words of Scripture, " tarry till I come."

By-the-bye, you give me a long account of some Phizes; but you omit something even more interesting—namely, a description of the last *Diables* and *Juif.*

Have you seen lately anything of our friend Gilbert, or procured any of his works ? I hope his style continues in good health.

Get in Wellington Street the *Illustration* for Sunday 8 December, being the one before last. I could not procure a copy in this place, they being all sold. It contains some capital Chams, some excellent Bertalls, and two or three landscapes by Calame of *rather* a sublime character.

You remember two or three cuts in our portfolio signed P.S.G. The name, I find, is Saint-Germain. The other day I actually saw, in a barber's shop on the port, some of the finest cuts from Vernet's *Napoleon* (among others, the Kremlin and the Battle of Wagram) cut out and pasted on some bottles of eau-de-Cologne. My blood boils within me as I write it.

The other night I went to Franconi's to see the horseman-ship. It certainly beats our Astley's. Franconi is the very image of the Duke of Wellington. There was a horse which danced the polka.

I have got the rest of the *Voyage* with the exception of one number. Unfortunately I do not know which it is. On my return however I shall endeavour to find out by reference to the numbers I bought last year, and shall order it accordingly.

I trust that Papa's sight has improved, or at least remains stationary. Mr. Maenza greatly admired the *Canto Marziale*, and was particularly delighted with the lines commencing " Sette siri ci colman di mali." I have a favour to ask for him as soon as I return to London. It is that Papa will make me a present of a *Salterio* for ——,[1] who admires his

---

[1] The name has been torn off—perhaps Siesto.

poetry exceedingly, and begged me, if possible, to coax him out of a copy.

We are still expecting Peppino. I anticipate his advent with great pleasure, since he will be a wonderful acquisition in the way of cheerfulness.

Love to all, especially Mamma. Love likewise from Mr. and Mrs. Maenza.

Your most affectionate Brother,
GABRIEL CHAS. ROSSETTI.

P.S.—Is Maria yet arrived ?

B 6.

My brother had just had at Boulogne an attack of small-pox, to which the opening passage in this letter refers. It left no trace behind.

[BOULOGNE.]   Wednesday 22 January 1845.

MY DEAREST MOTHER,

About a couple of hours ago I received your letter, and hasten to answer it. My health improves daily, so much so that yesterday and to-day I have been able to go out. The pustules have almost entirely disappeared, my eyes have not suffered in the least, and I feel much stronger. There is not the least necessity for my staying here after the present week. I shall return (by Folkestone, which the Doctor tells me is necessary) on Saturday or Sunday. He (Dr. R.) says there is not the slightest danger of contagion.

*　　*　　*　　*　　*　　*

I am sorry to say that we are all invalids here, inasmuch as Mrs. Maenza has a violent cold, and Mr. Maenza (who has been unwell in one way or another ever since my arrival) has been seized to-day with a pain in the leg, which troubles him much and almost prevents his walking. Both wish to be remembered to you, and the former says that she should have made it a duty to answer your letter, had she not been ill.

Did you not think Peppino greatly improved ? We have

agreed to keep up a weekly correspondence, in which I intend to spur him on to follow up his plan of making a water-colour for the exhibition. It is perfectly shameful that with his talents, which (in portrait, landscape, and in fact in everything except original composition) are of a very high order, he should consent to remain buried in a country-school.

Being afraid, dear Mamma, that any news I might have to tell would not be of a nature to interest *you*, I shall address it instead to William; hoping to see you all very soon, and begging you to believe me

Your affectionate Son,
GABRIEL CHAS. ROSSETTI.

C 4.

"The prospect of employment which had opened for me" was that which continued to abide with me up to the close of August 1894, when I retired from the public service. I entered the Excise Office (then in Old Broad Street, City, now Inland Revenue Office in Somerset House) as an extra clerk on 6 February 1845—being in my sixteenth year. The translation which my brother made from a Corsican ballad has perished. It is difficult to understand how he could have supposed the powers of his young friend Peppino Maenza, in sketching from Nature, to be "perfectly gigantic," though I dare say they were well up to the average, or even beyond that. Perhaps my brother contrasted these powers with his own—which in that direction were never strong.

[BOULOGNE. 22 *January* 1845.]

DEAR WILLIAM,

I was rejoiced to hear of the prospect of employment which has opened for you. Let us hope that it will be permanent.

Did Peppino show you his Gavarni book? If so, *vous m'en direz des nouvelles* on my return. If not, you will soon be able to console yourself with the store of treasures to be laid before your admiring eyes on the aforesaid occasion.

I have read several books lately, the principal ones being : *M. Dupont*, by Paul de Kock ; *Les Jolies Filles*, by Langon and Touchard ; and *Colomba* and other tales, by Prosper Mérimée. The first is excellent, of course, though not so good as some by the same author. The second is a combination of extreme stupidity with the highest pitch of disgusting obscenity.

As regards *Colomba*, it is perfectly sublime. There is about it a manly and vigorous style which has seldom indeed been equalled. It contains likewise some Corsican ballads, exactly in the style of the old English poetry ; one of which in particular pleased me so much that I took the trouble of translating it. It is, I am sorry to say, a fragment, consisting of a very few verses. Among the other tales in the same volume there is a supernatural one, called *La Vénus d'Ille*, which is unutterably fine.

I have read several other things : among the rest, a poem by Barthélémy entitled *L'Art de Fumer*, carried through three cantos with a most amusing cheek.

I have bagged a few sketches of Peppino's, with which I am sure you will be greatly pleased. Certainly, as long as he keeps to Nature, his powers are perfectly gigantic.

Having no more room, believe me

Your affectionate Brother,

GABRIEL CHAS. ROSSETTI.

B 7.

There are some rather strong utterances in this epistle.

"Lady Charles" was Lady Charles Thynne, a sister-in-law of the Marchioness Dowager of Bath. "Poor Maggy" (Maria) had become governess in the family of Lady Charles. She pretty soon gave up acting as a regular governess, and lived at home, giving lessons at the houses of pupils.

Our Mother, with Christina, was at Herne Bay when this letter was written ; other members of the family had been along with her, but were now back.

DEAR MAMMA,

Accompanying this is a letter from Mr. L., which has just come in time to send. The stupid seal alluded to we retain, as unworthy of carriage expenses. As to the non-sense about Christina's *Verses*, I should advise her to console herself with the inward sense of superiority (assuring her moreover that she will not be the first who has been driven time after time to the same alternative), and to consign the fool and his folly to that utter mental oblivion to the which, I doubt not, she has long ago consigned all those who have been too much honoured by the gift of her book.

I hope you told Lady Charles that that poor Maggy is not to be bullied and badgered out of her life by a lot of beastly brats ; and that Lady C[harles] fully understands the same, and has already provided the said Maggy with a bamboo.

You do not say a word of your own return, although you cannot but know how anxious we are on the subject.

Your affectionate Son,

G. C. ROSSETTI.

While William was away two tickets came from Maroncelli (directed to Christina) for a concert, where Jenny Lind sang her Swedish songs and several other things. As I abhor concerts, I gave them to the Heimanns, who, it appears, were greatly pleased. There was a hymn sung, with choruses, in honour of Pio Nono. I suppose you have not heard that the Austrians have been forced by a general rising to retreat from Ferrara. The papers also affirm, as a certain fact, that the Pope has said that, if this unjustifiable interference is continued, he shall first make a protest to all the Sovereigns of Europe against Austria ; that, in case this should fail, he will excommunicate both Emperor and people ; and that, when driven to the last extremity, he will himself ride in the van of his own army with the sword and the Cross, and that then five millions of Christians shall rise and follow him.

A 3.

This letter, and other subsequent letters as well, show that my brother had much reason to be thankful to our Aunt Charlotte Polidori for liberal assistance afforded to him at contingencies when he would otherwise have been in straits. Miss Polidori, having a regular and sufficient income from her exertions as governess, was, during his earlier professional career, a good deal better off than other members of the family, and was alone capable of producing a comfortable extra sum in hand. My brother speaks of "two men," to one or other of whom he thought of applying for practical artistic training, especially in colouring. One of these, to whom he actually did apply, was Ford Madox Brown, who thus became his life-long and most affectionate friend. I cannot say who the other may have been. He admired towards this time the paintings of Mr. C. H. Lear and Mr. W. D. Kennedy, as testified by some writings of his published by me in his *Collected Works* (vol. ii., pp. 495-6). Perhaps one of these was in his mind. I fear that both these artists are now forgotten, more especially Mr. Lear, who must not be confounded with the landscape-painter and author Edward Lear, writer of *The Book of Nonsense*, and of some books of travel, very sprightly but not at all nonsensical.

[50 CHARLOTTE STREET. ? February 1848.]

DEAR AUNT CHARLOTTE,

It is now several days since I received a very kind letter of yours, but it is not till now that I have been able to decide in my own mind whether or not I had any right to accept the offer it contains. I have at length resolved to do so ; and to this resolution I shall add no mere expression of a gratitude which I shall best prove by profiting as much as possible by the opportunity you so generously place within my reach. Nor do I forget that this is not the first time I have been equally indebted to you.

The motive which has induced me to lay myself under so great an obligation to you is the knowledge that, unless I obtain by some means the advantage which you have offered me, my artistic career will be incalculably retarded, if not

altogether frustrated. Every time I attempt to express my
ideas in colour I find myself baffled, not by want of ability—
I feel this, and why should I not say it?—but by ignorance of
certain apparently insignificant technicalities which, with the
guidance of an experienced artist, might soon be acquired.
Such an artist it is not very easy to find, out of the ranks of
those whose fame either makes them careless of obtaining
pupils, or renders their charges for instruction exorbitant. I
have got however two men in my eye who, possessing
abilities equal to the most celebrated, have by some unaccountable accident not obtained, except among their brother
artists, that renown which they merited. These therefore
would, I should think, be the persons to apply to; and, as
soon as I have communicated with either of them (which I
shall proceed to do immediately), I will write you the result.

I remain, my dear Aunt,
Your grateful Nephew,
GABRIEL C. ROSSETTI.

A 4.

This letter—of superior interest as showing my brother's first
acquaintance with Mr. Brown—calls for little elucidation. The
" work he is engaged upon " must have been the *Wiclif reading his
Bible to John of Gaunt*, or possibly *Cordelia watching the Bedside of
Lear*.

[50 CHARLOTTE STREET. April 1848.]

MY DEAR AUNT,

I dare say you will have thought my long silence
strange enough. The fact is that, when I wrote to Mr. Ford
Brown (one of the artists to whom I alluded in my last), I
affixed to my note the address which I found in the Exhibition Catalogue; but it turns out that he has moved since the
last time he exhibited, so that my letter probably wandered
about before reaching him. When he got it however he
called on me, and requested that I would go down to his

studio (which is in Clipstone Street), and see a work he is engaged upon. I accordingly went, and he entered on the subject of my becoming his pupil. He says that he is not in the habit of giving instruction in a professional way ; but that any assistance he can afford me he shall be exceedingly happy to impart as a friend, and that, even if I wish to go through a regular course of study under his direction—so long as he perceives that I have sufficient talent to make success probable—he most kindly consents to receive me, still as a friend. At the same time he advises me to join an evening academy held in Maddox Street, where students can draw from the living model at, I believe, a trifling expense. I shall of course follow his advice, and to that effect will avail myself of your kind offer—for which, believe me, I am none the less grateful because a fortunate chance (which could not have occurred without it) enables me to dispense with the full extent of the obligation.

On Monday evening next I shall join the academy in question. At the same time I shall of course settle respecting terms etc., whereof I will immediately render you cognizant.

Meanwhile, believe me, my dear Aunt, with renewed thanks,

Your affectionate Nephew,

G. C. ROSSETTI.

A 5.

My brother, in tendering some of his poems to Leigh Hunt for perusal, acted simply from a belief in the critical acumen and sympathy of that veteran writer. Hunt's book of *Lord Byron and some of his Contemporaries* was very familiar to my brother and myself, along with various specimens of his more strictly critical writings and of his poems—which last we relished without unmodified admiration. My brother did call once upon Hunt, in accordance with his invitation, and enjoyed the interview, yet I hardly think that he made any second call—owing not to any real reluctance, but to occupations, distractions, and lack of forwardness.

[50 Charlotte Street. 12 *April* 1848.]

Dear Aunt Charlotte,

For the whole of the past week I have been afflicted with a return of my old atrocious boils, which has effectually precluded the possibility of my stirring out. Of this, however, I dare say you have already been informed by Mamma, who thinks everybody's illnesses of consequence except her own. It was therefore not till last night that I was enabled to join the Maddox Street Academy, according to the recommendation of Mr. Ford Brown. I find that the terms are half-a-guinea monthly—rather more than I had been led to believe. However, as you had made me so kind an offer, I thought that I should not be exceeding the bounds of moderation in joining, which I did. In order to pay for the first month I was obliged to inform Mamma of our correspondence and its object; so that it will now be as well to forward to her, instead of to me, the half-guinea in question, which she disbursed. For all this I will not repeat my thanks, because it would perhaps appear an affectation, but I hope you will believe me nevertheless not ungrateful. The academy is a capital one. The hours are from seven to ten in the evening, and the model sits four times a week.

Notwithstanding illness, I have been for some days in a state of considerable exhilaration. Not long ago I sent some poems of mine to Leigh Hunt, requesting him to read them, and tell me if they were worth anything. His answer is so flattering that I cannot quote any part of it, lest it should seem like conceit. Moreover, he requests me, as soon as he has moved into another house (by reason of which removal he is at present in some bustle and confusion), to "give him the pleasure of my acquaintance"! ! ! !

A 6.

The poem which my brother sent to our Aunt in this instance must, I think, have been *My Sister's Sleep*. At a later date (see C 59 etc.) he certainly did not regard it as "my best thing as yet."

Leigh Hunt's reference to " Dantesque heavens " must have applied in chief to *The Blessed Damozel.*

[50 CHARLOTTE STREET.] *Sunday [? June* 1848].

DEAR AUNT CHARLOTTE,

Ever since I received your last letter (which I fear is very long ago) I have kept it lying on my table as a memento. The fact is that I should have answered it long ago, had I not wished my answer to be accompanied by the poem which I enclose, and which wanted a few finishing touches, which I have at last found time to give it. It is the one of my precious performances which is, I think, the most likely to please you as to style and subject. All the others are of course completely at your service, and shall be sent, if you so desire, immediately upon an intimation from you to that effect. I only refrain from doing so till then because I do not wish you to pay a heavy postage for things of such a little value. I hope you will not be displeased at my adding that I should not wish the verses to be seen by any one but yourself, as I think an unpublished poet is always rather a ridiculous character to appear in before strangers.

Where Hunt, in his kind letter, speaks of my " Dantesque heavens," he refers to one or two of the poems the scene of which is laid in the celestial regions, and which are written in a kind of Gothic manner which I suppose he is pleased to think belongs to the school of Dante. The other word about which you ask me I read as you do— viz., " round."

I continue going to the Life-school in Maddox Street, where I enjoy my studies much. During the day I paint at Mr. Brown's, who is an invaluable acquisition to me as regards the art, and moreover a most delightful friend. We are already quite confidential. His kindness, and the trouble he takes about me, are really astonishing ; I cannot imagine what I have done to deserve them. Yesterday I showed him some of my poetical productions, which he seemed to

By D G Rossetti.   1848

WILLIAM M. ROSSETTI.

like much, especially the one I send you. Indeed I think myself that it is perhaps my best thing as yet, being more simple and like nature.

C 5.

When this letter was written, I was staying at Brighton with our Mother, Christina, and our Grandfather Polidori. The picture on which my brother was then engaged was his first exhibited oil-picture, *The Girlhood of Mary Virgin.* "The first volume of *Keats*" means the first volume of Lord Houghton's *Life of Keats.* "*Joseph* and the *Stories*" mean Charles Wells's drama of *Joseph and his Brethren,* and his *Stories after Nature.* The lines " 'Twas thus, thus is," etc., must (need I say ?) be understood as *intentional* nonsense, or burlesque. "Your Mackay song" was an effusion of the same class, meant as a skit upon songs (such as "There's a good time coming ") by Dr. Charles Mackay. " Our next literary meeting" refers to certain meetings—monthly or the like—which the members of our family, with a very few intimates, held at this time, for reading recent verse-compositions, etc. These meetings rapidly died out.

[50 CHARLOTTE STREET.   20 *August* 1848.]

DEAR WILLIAM,

I write to you because I have a half-hour to spare and nothing else to do. If, being in the same predicament, you happen to answer, tell me what you do at dreary snobbish Brighton ; and, if you have written anything, send me a copy. I have not scribbled a line, but think of shirking the studio to-day, and doing so. I have made a study for the colour of my picture, but, not being quite satisfied therewith, am trying a second. I have also made a nude study for the figure of St. Anne. Hunt and I are now settled down quite comfortably, and he is engaged on the preliminaries for his picture of *Rienzi.*

I have not yet had time to get quite through the first volume of *Keats*, which is exceedingly interesting. He seems to have been a glorious fellow, and says in one place (to my great delight) that, having just looked over a folio of the first and second schools of Italian painting, he has come to the conclusion that the early men surpassed even Raphael himself!

I picked up the other day for sixpence a book I had long wished to see, called *An Exposition of the False Medium and Barriers precluding Men of Genius from the Public.* It is well worth a perusal, and makes mention of *Joseph* and the *Stories.* The date of publication is 1833.

Hunt and I went the other night to Woolner's, where we composed a poem of twenty-four stanzas on the alternate system. I transcribe the last stanza, which was mine, to show you the style of thing :—

> " 'Twas thus, thus is, and thus shall be :
> The Beautiful—the Good—
> Still mirror to the Human Soul
> Its own intensitude ! "

I saw your Mackay song, which is not at all bad. The other thing very poor. . . .

Our next literary meeting, as you will remember, comes off next Saturday. If you can be there, it will be all the better. Does Christina write? Love to Mamma etc.

Sincerely yours,

G. C. ROSSETTI.

C 6.

My brother and I at this time—and in a minor degree our sister Christina—were much addicted to writing sonnets to *bouts rimés*; one of us giving the rhyme-endings, and the other knocking-off the sonnet thereto as fast as practicable. A large proportion of the "poems" of mine published in *The Germ* had been thus composed. We were all three dexterous practitioners in this line, Gabriel the best. A sonnet would sometimes be reeled off in five or seven minutes—ten to twelve minutes was counted a long spell. The sonnets of which he speaks in the present letter had been concocted on this plan by my sister and myself at Brighton.

Hancock was a young sculptor of some repute. It seems that I had seen in Brighton some one whom I supposed to be Munro the sculptor.

50 CHARLOTTE STREET.   *August* 30, 1848.

DEAR WILLIAM,

First, of the sonnets. I grinned tremendously over Christina's *Plague*, which however is forcible, and has something good in it. Her other is first-rate. Pray impress upon her that this, and the one commencing " Methinks the ills of life," are as good as anything she has written, and well worthy of revision. Of your own, *The Completed Soul* and *The Shadow of the Flower* (as I should laconize it) are admirable. " I drink deep-throated of the life of life," splendid. *The Great Gulf Betwixt,* and *The Holy of Holies,* are also very good, though a shade less so. I do not think you have improved *The One Dark Shade* ; touching which, moreover, I hereby solemnly declare that " The trees waving which breezes seem to woo " is no verse at all, and should say " The waving trees." Let me earnestly assure you that this *is the fact.* As for *Thither,* you will never make sense of that till you cut away the simile about the poet. If you have written anything since, send it in your answer, which make as speedy as possible, as I am awfully low and want something to stir me up.

I have not read a line of anything since I wrote, and of course therefore have not finished *Keats.* I dare say, after all, you will have read it before I shall. The only book I have picked up is L. E. L.'s *Improvisatrice,* for which I gave ninepence. By-the-bye, have you got her *Violet* and *Bracelet* with you? I cannot find them in our library.

There was no meeting of the Literary Society on Saturday. Collinson was at the Isle of Wight (whither I did *not* go with him), Hancock also out of town, and Deverell of course anywhere but where he ought to be. He explained his former absence by saying two engagements kept him away, he having otherwise prepared a dramatic scene for the occasion. This I have not yet inspected ; but he sent me the other day a poem, something about a distressingly ideal poet yearning for the insane, which is not quite so incongruous, and contained one or two good things,

Munro has *not* been to Brighton; but the other day, in London, he fancied he saw *you* on the top of an omnibus. As he is a Scotchman, this is dangerous, or rather encouraging. There can be no doubt that one at least is to die. Pray to God that it may be you.

Apropos of death, Hunt and I are going to get up among our acquaintance a Mutual Suicide Association, by the regulations whereof any member, being weary of life, may call at any time upon another to cut his throat for him. It is all of course to be done very quietly, without weeping or gnashing of teeth. I, for instance, am to go in and say, " I say, Hunt, just stop painting that head a minute, and cut my throat"; to which he will respond by telling the model to keep the position as he shall only be a moment, and having done his duty, will proceed with the painting.

The Cyclographic gets on fast. From discontent it has already reached conspiracy. There will soon be a blow-up somewhere.

Hunt and I have prepared a list of Immortals, forming our creed, and to be pasted up in our study for the affixing of all decent fellows' signatures. It has already caused considerable horror among our acquaintance. I suppose we shall have to keep a hair-brush. The list contains four distinct classes of Immortality; in the first of which three stars are attached to each name, in the second two, in the third one, and in the fourth· none. The first class consists only of Jesus Christ and Shakespear. We are also about to transcribe various passages from our poets, together with forcible and correct sentiments, to be stuck up about the walls.

The night before last I sat up and made a design of Coleridge's *Genevieve*, which is certainly the best thing I have done. It took me from eleven to six in the morning. I have also designed very carefully *Hist, said Kate the Queen,* which has come well. I made the other day a small sketch for the *Death of Marmion,* which I mean to do larger, as it is a fine subject in spite of the muffs. I have not written a line.

I went the other night to see *Lucrezia* at Covent Garden. Grisi is most tremendous, and Alboni's song, with the funeral chaunt between the stanzas, very fine—in fact, the whole of the last scene is tremendous, as is also the denunciation at the end of the first act. In this Grisi screamed continuously for about two minutes, and was immense. We must go and see it together. Love to all.

Your affectionate Brother,

G. C. R.

B 8.

Clifton was a painstaking but not powerful painter, a member of the Cyclographic Society.—Collinson's poem of *The Child Jesus* stands published in *The Germ.*

[*Towards September* 1848.]

DEAR MAMMA,

William having suggested that you might perhaps like a note from me, I hasten to send you the same, which I would have done before, had I possessed any news which I thought would interest you. At present indeed I have not a jot more than then, except of that class which William gloats over, and all others scorn. This accordingly I must proceed to retail.

I have returned this minute from the Queen's Theatre in Tottenham Street, whither I went with Collinson and Clifton to witness a profoundly intense drama entitled *Kœuba the Pirate Vessel*, wherein are served up a British sailor and other dainties. One of the pirates wore trouser-straps—which I thought was a touch of nature, considering.

Have you seen Christina's and William's rhyme-sonnets? The second of C[hristina]'s is really good, so is the second of William's. His third is also good, but for the strange word "queer," wherein I recognize the influence of Christina's powerful mind. His fourth has some very good lines, but is wretched nonsense as it stands.

By-the-bye, I will transcribe you a howling canticle written by me yesterday—in what agony of tears let the style suggest. I hereby declare that if snobbishness consists in the assumption of false appearances, the most snobbish of all things is poetry.

THE FALL OF THE LEAF.

Know'st thou not at the Fall of the Leaf.

[Here follows the poem, in a less mature form than the printed version.]

The folio of the great Cyclographic continues its rounds. It is now with Collinson. Calling on him this morning, and finding that he had no sketch ready and did not mean to make one, I designed an angular saint, which we mean to send round under his name, to the mystification and sore disgust, no doubt, of the members in general. I expect we shall end by getting kicked out. The criticisms are becoming more and more scurrilous. Dennis has helped them materially in their downward course by telling Deverell that his last design is a re-version from Retzsch's outline of the same subject.

Collinson has almost finished his poem of *The Child Jesus*. It is a very first-rate affair. He has augmented it with two new incidents, by which addition it is now made emblematical of the " five sorrowful mysteries " of the Atonement. He thinks of leaving to-morrow for Herne Bay, with the intention of remaining there a few days. I may perhaps accompany him, but have not yet quite decided.

Having exhausted everything, believe me, dear Mamma,

Your affectionate Son,

G. C. ROSSETTI.

Will you tell William that our literary criticisms have *not* yet commenced ? I see no reason why he should not retain " grey meadows."

C 7.

James Collinson's brother was a bookseller at Mansfield in Nottinghamshire. I was at this time on a visit to James Collinson and his mother hard by, at Pleasley Hill. The question whether I had found a castle yet refers to my having projected writing a poem descriptive of a ruined castle. I did find one in a different neighbourhood, and composed the lines of blank verse published in

The Germ. The head of St. Anne in my brother's picture was painted from our mother—a very good likeness.

[50 CHARLOTTE STREET.]
Wednesday, 5 P..M. [*22 November* 1848].

DEAR WILLIAM,

I believe Collinson's brother has a subscription library. It has just struck me that he may possibly possess the *Stories after Nature,* or at least know where we might be likely to obtain a copy. I therefore write without delay, in order that you may make diligent enquiry on the subject.

I wrote yesterday the subjoined sonnet touching my picture, for the catalogue. You are going, I believe, to write to Christina, and can then tell me how you like it. I do not quite relish the fourth line, neither am I certain about "strong in grave peace." You will perhaps remember that in a translation of mine from Mamiani there is the expression " An angel-watered plant." This is not in Mamiani at all, but was my own addition, and therefore of course at my free disposal. I have here used it in allusion to the allegory of the picture.

Have you written anything or found a castle yet? St. Anne's head in my picture has succeeded beyond my expectations.

Commend me to Collinson—that is, if he is in a good humour ; and remember that I am

Your affectionate
GABRIEL DANTE ROSSETTI.

SONNET.

This is that Blessed Mary, pre-elect
   God's Virgin. Gone is a great while since she
   Dwelt thus in Nazareth of Galilee.
Loving she was, with temperate respect:
A profound simpleness of intellect
   Was hers, and extreme patience. From the knee
   Faithful and hopeful; wise in charity;
Strong in grave peace; in duty circumspect.
Thus held she through her girlhood; as it were
   An angel-watered lily that near God

Grows and is quiet. Till one dawn, at home
She woke in her white bed, and had no fear
At all, yet wept for a brief period;
Because the fullness of the time was come.

A 7.

The work here spoken of as " my picture this year " is again *The Girlhood of Mary Virgin*. The Marchioness Dowager of Bath—in whose family our Aunt Charlotte Polidori lived for many years, as governess and afterwards as companion—purchased the picture, some short while after the date of this letter. The notion of commissioning Gabriel to do some portraits may probably have come from the Marchioness; no such portraits were produced. The larger and smaller pictures which he was now contemplating must have been *Kate the Queen* and *The Annunciation* (otherwise named *Ecce Ancilla Domini*), which is in the National Gallery. The portrait which "Collinson did of Christina" is now in my possession. The *Art-Union* journal is the same publication which was afterwards termed *The Art Journal*. It did print a criticism of *The Girlhood of Mary Virgin*—and a laudatory one. The final question addressed to our Aunt—"Have you written any more poetry?"—refers to the fact that she had (by a sort of sudden impulse, for which she could not well account) thrown off some verses in a quasi-ballad form; my brother thought there was "something in them." This was a curious "sport" on her part, and remained solitary; for she was not in the least a poetical person, either in performance or in temperament. I will here give the verses, which I found among the papers left by Christina at her decease:—

He wanders on, he wanders on—
  I know not where he's gone:
I follow him, I follow him,
  Who has my heart as his.

He waxèd hot, he waxèd hot
  When gently I him told
My mother's fears, my mother's fears
  That he my peace would mar.

He called me cold, he called me cold;
  My hand from his he threw:
He would not hear, he would not hear
  My bitter words of grief.

O mother dear, O mother dear,
Break not thy heart for me:
I'll hasten on, I'll hasten on,
And then fall down and die.

The reader may perhaps observe that this is the first letter bearing the signature "Dante Gabriel Rossetti." It must therefore have been towards the close of his twenty-first year, or the beginning of his twenty-second, that he adopted this form of the Christian names, to which he ever afterwards adhered.

[? 50 CHARLOTTE STREET.]
Tuesday Morning [? *May* 1849].

MY DEAR AUNT,

I am much obliged to you for your note of yesterday, which I would have answered before this morning if my time had been less taken up.

As my picture this year has created some interest, it is desirable that I should come before the public next year as prominently as possible, so as to succeed in establishing at once some degree of reputation. I am therefore about to commence immediately another work, hoping thus to get two done before the next exhibition—one of some size, and another smaller. For this purpose I am now engaged on making drawings. These things considered, I should be unwilling to endanger my chance of finishing two pictures by employing my time on portraits, unless the latter were really to compensate me by a good remuneration.

My terms therefore would be as follows :—

For a small full-length in chalks (18 inches by 15 or thereabouts), £5 5s.

For a small portrait in oil, like the one Collinson did of Christina, £8 8s.

For a larger portrait in oil, the price would be proportionate according to the size.

I do not take miniatures ; and, as to the number of sittings, that must of course depend in a great measure on the patience of the sitter. Moreover, as I have not much practice in portraits, I cannot be positive in that matter.

Should these terms prove too high (as I almost anticipate

that they will), I hope that you will not consider me foolish in thus rejecting a linnet in the hand for the sake of two pheasants in the bush.

The other day I went to the Free Exhibition, with Millais, Hunt, and two or three other friends ; and we remarked one of the critics of the *Art-Union* journal standing before my picture for a quarter of an hour at least. I therefore anticipate, on the first of next month, to be either praised or regularly cut up in that paper. As the paper is very influential, I hope it will be the former. I have already been approved by the only two other journals whose opinion goes for anything in matters of art—the *Athenæum* and the *Builder*. As soon as the *Art-Union* makes its appearance I will take care that you are apprized of its contents in my regard, as I have reason to know of old how much kind interest you take in my unworthy self.

Mamma and the rest desire me to send you their loves with my own, with which valuable missive I remain

Your affectionate Nephew,

DANTE GABRIEL ROSSETTI.

Have you written any more poetry ?

C 8.

The main subject of this letter is the projected Præraphaelite magazine, shortly afterwards entitled *The Germ*. I was at Ventnor (Isle of Wight) when the letter was written. Collinson had accompanied me to Cowes, but was now gone again.

The joke " It doesn't show (so much) at night " is taken from one of Hood's funny poems, in which a negro's ghost is made to appear by daylight—

> "Because he was a Blackamoor,
> And wouldn't show at night."

Herbert, who is spoken of as one of the proprietors of *The Germ*, was the R.A. painter John R. Herbert, then well known to Collinson. He did not however actually become a proprietor. North was William North, an eccentric literary man, not without a spice of

genius, of whom we then saw a goodish deal—author of *Anti-
Coningsby, The Infinite Republic,* and other works. Not very long
after this he emigrated to the United States, and in 1854 committed
suicide.   Bliss was a young lawyer of some literary aspirations.
He also emigrated, to Australia.

Holman Hunt and my brother had at this time resolved to make
a little tour to Paris and Belgium, which soon afterwards came off.

Dickinson means Lowes (or else Robert) Dickinson, members
of a flourishing print-selling firm in Bond Street.   Mr. Lowes
Dickinson is now, as for many years past, a leading portrait-painter.
Williams, whom my brother had met at Dickinson's, was Mr. William
Smith Williams, the first discoverer of Charlotte Brontë's genius.
He was brother-in-law to Charles Wells, and became father-in-law
to Mr. Lowes Dickinson.

This letter shows the origin of my brother's poem *The Staff and
Scrip.*   I must have returned to him the synopsis of the subject
which he sent me.   I do not remember the "other plot of his
own devising."

"I want to know all about your poem."   This refers to a blank-
verse narrative poem which I was writing at Ventnor, intending
it for *The Germ.*   It first saw the light of actual publication in 1868,
in the *Broadway Magazine,* under the name of *Mrs. Holmes Grey.*
The notion of my brother's coming with Woolner to join me at
Ventnor did not take effect.

[LONDON. *Tuesday Night,* 18 *September* 1849.]

DEAR WILLIAM,

Feeling utter disgust at everything, I sit down to
write to you, hoping thereby to get myself into a philoso-
phical frame of mind.   I ought to have written before,
having somewhat to say, but in the daytime the awful bore
confronted me in too glaring a manner.   It doesn't show
(so much) at night.   This filthy joke is as a mill-stone round
the neck of my spirit, to sink it to the lowest abyss of
degradation, whence (having no further to descend) it can
now indite this epistle in a mood of sullen calmness.

I believe we have found a publisher for the Magazine—
viz., Aylott and Jones, 8 Paternoster Row.   I was introduced
to them about a week back by a printer, a friend of

Hancock's. They seemed perfectly willing to publish for us, and the only reason that we have not yet printed the prospectus with their names attached is that I wished first to be sure that the commission they ask (10 per cent, not on the profits only, but on the *entire sale*) is a just one. The duty of sifting this matter devolved on the dilatory Deverell —a fact which will fully account for its being yet in abeyance. I hope from day to day however to have the prospectus out. We have made enquiries about the printing of the etchings, which it appears would cost us about 2s. or 2s. 6d. a hundred, exclusive of the cost of paper. Our proprietors at present amount to nine (including Hancock, who has been enrolled, and Herbert, who I fear is rather a doubtful case). I cannot see why old Collinson should not be made to take a share. Endeavour to impress this on the amount of mind he possesses. I strongly suspect that the cost of printing a number will not be less than nearly £20. North however has given me an estimate of what it would cost with the printer who did his *Signs*, which brings it only to £13, including even prospectus. He swears positively that it can be done for this, and that a penny more will be cheating. On the other hand, the estimate given by the Tuppers is £13 for printing only, including, I think, paper. I am still waiting for a third estimate which Haynes, Hancock's friend, is to send me. Under these circumstances we must look out for as many proprietors as possible. I attended a meeting last night at Bliss's, where I had meant to bring up the subject and sound him. . . . For my part, I am certain that, as soon as the prospectus is printed, we shall be able, among the lot of us, to secure at least 250 subscribers before the thing is out at all, and this will be something. Tell Collinson, if he is writing to his brother, to ask him about the publishers' percentage. I have no doubt he could enlighten us.

Stephens is writing for the first number an article on Early Art which I have not seen. Hunt is at his etching ; he is now tremendously agog about the thing. I know not exactly when we shall start on our tour—probably next week. The

fact is, we ought not by rights to go at all. Hunt's background is still detaining him. Brown was in town for a day,
but is gone back again.

The other night I was at Dickinson's, where I met
Williams, who has lent me a tale by Wells not contained
in the *Stories after Nature*; as also a poem by Linton on
the affairs of Rome. I have not yet read it.

I have done but little in any way, having wasted several
days at the Museum, where I have been reading up all
manner of old romaunts, to pitch upon stunning words for
poetry. I have found several, and also derived much enjoyment from the things themselves, some of which are
tremendously fine. I have copied out an exquisite little
ballad, quoted in the preface to one of the collections.

I bought the other day the original editions of the lyrical
numbers of the *Bells and Pomegranates*, which you remember
contain variations; also Horne's *Orion* (original edition) and
Death of Marlowe; also (for 5s.) a translation, in two volumes,
of the *Gesta Romanorum*—a book I had long wished to possess.
I was however rather disappointed, having expected to find
lots of glorious stories for poems. Four or five good ones
there are; one of which (which I have entitled *The Scrip and
Staff*) I have considerably altered, and enclose for your
opinion, together with another plot of my own devising.
Both of these I contemplate versifying when free of existing
nightmares. Tell me what you think thereof; and please
to return them with your answer, as I may want them. Let
me also have Collinson's verdict. I have only written twelve
stanzas of *Bride-Chamber Talk* since your departure; but
hope to get through some more to-night before going to bed.

I want to know all about your poem—what the plot is,
and how much you have written. By-the-bye, I added three
stanzas yesterday to *My Sister's Sleep*, which I think were
wanted as stop-gaps. I wish if possible to have this in No. 1.

What is Collinson after? I suppose (ahem!) he works
like a horse; of course I mean a Jerusalem pony. I hope
to follow up this delicate compliment with a letter as soon

as possible ; meanwhile remember my brotherhood to him.
Millais is still in the country.   Write soon.

DANTE G. ROSSETTI.

P.S.—Going downstairs to get your address, I find Collinson
there, whose projected return I had quite forgotten.   He has
given me a vagueish notion of what you are writing.   Let
me hear from you *immediately*, as Woolner and I are going
forthwith into the country somewhere for a few days, and, if
accounts are good, the vine-branches of your rhetoric might
induce us to go up into the land and possess it with you.

C 9.

Some sonnets of mine are referred to in this letter.   *Her First
Season* appears printed in *The Germ*.   It was a *bouts-rimés* performance.   The sonnets on Death were earlier by, I think, a year
or two.   They have never been inflicted on the public eye.   My
sister's sonnet *Vanity Fair* was a sportive effusion also done to
bouts-rimés, and likely now to be soon published.   " A prospectus
of the *Thoughts* " means " a prospectus of the *Thoughts towards
Nature* "—this being the sub-title (at that date the intended title)
of *The Germ* magazine.   " Woolner's poems " included no doubt
My Beautiful Lady, printed in the first number of *The Germ*.

[LONDON].   *Monday* [24 *September* 1849].

DEAR WILLIAM,

Coming to Woolner's at the moment of his receiving
your last, I undertake (in consequence of a miserable pro-
stration produced in him by unmanly sloth) to answer it
for him.

In the matter of editorship, your objections are, I think,
set at rest by the fact that we have excluded from the title
the words " Conducted by Artists."   You are thus on exactly
the same footing as all other contributors.   The publishers
(whose names appear in the prospectus) are Messrs. Aylott
and Jones, who were found on enquiry to be highly respectable.   The prospectus is now at the printer's, and in a day
or' two I expect to send you a copy.   Patmore, to whom it

was shown, seemed considerably impressed in its favour, and was even induced thereby (open thine ears, eyes, or whatever other organs may be most available) to contribute for the first number a little poem of three stanzas called *The Seasons*, which I copy here, not to inflict on you the agony of hope deferred.

> "The crocus, in the shrewd March morn,
>   Thrusts up his saffron spear;
> And April dots the sombre thorn
>   With gems and loveliest cheer.
>
> "Then sleep the Seasons, full of might,
>   While slowly swells the pod,
> And rounds the peach, and in the night
>   The mushroom bursts the sod.
>
> "The Winter falls; the frozen rut
>   Is bound with silver bars;
> The white drift heaps against the hut;
>   And night is pierced with stars."

Stunning, is it not? But unluckily we are not to publish his name, which he intends to keep back altogether from all articles until his new volume is out. Woolner showed him some of your sonnets, which he thought first-rate in many respects, but wanting in melody. The *First Season* he said was in all points quite equal to Wordsworth, except in this one. ·The sonnets on Death he admired as poetry, but totally eschewed as theory, so much so indeed that he says it prevented him from enjoying them in any regard. This of course will not keep you awake at nights, since Shelley was with you, and watches (perhaps) from his grave Mrs. Patmore was greatly pleased with Christina's poems. I do not think that Coventry himself read much of them, but he was delighted with the sonnet *Vanity Fair*.

You seem to be getting on like fury with your poem. How the deuce can you manage to do 103 lines in a day? I agree however with Woolner as regards your surgeon, who is a wretched sneak—quite a sniggering squelch of a fellow. Do something, by all means, to pull him out of his present mire.

For my part I have done scarcely anything—having been sadly knocked about in the matter of this prospectus and other bores. I wrote last night to W. B. Scott, returning him his books, and saying that I should send him a prospectus of the *Thoughts* in a few days, with a request for contributions in the poetical or literary line.

I believe Hunt and self will start on Monday at the latest, so that I fear I may not see you. If you really think you will be up on Tuesday however, let me know, as I would then manage to defer our departure, and say good-bye to you personally. Moreover I long to hear your poem. I have done nothing to *Hand and Soul.* There is time however, as I believe the first number is to be delayed yet a month, in order to have it out at Christmas, which every one thinks desirable. *November* is at present in the prospectus ; but when I get a proof I shall alter it to *December.* I was at Collinson's the other evening, who seems to have been disgracefully lazy at the Isle of Wight. Seddon, who knows that ilk well, says that you should go on to a place called Niton, about six miles from Ventnor, and by far the best in the Island.

With respect to Woolner's poems, I can tell you that Patmore was stunned ; the only defect he found being that they were a trifle too much in earnest in the passionate parts, and too *sculpturesque* generally. He means by this that each stanza stands too much alone, and has its own ideas too much to itself. I think you will agree with me in thinking this objection groundless, or at least irrelevant. Write soon.

D. G. ROSSETTI.

C 10.

The project of visiting Brittany, " for the purpose of seeing Wells about his new edition "—*i.e.*, a new edition of *Joseph and his Brethren*, which my brother hankered after—did not take effect. The P.S. refers to my drawing—which I did on and off for a short while—from the living model, along with some other students.

[LONDON.] *Tuesday* [25 *September* 1849].

DEAR WILLIAM,

I find that by delaying our departure I should be inconveniencing Hunt. I therefore start with him for France and Belgium on Thursday at half-past one, without going at all into the country with Woolner. Either going or on our return we shall visit Brittany, if possible, for the purpose of seeing Wells about his new edition.

Even should the prospectuses be all printed before I go, I am almost certain of not finding time to send any of them about. Would you therefore undertake this job on your return to town, sending to every friend you can possibly think of, as well as to all literary men and artists of anything like our own views ? You must also look sharp about advertising, a certain amount of which is unfortunately indispensable.

I believe there is nothing more to be said. Farewell therefore till such time as I see you again.

DANTE G. ROSSETTI.

Seddon is anxious to know whether you intend joining in the model at his place. When in town, just write him a word or two about this matter. A note to T. Seddon Esq. Jun., Gray's Inn Road, will reach him.

C 11.

My brother was very averse from the idea of having, after his death, anything published which he had rejected as juvenile or inferior. When I was compiling his *Collected Works*, published at the end of 1886, I felt that some of the verses which appear in his letters of this period were fully good enough for insertion there. Other verses I have omitted from the *Collected Works*, but they do not seem to me unfitted to figure here, as forming a portion of his Family-letters.

At the end of the first snatch of blank verse, the last two fine lines may be recognized as having been utilized, in a somewhat altered form, in the poem which he himself published, *The Portrait*. He afterwards altered them in the blank verse, but I retain them here. The lines at Boulogne, " The sea is in its listless chime," etc., have also appeared in a revised form, and constitute one of my brother's most impressive lyrics.   In all these descriptive verses, about railway-travelling, etc., the reader will readily perceive that the writer was bent on the Præraphaelite plan—that of sharply realizing an impression on the eye, and through the eye on the mind.

BETWEEN LONDON AND PARIS.
Thursday 27 September 1849.

LONDON TO FOLKESTONE.
(Half-past one to half-past five.)

A CONSTANT keeping-past of shaken trees,
And a bewildered glitter of loose road;
Banks of bright growth, with single blades atop
Against white sky; and wires—a constant chain—
That seem to draw the clouds along with them
(Things which one stoops against the light to see
Through the low window; shaking by at rest,
Or fierce like water as the swiftness grows);
And, seen through fences or a bridge far off,
Trees that in moving keep their intervals
Still one 'twixt bar and bar; and then at times
Long reaches of green level, where one cow,
Feeding among her fellows that feed on,
Lifts her slow neck, and gazes for the sound.

There are six of us: I that write away;
Hunt reads Dumas, hard-lipped, with heavy jowl
And brows hung low, and the long ends of hair
Standing out limp.   A grazier at one end
(Thank luck not my end!) has blocked out the air,
And sits in heavy consciousness of guilt.
The poor young muff who's face to face with me,
Is pitiful in loose collar and black tie,
His latchet-button shaking as we go.
There are flowers by me, half upon my knees,
Owned by a dame who's fair in soul, no doubt:
The wind that beats among us carries off
Their scent, but still I have them for my eye.

Fields mown in ridges; and close garden-crops
Of the earth's increase; and a constant sky
Still with clear trees that let you see the wind;
And snatches of the engine-smoke, by fits
Tossed to the wind against the landscape, where
Rooks stooping heave their wings upon the day

Brick walls we pass between, passed so at once
That for the suddenness I cannot know
Or what, or where begun, or where at end.
Sometimes a Station in grey quiet; whence,
With a short gathered champing of pent sound,
We are let out upon the air again.
Now nearly darkness; knees and arms and sides
Feel the least touch, and close about the face
A wind of noise that is along like God.
Pauses of water soon, at intervals,
That has the sky in it;—the reflexes
O' the trees move towards the bank as we go by,
Leaving the water's surface plain. I now
Lie back and close my eyes a space; for they
Smart from the open forwardness of thought
Fronting the wind ——

——I did not scribble more,
Be certain, after this; but yawned, and read,
And nearly dozed a little, I believe;
Till, stretching up against the carriage-back,
I was roused altogether, and looked out
To where, upon the desolate verge of light,
Yearned, pale and vast, the iron-coloured sea.

FOLKESTONE TO BOULOGNE.

(6 *to* 9.—*Rough passage.*)

" Darkness, as darkness itself, and as the shadow of death; without any
order, and where the light is as darkness."—*Job.*
" If ye know them, they are in the valley of the shadow of death."—*Ibid.*

Friday 28.

AT BOULOGNE. UPON THE CLIFFS: NOON.

THE sea is in its listless chime,
  Like Time's lapse rendered audible;
  The murmur of the earth's large shell.
In a sad blueness beyond rhyme
  It ends; Sense, without Thought, can pass
  No stadium further. Since Time was,
This sound hath told the lapse of Time.

No stagnance that Death wins,—it hath
  The mournfulness of ancient Life,
  Always enduring at dull strife.

Like the world's heart, in calm and wrath,
    Its painful pulse is in the sands.
    Last utterly, the whole sky stands,
Grey and not known, along its path.

BOULOGNE TO AMIENS AND PARIS.

(3 *to* 11 P.M.; 3*rd class*.)

STRONG extreme speed, that the brain hurries with,
Further than trees, and hedges, and green grass
Whitened by distance,—further than small pools
Held among fields and gardens,—further than
Haystacks and windmill-sails and roofs and herds,—
The sea's last margin ceases at the sun.

The sea has left us, but the sun remains.
Sometimes the country spreads aloof in tracts
Smooth from the harvest; sometimes sky and land
Are shut from the square space the window leaves
By a dense crowd of trees, stem behind stem
Passing across each other as we pass:
Sometimes tall poplar-wands stand white, their heads
Outmeasuring the distant hills. Sometimes
The ground has a deep greenness; sometimes brown
In stubble; and sometimes no ground at all,
For the close strength of crops that stand unreaped.
The water-plots are sometimes all the sun's,—
Sometimes quite green through shadows filling them,
Or islanded with growths of reeds,—or else
Masked in grey dust like the wide face o' the fields.
And still the swiftness lasts; that to our speed
The trees seem shaken like a press of spears.

There is some count of us:—folks travelling-capped,
Priesthood, and lank hard-featured soldiery,
Females (no women), blouses, Hunt, and I.

We are relayed at Amiens. The steam
Snorts, chafes, and bridles, like three-hundred horse,
And flings its dusky mane upon the air.
Our company is thinned, and lamps alight:
But still there are the folks in travelling-caps—
No priesthood now, but always soldiery,
And babies to make up for show in noise,
Females (no women), blouses, Hunt, and I.

Our windows at one side are shut for warmth.
Upon the other side, a leaden sky,
Hung in blank glare, makes all the country dim,
Which too seems bald and meagre,—be it truth,
Or of the waxing darkness. Here and there
The shade takes light, where in thin patches stand
The unstirred dregs of water.

                         Hunt can see
A moon, he says; but I am too far back.
Still the same speed and thunder. We are stopped
Again, and speech tells clearer than in day.

Hunt has just stretched to tell me that he fears
I and my note-book may be taken for
The stuff that goes to make an " émissaire
De la perfide." Let me abate my zeal:
There is a stout gendarme within the coach.

This cursed pitching is too bad. My teeth
Jingle together in it; and my legs
(Which I got wet at Boulogne this good day
Wading for star-fish) are so chilled that I
Would don my coat, were not these seats too hard
To spare it from beneath me, and were not
The love of ease less than the love of sloth.

Hunt has just told me it is nearly eight:
We do not reach till half-past ten. Drat verse,
And steam, and Paris, and the fins of Time!
Marry, for me, look you, I will go sleep.

Most of them slept; I could not—held awake
By jolting clamour, with shut eyes; my head
Willing to nod and fancy itself vague.
Only at Stations I looked round me, when
Short silence paused among us, and I felt
A creeping in my feet from abrupt calm.
At such times Hunt would jerk himself, and then
Tumble uncouthly forward in his sleep.
This lasted near three hours. The darkness now
Stayeth behind us on the sullen road,
And all this light is Paris. Dieu merci.

                     PARIS. *Saturday Night,* 29.
Send me, dear William, by return of post,
As much as you can manage of that rhyme

Incurred at Ventnor. Bothers and delays
Have still prevented me from copying this
Till now; now that I do so, let it be
Anticipative compensation.
Numéro 4 Rue Geoffroy Marie,
Faubourg Montmartre, près des Boulevards.
Dear William, labelled thus the thing will reach.

C 12.

This letter is an amusing example of the one-sided and in great
part uninformed feeling about works of art which prevailed among
the Præraphaelites in their early days. My brother was now in the
twenty-second year of his age. In later years he heartily admired
Delacroix, and worshipped Michelangelo; while for Hippolyte
Flandrin he would have felt little beyond a tepid and critical
respect.

The "monosyllable current amongst us" occurs further on in the
letter—viz., slosh. This term (quasi slush) was applied to paintings
of the over-facile and inaccurate kind.

4 RUE GEOFFROY MARIE, FAUBOURG MONTMARTRE, PARIS.
Thursday [4 *October* 1849].

DEAR WILLIAM,

Send me your poem *immediately*, with no more delay
than is quite unavoidable. Sit up all night copying, and
send it. Copy it on thin large sheets in double columns
(like my journal, which I posted the other day for the Isle
of Wight, and which no doubt you can get by sending
thither), and I have no doubt the postage will not be ruinous.
I gather from the outside of your note that you paid 1s. 3d.
for it in London; whereas Maria's (being, I presume, unpaid)
reached me for sixteen sous. It is therefore evident that,
unless the heavy postage was owing to the weight of your
letter, it will be advisable to leave me to pay for letters. I
presume that my journal (which, by-the-bye, is not in *rhyme*
but in blank verse), as well as a joint letter from Hunt and
self to Stephens and Woolner, will reach free of expense, as
they were paid for here. Let me know about this, as it is
as well to understand the postage. I should have paid for

the first note I sent to Maria, but it was too late in the day to do so.

I am obliged to write this on English note-paper, as Hunt has ruined the last sheet of French we possessed by endeavouring to concoct an undecipherable monogram of P.R.B. to be signed to passports etc. The paper however is very thin, and I think will not incur additional postage.

We have made the acquaintance here of two very nice French fellows, named Cotourrier and Levasseur. Perhaps Woolner remembers them as they do him. We climbed with them the other day to the very top of Notre Dame, whence we had a most glorious view of Paris, and shouted in the spirit. The Cathedral itself is inconceivably stunning, and contains most glorious things to put in pictures. While climbing, a sonnet came whole into my head, which however I have almost forgotten, owing to the hurry of the moment and the talk, I suppose. I am trying constantly to remember it, and will copy it in my next note if I succeed.

There is also a little English cove here of the name of Broadie, who is very obliging and really rather clever. We see him a good deal. . . .

I bought yesterday a great number of Gavarni's *Charivari* sketches at two sous each. I have no doubt of being able to pick up more. The number of book and print stalls is quite incredible. Hunt and I begin to like Paris immensely—the city itself, I mean.

At the Luxembourg there are the following really wonderful pictures—viz., two by Delaroche, two by Robert-Fleury, one by Ingres, one by Hesse ; others by Scheffer, Granet, etc., are very good. The rest, with a few mediocre exceptions, we considered trash. Delacroix (except in two pictures which show a kind of savage genius) is a perfect beast, though almost worshipped here. The school of David got at first frightfully abused for making a stand against him on his appearance. They were quite right, being themselves greatly his superiors, and indeed some of them men who I have no doubt would have done much better in better times.

We ran hurriedly through the Louvre yesterday for the first time. Of course detail as yet is impossible, and indeed, to say the truth, there is a monosyllable current amongst us which enables a P.R.B. to dispense almost entirely with details on the subject. There is however a most wonderful copy of a fresco by Angelico, a tremendous Van Eyck, some mighty things by that real stunner Lionardo, some ineffably poetical Mantegnas (as different as day from night from what we have in England), several wonderful Early Christians whom nobody ever heard of, some tremendous portraits by some Venetian whose name I forget, and a stunning *Francis I.* by Titian. Géricault's *Medusa* is also very fine on the whole. We have not yet been through all the rooms. In one there is a ceiling by Ingres which contains some exceedingly good things. This fellow is quite unaccountable. One picture of his in the Luxembourg is unsurpassed for exquisite perfection by anything I have ever seen, and he has others there for which I would not give two sous—filthy slosh. I believe we have not yet seen any of Scheffer's best works. Delaroche's *Hémicycle* in the Beaux Arts is a marvellous performance. In the same place is a copy of Michelangelo's *Judgment* —an admirable copy, I believe, but one of the most comic performances I ever saw in my life.

Now for the best. Hunt and I solemnly decided that the most perfect works, taken *in toto*, that we have seen in our lives, are two pictures by Hippolyte Flandrin (representing Christ's Entry into Jerusalem, and his departure to death) in the Church of S. Germain des Prés. Wonderful! wonderful!! wonderful!!! Tell Hancock of this.

D. G. R.

C 13.

I ought perhaps to apologize for publishing the earlier portion of this letter, criticizing as it does with more than brotherly indulgence my blank-verse narrative poem *Mrs. Holmes Grey*. The feelings which have withheld me from cutting it out will no doubt be intelligible, in whole or in part, to the reader, and I will say no more on the subject.

The informing idea of the poem was to apply to verse-writing the same principle of strict actuality and probability of detail which the Præraphaelites upheld in their pictures. It was in short a Præraphaelite poem. The subject is a conversation about the death of a lady, a surgeon's wife, who had died suddenly in the house of another medical man for whom she had conceived a vehement and unreciprocated passion; and a newspaper report of the coroner's inquest occupies a large space in the composition. At this time the proposed title of the piece was *An Exchange of News*.

The sonnet on the Place de la Bastille, somewhat modified, is published in my brother's *Ballads and Sonnets*, 1881. That on the *Venetian Pastoral by Giorgione*, also modified, is in the *Poems*, 1870 and 1881. It had previously been printed in *The Germ*. In another sonnet occurs a reference to laziness on the part of Mr. Woolner. This is mostly a joke. From the sonnet on the Salle Valentino I have been compelled to omit some phrases which express, in terms unprintably energetic, the writer's disgust at the grossnesses of the scene.

Cottingham, mentioned towards the close of the letter, was an architect of some name. He showed a disposition to purchase something of my brother's, but never did so. Mr. Morrison was, I think, a landscape-painter. Signor Ronna was an Italian refugee in Paris, an old acquaintance of our Father.

"The sonnets on Keats" were three poor sonnets of my own composition, and a better one by Christina. Possibly my brother did some also—now lost.

[RUE GEOFFROY MARIE 4, PARIS.
Monday 8 October 1849.]

DEAR WILLIAM,

The arrival of your poem yesterday was about the best thing that has happened since my arrival here. I read it at once twice through, to the very great satisfaction of Hunt and myself. The points that we noted in any way especially I will now proceed to communicate. But first of all we both think that a better title might be found. I dare say you will manage to think of one.

I do not know if you remember that at the beginning of the *Eve of St. Mark* there are the lines—

> "The city streets were cool and fair,
> From wholesome drench of April rains."

This is like the beginning of your poem; and, though of course the statement of a fact from observation cannot even be a reminiscence of what has been done before, still I think it is perhaps as well not to have at the very outset a line which some people might manage to draw conclusions from. The expression " fish *flapping* about " might I think be altered to something newer, and even more strikingly truthful.

The 2nd paragraph is excellent; the 3rd is good. In the speech of Harling (4th paragraph) I think some little bright detail might still be introduced to increase the force. The 5th is admirable—last line especially so. In the 6th the word *rustling* is rather old, and the last line a trifle common and awkward. In the 7th I see no necessity for second line, which I think makes too much of a trifling point in so serious a poem. Would not " Loosed itself and touched along his forehead " etc. be quite sufficient? Both Hunt and I thought you might alter " Something at a window." It is rather melodramatic perhaps. "What was at a window" suggested itself to me, but I believe this is too Tennysonian. In the 8th I do not like the position of the man altogether; it seems a little violent. One can fancy some of the Adelphi people doing it. The 9th and 11th will do very well; the 10th is first-rate. In the 12th, I think (as they had been always in correspondence) that Harling might in some way allude to their letters—quite slightly of course, by a word. At present it seems rather abrupt, and at first looks as if they had known nothing whatever of each other for years. In the 13th the " Sir " belongs, as of course you must be aware, to the French school of ultra-metaphysics. 14th to 21st all capital. The last line of the 22nd appears to me scarcely in character with Grey. I have something of the same sort in my *Bride-Chamber Talk*, but I will have the

cheek to say that I think it is there more appropriate to the
personage.   23rd excellent.   The line composing 24th seems
rather common.   What do you think of "that his laugh
troubled him," or "It seemed to Harling the laugh was not
his"?   25th admirable.   Perhaps at the end "I am one"
would be more absolutely conversational than "I am such."
26th capital; 27th first-rate; 28th excellent; 29th and 30th
very good, except that the lady would be employed in a
more feminine and I believe equally natural manner, were
she helping the wounded instead of fighting.   31st and 32nd
very good; perhaps the last two lines a little crackjaw.   In
the 33rd the "divided into oblongs" business reads as trivial.
The last line of 34th a little common.   35th very good.
Something newer, I think, might be done at the end of
36th.   There might be, especially in Grey, a kind of shaking
of the jaw and pressing into the clavicle which could be made
very fine.   37th excellent; 38th remarkably fine.   39th not
quite so good.   40th and on as far as the inquest exceedingly powerful.   I think certainly that the piece about the
lilac dress and the hair is rather Gallically introduced, and
Hunt remarked that the "worn plain" is an expression more
likely to be used by a woman than a man.

Now for the inquest.   I do not think that "disclosures
extraordinary" is the newspaper phrase, but "extraordinary
disclosures."   If so, I would be careful to alter this, as it may
be taken for a poetical inversion.   "The worthy coroner" is
a little strong; but I shall not argue this, as no doubt you
consider it the hinge of the poem.   At "accommodated with
a chair" Hunt suggested "a seat" instead, as being a trifle
less comic.   "A something trembled at her lips" appears to
me, on the other hand, too poetical for evidence.   In my
copy the line "So she assured that should come to pass" has
had some syllable omitted by mistake, I suppose.   There is
one man in England who will understand the phrase "the
living-up of her old love": his name is Alfred Tennyson.
If you write for any other Englishman, this must be cut out.
"That in the first letter you sent deceased" is rather a harsh

line. All the passage about the familiarities looks rather ambiguous. I do not know whether you mean it to be so. In the woman's letter, the "looking strange" Hunt suggested might be altered to some impression which she could more clearly realize to herself. I however do not feel certain as to this. The Christ business is very good as it is, and the line about the stone has also something appropriate in it. The following adaptation suggested itself to me, as uniting the qualities of both :—

> "And prayed of Christ (he knowing how it was)
> That, if this thing were sinful unto death,
> He would himself be first to throw the stone.
> So then I entered," etc.

Your inquest is, on the whole, I think, a very clever and finished piece of writing,—wonderfully well-managed in parts and possessing some strong points of character. The woman's letter is exceedingly truthful and fine. The rest of the poem is very first-rate indeed—some passages really stunning. Hunt suggested that "Who ever heard of *Dr.* Luton yet?" would more thoroughly explain Grey's intention, and I fancy he is right. True, Luton is a surgeon, but surgeons are constantly called doctors by courtesy. I am not certain whether a few additional lines after the last one would not finish the poem more soberly.

I will now sum up, with "the worthy coroner." I think your poem is very remarkable, and altogether certainly the best thing you have done. It is a painful story, told without compromise, and with very little moral, I believe, beyond commonplaces. Perhaps it is more like Crabbe than any other poet I know of ; not lacking no small share of his harsh reality—less healthy, and at times more poetical. I would advise you, if practicable, to show it to any medical man at hand—Dr. Hare, for instance. He might discover some absurdity which escapes us, or suggest something of value to the story.

Now for myself. I am ashamed to declare I have nothing

yet to offer you in return for your 700 lines but "*quelques méchants sonnets*"—real humbugs, which it is almost absurd to send, lest they should be taken for a compensation. Moreover one or two of them are sloshy in the rhymes of the first half. I think however I could find authorities among the early Italians. Here is the one which came into my head on the staircase of Notre Dame, and which I have since remembered, though I fancy with some deterioration.

> As one who, groping in a narrow stair,
> Hath a strong sound of bells upon his ears,
> Which, being at a distance off, appears
> Quite close to him because of the pent air;
> So with this France. She stumbles file and square,
> Darkling and without space for breath: each one
> Who hears the thunder says, "It shall anon
> Be in among her ranks to scatter her."
> This may be; and it may be that the storm
> Is spent in rain upon the unscathed seas,
>   Or wasteth other countries ere it die:
> Till she,—having climbed always through the swarm
> Of darkness and of hurtling sound,—from these
>   Shall step forth on the light in a still sky.

I forget whether I told you that it was the ringing of the bells as we climbed the staircase which gave me this valuable inspiration.

The other day we walked to the Place de la Bastille. Hunt and Broadie smoked their cigars, while I, in a fine frenzy conjured up by association and historical knowledge, leaned against the Column of July, and composed the following sonnet :—

> How dear the sky hath been above this place !
> Small treasures of this sky that we see here,
> Seen weak through prison-bars from year to year—
> Eyed with a painful prayer upon God's grace
> To save, and tears which stayed along the face
> Lifted till the sun went. How passing dear
> At night when through those bars a wind left clear
> The skies and moonlight made a mournful space !

This was until, one night, the secret kept
  Safe in low vault and stealthy corridor
    Was blown abroad on a swift wind of flame.
    Above, God's sky and God are still the same;
  It may be that as many tears are wept
  Beneath, and that man is but as of yore.

I find I must adopt the plan of writing only on one side for it is candle-light now, and I cannot see distinctly.

The other day, pondering on the rate of locomotion which the style of the old masters induces in us at the Louvre, I scribbled as follows :—

Woolner and Stephens, Collinson, Millais,
  And my first brother, each and every one,
  What portion is theirs now beneath the sun
Which, even as here, in England makes to-day ?
For most of them life runs not the same way
  Always, but leaves the thought at loss: I know
  Merely that Woolner keeps not even the show
Of work, nor is enough awake for play.
Meanwhile Hunt and myself race at full speed
  Along the Louvre, and yawn from school to school,
    Wishing worn-out those masters known as old.
And no man asks of Browning; though indeed
  (As the book travels with me) any fool
    Who would might hear Sordello's story told.

There are very few good things at the Louvre besides what I mentioned in my last. There is a wonderful head by Raphael however; another wonderful head by I know not whom ; and a pastoral—at least, a kind of pastoral—by Giorgione, which is so intensely fine that I condescended to sit down before it and write a sonnet. You must have heard me rave about the engraving before, and I fancy have seen it yourself. There is a woman, naked, at one side, who is dipping a glass vessel into a well ; and in the centre two men and another naked woman, who seem to have paused for a moment in playing on the musical instruments which they hold. Here is my sonnet :—

Water, for anguish of the solstice,—yea,
  Over the vessel's mouth still widening,
  Listlessly dipped to let the water in
With low vague gurgle. Blue, and deep away,
The heat lies silent at the brink of day.
  The hand trails weak upon the viol-string
  That sobs; and the brown faces cease to sing,
Mournful with complete pleasure. Her eyes stray
In distance; through her lips the pipe doth creep
  And leaves them pouting: the green shadowed grass
  Is cool against her naked flesh. Let be:
Do not now speak unto her lest she weep,—
  Nor name this ever. Be it as it was:
  Silence of heat, and solemn poetry.

Last night we went to Valentino's to see the cancan. As the groups whirled past us, one after another, in an ecstasy of sound and motion, I became possessed with a tender rapture and recorded it in rhyme as follows:—

(N.B.—The numerical characteristics refer to the *danseuses*.)

The first, a mare; the second, 'twixt bow-wow
  And pussy-cat, a cross; the third, a beast
  To baffle Buffon; the fourth, not the least
In hideousness, nor last; the fifth, a cow;
The sixth, Chimera; the seventh, Sphinx; . . . Come now,
  One woman, France, ere this frog-hop have ceased,
  And it shall be enough. A toothsome feast
Of blackguardism . . . and bald row,
No doubt for such as love those same. For me,
I confess, William, and avow to thee,
  (Soft in thine ear) that such sweet female whims

*   *   *   *   *   *

Are not a passion of mine naturally.

*   *   *   *   *   *

This sonnet is rather emphatic, I know; but, I assure you, excusable under the circumstances. My dear sir, we have not seen six pretty faces since we have been at Paris, and those such as would not be in the least remarkable in London. As for the ball last night, it was matter for spueing; there is a slang idiocy about the *habitués*, viler than gentism. And the females . . . my God! As for Gavarni, he is a liar and the father of it.

I bought some more of his things the other day, and have got a great number now—more than I care to count. I wish, if you have leisure, you would go to Brown's study, and look up, among our portfolios there, all such Gavarnis as they may contain—since on my arrival in London I will get them bound into a volume with those I have bought here; and it is as well they should not go knocking about among all the jumble of those same portfolios any longer, as the paper of them is somewhat frail.

Hunt and I have likewise bought three stunning etchings by Albert Durer, and one or two other little things.

The other night we went to the Gaîté to see a piece called *La Sonnette du Diable*, which is an adaptation of Soulié's *Mémoires*. It was most execrably played, and so stupefied us that we lost ourselves in coming home.

P.S.—The other night we were inexpressibly astounded by Rachel, in a piece by Scribe called *Adrienne Lecouvreur*.

I am indeed rejoiced to hear that Papa is so much better. I shall write to him immediately almost; also to Cottingham, with whom I ought by rights to have communicated before leaving London.

Stephens must have forgotten that he himself and Hunt, as well as I, were at first all agog for the title of *P.R.B. Journal*, though we afterwards all abandoned it. As for the sonnets on Keats, I cannot see any call for their appearance in No. 1. As for our title, I think "towards" is much the better—"toward" being altogether between you, me, and Tennyson; and it is well to seem as little affected as possible.

I suppose you have by this time got over the insane exultation incident on finding *Joseph and his Brethren*, which Williams brought, together with the *Stories*, the night before we left. The latter I have taken with me, as they might possibly be wanted somehow in case we see Wells. Love to our family, the P.R.B., and all. We have not yet delivered the letters of Messrs. Brown and Morrison, nor the one from Papa to Ronna ; but shall do so as soon as possible. I hope Brown is well, and trust to write to him very shortly.

C 14.

The sonnets on the picture of *Ruggiero and Angelica* by Ingres were published in *The Germ*, and afterwards in my brother's *Poems.* The *Last Sonnets at Paris* show—what indeed was very marked throughout his life—that my brother was in many respects an Englishman in grain—and even a prejudiced Englishman. He was quite as ready as other Britons to reckon to the discredit of French-men, and generally of foreigners, a certain shallow and frothy demonstrativeness; *too* ready, I always thought. In the prose part of his present letter, the phrase "a lot of scientific and industrial silliness" bewrays another weak point—his constitutional indifference, or indeed dislike, to anything that had not an artistic or imaginative appeal. However, the phrase must not be taken overmuch *au pied de la lettre.* "Hans Hemmling" (named in one of the blank-verse pieces) means "Memling": my brother at this date supposed "Hemmling" to be the correct name—and indeed I fancy the right spelling was then a matter of dispute.

Lyell, named as the destined recipient of a prospectus of *The Germ*, was Mr. Charles Lyell, godfather to my brother.

"The Bermondsey murder" was the notorious affair which brought Mr. and Mrs. Manning to the scaffold. My brother always, or at any rate until the last few years of his life, took a certain interest in "horrid murders."

LAST VISIT TO THE LOUVRE.

THE CRY OF THE P.R.B., AFTER A CAREFUL EXAMINATION OF THE CANVASES OF RUBENS, CORREGGIO, *et hoc genus omne.*

Non noi pittori! God of Nature's truth,
    If these, not we ! Be it not said, when one
    Of us goes hence: "As these did, he hath done;
His feet sought out their footprints from his youth."
Because, dear God ! the flesh Thou madest smooth
    These carked and fretted, that it seemed to run
    With ulcers; and the daylight of thy sun
They parcelled into blots and glares, uncouth

With stagnant grouts of paint. Men say that these
   Had further sight than man's, but that God saw
   Their works were good. God that didst know them foul!
In such a blindness, blinder than the owl,
Leave us! Our sight can reach unto thy seas
And hills; and 'tis enough for tears of awe.

LAST VISIT TO THE LUXEMBOURG.

ROGER RESCUING ANGELICA; BY INGRES.

I.

A REMOTE sky, that meeteth the sea's brim;
   One rock-point standing buffeted alone,
   Vexed at its base with a foul beast unknown,
Hell-spurge of geomaunt and teraphim:
A knight, and a winged creature bearing him,
   Reared at the rock: a woman fettered there,
   Leaning into the hollow with loose hair
And throat let back and heartsick trail of limb.
The sky is harsh, and the sea shrewd and salt.
   Under his lord the griffin-horse ramps blind
      With rigid wings and tail. The spear's lithe stem
Stands in the roaring of those jaws; behind,
The evil length of body chafes at halt.
   She doth not hear nor see—she knows of them.

II.

Clench thine eyes now,—'tis the last instant, girl:
   Draw in thy senses, loose thy knees, and shake:
   Set thy breath fast: thy life is keen awake,—
Thou mayst not swoon. Was that the scattered whirl
Of its foam drenched thee? or the waves that curl
   And split—bleak spray wherein thy temples ache?
   Or was it his thy champion's blood, to flake
That flesh which has the colour of fine pearl?
Now silence: for the sea's is such a sound
   As irks not silence, and except the sea
      All is now still. Now the dead thing doth cease
To writhe, and drifts. He turns to her; and she,
Cast from the jaws of Death, remains there bound,
   Again a woman in her nakedness.

LAST SONNETS AT PARIS.

I.

CHINS that might serve the new Jerusalem;
  Streets footsore; minute whisking milliners,
  Dubbed graceful, but at whom one's eye demurs,
Knowing of England; ladies, much the same;
Bland smiling dogs with manes—a few of them
  At pains to look like sporting characters;
  Vast humming tabbies smothered in their furs;
Groseille, orgeat, meringues à la crême—
Good things to study; ditto bad—the maps
  Of sloshy colour in the Louvre; *cinq-francs*
  The largest coin; and at the restaurants
Large Ibrahim Pachas in Turkish caps
  To pocket them. *Un million d'habitants:*
Cast up, they'll make an Englishman—perhaps.

II.

Tiled floors in bedrooms; trees (now run to seed—
  Such seed as the wind takes) of Liberty;
  Squares with new names that no one seems to see;
Scrambling Briarean passages, which lead
To the first place you came from; urgent need
  Of unperturbed nasal philosophy;
  Through Paris (what with church and gallery)
Some forty first-rate paintings,—or indeed
Fifty mayhap; fine churches; splendid inns;
  Fierce sentinels (toy-size without the stands)
    Who spit their oaths at you and grind their r's
If at a fountain you would wash your hands;
  One Frenchman (this is fact) who thinks he spars:—
Can even good dinners cover all these sins?

III.

Yet in the mighty French metropolis
  Our time has not gone from us utterly
  In waste. The wise man saith, "An ample fee
For toil, to work thine end." Aye that it is.
Should England ask, "Was narrow prejudice
  Stretched to its utmost point unflinchingly,
  Even unto lying, at all times, by ye?"
We can say firmly: "Lord, thou knowest this

Our soil may own us." Having but small French
Hunt passed for a stern Spartan all the while,
Uncompromising, of few words: for me—
I think I was accounted generally
A fool, and just a little cracked. Thy smile
May light on us, Britannia, healthy wench.

FROM PARIS TO BRUSSELS.

(11 P.M. 15 *October to half-past* 1 P.M. 16.)

PROEM AT THE PARIS STATION.

IN France (to baffle thieves and murderers)
A journey takes two days of passport work
At least: The plan's sometimes a tedious one,
But bears its fruit. Because, the other day,
In passing by the Morgue, we saw a man
(The thing is common, and we never should
Have known of it, only we passed that way)
Who had been stabbed and tumbled in the Seine,
Where he had stayed some days. The face was black,
And, like a negro's, swollen; all the flesh
Had furred, and broken into a green mould.
Now, very likely, he who did the job
Was standing among those who stood with us,
To look upon the corpse. You fancy him—
Smoking an early pipe, and watching, as
An artist, the effect of his last work.
This always if it had not struck him that
'Twere best to leave while yet the body took
Its crust of rot beneath the Seine. It may:
But, if it did not, he can now remain
Without much fear. *Only*, if he should want
To travel, and have not his passport yet,
(Deep dogs these French police!) he may be caught.

Therefore you see (lest, being murderers,
We should not have the sense to go before
The thing were known, or to stay afterwards)
There is good reason why—having resolved
To start for Belgium—we were kept three days
To learn about the passports first, then do
As we had learned. This notwithstanding, in
The fullness of the time 'tis come to pass.

ON THE ROAD.

OCTOBER, and eleven after dark:
Both mist and night. Among us in the coach
Packed heat on which the windows have been shut:
Our backs unto the motion—Hunt's and mine.
The last lamps of the Paris Station move
Slow with wide haloes past the clouded pane;
The road in secret empty darkness. One
Who sits beside me, now I turn, has pulled
A nightcap to his eyes. A woman here,
Knees to my knees—a twenty-nine-year-old—
Smiles at the mouth I open, seeing him:
I look her gravely in the jaws, and write.
Already while I write heads have been leaned
Upon the wall,—the lamp that's overhead
Dropping its shadow to the waist and hands.

Some time 'twixt sleep and wake. A dead pause then,
With giddy humming silence in the ears.
It is a Station. Eyes are opening now,
And mouths collecting their propriety.
From one of our two windows, now drawn up,
A lady leans, hawks a clear throat, and spits.

Hunt lifts his head from my cramped shoulder where
It has been lying—long stray hairs from it
Crawling upon my face and teazing me.
Ten minutes' law. Our feet are in the road.
A weak thin dimness at the sky, whose chill
Lies vague and hard. The mist of crimson heat
Hangs, a spread glare, about our engine's bulk.
I shall get in again, and sleep this time.

A heavy clamour that fills up the brain
Like thought grown burdensome; and in the ears
Speed that seems striving to o'ertake itself;
And in the pulses torpid life, which shakes
As water to a stir of wind beneath.

Poor Hunt, who has the toothache and can't smoke,
Has asked me twice for brandy. I would sleep;
But man proposes, and no more. I sit
With open eyes, and a head quite awake,
But which keeps catching itself lolled aside
And looking sentimental. In the coach,
If any one tries talking, the voice jolts,
And stuns the ear that stoops for it.

Amiens.

Half-an-hour's rest. Another shivering walk
Along the station, waiting for the bell.
Ding-dong. Now this time, by the Lord, I'll sleep.

I must have slept some while. Now that I wake,
Day is beginning in a kind of haze
White with grey trees. The hours have had their lapse.

A sky too dull for cloud. A country lain
In fields, where teams drag up the furrow yet;
Or else a level of trees, the furthest ones
Seen like faint clouds at the horizon's point.
Quite a clear distance, though in vapour. Mills
That turn with the dry wind. Large stacks of hay
Made to look bleak. Dead autumn, and no sun.

The smoke upon our course is borne so near
Along the earth, the earth appears to steam.
Blanc-Misseron, the last French Station, passed.
We are in Belgium. It is just the same :—
Nothing to write of, and no good in verse.

Curse the big mounds of sand-weed! curse the miles
Of barren chill,—the twentyfold relays !
Curse every beastly Station on the road !

As well to write as swear. Hunt was just now
Making great eyes because outside the pane
One of the stokers passed whom he declared
A stunner. A vile mummy with a bag
Is squatted next me : a disgusting girl
Broad opposite. We have a poet, though,
Who is a gentleman, and looks like one;
Only he seems ashamed of writing verse,
And heads each new page with "*Mon cher Ami.*"
Hunt's stunner has just come into the coach,
And set us hard agrin from ear to ear.

Another Station. There's a stupid horn
Set wheezing. Now I should just like to know
—Just merely for the whim—what good that is.
These Stations for the most part are a kind
Of London coal-merchant's back premises;
Whitewashed, but as by hands of coal-heavers;
Grimy themselves, and always circled in
With foul coke-loads that make the nose aroint.

Here is a Belgian village,—no, a town
Moated and buttressed. Next, a water-track
Lying with draggled reeds in a flat slime.
Next, the old country, always all the same.
Now by Hans Hemmling and by John Van Eyck,
You'll find, till something's new, I write no more.

(4 HOURS.)

There is small change of country; but the sun
Is out, and it seems shame this were not said:
For upon all the grass the warmth has caught;
And betwixt distant whitened poplar-stems
Makes greener darkness; and in dells of trees
Shows spaces of a verdure that was hid;
And the sky has its blue floated with white,
And crossed with falls of the sun's glory aslant
To lay upon the waters of the world;
And from the road men stand with shaded eyes
To look; and flowers in gardens have grown strong
And our own shadows here within the coach
Are brighter; and all colour has more bloom.

So, after the sore torments of the route :—
Toothache, and headache, and the ache of wind,
And huddled sleep, and smarting wakefulness,
And night, and day, and hunger sick at food,
And twentyfold relays, and packages
To be unlocked, and passports to be found,
And heavy well-kept landscape ;—we were glad
Because we entered Brussels in the sun.

L'ENVOI: BRUSSELS, HÔTEL DU MIDI: 18 OCTOBER.

IT's copied out at last: very poor stuff
Writ in the cold, with pauses of the cramp.
Direct, dear William, to the Poste Restante
At Ghent—here written Gand. . . .
We go to Antwerp first, but shall not stay;
After, to Ghent and Bruges; and after that
To Ostend, and thence home. To Waterloo
Was yesterday. Thither, and there, and back,
I managed to scrawl something,—most of it
Bad, and the sonnet at the close mere slosh.
'Twas only made because I was knocked up,
And it helped yawning. Take it, and the rest.

ON THE ROAD TO WATERLOO: 17 October.

(En vigilante, 2 hours.)

It is grey tingling azure overhead
    With silver drift. Beneath, where from the green
    The trees are reared, the distance stands between
At peace: and on this side the whole is spread
For sowing and for harvest, subjected
    Clear to the sky and wind. The sun's slow height
    Holds it through noon, and at the furthest night
It lies to the moist starshine and is fed.
Sometimes there is no country seen (for miles
    You think) because of the near roadside path
    Dense with long forest. Where the waters run
They have the sky sunk into them—a bath
Of still blue heat; and in their flow, at whiles,
    There is a blinding vortex of the sun.

A HALF-WAY PAUSE.

The turn of noontide has begun.
    In the weak breeze the sunshine yields.
    There is a bell upon the fields.
On the long hedgerow's tangled run
    A low white cottage intervenes:
    Against the wall a blind man leans,
And sways his face to have the sun.

Our horses' hoofs stir in the road,
    Quiet and sharp. Light hath a song
    Whose silence, being heard, seems long.
The point of noon maketh abode,
    And will not be at once gone through.
    The sky's deep colour saddens you,
And the heat weighs a dreamy load.

ON THE FIELD OF WATERLOO.

So then, the name which travels side by side
    With English life from childhood—Waterloo—
    Means this. The sun is setting. "Their strife grew
Till the sunset, and ended," says our guide.
It lacked the "chord" by stage-use sanctified,
    Yet I believe one should have thrilled. For me,
    I grinned not, and 'twas something ;—certainly
These held their point, and did not turn but died:

So much is very well. " Under each span
  Of these ploughed fields" ('tis the guide still) " there rot
   Three nations' slain, a thousand-thousandfold."
  Am I to weep ? Good sirs, the earth is old :
  Of the whole earth there is no single spot
But hath among its dust the dust of man.

RETURNING TO BRUSSELS.

UPON a Flemish road, when noon was deep,
  I passed a little consecrated shrine,
  Where, among simple pictures ranged in line,
The blessed Mary holds her child asleep.
To kneel here, shepherd-maidens leave their sheep
  When they feel grave because of the sunshine,
  And again kneel here in the day's decline ;
And here, when their life ails them, come to weep.
Night being full, I passed on the same road
  By the same shrine ; within, a lamp was lit
Which through the silence of clear darkness glowed.
   Thus, when life's heat is past and doubts arise
  Darkling, the lamp of Faith must strengthen it,
   Which sometimes will not light and sometimes dies.

[18 *October* 1849.]

DEAR WILLIAM,

    I have been thinking whether Brussels offers materials
for a sonnet, but have come to the conclusion that not even
thus much is to be got out of its utter muffishness. I will
therefore fill this last column with as much prose as I can
afford you. However, the verse must stand for a letter this
time ; though, with the exception of two or three of the
sonnets, I fear it is not even so good as what I have already
sent you. The fact is, a journey in fair and foul weather are
two very different things, and the verse gets its measure of
estro accordingly. But I will not grunt about past evils, for
the weather, these days in Brussels, has been like the finest
summer.

    There is a most servile aping of the French here, notwith-
standing that they seem to be held in hatred. The English
are victimized to a beastly extent everywhere. One of the
great nuisances at this place, as also at Waterloo ,is the plague

of guides, from which there is no escape. The one we had at Waterloo completely baulked me of all the sonnets I had promised myself, so that all I accomplished was the embryo bottled up in the preceding column. Between you and me, William, Waterloo is simply a bore.

I believe we saw all the town to-day, except a lot of scientific and industrial silliness, and one room at the Museum which we perceived was full of Rubenses, and so held aloof. There are a few very fine early German pictures, among them a wonderful Van Eyck. I believe we shall see no end of these stunning things at Antwerp, Ghent, etc.; and, as I am convinced they will drag me into rhyme, I almost fear that I shall not do much, if anything, to *Bride-Chamber Talk* till my return. Before leaving Paris, we went to the Hôtel de Cluny, a first-rate place, which will be of great use to me in finishing this poem. Could I do it on the spot, I fancy I should be a made man. I fear there is no chance now of going to Brittany.

All further matters concerning your poem we can discuss on my return, which will be much shorter work. I will only mention one thing which I forgot to include in my last. I think the penultimate line of the poem would perhaps be more forcible if it stood thus : "I can wait, John, but is not *the whole* due?"

You can have no conception of the intense sweating exasperation incident on passport-hunting. We had three days of it before leaving Paris.

You talk about printing my blessed journal. I fear this would never do. There is too much of a kind of exclusive matter belonging only to ourselves ; and moreover, among the things I have written since leaving London, there are only three sonnets which have received any consideration— viz., the two on Ingres' picture, and the one On the Road to Waterloo—all in the present letter.

I believe it is very probable that you will receive before my return a large volume of old *Charivaris* containing Gavarni's sketches, which I left with Broadie at Paris, to be bound and forwarded to you, in order to escape paying double duty both in Belgium and England. They will be bound anyhow, provisorily, merely that they may go in the book-form, and not have to pay a penny apiece, as prints, at the Custom-House.

Of the two prospectuses you sent me, I gave one to Broadie, and the other has somehow got all covered with ink. I must therefore let the sending to Lyell and Cottingham stand over for the present. We can discuss advertising at length when we are all together. I quite agree with you about the in-advisability of getting any more proprietors as yet. . . .

It appears to me quite unnecessary to begin sending about prospectuses at present in any great quantity.

You speak of the uncertainty of Haynes' estimate coinciding with Tupper's. If Tupper is more moderate, let us print by all means with him.

Will you tell Papa that while in Paris I called with his letter for Ronna at the address which it bears, and saw a crusty old woman who said he had been gone some time and she did not know whither, but that if I called next day perhaps some one would be there who knew? The quarter of Paris however was one we never had occasion to be in, and which is infamously paved. The consequence was that we put off calling again till it was too late. Owing to the number of things we were obliged to run after, several other letters with which we had been entrusted shared the same fate.

To Papa, Mamma, and Collinson, I intend to write as soon as possible. I hope they have made allowances hitherto. A letter is also due to Christina which still lies unattempted. I have likewise to answer Woolner, and to redeem my promise to Hancock.

Write at once, and if you have done anything send it: if not, something of Christina's. Remember me warmly to all friends, who by my good fortune are too numerous to par-ticularize. I trust Papa's health holds good. By-the-bye, I hear nothing of the Bermondsey murder.

A 8.

[LONDON. ? *January* 1850.]

MY DEAR AUNT,

I am quite ashamed, and have been ashamed from day to day for a long while, of not having ever thanked you yet for the kind present you made me some while back. I can scarcely hope that you will believe me nevertheless to be none the less thankful for not having said so, and can scarcely with any countenance assure you that such is the case. The fact is, and I am sorry for it, that my laziness is so great as to account for many things which it cannot excuse. I need not tell you how timely your gift was.

I am now beginning a large picture containing about thirty figures, and concerning the love of a page for a queen, as treated of in one of Browning's songs—a subject which I have pitched upon principally for its presumptive saleableness. I find unluckily that the class of pictures which has my natural preference is not for the market.

I have nearly finished the sketch in colour for my picture, have made many of the studies, and am beginning to draw it in on the canvas; so that I am at least setting to work in time; but it will be a long job.

I trust that this note will find you in a state of robust muscularity.

F I.

This laughable sonnet was sent in a letter to our sister Christina, then in Brighton, towards 20 January 1850. The letter has perished, but the sonnet survives, and may serve as a small pen-and-ink sketch of my brother's domicile at that now remote date. He had taken a first-floor studio in a house in Newman Street in which a dancing-academy was held; this he terms "the hop-shop." Hancock's "accents screechy" are not an arbitrary make-rhyme to Beatrice (according to the Italian pronunciation of that name), but a tolerably true definition of his voice, which was small and high-pitched. He was now doing a statue of Dante's Beatrice, as seen by the poet in the Garden of Eden. The "engraving of his bas-relief" was taken from a work which he had produced, and which had gained an

Art-Union prize, *Christ's Entry into Jerusalem.* Bernhard Smith
was a very tall and stalwart young man, of florid English presence,
handsome and good-humoured; a sculptor, who painted one or two
small pictures as well, and came near to being enlisted as a P.R.B.
Soon afterwards he emigrated, along with Woolner, to Australia,
and in course of time became a police-magistrate there. He died
in or about 1885. This sonnet was headed *St. Wagnes' Eve,* and
was written on St. Agnes' Eve, 20 January.

[*20 January* 1850.]

The hop-shop is shut up: the night doth wear.
  Here, early, Collinson this evening fell
  "Into the gulfs of sleep"; and Deverell
Has turned upon the pivot of his chair
The whole of this night long; and Hancock there
  Has laboured to repeat, in accents screechy,
  "Guardami ben, ben son, ben son Beatrice";
And Bernhard Smith still beamed, serene and square.
By eight, the coffee was all drunk. At nine
  We gave the cat some milk. Our talk did shelve,
    Ere ten, to gasps and stupor. Helpless grief
Made, towards eleven, my inmost spirit pine,
  Knowing North's hour. And Hancock, hard on twelve,
  Showed an engraving of his bas-relief.

C 15.

When this letter was written I was in Edinburgh for a brief
holiday. My brother knew nothing then of the Scottish capital;
nor I think did he ever do more than pass through it. The
phrase "Millaian squalor" must be a jocular allusion to press-
attacks on Millais's picture termed *The Carpenter's Shop.*

"The Browning picture" has been already mentioned—*Hist,
said Kate the Queen.* The subject from *Much Ado about Nothing*
which my brother thought of designing and painting was the final
scene where Benedick stops Beatrice's mouth with a kiss. A design of
the subject survives, but the picture was never undertaken. "The
Gurm" means *The Germ.* Cayley's MS. was a portion of the translation, by Charles Bagot Cayley, of Dante's *Commedia.* The work
was published not very long afterwards, and it remains to this day, I
think, the best translation of the poem, all things considered. Mr.
Cayley died in December 1883.

[LONDON.] *Tuesday 3 September* 1850.

DEAR WILLIAM,

Your letter received two days back (and which I should have answered before) is the most pitiful apocalypse of dreariness that I remember to have seen. What can you be doing? Of what avail are mere gateways and staircases and gables, be they even of Millaian squalor? Verily they shall not suffice.

I would advise you, if you wish "to elude madness," to make with some speed for the Lakes or the Highlands, and shake off the dust of Edinburgh, which is just a place where people tell lies in Scotch.

Or, should you remain, being stiff-necked, and have not reached that state of whining impotence which precludes you from society, I shall be able in a day or two to send you some letters from Stephens and Hannay for fellows in Auld Reekie, the fallacious expectance whereof has indeed caused this letter to be thus delayed.

I have no news scarcely. . . .

Having found it impossible to get the Browning picture ready for next exhibition, I have designed the subject I mentioned to you from *Much Ado about Nothing*, and shall begin to paint it in a very few days. I think it will come well. I have also made one or two other sketches for different subjects.

Mamma the other day pitched somehow on a paper called *The Guardian* which contains a flare-up review of *The Gurm*. It is the number for 28 August.

I went the other night to see the *Legend of Florence*, which is much more poetical on the stage than I anticipated. Miss Glyn is godlike.

Why do you not write something? By which I mean neither an incubus nor a succubus. I have just read your review in *The Critic* of the British Institution, many parts of which I do not understand. What do you mean by the "enforcement of magnificence having a tendency to impair the more essential development of feeling?" This smacks villainously of Malvolio's vein.

Can you explain the following ?—

> She knew it not,—most perfect pain
> To learn ; and this she knew not. Strife
> For me, calm hers, as from the first.
> 'Twas but another bubble burst
> Upon the curdling draught of life :—
> My silent patience mine again.
>
> As who, of forms that crowd unknown
> Within a dusky mirror's shade,
> Deems such an one himself, and makes
> Some sign ; but, when that image shakes
> No whit, he finds his thought betrayed,
> And must seek elsewhere for his own.

This may not reach you, as I have lost your letter, and am uncertain of your number.

D. G. R.

Mamma sent Cayley's MS., which I suppose you have got.

B 9.

My brother had gone on 23 October with Mr. Holman Hunt to Sevenoaks to discover and paint a suitable background for a picture. He painted on a moderate-sized canvas a woodland background, which remained unutilized for a great number of years.

MRS. HEARNDEN'S, HIGH STREET, SEVENOAKS, KENT.
[24 October 1850.]

DEAR MAMMA,

. . I reached here yesterday evening, and seem to have come in for the most rascally fortnight of the year. The wet seems regularly established, being nevertheless anything but respectable on that account. I went out this morning with Hunt in search of an eligible spot, and found what I wanted ; but was unable to make more than a sketch, since, after an interval of extreme anguish, Hunt and myself were obliged to beat a retreat, soaked to the bone.

I find I shall never be able to get on without a change of nether garments, which article of dress proved this morning

unable to withstand a three hours' cataract. Will you therefore take the trouble to send me somehow my other breeches
(the pair with straps), and to wrap in them any Italian
grammar you can spare, as Hunt wishes to avail himself of
my lore in that language? I find that two other indispensable
articles will be a pair of goloshes and a rug to wrap round the
legs, both of which I shall be able to procure here at no very
desperate outlay.

I am become loathsomely matutine, and was up this
morning at seven.

Love to all at home from myself, and best remembrances
from Hunt and Stephens.

A 9.

The address given to this letter, 17 Red Lion Square, was that of
Walter Deverell's studio. My brother worked there for a short time
between his leaving Newman Street and settling in Chatham Place.
The date of the letter is approximately fixed by the reference
to Lord Compton's succession to the Marquisate of Northampton—
an event which took place on 17 January 1851. I cannot say which
was the picture that the Marquis thought of buying—possibly the
Beatrice at a Marriage-feast. He certainly did not buy that work,
nor, so far as I know, any other. I am not sure that my brother
ever became personally known to him—but I think he did.

There follows a reference to a small picture which had been
begun as a substitute for a large one abandoned. The large one is
no doubt *Kate the Queen.* The small one appears to be the same
which is afterwards spoken of as attracting Mr. Combe of Oxford
(the Director of the University Press). It may have been the water-
colour of *Dante drawing an Angel in Memory of Beatrice,* which
was in the possession of Mrs. Combe up to the date of her death
in 1894, and was bequeathed by her to the Oxford University
Gallery. Its *first* owner however was Mr. McCracken of Belfast.

"Unless I should immediately get rid of my last year's picture."
This phrase relates to the picture of *The Annunciation.*

I cannot now well understand my brother's statement that his
"present engagement consists in making some drawings on wood,"
especially as coupled with the reference to its "yielding just the

means of daily subsistence." To the best of my recollection the very first woodcut he actually produced was the one, published in 1855, to Allingham's poem *The Maids of Elfin Mere.* I have by me however a wood-block on which he has drawn a design of a monk painting, with other monks looking on. This may date in or about 1851. It was never cut. Whether he expected to be paid for it, and by whom, I do not now remember. In his letter he speaks also of "writing," in the same connexion with "the means of daily subsistence." This does not however clearly imply that he was actually thus writing; nor have I the least recollection that he was— save only that he did, in 1851 or '52, a *little* of the translating-work for a book which was published in the latter year, the *Memoirs and Correspondence of Mallet du Pan.* Mr. Benjamin H. Paul (a Scientific Chemist, whom we knew in James Hannay's set) was the chief translator, along with myself, and the female members of my family did something substantial.

17 Red Lion Square [London].
Thursday [? *February* 1851].

My dear Aunt Charlotte,

Having been staying for two days at Chelsea with my friend Hunt, I got your first missive only last night at about eleven, and your second this morning. I am very sorry that your generosity to me should have resulted in any uneasiness to yourself.

I shall not dwell, as I know you do not wish it, upon my obligation to you for this new act of kindness. Indeed, I should scarcely know how to express my thanks for so many repeated proofs of affectionate interest on your part, whom I now see so little of, and who know so little of me that can render me deserving in your eyes.

I am afraid in particular that you must have thought me most ungrateful for not answering during all this time a letter of yours received several months back. The reason why I deferred doing so at the time was that I was then in constant expectation of selling a small picture of mine which Lord Compton (now, by his father's death, Marquis of Northampton) had requested, through a friend, might be sent to him for examination. I dare say Mamma may have told you about this at the time. I hoped, by delaying my answer to you, to be able to decline your generous offer at the same time that I sincerely thanked you for making it; but unfortunately I heard no further from the Marquis, whose good pleasure I am still waiting for, having only learnt that he wishes to be introduced to me—for which however he has as yet given me no opportunity. Nothing could give me more pleasure than to sell my picture; but I confess that one thing I cannot manage to do is thrusting myself on the acquaintance of a Lord.

Just then I was commencing a small picture, having abandoned the one I had been engaged on for some time, on account of its being too large to get done for the Academy. On this smaller picture however I was unwilling to risk any one's money except my own; since, being rather a hurried affair, and got up chiefly to keep my name before the public, it might possibly not sell after all. Therefore, hearing no more from Lord Northampton, and having determined that I would be no further drag upon my parents, I abandoned the small picture I speak of, and preferred undertaking, for the time being, one or two odd jobs which had turned up, and which might enable me to wait. On these I am still engaged, and they will now before long bring me in sufficient money to discharge what few debts I have remaining after your present; among others, several pounds which I have been forced to borrow of Mamma from time to time. I shall also have a little left for myself; but, I must frankly tell you, far from sufficient to go on with my large picture, upon which, through the lapse of time, it is now absolutely necessary that I should get to work again at once.

I have been induced to give you all these details concerning my affairs because, unless I should immediately get rid of my last year's picture, I shall be necessitated, as soon as my present engagement (which consists in making some drawings on wood) leaves me free for my real work, to be obliged to write to you, accepting those means of pursuing my studies which you have so freely offered me. Indeed, were I not to do so, I think I should be guilty of injustice to myself, as well as of ingratitude to you; since I think there can be little doubt at present of my selling a picture, if I have the means to get it *properly* done. Indeed, a Mr. Combe of Oxford, a patron of my friend Millais, has expressed a desire to have a picture of mine, and is greatly pleased with the subject of my present one. If therefore I could get it satisfactorily advanced, I think it very probable indeed that he might purchase it.

I am sure you will agree with me that it is very necessary I should, if possible, occupy myself constantly with my real career as a painter, and put aside that kind of minor employment, either in writing or designing, which, while yielding just the means of daily subsistence, would be causing me to lose entirely what ground I have already gained with the public; which, I may add without vanity, is much more than most young men have gained upon the strength of two small pictures.

Thus I need not say of what incalculable value to me, at this juncture, will be the means of dispensing with further delay in my picture, nor with how much gratitude to you I shall accept them, from a sense of duty towards myself; seeing that they may probably be instrumental in enabling me before long to be of no further charge to any one. I may add an assurance that I should consider all such sums strictly as a loan, to be returned when the sale of a picture enabled me to do so.

I am sure therefore that, should you hear from me again on this subject within a short period, you will not think the worse of me for thus taking advantage of your generosity.

Believe me always, my dear Aunt,
Your grateful and affectionate Nephew,
D. G. ROSSETTI.

P.S.—I cashed the cheque as soon as it reached me—*i.e.*, this morning.

C 16.

I can remember something of the "Electro-biology" to which the following note refers. It was a public display, conducted either by Dr. Marshall Hall, or by an over-plausible and fresh-complexioned Irish-American whom my brother characterized as "the Pink Owl." The Electro-biology was in the nature of clairvoyance, or what we now call hypnotism. For anything of this kind, including table-turning and spirit-rapping, my brother had a rather marked propensity and willing credence. He did not however believe in the "Pink Owl." "Johnny" is Millais.

The "notice of Poole"—his picture of *The Goths in Italy*—was volunteered for insertion amid the review of the Royal Academy Exhibition which I, as Art-critic of the *Spectator*, was then writing for that journal. It appeared in the *Spectator*, and is reproduced in the *Collected Works* (vol. ii., p. 501).

[LONDON. 9 *May* 1851.]

DEAR WILLIAM,

I believe Millais, Hunt, and self, are going to-morrow night to have another shy at seeing the Electro-biology. Do you like to come? I suppose I shall be at Johnny's about half after six or so. I shall be at Hannay's late.

I send you a notice of Poole. Please to print all, or not to print any.

C 17.

I insert this scrap as giving me the opportunity of mentioning a poet, some of whose pieces were much admired by my brother in his early manhood, and to the last regarded with esteem and predilection. The "some one at Hannay's" was Thomas Buchanan Read, an American poet, and a painter by profession as well, author of *Rural Poems, Lays and Ballads*, etc. My brother and I had seen a few of his lyrics in some newspaper—perhaps in 1848 or 1847. Read died several years ago. He was a curiously small man in stature, and had at this time a pleasant little wife (I think he re-married afterwards) on exactly a corresponding scale.

[LONDON.] 13 *August* 1851.

DEAR W——

Some one is at Hannay's to-night whom you will be surprised to see. Come if you can. This is written from there.

A 10.

The subject from the *Vita Nuova* which my brother was now attending to was probably the water-colour entitled *Beatrice at a Marriage-feast denies Dante her Salutation.* It was hung soon afterwards in a small exhibition. A water-colour of *The Return of Tibullus to Delia* was also, I believe, produced in 1851; but the principal water-colour of this subject belongs to a much later date, 1866-7. "My little picture," the sending of which to the Liverpool Exhibition had been suggested, must be *The Annunciation*, which had been exhibited in London (Free Exhibition) in 1850, but had not as yet found a purchaser.

17 NEWMAN STREET [LONDON].
Wednesday [? *August* 1851].

MY DEAR AUNT,

Pray accept my acknowledgments for the receipt of the money-order, which came duly to hand this morning.

I have at present two subjects *en train*—one from Dante's *Vita Nuova*, and one from the Poems of Tibullus. I am still in doubt, though I shall be obliged to decide in a day or two, upon which to turn my principal attention. The latter, as being rather the smaller, would be likely to secure a better place in the Exhibition. I think that, as to sale, the chances are about equal.

As regards Lady Bath's idea about sending my little picture to Liverpool, I should certainly have done so (or else to Manchester or Birmingham) last year, had the thing been of a more popular character. Even were it only a *little* less peculiar, I would have done so for the sake of the chance; but, as it is, I know by experience that you might as well expect a Liverpool merchant to communicate with his Chinese correspondent without the intervention of some one who knows the language as imagine that he could look at the picture in question with the remotest glimmering of its purpose. This is the reason which has prevented me from sending it anywhere; particularly as it would be sure to come back with the frame knocked to pieces, and as it is a very bad thing for any artist, without some definite chance of sale,

to exhibit any picture a second time, and to let every one
know that he has not sold it.

C 18.

When this note was written I was staying at Newcastle-on-Tyne
with Mr. and Mrs. William Bell Scott.   During my absence from
London, Gabriel accommodated me by keeping-up the writing that
was due from me for the *Spectator*, of which Mr. Rintoul was editor.
The "pamphlet" which he speaks of was Mr. Ruskin's pamphlet on
Præraphaelitism.   The "exposure at Lichfield House" was an
"Exhibition of the Modern Pictures of all Countries."   My brother
wrote the notice of this, reproduced in his *Collected Works* (vol. ii.,
p. 476).   "The *Vita Nuova*," mentioned in this letter, is my brother's
translation of that work, subsequently published (but not by Murray)
in his volume *The Early Italian Poets*, now named *Dante and his
Circle*.   Mr. Taylor was John Edward Taylor, a printer and a man
of literary cultivation, an old friend of our father's—author of
Michelangelo considered as a Philosophic Poet, etc.

[LONDON. *Monday 25 August* 1851.]

MY DEAR WILLIAM,

I have felt so very ill to-day and yesterday as to have
been quite unable to write anything which could be printed
about the pamphlet etc.   I have lost your note, but believe
you said the article should be sent off to-night.   I suppose
you have not still time to write it yourself.   Rintoul however
has just sent me an order to go to that blackguard exposure
at Lichfield House.   I am not well enough to stir out to-night
(the order being for to-night only), but will write an article
from recollection and catalogue—which Brown has got.   This
I suppose will be sufficient for the present week.   The P.R.B.
business will not lose, I think, by waiting till the other papers
have had their say.

Will you thank Scott for the *Vita Nuova* and for his note,
which I shall answer immediately?

He is quite right, I know, in all he says of ruggedness etc.,
and I shall pay every attention to those matters.   I have

sent the thing to Mr. Taylor, and it seems there is a chance of its coming out with Murray, which would be a capital advertisement for my next picture.

D. G. R.

Remember me most kindly to your host and hostess.

C 19.

My brother did write, as proposed, a notice of the "Exhibition of Sketches." It appears in his *Collected Works* (vol. ii., p. 485). Egg was the painter of that name.

[LONDON.]   *Saturday* [30 *August* 1851].

DEAR WILLIAM,

I hope this will reach you before you leave Newcastle. Rintoul has sent me an order for Pocock's Exhibition of Sketches just opened at the Old Water-colour ; also an intimation about some blessed Dioramas ; also a notice about an Art-Union print ; also a letter saying that there will probably be more of the same kidney. I wrote a very long notice (at least I found it very long to write) of the rubbish at Lichfield House, and will see to the Sketches, though I cannot go to-day, as, being the private view, I should be sure to pitch upon some Associate or Academician. I have written to Rintoul saying that the Dioramas can, I suppose, stand over.

As I have got the notice of the sketching geniuses to write, you had better do the Ruskin business yourself. Indeed, as I hear that Egg had been told by some one that I wrote the *Spectator* notices (regarding which Hunt was obliged to undeceive him by telling him that *you* did), I had rather not have anything to do with it. Do not omit to mention my name however (though of course not obtrusively), and to dwell particularly on the fact that my religious subjects have been entirely independent in treatment of any other corresponding representation, and indeed altogether original in the inventions.

I have been queer ever since I wrote to you, and to-day am exceedingly disordered and uncomfortable.

Your affectionate Brother,
D. G. R.

Remember me to Mr. and Mrs. Scott.

C 20.

I had now written for the *Spectator* an article on *Præraphaelitism*, consequent partly on Mr. Ruskin's pamphlet. The Editor (no doubt rightly) demurred to my treatment of the subject; another paper was then written by me, and was approved and published. It is to the first of these papers that my brother's letter adverts. The statement that I had "not referred to any work of Hunt" can only mean that I had not mentioned any such individual work, for I must assuredly have given due prominence to Hunt himself in general. My brother's reference to his picture of the *Girlhood* will be understood as relating to his first picture, *The Girlhood of Mary Virgin.*

[LONDON. September 1851.]

DEAR W——

I have read your paper on the P.R.B., and agree with Rintoul that it is too full of details and particular instances. Moreover it dashes too much at once into these, and seems as if you were too well up and habituated to the subject. Are you aware too that you have not referred to any work of Hunt, though giving a minute analysis of one of Millais, and of mine? I would not for the world that the long paragraph about me should appear without any reference to Hunt. Indeed I think it too long in any case, and would seem like personal bias to some. I wish too you would put the one about Millais first ; also that you would not attempt to defend my mediævalisms, which *were* absurd, but rather say that there was enough good in the works to give assurance that these were merely superficial. My picture should be described as the *Girlhood*, and by no means *Education.*

F 2.

"The Sid," first mentioned in this letter, and more frequently afterwards under her name Lizzy, was Elizabeth Eleanor Siddal.

My brother's things sent "from Highgate" must have been forwarded, I think, from a house rented by Mr. Bateman, a decorative artist, who had emigrated to Australia with Mr. Woolner and others. Mrs. and Miss Howitt (the late Mrs. Howitt-Watts) were then staying in the house, and were on very cordial terms both with my brother and with Miss Siddal. My brother's proposed trip to Hastings was for the purpose of rejoining Miss Siddal, who stayed there on various occasions for health's sake.

This amusing letter was written to Christina while she was on a visit to the family of Mr. Swynfen Jervis, at Darlaston in Staffordshire. It contains a pen-and-ink sketch, described towards the close. The whole thing is "chaff," and should not be understood as seriously ill-natured to Mr. Jervis, who was something of a Shakespearian commentator, and something also of a verse-writer. The sketch represents Christina either drawing a portrait of Mr. Jervis or transcribing verses from his dictation. Mr. Jervis, goose-quill in hand, rests his right elbow on the plinth of a bust of Shakespear. This bust has a sly glance, as if Shakespear took a view of Mr. Jervis's lucubrations rather different from that gentleman's own view. On the plinth is inscribed "We ne'er shall look upon his like again"; to which Mr. Jervis has appended the words, "Oh ah ! S. J."—A mushroom grows at the base of the plinth. In the background appears a totally unrecognizable scribble of Westminster Abbey. Christina's profile is caricatured, but expressively so.

[LONDON. 4 *August* 1852.]

MY DEAR CHRISTINA,

Maria has just shown me a letter of yours by which I find that you have been perpetrating portraits of some kind. If you answer this note, will you enclose a specimen, as I should like to see some of your handiwork? You must take care however not to rival the Sid, but keep within respectful limits. Since you went away, I have had sent me, among my things from Highgate, a lock of hair shorn from the beloved head of that dear, and radiant as the tresses of Aurora, a sight of which may perhaps dazzle you on your return. . . .

I am rejoiced to hear of your improved health, and hope it may prove lasting. I was lately in company with Mrs. and Miss Howitt, with whom you are a considerable topic. I believe Mamma forwarded you an intelligent Magazine by Mrs. H[owitt] to which you are at liberty to contribute. That lady was much delighted with your printed performances, and wishes greatly to know you. Her daughter . . . has by her, singularly enough, a drawing which she calls *The End of the Pilgrimage*, made by her some years back, which furnishes an exact illustration of your *Ruined Cross*.

On the opposite page is an attempt to record, though faintly, that privileged period of your life during which you have sat at the feet of one for whom the ages have probably been waiting. The cartoon has that vagueness which attends all true poetry. On *his* countenance is a calm serenity, unchangeable, unmistakable. In yours I think I read awe, mingled however with something of that noble pride which even the companionship of greatness has been known to bestow. Are you here transcribing from his very lips the title-deeds of his immortality, or rather perpetuating by a sister art the aspect of that brow where Poetry has set-up her throne? I know not. The expression of Shakespear's genial features is also perhaps ambiguous, though doubtless not to him. Westminster Abbey, I see, looms in the distance, though with rather an airy character.

I shall very possibly be going to Hastings in a few days. Meanwhile, till I hear from you or see you again, believe me, dear Christina,

Your affectionate Brother,

D. G. ROSSETTI.

I forgot to say that Mamma considers 2s. 6d. sufficient to give the maid—in which, I may add, I do not coincide. Mamma however says *you* must judge.

C 21.

I had gone for two or three days to Holman Hunt's lodgings at
Chelsea, near the Old Church, to sit to him for a head or what not
in one of his pictures. My brother at the same time wanted me to
sit to him for something else; I think it was the head of Dante in
his water-colour of *Dante drawing an Angel in Memory of Beatrice.*
Hence this note. The opening phrase refers to the subsiding of
some extraordinarily heavy rains.

[LONDON.] *Friday at breakfast,* 13 *August* 1852.

DEAR W——

Now that Chelsea and London are again one continent, I think you could not do better than return to your
Lares, who are pining for you with a pencil in one hand and
an india-rubber in the other. Or, as I have abandoned poetry,
I had better plainly inform you that, almost immediately
after your abrupt bolt the other morning, I descended to the
parlour with a request in reserve that you would come and
sit, but found only that *vacuum* which Art on this occasion
concurred with Nature in abhorring.

If you do not come at once, I am really afraid that I shall
not be able to do what I want from you, though it is not
much, before you start for Hastings or elsewhither as the
case may be. So be a good fellow and come, and tell Hunt
I shall cut him if he tries to keep you.

Your affectionate executioner,

D. G.

B 10.

"Wells Street" must mean the Church in Wells Street, Oxford
Street, at which there were services of more than common musical
beauty, attended at this time by our Mother and sisters, and sometimes by my brother as well. "The press" was the printing-press
which our Grandfather Polidori kept for his private convenience. It
seems that Mr. Tupper the printer was now thinking of buying this
press—perhaps he did so. Teodorico was our cousin Teodorico
Pietrocola-Rossetti, who was settled in London in these years.

[14 CHATHAM PLACE, BLACKFRIARS BRIDGE.]
Wednesday [towards end of 1852].

MY DEAR MAMMA,

. . . I think the other day named by Christina (whose note I cannot find) was Sunday. If I am able to get round to Wells Street in the morning, I shall come to dine with you afterwards, and may possibly see you this evening, if Tupper and I go to Grandpapa's about the press. I trust he continues better.

. . . I did a sketch of Teodorico last night, but suspect that it was a perfect failure. He has got it, and I believe means to show it you. I am getting to work here.

C 22.

My brother's proposal that I should review in the *Spectator* Miss Howitt's very pleasant and taking book, *An Art-student in Munich*, did not come to fulfilment. The work was reviewed, but not by me. I think it had been assigned or bespoken before I had an opportunity of addressing the Editor.

Edwards is Mr. Sutherland Edwards, the musical critic and author. Browning's play must have been *Colombe's Birthday*. I don't know why my brother should have been "bored to death" in case he had gone to see the play acted in the company of Mr. Edwards, without mine as well. He intensely admired Browning and his works, and had no sort of antipathy to Mr. Edwards; possibly he expected the drama to be spoiled in the acting. But wilfulness and waywardness governed him in matters of this kind.

[CHATHAM PLACE.] *Saturday [23 April* 1853].

MY DEAR WILLIAM,

Let me remind you again to speak to Rintoul, if you have not already done so, about giving you Miss Howitt's *Art-student in Munich* to review. Pray make him do so, as I have promised that you will. I fancy the book may be out by this time, or will be in a day or two.

D. G. R.

Edwards came here last night, and has an idea that he can get some orders for the Haymarket on Monday to see

Browning's play. Will you be here at six and go? Do come, as I now regret I engaged to go, and shall be bored to death if you do not.

B 11.

My Mother was at Frome Selwood, Somerset, when this letter was written; settled there, along with my Father and Christina, for about a year. The "very undignified" verses which Christina had sent up were, I fancy, a few which begin "In my cottage near the Styx"; for I know that Maria was (as intimated in this letter) singularly amused by that effusion. It may soon be published. Mr. Stewart was the medical man who attended our family for several years, succeeded after a while by his son, whose kind and skilful treatment proved invaluable to my Mother, Christina, and other members of the family. The "sketch of Papa" is the one which appears in this book—a very accurate likeness.

CHATHAM PLACE. Thursday [12 May 1853].

MY DEAR MAMMA,

I came down here again yesterday, having stayed till then at home. I got Christina's note, but I am sure that she will prefer that I should write to you instead of answering her. I must owe her a letter till I have more news. I certainly owe her, and may pay her if my "muscles" permit, a copy of verses also for that very undignified one of hers, which however is exceedingly good. The slightest allusion to it, ever since its arrival, brings to light a neatly-paved thorough-fare between Maggie's ears.

My boil has subsided. . . . Mr. Stewart called here yesterday, and said he would send me some other kind of medicine, as the old is finished. He seemed to like the situation much, and did not consider the rent at all high. I showed him that *Annunciation*, having nothing else at hand. He said it would be very pretty when finished, but I suspect was rather impressed by it with the idea that the doctor I most needed resided at Hanwell. I showed him also the sketch of Papa, which I have not yet managed to get to the frame-maker, but hope to do so to-day, as Green's man is going to call and fetch

MacCracken's picture.   Mr. S[tewart] thought the governor extremely like.   Since you went I have added the cupboard and a piece of chimney-piece in his background, which improves him much.   You will get him before long.   If you answer this, pray let me know how the original of the sketch gets on, as we have heard as yet nothing particular about him·

I want to get into the country immediately. . . .

Calder Campbell has just been in here, and detained me some time talking, and I must now set about doing something or other.   And indeed I have no more news—or rather no news at all, for that is about the contents of this note.   However, I know you have the weakness to care about every detail concerning my health, and so have written, though without mood or material for a letter—remaining, my dear Mamma,

Your affectionate Son,

D. G. ROSSETTI.

A 11.

Osborne, here mentioned, was a cabman, much employed as a jobbing man in our Grandfather's family.   The reason why my brother saw an improved prospect for the sale of his pictures (as notified at the close of his letter) was, I think, that he had now established a connexion with Mr. Francis MacCracken of Belfast—a merchant or packing-agent, who evinced a very great liking for Rossetti's work, bought various examples of it, and would probably have continued his purchases, but he died some three or four years after this date.

[CHATHAM PLACE.]

Wednesday [15 *June* 1853].

MY DEAR AUNT CHARLOTTE,

I am going to or near Newcastle with our friend Mr. Scott for a week or so, and find on enquiry that there is no valise or carpet-bag, or anything of the sort, I can take, at home.   Have you any such thing that you could kindly spare me?   I shall not want it for long.   Maria will send Osborne to you this afternoon for your answer, and, if you can lend me a carpet-bag, he will bring it me.   You may depend on my taking care of it.

This however is not the only request with which I have to trouble you. I am obliged to leave town without more delay, by continually returning illness, which I ought to have tried to shake off before by change of air. I am doing some work which will not take long to finish on my return, and for which I shall get paid immediately. Meanwhile, if you could increase my obligations to you by a loan of ten or twelve pounds, I would engage faithfully to return it as soon as I get the money in question, of which there is no doubt.

Maria good-naturedly says that she will be at Park Village this afternoon, in case you should be there, to speak to you about this—as I have mentioned it to her, and am myself obliged to be at my study. I think I am going to start to-morrow for Tynemouth, which is a watering-place near Newcastle. I hope the sea-air will do me some good, as I have long been in want of it. I shall bathe, and try to set myself up.

I am glad to say that I am now beginning to see my way much more clearly as regards the sale of whatever pictures I do, and shall without doubt be able to repay you before long, should you kindly oblige me just now.

B 12.

The hope here expressed "that Christina is energetic in her pursuit of art" refers to certain endeavours in drawing and painting which she was then making. They might have come to something eventually, but were not pursued far. There is an allusion to the same matter in a previous letter, F 2.

3 St. Thomas Street, Newcastle-on-Tyne.
Monday [20 *June* 1853].

My dear Mother,

I left town on Friday morning at 7, and arrived here between 9 and 10 P.M. with Scott. I have got out as yet but little, compared to what I should have wished, as the weather has not been very pleasant for walking. I do not know exactly what my next move will be, but I do not think of staying here, as it is rather a dreary place, and

Scott's inertia is so much akin to my own that I am afraid
I shall not get much benefit of exercise as long as I am here.
I think of going to the sea-side at Tynemouth; but may
perhaps adopt the plan of going there in the mornings and
coming back here at night, as it seems the journey takes
only half an hour, and I need not then bother about a
lodging. Mrs. Scott is in town still for the present.

I suppose perhaps you have William with you by this
time. I should like to know what are his plans during his
holiday, as we might perhaps combine sooner or later. I
fancy I feel rather better than I did in London; but this
atmosphere is so stagnant (intellectually speaking) that I
really scarcely know, nor can exert myself to think whether
I have anything to say. I do not know though that I should
have in any case. I occupy my time chiefly in chaffing
Scott about his brother David's works, and made a grand
allegorical design yesterday in that worthy's style, which
I declared was as fine as anything of his, and which Scott, I
believe, considers secretly to be really a grand work, though
I myself do not understand it.

I trust the governor's health continues in the improved
state which was the last I heard of it, and also that Christina
is energetic in her pursuit of art. Perhaps it would be as
well for you not to take the trouble of writing to me at
present, as I am uncertain as to my movements. I shall get
away from here I think before long. I have already caught
meteoric glimpses of the bore, and foresee that he will shortly
commence tossing his Briarean arms in various directions,
if I stay.

A 12.

3 St. Thomas Street, Newcastle-on-Tyne.
Monday 20 June 1853.

MY DEAR AUNT CHARLOTTE,

I got here on Friday night, and this morning have set
about letter-writing. I ought before to have thanked you
for the remittance which your kindness supplied so immediately, and which I shall not forget to return as soon as

possible. The carpet-bag was exactly suited to my requirements, which were very small ; indeed anything larger would
have been quite unnecessary.

*   *   *   *   *   *

My friend Mr. Scott, at whose house I am, is a very
delightful man, but the family-atmosphere is rather inactive,
and his inertia encourages mine. I fancy the sea-air at
Tynemouth will be the thing for me.

I send this letter to Maria, as I am uncertain about your
exact address. This morning I have written also to Mamma,
to whom I lately sent the sketch I made of Papa, which I
got framed in London. I fancy William must be at Frome
by this time.

Please remember me kindly to all members of the family
whom you may see, and believe me

Your affectionate Nephew,
D. G. ROSSETTI.

C 23.

David Scott, R.S.A. (mentioned also in a preceding letter), was
the brother, deceased in 1849, of William Bell Scott. Gabriel's
observation that he was "a tremendous lark" represents his opinion
only in a certain sense. He saw the singularities and aberrations
of David Scott's genius, but really admired it in a high degree.
His deliberate judgment is expressed in some observations introduced into Gilchrist's *Life of Blake*, and re-printed in the *Collected
Works* (vol. i., pp. 450—452). My brother never produced the
etching which he contemplated for W. B. Scott's poem of *Rosabell*.
The Artist was a short-lived serial with which I had something to
do. It did not publish any etchings either by Scott or by Madox
Brown. The Commonwealth etchings of Scott were a set executed
several years before the date of this letter, relating to the English
civil war of the seventeenth century.

NEWCASTLE-ON-TYNE. 20 June [1853].

MY DEAR WILLIAM,

I have been here since Friday, and do not exactly
know what I mean to do. Let me know what your moves
are to be, how long your holiday is, etc., in case we should

be able to combine at all—and whether you have any plans about the *rent*, which is due on the 24th. I think I shall not stay here long, as I find the general stagnation too like the spirit of Banquo, except for a strenuous dog, from whom also I suffer much. David Scott is a tremendous lark.

I want to tell you that Lizzy is painting at Blackfriars while I am away. Do not therefore encourage any one to go near the place. I have told her to keep the doors locked, and she will probably sleep there sometimes.

Tell me any news; I have none to tell. I suppose you are probably at Frome. . . .

I have heard several of Scott's poems, some very fine, and am going to do the etching for his *Rosabell*, as I proposed. By-the-bye, I mentioned to him that affair of *The Artist*, and that they would have etchings; that Brown was doing one, etc. ; and he asked me yesterday whether I thought it could be managed to get them to buy some of those Commonwealth etchings of his. They are really very good, but I do not know whether you could mention it at any time. You will know best.

Your affectionate Brother,
D. G. ROSSETTI.

I suppose, if you write to me here, it can be sent on in case I have left.

C 24.

" The town-subject " must be the picture—then I think already begun, but never quite finished—entitled *Found*. My brother's project of going to Nuremberg did not take effect at this time—nor at any. Deverell's father was the Secretary to the Schools of Design, now enlarged into the Department of Science and Art.

NEWCASTLE. Friday [1 July 1853].

MY DEAR WILLIAM,

I ought to have answered you before, but have been unable to come to any conclusion as to my plans hitherto.

Yesterday and the day before Scott and I made an excursion to Wetheral, Carlisle, and Hexham, and I rather think I shall settle at either the first or last for a little while, and begin my picture there. I wrote to MacCracken in answer to what he said about the *House of John*, and told him that I should have no objection to paint something else instead, mentioning the two pictures I had in contemplation—viz., the *Magdalen at the door of Simon*, and the town-subject, but without describing the latter, or mentioning price for either. I also offered him the Dante water-colour, begun in London, for thirty-five guineas. This last he snatches at. . . . I shall send for the drawing from London, and finish it here somewhere.

Do you know, I fancy after all I had rather go to Belgium than to Paris, which I expect would turn out a bore. But it strikes me that the best (and this I would *positively* do for a week or ten days, money permitting) would be to go to Nuremberg, and see the Durers etc. I suppose we could include Cologne in such a trip, but have no idea whether the expense (should you be equally inclined for this as the other) would be greater. I fear however that my delay will cause this to reach town after you have left. In this case you will get it elsewhere, and can then write to me at once where you are and what you mean, and I will answer *at once* with any proposal I may have to join you anywhere. . . .

I have done little here. However I have made a little water-colour of a woman in yellow, which I shall be able to sell, I have no doubt. I have also made sketches for an etching which I mean to do for Scott's book, and for the picture of the Magdalen. Scott and I have looked through his poems together, and have made some very advantageous amendments between us. *Rosabell* especially is quite another thing, and is now called *Mary Anne*.

MacCracken has written a long letter inviting me to Belfast, but I have no idea of going. I heard this morning from Deverell that his father is dead.

I do not find myself much better, I think, at Newcastle than in London. This is a beastly place. But in our late country excursion I felt very different ; I shall be much better I am sure if I settle for a little while.

Remember me most particularly to all at home if you are still there.

B 13.

The reference to our Father's face as being only partially visible must be founded on the fact that he wore a cap with a large projecting shade, to protect his eyesight; the sight of one eye having been lost for some years, and that of the other being alarmingly precarious. " Christina's almost stereotyped smile " is a more decidedly jocular allusion—being meant to indicate an expression (real or supposed) of settled gloom, as illustrated in the letter by a sketch scribbled in.

RED HORSE INN, STRATFORD-ON-AVON.
Tuesday Night, 12 July [1853].

MY DEAR MOTHER,

I left the North towards the end of last week after seeing several interesting places. Carlisle and Hexham especially delighted me, with all the country thereabouts. Newcastle however, where I was mainly staying, I found a horrid place, and the weather had been generally very shabby. Indeed till I came down into Warwickshire here I had felt but little better, but do now.

I came straight from Newcastle to Coventry by rail, and since that I have had no more of that disgusting work, but have walked always from place to place. To-day I walked from Kenilworth to Stratford—twelve miles. I never feel in the least tired, as it is quite another thing walking here from what it is in London or about beastly Newcastle. Coventry, Warwick, and Kenilworth, are all very interesting places, and the country about here lovely. After getting to Stratford this evening, I walked out again and saw Shakespear's house, to which I must pay a second visit. I shall stay here one or two days longer, and then back to London to get about work, though I shall probably leave again almost immediately to paint a background in the country. I want to find my way to Frome, and see your dear face again before long—also as much as is visible of the governor's, and Christina's almost stereotyped smile.

I suppose my letter reached Frome too late for William, from whom I have not heard, though no doubt you sent it on. I imagine he must nearly have finished his trip by this time.

MacCracken is in a state of wild excitement about some subjects I have been mentioning to him, and wrote me a long letter with full directions as to how I was to get to Belfast at once, and stay with him a little while, when we could arrange everything. He has closed with an offer I made him of a sketch, begun in London, for 35 guineas. It is of the same size as those I have sold before for 12, so that this is not amiss. I shall finish it on my return, and send it to him. I shall not go near him for the present, as I think it would be unwise. I have made one or two sketches while in the country which I shall be able to sell. You will hear from me when I reach London. Meanwhile I am, dear Mamma,

Your affectionate Son,

D. G. ROSSETTI.

B 14.

The opening of this letter refers to a carbuncle (or possibly, as he says, a large boil) which my brother had been troubled with. He wrote from No. 38 Arlington Street, Mornington Crescent, which had for more than two years been the residence of our family, but not now of Gabriel himself, who was housed in Chatham Place, Blackfriars.

ARLINGTON STREET.
Wednesday [Summer 1853].

DEAR MAMMA,

As I have no doubt you have been getting into a state about me, like a dear old thing as you are, I write to-day to tell you that I am come down into the parlour, and am all right again, except that the thing is not healed up yet. I have no poultice on however to-day, but some ointment. I doubt, after all, whether it has been more than a boil, though a large one.

I hear you are reading Haydon's Life, as I have been, and am now some way through vol. iii. It gets very melancholy reading as it goes on ; but altogether the book gives one a very high opinion of him, I think. I cannot see, after all, that he was so conceited as that fellow Tom Taylor wants to make out, with the insolent pity of a little snob. He was always, or nearly so, dissatisfied with his own work, though certainly he was always saying he could see a great thing before him, which thing he really *did* see. The fact is that, when a man near the top of a hill begins going into raptures about the view which his position commands, it is necessary that one should be something more than an ant even to understand him, since the ant cannot even look high enough to see that the hill is there at all. I hate that sneak Wilkie. After all, Haydon does not seem to have been extravagant, or even very improvident.

I shall get back to my study as soon as possible, and hope I shall not have any more plagues to prevent my getting to work. I got a letter from MacCracken towards the end of last week, saying he should be in London the early part of this, and would call at my study. I am convinced he has come chiefly to see Hunt and myself, and I fear he may miss both, as Hunt is at Ewell. However, I shall be back there as soon as I am quite well, and should really like to see him, if possible. Meanwhile I have left a note for him with the housekeeper explaining.

Remember me most affectionately to Papa and to Christina.

B 15.

The *Arpa Evangelica*, a volume of religious poetry composed by our Father, had now been printed abroad. It formed his last publication,

[14 CHATHAM PLACE.]
Monday [August 1853].

MY DEAR MAMMA,

Maggy's going to Frome this morning recalls to me even more strongly than usual how glad I should be myself to see you again, and how I neglect, through wretched laziness as a correspondent, the only means of communicating with you just at present. I need not say how sorry I was to hear that your health had not been quite so good lately. I trust however that you will not long have this additional trouble. I am much better than I have been, though these hot days make one feel sick and queer. My sketch for MacCracken, which had languished with my health, is very forward now, and I hope soon to get the tin, and soon after that to be able to speak in the same manner of the even more important progress of his picture, on the subject of which his excitement continues unabated, or rather on the increase. MacCrac was, as perhaps I told you, to have come to London for a few days, but, finding on a sudden that the R.A. had closed, he withheld his (yearned-for) visit.

I have seen scarcely any one lately. Read, the American poet whom you wot of, has been here again with his wife and children, on their way to settle in Italy, and consequently bored me for a brief gasping interval. . . .

I am quite sorry to hear of the difficulties which delay the arrival of the *Arpa Evangelica*, which must be very disappointing. Pray remember me most affectionately to its author, for report of whose manners and habits the mental eye needs no telescope.

I have finished Haydon's Life, which afforded me very great enjoyment. I am now reading that of Benvenuto Cellini, which Grandpapa gave me some time back. This also is most interesting, and I am perhaps the more able to enter into the writer's character from the surprising resemblance which I find in it to that of poor Sangiovanni. The book, as you know, is an autobiography, and at every page it is absolutely like hearing Sangiovanni speak. This is curious to remark, as S[angiovanni]'s speciality in art was much of the same kind as Benvenuto's, and I dare say under equally fortunate conditions might have been developed to as high a degree.

I am uncertain as to where I shall move to, or whether at all unless my picture absolutely requires it. Scott's holiday at Hexham is now nearly over, so that I should probably not go there now, as I have been prevented hitherto ; though indeed the old market-town is attractive enough of itself, but the distance is so very great. I hope still to be able at no distant period to snatch a week or so at Frome, when I should be able to examine the neighbourhood as well as to see your dear old eye.

*   *   *   *   *   *

A 13.

The small matter with which this letter opens appears to have stood thus. My brother had done, for insertion in our Aunt's workbox, some sketches, which she shortly handed over to Lady Bath. He then made another sketch for the workbox.

[14 CHATHAM PLACE.]
Friday [*2 September* 1853].

MY DEAR AUNT,

I am very glad the sketches pleased you, and that they served your object by pleasing Lady Bath. But—that the original box may not bewail its honours—I send you a little sketch for the inside. It is a recollection from Nature —a little girl whom I saw wheeling a baby in just such a barrow. Would it not make a capital picture of the domestic class to represent a half-dozen of girls racing the babies entrusted to their care—babies bewildered, out of breath, upset, sprawling at bottom of barrow, etc. etc. ?

I think this sketch ought to have another piece of paper pasted *underneath* it, or I fear the printing on the box would show through. You should use the paste rather dry also, or the ink may run.

*   *   *   *   *   *

As to what I hope to show you, I merely referred to what I am about for Mr. MacCracken of Belfast, of whom you have heard—which performances I trust to see finished at some indefinite period.

I have seen extracts from Sir H. Lowe's Journal, but, to tell you the truth, should be rather doubtful, as far as I have seen, whether he might not have treated poor Bony a little better than he did, without injustice to his own Government. I have been reading Haydon's Autobiography—a most interesting book, which I recommend to you if it should come in your way.

B 16.

As to "Uncle Philip" see the Note to C 1. The "brick wall, and white heifer tied to a cart," were wanted for my brother's picture *Found*. It is worth noting that he speaks of a "heifer" (not "calf"); one might infer that he intended the heifer, bound for butchering, to have a symbolic analogy with the outcast woman of his picture. *Nick* was a grotesque prose-tale written by Christina. It had apparently been entrusted, or was to be recommended, to Hannay, with a view to publication—which did not take place at that time. The tale was finally included in the volume named *Commonplace, and other Stories*. George Tupper and two others are mentioned towards the close of the letter in the character of creditors, Mr. Tupper being anxious to close the money-accounts of the long-defunct *Germ*. Reeves was an artists' colourman, and Coleman a tailor. "Maggy" always means our sister Maria.

The letter opens by repelling the idea that Gabriel, in his Mother's opinion, "thought it a bore writing to her." He received a reply, 3 October, from which I will quote a few maternal words. "Read my letter again, and you will see that I never said that you thought it a bore to write to me; but that my letters are so barren that *they* might well prove a bore to you to read. You have always had a fund of affection for me; and the remembrance of how, when quite little, you came forward in my defence if I was attacked, and tried to console me if I seemed unhappy, is one of the dearest reminiscences of my heart."

MY DEAR MAMMA,

I received your very welcome note, the only at all
unsatisfactory thing in which is your hint that I think it
a bore writing to you.   Is this really quite fair, when I sent
a letter by Maria? and even before that think (though am
not certain) that I had been the last to write.   At any rate,
I know I am a better correspondent to you than to almost
any one, as my friends could testify.

I have just come in from taking tea at Park Village, where
I am glad to inform you that I found all well, including
Grandpapa, who conversed with me on a variety of subjects,
though his memory seems now and then to be at fault.
Uncle Philip seemed much gratified at your having written
to him, and repeated at intervals, with a certain tendency to
defiance, that the letter was good English.

I know you will be pleased to hear that I am painting
Aunt Charlotte's portrait, to be given to Grandpapa.   I had
the second sitting to-day, and have got very forward with it,
though at the close of to-day I discovered a radical defect
in the nose, and erased that important feature, whereby the
portrait no doubt gains a temporary sublimity by resembling
many antique statues.   I am confident it will be very like
when done.   I find they have an old frame at Park Village,
which I think can be made to suit it.

I am progressing with my works for MacCrac, the water-
colour being at last nearly done, as it ought to have been
long ago ; but I shall never, I suppose, get over the weakness
of making a thing as good as I can manage, and must take
to charging on that principle.   As for the present drawing,
the stipulated 35 guineas is absurdly under its value now,
and I think I must give MacCracken to understand as
much.

I believe I shall be wanting to paint a brick wall, and a
white heifer tied to a cart going to market.   Such things are
I suppose to be had at Frome, and it has occurred to me

that I should like if possible to come and paint them there. There is a cattle-market, is there not? Have you ever seen such an article as the heifer in question, and have you or Christina any recollection of an eligible and accessible brick wall? I should want to get up and paint it early in the mornings, as the light ought to be that of dawn. It should be not too countrified (yet beautiful in colour), as it is to represent a city-wall. A certain modicum of moss would therefore be admissible, but no prodigality of grass, weeds, ivy, etc. Can you give any information on these heads? I suppose Christina's pictorial eye will by this time have some insight into the beauties of brick walls—the preferability of purplish prevailing tint to yellowish, etc.

I suppose Christina has not been working much at the Art? Will you tell her that I am quite ashamed of not being able yet to tell her anything positive about *Nick*? I am constantly remembering it when Hannay is not in the way, and always forgetting it when he is. I have now resolved to remember it the next time I see him, and, if I am baulked again, to write to him the next time I think of it.

I was rejoiced at the arrival of the *Arpa Evangelica*, in thinking how much pleasure it would give Papa, to whom pray give my sincere love. I have been looking through the volume, and hope before long to have read it through. Its whole plan and arrangement seem to me highly artistic and admirable.

I have been thinking whether anything is left to say; but can only find that George Tupper is still uncompromising, Reeves strenuous, Coleman sleepless, and MacCrac the same frenzied enthusiast; facts which demand that the present writer should be a philosopher of some eminence, as well as being

Your most affectionate Son,

DANTE GABRIEL ROSSETTI.

Give my best love to Maggy and Christina, the former of whom no doubt I shall soon see again.

E 3.

This letter to our Father, and the following one, may as well appear in their original Italian: I subjoin translations. A suggestion had been made by our Father in a letter dated 4 October, that Lady Bath, the purchaser of *The Girlhood of Mary Virgin*, might probably commission Gabriel for a portrait of herself. It will be seen from the letter that Mr. MacCracken was now the owner of the *Annunciation* picture.—I will give one passage from our Father's letter: "Remember, my much-loved son, that you have only your own ability upon which to thrive. Remember that you were born with a decided aptitude [for painting]; and that, even from your earliest years, you made us conceive the highest hopes that you would prove a great painter. And such you will be, I am assured."

Saturday.

MY DEAREST FATHER,

I learned yesterday with great concern, from Mamma's letter to Maria, that you have had in these last days a severe attack of diarrhœa ; but I thank God for the decided improvement of which that letter also assures me. May your health strengthen always from day to day with the fine air of the country, from which I hoped much when you left London.

I would not have delayed so long in answering your dear and affectionate letter, but that I was wishing to speak somewhat, in my reply, about the *Arpa Evangelica*, and to read it in full before writing to you. Nor have I yet, being much occupied just now, found time for a deliberate reading. I have read the whole second series, the *Solemnities of the Church*, which I liked well ; but more perhaps than any of the compositions there I like the last composition in the fifth series, *The Penitent Woman on the Crucifix*, which appeared to me very fine, and which might almost appertain to the argument of the second series. The other evening, in my Grandfather's house, I read with him some of the *Arpa* ; and he particularly indicated to me the poem on the *Fall of Jerusalem*, and I joined him in admiring it. I have also read the first of the three cantos of *The Redemption*, which seems to me worthy of the other two, which I already knew.

I trust that perhaps I may soon be able to come and see you at Frome, when I hope to find your health improved, and that of Mamma and Christina vigorous. The portrait of my Aunt Charlotte will perhaps require one other sitting, but it is already nearly finished ; I think it is now very like. I fear there is not any ground to suppose that Lady Bath wants her own portrait, as she has lately had it painted twice —one in miniature, another in oil. Nor perhaps could I just now undertake it, being bound to paint a picture for that Irish gentleman who owns my *Annunciation*. For him is likewise the water-colour which I am now finishing, and of which Mamma will certainly have spoken to you.

Please tell Mamma that I have not forgotten her last letter, and will not fail to reply. Assure her, and also Christina, of my sincere affection, and believe me always

Your very affectionate Son,
D. G. ROSSETTI.

14 CHATHAM PLACE, BLACKFRIARS BRIDGE.
SABATO [October 1853].

MIO CARISSIMO PADRE,

Ho saputo ieri con gran rammarico, dalla lettera di Mamma a Maria, che avete avuto in questi ultimi giorni un severo attacco di diarrea, ma ringrazio Iddio del miglioramento deciso che quella lettera anche mi assicura. Possa la vostra salute invigorirsi sempre di giorno in giorno coll' aria benefica della campagna, dalla quale ho sperato molto quando lasciaste Londra.

Non avrei indugiato tanto nel rispondere alla vostra cara ed affettuosa lettera, se non avessi desiderato di parlare alquanto, nella mia risposta, dell' *Arpa Evangelica*, e di leggerla tutta prima di scrivervi. Nè ancora, essendo molto occupato in questo momento, ho io trovato tempo per una lettura accurata. Ho letto intiera la seconda serie delle *Solennità della Chiesa*, la quale mi piace assai, ma forse più ancora che qualunque delle composizioni contenute in essa mi piace l'ultima composizione della quinta serie, *La Penitente sul Crocifisso,* la quale mi è paruta bellissima, e che apparterrebbe quasi all'argomento della seconda serie. L'altra sera, a casa di mio avo, ho letto con lui qualche squarcio dell' *Arpa,* ed esso mi ha indicato specialmente la poesia sulla Caduta di Gerusalemme, ed io mi sono unito con lui nell' ammirarla. Ho letto anche il primo dei tre Canti della *Redenzione,* che mi pare degno dei due altri, i quali io già conosceva.

Spero che forse fra poco io potrò venire a visitarvi a Frome, dove spero di trovare ristabilita la vostra salute, e vigorosa quella di Mamma e di Cristina. Il ritratto di mia zia Carlotta richiederà forse un' altra seduta, ma è già quasi finita ; mi pare che adesso somigli molto. Temo che non ci sia affatto luogo di credere che Lady Bath vorrà il proprio ritratto, poichè se l'ha fatto dipingere ultimamente due volte, una in miniatura, un' altra ad olio. Nè io forse in questo momento lo protrei intraprendere, avendo l'incombenza di fare un quadro per quel signore irlandese che possiede la mia *Annunziazione.* Per lui anche è l'acquarella che finisco ora, e di cui Mamma vi avrà certamente parlato.

Vi prego di dire a Mamma che non mi sono scordato della sua ultima lettera, e che non mancherò a risponderci. Assicurate lei, come anche Cristina, del mio sincero affetto, e credetemi sempre

il vostro affettuosissimo figlio,

D. G. ROSSETTI.

B 17.

Williams, here named, was a jobbing man, employed in our family to black boots, etc. : he entertained a special predilection for Gabriel. In earlier years he had been a police-constable in Wales ; he had good natural intelligence, and a characteristic face, which Gabriel painted as St. Joachim in his *Girlhood of Mary Virgin.* No opportunity offered to my brother of painting our Mother's portrait at Frome. In laughing at the statement that Woolner was " a gentleman of very affable and agreeable manners," Gabriel did not intend any sneer at his friend : only that Woolner was much more laudable for

By D. G. Rossetti.

CHARLOTTE L. POLIDORI.

1853.

sturdy independence and resolute decision than for anything to be classed under the term "affable."

Thursday evening [*Autumn* 1853].

MY DEAR MOTHER,

I have been putting off writing to you under the idea that, by doing so, I should be able to speak positively as to my possible visit to Frome; but find myself as yet still unable to do so, and will no longer defer writing.

I have been working a great deal lately, but somehow it seems impossible to finish anything. I have received £20 in advance towards the payment of the drawing for MacCrac, which is at last nearly done; and have been getting under way with his picture, which I hope, when once fairly afoot, will soon be very forward, as I have been making careful preparations, and caution at first is always the shortest in the long run. Aunt Charlotte's portrait is done to all intents and purposes, though I shall have another sitting. I think it is now a great deal like. I showed it to-day to Williams, who was sitting to me, and he recognized it immediately. As soon as I am able to come to Frome I mean to paint a similar portrait of you; and should like also to do one of Papa, but fear he would find the sitting too wearisome. Aunt Charlotte's is done very carefully—the head quite as finished as anything I have painted.

You will be glad to hear that I have at last some news of Woolner and B[ernhard] Smith. The former has written to his father, and the latter to his brother. At Edward Smith's last night we had a regular meet for reading the letters. It seems that the two went in succession to all the Diggings, or nearly so, during a period of seven months, and were uniformly unsuccessful, working always as hard as navigators, or harder. . . . After the seven months' digging W[oolner] resolved on returning to Melbourne to try his luck at sculpture, and here, I am delighted to say, he seems in a fair way of complete success. He has done several medallions at £25 each—one of Mr. La Trobe, the Governor of the Settlement —and there is a prospect of his getting a commission for a statue of the Queen to be erected there ; in which case we may probably see him back as soon as next summer to work at it in London. He has sent two Australian papers in which he is spoken of most highly, and both of which quote William's notices of his works, from the *Spectator*, as conclusive as to his position in England ; so that William has probably been of some real use to him. One of them says that " Mr. Woolner is a gentleman of very affable and agreeable manners," which is rather rich. One bad thing is that the present Governor, who has been very friendly to Woolner, and is a cousin of Bateman, has been recalled, and will shortly leave the Colony. It is to be hoped W[oolner]'s luck will not go with *him*. W[oolner] is staying with Dr. Howitt (brother of W. Howitt), who as well as all his family are most kind to W[oolner], and greatly taken with him—as I know from some letters Mrs. Howitt here has had from them . . . Bernhard has gone to the farm of a brother of his about thirty miles from Melbourne, and I believe has been making interest to get into the " Gold Commission."

Will you tell Christina that Mrs. Howitt asked me the other day whether she could print the *Summer Evening* in a collection of translations from the German which are to be splendidly illustrated, and to which the publishers have asked her to add a few original English ones ? For the same collection she asked me to contribute something, and I gave a ghastly ballad called *Sister Helen*. The *Aikin's Year*, where Christina's poem was to have been, it seems, is delayed for the present.

I fear there is not much more news. Hunt and Brown are both I believe well, though I have seen neither very lately. I called the other night on poor Deverell, who is very ill indeed, and I have heard even that his doctor says he cannot live over next summer, if so long. But I hope this is an exaggeration. He is in good spirits, the same as ever, and I told him it was all stuff. He is full of troubles as to maintaining the family since his father's death.

*   *   *   *   *   *

F 3.

" Miss Barbara Smith " is better known to the present generation as Mrs. Bodichon; a most admirable woman, full of noble zeal in every good cause, and endowed with a fine pictorial capacity. Mrs. Orme—whom Thackeray called "a jolly fellow "—was the sister-in-law of Mr. Coventry Patmore. Hers too was a rich abundant nature, only partially indicated in Thackeray's phrase, for her whole type of character was most essentially that of a woman, and not a man ; among many kind friends of my youth she was nearly the kindest of all. Marshall, who was consulted in Deverell's illness, was the Mr. John Marshall so often mentioned in these pages. Mr. Burrows (afterwards a Canon of Rochester) was the Incumbent of Christ Church, Albany Street, which my female relatives attended with extreme constancy.

I am sure that some of my readers will laugh over the sonnet (or rather quasi-sonnet of fifteen lines) on MacCracken, parodied from Tennyson. It is (otherwise I would not publish it) a mere piece of rollicking fun, without the least real sting in it ; for MacCracken was my brother's mainstay in his most struggling years, and was well recognized and appreciated as such by my brother himself. Of course the inspiration of the sonnet is the resemblance between the sounds Kraken and MacCracken ; and Mr. MacCracken would never have been accused of " spungings," of perpetrating a " secret sell," and of a determination to "lie," had it not been that Tennyson's sonnet contained similar words or sounds, and the temptation to misapply them was irresistible. As a specimen of parody, I know not where to find a more felicitous thing than this. As a picture of facts its value is less than nil : except indeed for its clear implication that Rossetti would have liked to get bigger prices for his performances, from MacCracken or from any one, if only he could have got them.

Tuesday [8 *November* 1853].

DEAR CHRISTINA,

I have written lately to Papa and Mamma (by the bye, has the former got my letter ?), but it is some time since I have enlightened you. Maria showed me the other day two poems of yours which are among the best you have written for some time : only the title of one—*Something like Truth*—seems " very like a whale." What does it mean ?

The latter verses of this are most excellent; but some, which I remember vaguely, about "dreaming of a lifelong ill" (etc. etc. *ad libitum*), smack rather of the old shop. I wish you would try any rendering either of narrative or sentiment from real abundant Nature, which presents much more variety, even in any one of its phases, than all such "dreamings."

Allingham has just come to town, and with him and William I went last night to the Howitts. Anna Mary's excitement on your subject has not subsided, and she still hopes, when you come to town, not to miss you again. She has painted a sunlight picture of *Margaret* (*Faust*) in a congenial wailing state, which is much better than I fancied she could paint. I am going down some time by daylight to give her some hints about the colour. I wish there were any chance of my ever doing the same for you, but I am afraid you find art interfere with the legitimate exercise of anguish. Ah if you were only like Miss Barbara Smith! a young lady I meet at the Howitts', blessed with large rations of tin, fat, enthusiasm, and golden hair, who thinks nothing of climbing up a mountain in breeches, or wading through a stream in none, in the sacred name of pigment. Last night she invited us all to lunch with her on Sunday; and perhaps I shall go, as she is quite a *jolly fellow*—which was Thackeray's definition of Mrs. Orme.

Mr. Orme has just received a letter from Woolner, which I think I may perhaps be able to send you when it shall have been seen to-night at a supper which Allingham gives to Hunt, Hannay, Stephens, W[illiam], and self. Hunt still talks of starting for Paris on the 15th, whence he will proceed with Seddon to Egypt possibly, or at any rate somewhither. Millais, I just hear, was last night elected Associate.

"So now the whole Round Table is dissolved."

You know—do you not?—of poor Deverell's illness. Marshall, whom you have heard me speak of, went the other day to see him, and quite confirmed his own doctor's decision (which I had hoped might be a mistaken one) that he does not seem to have six months' life in him.   He says, however, there *may* be a chance if he is very careful.   I wanted him to come and take possession of one of my rooms, thinking it would be more cheerful for him ; but it seems he must not think of stirring out.   I fear he does not know his danger, as he talks still of going, as soon as he is better, to paint the background of a picture at the London Docks.   He has, strangely enough, begun another picture which he calls *The Doctor's Last Visit*—where a doctor is trying to explain to the assembled family of a sick man that there is no hope. His spirits are, I think, the same as ever, and in the evenings he does not seem to suffer much . . . but in the morning, I believe, is his worst time.   His complaint is described as " Dr. Bright's disease of the kidneys."

This is not very cheerful.   Sunday night Maria and I went to see Mr. Burrows after attending service at his church. I liked him very well, but he rather reminded me of Patmore in manner.   The decorations at Christ Church are very poor —four gilt Corinthian capitals ; item, one pulpit-cloth with seven white stars, etc. etc.

I managed to finish Aunt Charlotte's portrait before she left town, except that I find I shall want one more sitting to work on the hands.   I have ordered the frame, and, when that comes, shall take the picture to Park Village.   Aunt Eliza is coming here to-morrow (9th November) to bask in the ecstasy of the Lord Mayor's Show !

I do not know that I have any more to say, except that I will subjoin two sonnets—one by Tennyson, and the other a parody on it.   The latter, I must say, is perhaps rather a stern view of the character.

Love to all.

THE KRAKEN.

BY A. TENNYSON.

" Below the thunders of the upper deep—
    Far far beneath in the abysmal sea—
His ancient dreamless uninvaded sleep
    The Kraken sleepeth. Fainter sunlights flee

About his shadowy sides: above him swell
   Huge sponges of millennial growth and height:
   And far away into the sickly light,
From many a wondrous grot and secret cell,
Unnumbered and enormous polypi
   Winnow with giant fins the slumbering green.
There he has lain for ages, and will lie,
Battening upon huge sea-worms in his sleep,
Until the latter fire shall heat the deep.
   Then, once by men and angels to be seen,
In roaring he shall rise, and on the surface die."

MACCRACKEN.

BY D. G. ROSSETTI.

Getting his pictures, like his supper, cheap,
   Far far away in Belfast by the sea,
His watchful one-eyed uninvaded sleep
   MacCracken sleepeth. While the P.R.B.
Must keep the shady side, he walks a swell
   Through spungings of perennial growth and height:
   And far away in Belfast out of sight,
By many an open do and secret sell,
Fresh daubers he makes shift to scarify,
   And fleece with pliant shears the slumbering 'green.'
There he has lied, though aged, and will lie,
Fattening on ill-got pictures in his sleep,
Till some Præraphael prove for him too deep.
   Then, once by Hunt and Ruskin to be seen,
Insolvent he will turn, and in the Queen's Bench die.

E 4.

Translation.

Thursday evening.

DEAREST FATHER,

   Excuse me for having so long ago received your dear
letter without as yet replying. I heard lately with the
greatest sorrow the bad news of your health. But from what
I hear now I trust that you find yourself a little better. I
would like to say, *much.*

   I can't yet say that I have read the *Arpa Evangelica* right through ; but I have read many compositions in it since I wrote last, and I specially remember that addressed *To the Guardian Angel* as one of the most beautiful, and on an idea which has always seemed to me one of the most poetical that can be treated.

Some days ago I showed the *Arpa*, as your latest work, to a certain Signor Ventura, who came to me as the only Rossetti he could find in the Directory, and thinking that here he would find *you*. He brought you the respects of a certain Signor Palizzi of Vasto, and also of the brothers of the latter, all of them readers of yours. Ventura himself seemed to know all your works, except this last one ; he informed me he does not belong to Vasto, but to Central Italy. I told him I would give you his message when first I wrote.

I greatly grieve, as we all must, for the death of my dear Grandfather, for whom I have always entertained a sincere affection. It would at least have been a slight consolation if he could once have recognized his family before passing away.

In your letter, my dear Father, you speak of my profession. I can assure you that now I am not negligent in that respect. With me progress always is, and always will be, gradual in everything. Of late also health has not been favourable to me ; but now I am well and at work, and I also find pur-chasers, and I can see before me, much more clearly than hitherto, the path to success. How much do I owe you, and how much trouble have I given you, dearest Father, in this and in all matters ! Needless were it to ask your loving heart to pardon me ; but I must always beg you to believe in the real and deep affection with which I remain

Your loving Son,

DANTE GABRIELE ROSSETTI.

The Signor Palizzi mentioned in this letter may probably be (or may have been, for I assume that he is no longer alive) a painter of considerable repute for pictures with telling groups of goat-herds, etc. ; he stood well in the annual Paris Exhibitions. This was

Filippo Palizzi ; one of his brothers, Giuseppe, was also a painter of good position.—Our Grandfather, Gaetano Polidori, had died of apoplexy on 16 December 1853. He had reached the age of eighty-nine, retaining, not much impaired, his strength and faculties to the last.

GIOVEDÌ SERA.
12 *January* [1854].

CARISSIMO PADRE,

Scusatemi che da tanto tempo ho ricevuto la vostra cara lettera, senza averci ancora risposto. Ho sentito ultimamente con grandissimo rammarico le cattive nuove della vostra salute. Ma, da quel che sento ora, spero che vi trovate un poco meglio ; vorrei dir, *molto*.

Non ancora posso dirvi di aver letta in tutto *l'Arpa Evangelica* ; ma ne ho lette parecchie composizioni da che vi ho scritto l'ultima volta, e specialmente mi rammento quella diretta *All' Angelo Custode* come una delle più belle, e sopra un' idea che mi è sempre paruta una delle più poetiche che si possa trattare.

Giorni fà, ho mostrato *l' Arpa*, come ultimo vostro lavoro, ad un certo Signor Ventura, il quale venne da me come essendo il solo Rossetti trovato da lui nel *Directory*, e pensando che qui vi troverebbe. Esso vi portò i rispetti d'un certo Signor Palizzi del Vasto, ed anche dei fratelli di questo, tutti lettori vostri. Anche questo Ventura pareva conoscere tutte le vostre opere, eccetto quest 'ultima : esso mi disse non essere del Vasto ma dell' Italia Centrale. Io gli dissi che vi darei il suo messaggio, quando prima vi avrei da scrivere.

Io mi dolgo grandemente, come dobbiamo fare tutti, della morte del mio caro avo, pel quale ho avuto sempre un sincero affetto. Sarebbe stato almeno qualche poco di consolazione s'egli avesse potuto riconoscere una volta la famiglia prima di spirare.

Nella lettera vostra, caro padre, mi parlate della mia professione. Vi posso assicurare che non sono trascurato adesso in questo riguardo. Con me il progresso è sempre, e sarà sempre, graduale in tutto, nè ultimamente mi è stata favorevole la salute ; ma adesso sto bene, e lavoro, e trovo anche compratori ; e mi veggo innanzi, molto più chiaramente che sin' adesso, la via della buona riuscita. Quanto vi debbo, e quanta pena vi ho dato, carissimo padre, in questo e in tutto ! Non ci è bisogno ch' io domandi al vostro amoroso cuore di perdonarmi ; ma debbo sempre pregarvi di credere al vero e profondo affetto con cui mi segno

il vostro amoroso figlio,
DANTE GABRIELE ROSSETTI.

C 25.

[LONDON.
Friday 3 February 1854.]

DEAR WILLIAM,

I had already heard from the family of poor Deverell's death.

I should like to meet Millais this evening, but do not know whether I shall feel in sufficiently good spirits to come out.

C 26.

" Allingham [Mr. William Allingham the poet—he died in 1889] has been looking over her poems " : this means " looking over Christina's poems "—not Lizzy's.   The " publisher " desiderated was not secured until 1862.

[14 CHATHAM PLACE.]
Tuesday [28 *March* 1854].

MY DEAR WILLIAM,

*   *   *   *   *   *

Tell Christina that, if she will come here on Thursday, Lizzy will be here. . . . I shall be glad if she will come, as I have told Lizzy she mentioned her wish to do so.

Allingham has been looking over her poems, and is delighted with many of them. I am going to lend them him (trusting in her permission to do so), that he may give his opinion as to which will be the best for a volume. Lizzy will illustrate, and I have no doubt we shall get a publisher.

B 18.

As to "Robertsbridge" and "Wilkinson" the Memoir gives
needful explanation ; Scalands near Robertsbridge being the
property of Miss Barbara Leigh Smith, and Dr. Wilkinson being
an eminent Homœopathic Physician whom the Howitts had
recommended Miss Siddal to consult.

(*My address will be*) 5 HIGH STREET, HASTINGS.

[*May* 1854.]

MY DEAR MAMMA,

    *   *   *   *   *

I found Lizzie apparently rather better than otherwise ; at any rate not worse, either by her own account or
by appearances. Some of her bad symptoms are certainly
abating, and her spirits, she says, are much better. I have
been staying at the Inn here ; but move to-day to Mrs.
Elphick's, 5 High Street, where Guggum is, and where
my lodging will cost 8s., I believe. Barbara Smith and
Anna Mary came down to see Lizzie yesterday from Robertsbridge, some miles from here, where they are staying ; and
we all took a walk together, which did not seem to fatigue
Lizzie much. There are several other ladies who have been
most attentive to Lizzie, and every one adores the dear. No
one thinks it at all odd my going into the Gug's room to sit
there ; and Barbara Smith said to the landlady how un-
advisable it would be for her to sit with me in a room
without fire.

I wrote yesterday, from her own lips, a most minute
account of her state to Wilkinson, and expect his reply. I
cannot think that there is any need of her going into the
Sussex Infirmary as proposed.

She and I are going to Robertsbridge to-morrow to spend
the day. The weather has turned, and become most delicious.
The sea to-day looks like enamel in the sun, and there is
a cool breeze. I write this waiting for breakfast at 8 a.m. (!)
Yesterday I saw the sun rise ! ! ! over the sea—the most
wonderful of earthly sights. This morning I was awake

in time too; but there was less beauty in the dawn, though the day promises to be even more lovely than yesterday.

But I fear you cannot even yet be much in a mood for hearing of these things. I myself feel more at ease since seeing Lizzie, but nevertheless was not the merriest of our party yesterday.

Bye-bye, Bunk. Love to all.

Your most affectionate Son,

D. G. ROSSETTI.

P.S.—Perhaps I may be bothering William before long to send some painting-things from my rooms, but am not sure how long I stay. Will he go round and see if Ruskin's books have reached there for me, and will you let me know if you write?

C 27.

"Ruskin's letter" was the letter about the Præraphaelites which Mr. Ruskin got printed in the *Times* about this date. Collins was Charles Allston Collins, a young painter much under Millais's influence, and (though not a member of the "Brotherhood") practically a Præraphaelite. That my brother should have regarded "£50 for the water-colour" (I think the water-colour of *Dante drawing an Angel*, previously referred to) as "a princely style of thing" shows how scanty was then the market for his productions; although of course it was liberal in Mr. MacCracken to pay £52 10s. (I apprehend that to be the exact sum) for a work which he had originally (as previous letters show) commissioned for £36 15s.

5 HIGH STREET, HASTINGS.
Thursday [11 *May* 1854].

MY DEAR WILLIAM,

I wish you would tell people I am not dead, but by no means encouraging the idea of such an amount of life as at all facilitates human intercourse. It is rather slow here, and generally very windy, though often glorious sunlight. Tell Allingham if you see him that, should he have an idea of coming to Hastings, I wish he would carry it out; and that, if he can only spare a day or so, his best plan would be to take a return ticket on Saturday, which costs £1 (second class), and will bring him back by the last train on Monday. Or if you could do this yourself, do. I want to know something of all things—how do people talk of Hunt's pictures? I saw Ruskin's letter. Had the *Times* been cheeky? How is Collins hung? And is there anything worth description in the R. A.? I suppose you have begun in the *Spec.* If you could send me that public organ I should be thankful.

Lizzy seems upon the whole a little better, and Wilkinson judges so from the long account of her symptoms which we sent. She and I spent a pleasant day on Monday at Scalands, where Barbara and Anna Mary have been staying. They made themselves very jolly, and it is a most stunning country there. I heard from MacCrac, who offers £50 for the water-colour, with all manner of soap and sawder into the bargain—a princely style of thing.

There seem to be several places tolerably within range hereabouts which we ought to see, and shall set about seeing; but Lizzy is not capable of too much exertion. I dare say I shall very soon be boring you to send my painting-things from London, but almost think I shall have to come myself when I want them. . . .

Your
D. G. R.

There is a very rich skit on A. Smith, *Balder*, etc., in *Blackwood*, professing to be a review of *Firmilian, a Tragedy by Percy Jones.* You should see it, and tell Allingham.

C 28.

The "relative" of Miss Barbara Smith, connected with a Sanatorium, was probably the celebrated Miss Nightingale, who towards the close of 1854 went out to the Crimea. Miller must be Mr. John Miller of Liverpool—an elderly Scotch gentleman, a merchant, a prime mover in artistic matters in Liverpool, and admirably kind and energetic in all his doings. He had apparently some claim upon Deverell's picture of *Twelfth Night*, and there was a proposal of raffling it for the advantage of the painter's surviving relatives. Mr. Gambart (I need perhaps hardly say) was at this time the most enterprizing picture-dealer in London.

5 HIGH STREET, HASTINGS.
14 *May* 1854.

MY DEAR WILLIAM,

As you ask about the weather here on behalf of some invalid, I write to say that it is just beginning to be decidedly warm—to-day rather oppressively so, seeming to forebode a storm. After which I hope the air may be purer and no less genial. Till the last day or two it had been almost uniformly windy, though often fine weather.

Lizzy went this morning to see a Dr. Hale, to whom Dr. Wilkinson has recommended her, and who advises her to leave this part of Hastings as being liable to get too hot at this time of year, and to go nearer the sea. He thinks her state requires the very greatest care, and gave her some directions. She seems much the same, in fact, I think, though sometimes rather weaker or stronger.

*   *   *   *   *   *

I see the *Athenæum* here, so need not trouble you for it, but should be glad of the *Spec*. What do you think of Poole's picture? and of Collins?

The indefatigable and invaluable Barbara has been getting up a plan for Lizzy's entering another place, since we rejected the Sussex Hospital. This is the "Sanatorium" which she describes as being in *Harley Street, New Road, London,* "where governesses and ladies of small means are taken in and cured." It contains only about twenty or thirty patients or so, and is, she says, most admirably managed, the object being to make it as much like a home as possible. It seems Miss Smith has a relation connected with the management of this place, and has already made arrangements by which Miss Siddal can enter at once if she likes, or else put it off for a little and then enter. She wrote to her about it this morning, and certainly it seems a not unpleasant plan if necessary. I wish now that Maggy would oblige me by enquiring of Aunt Charlotte, or any one else who might be at all likely to have heard of the place, any particulars that could be got, and writing them to me as soon as possible. I should be much obliged.

Love to all.

Yours,

D. G. R.

I wish I had thought of getting that shawl which Aunt Charlotte kindly promised me for Lizzy before I left London, as it would be just the thing. Remember me most kindly to Scott if you see him.

If you are seeing Millais, I wish you would ask him whether he knows anything of Deverell's *Twelfth Night* which Miller sent to Gambart, or of the projected raffle. I called one day at Gambart's, but he was then out of town.

C 29.

"I wrote at some length to Ruskin the other day." The acquaintance of my brother with Mr. Ruskin began in April 1854, when Ruskin addressed him by letter. The initials which I give—A. B, and D—are not the *correct* initials.

[SCALANDS.]
17 *May* 1854.

DEAR WILLIAM,

*   *   *   *   *   *

I return the *Spec.*, for which thanks. Lizzy is obliged for Maggie's information about the Sanatorium. I wrote at some length to Ruskin the other day. Why do you not mention Collins in the *Spec.*? Munro writes to me that there is mention of me with Hunt and Millais in Ruskin's Lectures just out. Have you seen or can you tell me of it?

Calder Campbell writes to me, " Surely you will not continue to respect the woman who weds [A. B.]." Can you interpret? I can conceive no one he can mean but Miss [D.], and this seems impossible. Besides, I thought [A. B.]

was married. But I know old C[alder] C[ampbell] dwells
in a region of unnamed horror and Juvenalian combination,
and this may be a fowl of the air after its kind. I have
written to him to ask an explanation.

I shall soon, I think, be back in town when I have any tin
to take me there, which I have not at present. I must come
up to see about replenishing my colour-box, etc., before
beginning *Found*, even if I come down here again; also to
fetch various things.

    *   *   *   *   *   *

This a stunning crib, but rather slow. Remember me to
every one. Lizzy is much the same. Where do you think
of going this summer?

    *   *   *   *   *   *

C 30.

[HASTINGS.]
Thursday 25 May 1854.

DEAR WILLIAM,

I think I shall not be in town till the beginning of
next week, though I thought to have been there before this.
Lizzy seems rather weaker the last day or two, though I trust
not permanently, and I do not like to leave her just at this
time.

I heard from Millais yesterday, who it seems is leaving
or has left London, and tells me Allingham is going back to
Ireland and the Customs. I trust not till I can see him
again.

Miss Smith has lent me Ruskin's *Lectures*, where there is
only a slight though very friendly mention of me. They are
very interesting.

I am sending you back the *Spec.*, and write these few words
to tell you of my delay in leaving here, but am not in any
writing mood, so good-bye.

Your affectionate Brother,

D. G. ROSSETTI.

Love to Mamma and all.

A 14.

The oil-picture here mentioned must apparently be *Found*.

14 CHATHAM PLACE.
Monday [August 1854].

MY DEAR AUNT CHARLOTTE,

I am afraid you will guess, before reading this letter, what it is likely to relate to. I am in a very great difficulty for money, and unless by your kind assistance (if you are able to afford it me) really do not know how to extricate myself from it. I have two water-colours in hand, and am beginning an oil-picture. The last, and one of the former, I believe I may consider already sold (to Messrs. Ruskin and MacCracken) as soon as they are finished; but meanwhile I am utterly at a loss for the means of getting models etc. to carry them on. One of the water-colours, at any rate, I hope will not be very long before it is finished, if I am only able to go on with it without being utterly swamped for want of money. I assure you I have not forgotten your kindness last year in lending me £12, nor my promise to return the loan; but I assure you that this has been hitherto simply impossible. If you can and will now assist me again, and I am thus enabled to get through with the works I have in hand, I have every reason to hope that I shall then have it in my power (as I shall most sincerely wish and intend) to return you, if not all at once at least by degrees, both this and the former loan. It is my hope indeed to return one day all that you have so kindly lent me from time to time; but I feel almost discouraged from saying so, lest, in my present inability to do so, it should seem like a mere pretence.

I have long been hoping to get through with something, and obtain some money without the necessity of trespassing again on your kindness. But I now find that, unless I do so, I can see before me no means of proceeding with my work; besides that some rent which I already owe here is being continually applied for, and worrying me to such an extent as to deprive me of the peace of mind necessary for working well.   Nor, even had I paid this rent, could I get rid of one source of expense by leaving these rooms—at least not without great detriment to my work, besides great interruption—since the oil-picture I am beginning is an open-air scene, requiring absolutely a large amount of light, which I should have difficulty in finding elsewhere so well as here.

Could you lend me £25, or if possible £30?   But perhaps I am asking much more than I have any right to ask, or than your circumstances (even if you are willing again to afford me this chance) will permit you to grant. Less than £20 it would be of little service to me to ask, as it would be merely to fall into difficulties again immediately, before I had been able to make any considerable progress with my pictures.

I know you must indeed be weary of applications like this from me, and am almost hopeless of my ever making that way in my profession which I ought to make, and placing myself in an independent position.   But, if I am only able to get my present works done, no time could well be more favourable than the present for making a sure step in advance, as anything I finish now is almost if not quite certain of sale.

I must now leave what I have said to your consideration. If you consider yourself justified in rendering me this assistance, I know your kindness too well to suppose that you will not do so.   And I hope indeed that you may think so ; since it is the only means I can see of avoiding a complete interruption to my work at a moment when it is most important to me that I should continue it.   When you were last in town I was still hoping to avoid the necessity of making this request, but I find now that there is really no other way.   I shall await your answer most anxiously—and remain

Your affectionate Nephew,

D. G. ROSSETTI.

A 15.

Muntham was the seat of Lady Bath—not far from Arundel in Sussex. My brother's landlord in Chatham Place was a legal gentleman, Mr. Benthall.

[14 CHATHAM PLACE].
Wednesday morning [August 1854.]

MY DEAR AUNT,

Many thanks indeed for the great kindness and promptness of your answer and enclosure; it rescues me from a greater difficulty than I have been in for some time. I trust most sincerely that you will hear of and see some results from it before many months, in the shape of work finished. I really do not know how to thank you enough. I dare say there will be no difficulty about the form of the order, but, if there is, I will send it back at once, as you direct.

I heard two days ago from Mr. Ruskin, who is at Chamounix, and received from him the very valuable present of all his works—including eight volumes, three pamphlets, and some large folio plates of Venetian architecture. He wished me to accept these as a gift, but it is such a costly one that I have told him I shall make him a small water-colour in exchange—which idea seems to please him. Besides this he wants a sketch of mine as a commission. If you at any time wish to read any of his works, I have them at your service.

I suppose it is as hot at Muntham as here. Here it has been almost insufferable these two days—very favourable, I fear, to the spread of cholera. Yesterday the smell from the river was so bad that I was obliged to go out. To-day I am glad to find it much decreased.

I was lately at the Crystal Palace at Sydenham, which is really well worth a visit, or indeed more than one. The Mediæval and Byzantine Courts interested me especially. The Alhambra also is very beautiful.

Believe me, my dear Aunt,
Your most affectionate Nephew,
D. G. ROSSETTI.

P.S.—On getting the order, I sent it to my landlord, to see if he could get it cashed at once, and pay his rent out of it—making sure he would find it all right. He tells me, however, that it is necessary that Lady Bath should write her initials across the face of Her Majesty on the stamp ; also that *you* should write on the back of the order, at the end where the stamp is, " Pay D. G. Rossetti Esq., or order, C. Polidori " ; and finally that I should write my signature after yours before presenting it at the Bank. These preliminaries, he says, are now indispensable (being perhaps recently introduced, for what I know) ; so it is a good thing the bill is dated for Saturday, as there will be time for its return to London by then, if you will kindly attend to these particulars. My landlord, who is a most excellent and civil fellow, did not make these objections in any captious spirit, but he assured me that he was quite certain there would be a difficulty made at the Bank, if they were not attended to.

C 31.

This letter was written from the house of Mr. Madox Brown at Finchley. My brother was staying there awhile—painting, I think, the calf in his picture of *Found*. The Rintouls were the family of the editor of the *Spectator*.

"Tin," in the sense of "money," and a few other items of schoolboy slang, occur *passim* in my brother's letters. He and I had been schoolboys together, and a sort of uninterrupted tradition of schoolboy *bonhomie* lingered about the use of such words between us.

FINCHLEY.
Sunday night [19 *November* 1854].

DEAR WILLIAM,

Is the ticket of Ruskin's that you have for me transferable ? If so, will you send it on to Lizzy, as she would like to use it, I believe ? Does it admit more than one person ? If not available for her, will you let me know at once, and also whether you will be in the way of getting more without bother, and can furnish her and Miss Howitt, and Barbara if possible? as otherwise I shall write to Ruskin, I think, myself. If you *will* be able to get such three tickets, would you send them to Lizzy at my place, as I should like her to do the civil by sending them to Barbara Smith and Anna Mary Howitt? I mean, of course, if you're going about tickets for Rintouls or others.

Can you fix a day to come and dine with Brown at six— or on Sunday earlier if you like? He tells me to ask you. Brown adds, if you come on Sunday you will have the anguish of missing *me*. Please don't forget—but I know you won't— about that tin—as soon and as much as you can manage. . . .

Hoping to hear soon,

Yours,

D. G. R.

C 32.

Where a —— is printed in this letter, the original gives a rapid hieroglyphic of a dove, by which my brother indicated Miss Siddal.

[14 CHATHAM PLACE.
12 *April* 1855.]

DEAR W——,

I'm wanting much to see —— this evening; and, as I have not found her in just now, must go again this evening, and am dining meanwhile with Hannay. I therefore apologize duly for not meeting you, and going on to see Ruskin, whom I saw this morning, and who is going to settle £150 a year immediately on ——!!! This is no joke, but fact. I shall bring her on Saturday to tea.

A 16.

The College here mentioned is the Working Men's College founded by the Rev. Frederick D. Maurice; Mr. Ruskin had a drawing-class there, and had prompted Rossetti to undertake another. Lord Ashburton was a near relative (I think brother) of Lady Bath.

BLACKFRIARS BRIDGE.
Thursday [3 *May* 1855].

DEAR AUNT CHARLOTTE,

If, as you propose, Lady Bath and Lord Ashburton will drive to the College any time between half-past seven till ten on Monday evening, and ask for me, that will do well ; or, if she preferred my meeting her anywhere else, I should be happy to do just as she liked.   To see the system of teaching in full force, they ought by rights to visit Mr. Ruskin's class some Thursday evening as well—as his class is of longer standing and far better organized than mine.   After your first message (viz., that Lady Bath wished to go some Thursday evening, which I find was owing to a misapprehension) I asked Mr. Ruskin about it, and he said it would give him much pleasure.

Thanks for your sympathy with Miss Siddal, whose good fortune could not have been better deserved, or more gratifying to her than to me.   I hope to introduce her to you some day at Albany Street.   Mr. Ruskin has now settled on her £150 a year, and is to have all she does up to that sum.   He is likely also to be of great use to me personally (for the use to her is also use to me), and I am doing two or three water-colours for him.   He is the best friend I ever had *out of my own family*; or, at any rate, I never had a better, not to do injustice to one or two more.   I hope to go with you one day to the College, as you say, and wish you could make one of our party to-day.   A modelling class is immediately to be added to our drawing-classes, the masters of which will be my friends Woolner and Munro.

B 19.

This long letter seems to call for only one note—viz.: that my brother was mistaken in supposing that the Marchioness of Waterford was the same person as " Lady Seymour, Queen of Beauty at the [Eglintoun] Tournament."

[14 CHATHAM PLACE].
Sunday night, July 1st [1855.]

DEAR MAMMA,

Ever since you left I have been intending to write to you, and 1 hope you have not fancied I forgot you, as I know you would not forget me.   I have been busy at times, and at times very ill at ease, though indeed neither of these is really an excuse for so long a silence, which your affection will best make allowance for.   I have been pleased to hear such good accounts of Christina, who I hope continues equally stronger and better.   But I also hope you are better now, and was truly grieved to hear you had been so far from well. I often fancy you together at Hastings, taking some of the trips probably that I took last year, and certainly rambling about the hills, which grow rather monotonous, but I dare say you have · longer patience with them.   You know, no doubt, that spot on the East Hill where there is something which looks far off like a ruin, but proves, if I remember rightly, to be nothing but a blocked-up door of some kind. On its side Lizzy and I scratched our initials last year— along the corner of one side, I think.   If you are that way, will you try and discover them ?   Is a very dark gipsy-looking little girl of about thirteen still in the habit of running about on the East Hill with a very fine baby sister ? I made a sketch of them, and Lizzy had the girl home and drew her.   I used always to think her the image of savage active health ; but Lizzy afterwards discovered that, as soon as the cold weather came on every year, she was seized with ague and unable to stir out in the winter ; owing no doubt to long disregard of weather and frequent privation of food.

Another place where L[izzy] and I scratched our initials was a stone at the Old Roar, a very pretty place indeed and not very far—I forget now in precisely what direction, but you would easily find out.   But perhaps you have been.   *Our* stone would lie to your right as you stood with your back to the fall, and a little way in front of you.   By the bye, the fall seems to have fallen most completely and successfully, for we couldn't see it.

I fancy Barbara Smith must now be again at her brother's farm near Robertsbridge, a railway trip from Hastings. If you would like it, I would find out whether this is the case, and if so write B[arbara] S[mith] word of your whereabouts, as she must often be at Hastings, and has long greatly wished for Christina's acquaintance; so no doubt she would soon turn up if you have any fancy for a little society, and would invite you to spend a day sometimes at the farm, a very lovely place. Another acquaintance of mine—Mr. Smith, chemist of George Street—you might have an opportunity of patronizing if you liked. . . .

I dare say you will have heard something of Lizzy's and my movements from Maggie. She is somewhat better from her trip to Clevedon, and will very soon be in the country again, I trust. She, Maggie, and I, are going to dine with Ruskin on Friday next. Ruskin has been to Tunbridge Wells and Dover; he was far from well, but has returned looking and being much better. He is very hard at work on the third volume of *Modern Painters*, who, I tell him, will be old masters before the work is ended. Have you seen his pamphlet on the R. A. Exhibition? If you would care to see it, I shall have the 3rd edition from him, I believe, in a day or two, and would send it you. Gift-books have rather poured in on me lately : Hannay's new novel, *Eustace Conyers*, very first-rate in Hannay's qualities, and a decided advance on *Fontenoy* ; Allingham's new collection of Poems, where there are some illustrations by Hughes, one by Millais, and one which used to be by me till it became the exclusive work of Dalziel, who cut it. I was resolved to cut it out, but Allingham would not, so I can only wish Dalziel had the credit as well as the authorship. I have also a very well-written pamphlet on the War by one Lushington, a new acquaintance of mine on the Council of the W[orking] M[en's] Coll[ege], and a book on Proverbs (I think) by Trench, given me by another Working Men's Councillor.

Any of these I could send you to read. I think you would like the pamphlet, and probably the last, which I haven't read. I have also, by the bye, Cayley's volume of Notes to Dante. And lastly, a pamphlet on Freemasonry, sent to me *for poor Papa* by one Mr. Taylor of Liverpool. I'll put in with this the letter which came with it, and which I answered.

While Ruskin was at the seaside I painted and sent him a water-colour of *The Nativity*, done in a week, price fifteen guineas. I thought and think it one of my best, but R[uskin] disappointed me by not thinking it up to my usual mark. I shall do him another instead, and sell that to some one else. At present I am doing two for him, one from Dante, and one begun some time ago of the Preparation for the Passover in the Holy Family. An astounding event is to come off to-morrow. The Marchioness of Waterford has expressed a wish to Ruskin to see me paint in water-colour, as she says my method is inscrutable to her. She is herself an excellent artist, and would have been really great, I believe, if not born such a swell and such a stunner. I believe that, as Lady Seymour, she was Queen of Beauty at the Tournament, and is, I have often heard, gloriously beautiful, though now rather past her prime. To-morrow she has appointed to come and see me paint, but whether I shall be able to paint at all under the circumstances I have my doubts. However, I have told a little boy to come, to paint the head of Christ from. He is a very nice little fellow whom I picked out from the Saint Martin's School the other day. He has a lovely head, and such a beautiful forehead that I thought he must be very clever, but on enquiring as to his favourite pursuit he rather threw me back by answering "buttons." Little Owens has also been sitting to me. I asked him whether he was often ill, as he seems very delicate, and was concerned (his sister, you know, having lately died of consumption) to be answered that he often was. Enquiring further into his symptoms, their leading character appeared to be stomach-ache, and, on continued analysis of the cause usually leading to this result, I arrived at " gooseberries."

But the funniest boy of all was one of whom Lizzy told me, who accompanied her on a donkey-ride at Clevedon lately. He was about twelve, and after a little while opened a conversation by asking if there was any lions in the parts she comed from. Hearing *no*, he seemed disappointed, and asked her if she had ever ridden on an elephant there. He had last year when the beastesses was here, and, on mounting the elephant for a penny, he felt so joyful that he was obliged to give the man his other twopence, so he couldn't see the rest of the fair. He wished to know whether boys had to work for their living there, and said a gentleman had told him that in his country the boys were so wicked that they had to be shut up in large prisons. He never knew hisself no boy what stole anything, but he supposed in that country there was nothing but fruit-trees. He pulled a little blue flower growing out of a rock, and said that he liked to let flowers grow in the fields, but he liked to " catch " one when it grew *there* and take it away, because it looked such a poor little thing. He had a project for leading donkeys without beating, which consisted in holding a handful of grass within an inch of their noses, and inducing them to follow it. Being asked whether that would not be the crueller plan of the two, he said he had noticed donkeys would always eat even when they were full, so he had only to fill his donkey first. All that could be got in explanation of why he thought Lizzy some outlandish native was that he was sure she comed from very far, much further than he could see.

I spent two or three very delightful days at Clevedon. Did you go near it when living at Frome? The junction of the Severn with the Bristol Channel is there, so that the water is hardly brackish, but looks like sea, and you can see across to Wales, only eight miles off, I think. Arthur Hallam, on whom Tennyson wrote *In Memoriam* (and who was the author of a pamphlet on Papa's view of Dante), is buried at Clevedon, and we visited his grave. We made several longish excursions, and saw the country for ten miles round, and many lovely things. Lizzy and I pulled up a quantity of golden water-flags, which I brought to London, and am having planted for my balcony.

Besides Clevedon, I went to Oxford some weeks ago when Guggum was there, and met some nice people, Dr. Acland and his family, who, as well as many others, were most kind to her there—too kind, for they bothered her greatly with attentions. Acland wanted her to settle at Oxford, and said he would introduce her into all the best society. All the women there are immensely fond of her— a sister of Dr. Pusey (or daughter) seems to have been the one she liked best. A great swell, who is Warden of New College . . . showed her all the finest MSS. in the Bodleian Library, and paid her all manner of attentions ; winding up by an invitation to a special treat at his own house, which consisted in showing her a black beetle painted by Albert Dürer, and having a real one fetched up from the kitchen to compare the two with a microscope. This she never went to enjoy. Acland examined her most minutely, and was constantly paying professional visits—all gratuitously, being an intimate friend of Ruskin. I went down on purpose to have a conversation with him about her health, and was glad to find that he thinks her lungs, if at all affected, are only slightly so, and that the leading cause of illness lies in mental power long pent up and lately overtaxed. Of course, though, he thinks very seriously of her present state, and of the care necessary to her gradual recovery. By his advice, she is likely to leave England, probably for south of France, before the cold weather comes on again, and must abstain from all work for some months yet.

They were all most friendly to me at Oxford, and Dr. Acland sent me afterwards an invitation to go there on the great occasion of laying the first stone of the New Museum the week before last ; but I did not go because of time and expense. I afterwards heard Tennyson and his wife had been there, and staying chiefly at Acland's ; I was sorry to have missed them.   I am asked by the architect to do some designing for the Museum, and probably shall.   Good-night, dear Mamma.

Your affectionate Son,
GABRIEL.

B 20.

" The Queen and Women Sewing " is the same as *Hist, said Kate the Queen*—a subject founded upon a song in Browning's *Pippa Passes*.

Wednesday [*September* 1855].

DEAR BUNKUM,

Can you come to tea with Guggum and Mr. and Mrs. K[incaid] on Saturday evening ?   Mrs. K[incaid] will sleep here, and then she and Liz start at seven on Sunday morning from the Docks for Hâvre. . . .

If I don't see you this evening, would you tell Williams . . . to let me have *early to-morrow* that sketch of the Queen and Women Sewing which Aunt Charlotte has of mine and I'm sure she'd lend me a few days, as I want to show it to Browning ?

A 17.

The Mr. Marshall here named (not to be confounded with two other Marshalls known to my brother) was a millionaire from Leeds, who had a large estate in Cumberland.   In all probability he became owner of the *Kate the Queen ;* as my Aunt certainly closed with my brother's offer, and got him to paint a portrait of her younger sister Eliza Harriet Polidori.

14 CHATHAM PLACE, BLACKFRIARS.
Thursday [15 *May* 1856].

MY DEAR AUNT CHARLOTTE,

In writing this note, I must premise quite sincerely that I only wish to consult your own wishes, and that the matter is put for your unbiased consideration.

A Mr. Marshall, of Eaton Square, who has bought several

drawings of mine, and commissioned me for others, has taken a really violent fancy to that oil-sketch of the Queen and Page belonging to you and still at my study. I told him it was not mine ; but, as he still continues hankering after and regretting it, I thought I would propose a bargain to you, in case you should not be unwilling—*i.e.*, in case you should *really* prefer what I propose. Thus then : Would you prefer if I were to paint you, instead of that little picture, a portrait in oil of Mamma, or of either of my aunts, or other member of our family ? and in that case sell the Queen and Page to Mr. Marshall, who I suppose would give me thirty or forty guineas for it. He is disposed to be very useful to me, I think, in purchasing my works, and also in very generously paying for them, as he always declares the prices I ask to be trifles ; and for these reasons I should like to oblige him, if you would *really prefer* (once again) the course I propose—without speaking of the convenience which it would also very decidedly be to me at present.

In case you should decide in the affirmative, I would immediately fix a day of sitting next week with Mamma, or whomever you might wish me to attack ; and meanwhile and ever am

Your affectionate Nephew,

D. G. ROSSETTI.

A 18.

The drawing (water-colour) from Dante's *Vita Nuova* appears to be *Dante's Dream*—a composition essentially different from the large oil-picture of that name now in the Walker Gallery of Liverpool. *The Monk* must be the same subject which is entitled *Fra Pace*. This letter comes to me as a half-sheet, and is, I think, incomplete.

[14 CHATHAM PLACE.]
Monday [19 *May* 1856].

MY DEAR AUNT CHARLOTTE,

I will certainly paint Aunt Eliza for you as soon as she comes to town. It will not be any great tax on my time, as a portrait is a thing needing no forethought, and to be taken up at any moment.

If Lady Bath wishes to favour me with a visit, the best time would be now, as I happen to have two or three things just finished, still by me—especially a drawing from Dante's *Vita Nuova*, which I should have much pleasure in showing her, and better worth seeing than *The Monk*, which is not yet finished, but which I could show her also. I should also very much like to show *you* the things, if you come with Lady Bath, supposing she is able to give me that pleasure.

C 33.

This letter shows that I was about to leave London, and the P.S. mentions Freshwater; but I don't think I went to the Isle of Wight—only to Southampton, and thence to Normandy. Plint was a Stockbroker in Leeds. I forget which of my brother's pictures was at this date commissioned by him. The passage about Moxon and woodblocks refers to the designs upon which my brother was now engaged for Moxon's illustrated edition of Tennyson. Windus was a Liverpool painter who had lately exhibited in London a picture, which my brother heartily admired, from the old ballad of *Burd Helen*.

[14 CHATHAM PLACE].
Saturday [2 *August* 1856].

DEAR W——,

I've only this moment got your note, and will attend to it when I get the cash; but the order for it, being on Leeds, had to be negotiated through a banker (of course without discount), and this has not yet been accomplished. I have no doubt it will be by Monday. If you want any, pray send *at once* (for obvious reasons), and I will send it forthwith.

I wish to Heaven I could have come with you; but am at the last gasp of time with those woodcuts, which are, however, getting a little better forward now, I think, and cannot stir a foot till something more be done towards them. It keeps me also from beginning Plint's picture, which I must begin soon. Ten days or a fortnight hence I might be more at liberty, or even a week hence perhaps, and probably at that time too may have to fly London and Moxon while I do the other woodblocks, as I cannot endure his pestering. So would you drop me a line at each of your leading movements, as nothing would give me more pleasure than to join you, if practicable. I shall have plenty of tin at present, I trust, from woodcuts, and a water-colour I have just finished and which I suppose some one will buy.

I've little news. Windus wrote to me the other day asking me to superintend the drawing of his picture, on wood, which he has been asked to allow for the *National Magazine,* a new *People's Journal* thing coming out by Saunders & Marston. I have been twice to see Ristori—her two last nights—with a Rev. William Elliott, a friend of Patmore and Woolner, who is a tremendous Browningian. I liked her prodigiously in *Rosmunda* and in a little comedy, and think her very beautiful—not quite Rachel though, yet, or ever. I saw her in that beastly bosh Pellico's *Francesca* too, of which no acting can make anything. In going out of the theatre one night I met —— and her mother; and, after offering to call their carriage for them and being told they had it not, only having to go home over the way, I stupidly forgot the next duty, of seeing them to their door, which I remembered as soon as they were out of sight. I wish if possible you'd take some opportunity of telling them what an ass I thought myself.

Your affectionate Brother,

D. G. R.

Mamma sent three or four letters to Freshwater for you. Did you get them? One of them was "On Her Majesty's Service," and was sent on *without paying*.

C 34.

The date of this letter marks the period when my brother began, or was about to begin, his tempera-pictures in the Union Hall in Oxford. The Seddon subscription was a subscription for purchasing for the National Gallery Mr. Thomas Seddon's picture of *Jerusalem*, just after his decease.

87 HIGH STEET, OXFORD.
[12 *August* 1857.]

DEAR W——,

I send you a cheque for the Seddon subscription. I am here for a few days only perhaps, but perhaps rather longer.

Yours,
D. G. R.

Please acknowledge at once, as it isn't crossed.

B 21.

Miss Siddal had gone to Matlock to try the hydropathic system, and my brother accompanied or followed her thither. The "anxiety" caused to our Mother is not quite clearly defined; perhaps she had for a while been uncertain as to where my brother had gone to, and only knew he was no longer in Oxford. I may add that he always retained a kindly feeling for the Cartledge family, with whom he had lived at Matlock, and did his best later on to befriend them in times less prosperous for themselves.

AT MR. CARTLEDGE'S,
LIME TREE VIEW, MATLOCK, DERBYSHIRE. [? 1857.]

MY DEAREST MAMMA,

I am most grieved that you should have been suffering anxiety on my account, as I now know you must have done. Had there been the least necessity, I should not have failed to let you know, but there has been none whatever. I do not know how many days I may remain here at present; but it will probably not be long before I am in London, at any rate for a day or so, when I trust not to miss seeing your dear face. You have heard no doubt from Jones, who opened the letter at Oxford. I have only got it this morning. It would be absurd in me to thank you for another proof of the affection which you have lavished on me all my life, and which is often but too little deserved. I am most ashamed of my disgraceful silence all the time I have been at Oxford;

but I am getting worse than ever as a letter-writer, though this should hardly apply in your dear case.

Will you thank William for his note, and say that, as far as I am concerned, this would not be the time to see the Union, as my own work there has been interrupted for some weeks? I hope to be finishing it sooner or later. This is an interesting and beautiful part of the country. I was yesterday at Haddon Hall, a glorious old place in some respects.

C 35.

Some friends were proposing to accompany me to see the pictures of my brother and his colleagues in Oxford. I forget who the friends were, except Mr. Holman Hunt, who alone joined me when I actually went.

13 GEORGE STREET, OXFORD.
Friday [30 *October* 1857].

DEAR W——,

I think it would be much better if you all came a week later as regards the pictures, since things are peculiarly in a muddle just now. Do put it off for a week or fortnight, and then come and see something finished.

Pray give my love to Mamma, Maria, and Christina. I am quite enraged at myself for not having written, and shall still immediately to Mamma. But I have not to any one, though this is no excuse whatever.

A 19.

Lady Bath's offer of "the loan of my picture" must have been an offer to re-consign to Rossetti the picture of *The Girlhood of Mary Virgin*, with a view to its being reconsidered (at his own suggestion) and in some particulars improved. It did ultimately reach him; and I think he did next to nothing to it, save perhaps to the head of the child-angel.

The pen-and-ink drawing I consider to be *The Magdalene at the door of Simon the Pharisee*. The oil-picture of this composition, though well begun on a large canvas, was never finished. As to the Llandaff picture, see A 23.

Miss Baring was a sister (or possibly niece) of Lady Bath. The "Hogarth Club ticket" was a ticket of admission to a small collection of paintings, some of them by my brother, at the premises of the then Hogarth Club.

[14 CHATHAM PLACE.]
Thursday [1859.]

MY DEAR AUNT,

I am sorry to have left you so long unanswered. Pray pardon, but I have been very busy and much interrupted.

I do not think I will avail myself, after all, of Lady Bath's kindness just yet, as regards the loan of my picture ; but will do so as soon as I feel sure of being able to work on it at once, as I would not like to be keeping it for ever.

The pen-and-ink drawing may be, I fear, higher in price than you expected. Its price would be £50 ; in explanation of which I may say that it will contain, when finished, fully as much work as, if not more than, a water-colour of the same size, for which I should ask considerably more (as for the one of *Mary and St. John* which you saw, a good deal smaller, for which Lady Trevelyan paid me 100 guineas). Moreover, it is the first design for a work of some importance, and therefore more valuable.

Should Lady Bath wish to have it, I may add (since you say it was her first intention) that an immediate sale would be most convenient to me, as I am sure to have several applications for it, I trust and believe, before the Spring, when you tell me Lady Bath will be in London. I should however have to keep it by me for a time after it was sold, both to finish it, and to make use of it in carrying out my picture. In case of Lady Bath's still entertaining the idea of buying it, and wishing to see it first, I would be happy to send it to her to look at, if she did not object to paying the expense of packing and carriage ; but I fear I could not spare it just now for more than a day.

You ask me whether I sketch my pen-and-ink drawings

first in pencil. I always do so, as far as indicating the composition goes, but little more.

I am at work now both on my pictures for Llandaff Cathedral (which I think you saw begun) and on the *Mary Magdalene*. I feel quite emancipated in getting to work of so large a size. I trust to have something considerable done to show you when you are next in London.

I shall have much pleasure in Lady Bath's and Miss Baring's proposed visit. I have been hunting for a Hogarth Club ticket, but find I have none, and fear they are being re-printed just now; so that I may not be able to send you one for a few days, but will be sure to do so.

A 20.

The drawing which Miss Baring contemplated buying must have been *The Magdalene* mentioned in the previous letter; my Aunt has noted in the present letter that Miss Baring *had* decided to purchase it without any further inspection. Halliday was Mr. Michael Halliday, a semi-professional painter, much influenced by Mr. Holman Hunt. The sketch (or picture) mentioned in this letter was named *The Blind Basket-maker's First Child*: I think it was engraved, and became more than moderately popular.

[14 CHATHAM PLACE.
1859.]

MY DEAR AUNT,

Do I understand you rightly that Miss Baring wishes me to consider the drawing as hers *now?* If so, I will send it her as soon as finished, but should have to borrow it for a short time further, to be photographed. My question is put because it is quite contrary to my practice to send a work of mine to be seen by any one before purchase; though I was happy to break through this rule, for the first time, the other day, on account of *your* connexion with the matter.

I understand, from certain members who have been looking up fresh rooms for the Hogarth Club, that they will not improbably take some they have seen in Waterloo Place, and which appear to be more commodious, though also dearer, than those in Piccadilly.

You ask me about Halliday's sketch. I think that, like all he has done, it is very satisfactory, considering that it is only a few years ago that he began painting figures, and that at a later time of life than most men begin at. The subject is a good one of its class; but I do not sufficiently recollect the head of the mother to be sure whether I agree with your criticism. The artist might plead, however, that grief for the father's want of sight at that moment might predominate at least as justly as joy at the child's birth.

A 21.

I do not know who were the "*protégés*" referred to in this letter; perhaps some village children near Muntham. The directions given by my brother are in general conformity with the teaching of Mr. Ruskin at the Working Men's College.

[14 CHATHAM PLACE.]
Thursday [? *February* 1859].

MY DEAR AUNT,

I am very sorry that I have really nothing by me that I could send which would be of the least use to such beginners as your *protégés*. What they ought to do in reality would be to take a piece of mossy bark, or something that would not decay, and try to imitate it on its own scale as exactly as possible—at first in pencil or Indian ink, and afterwards in colour. This would be a work of time, and perhaps requires in the first instance that some one should be by to rouse the beginner to a full consciousness of how close a fidelity he ought to aim at, and to be able, by mere industry, to attain. But, if they liked to make any such attempt, and you would forward me the result, I would gladly give what advice I could from a distance. The best gift you could make them would be of a plaster cast or two of natural leaves, and the materials necessary for drawing them, which could all be got cheaply enough. I will get you these if you like, and send them. If you and they still wish for a figure-piece of some sort, the most advisable would be one of the large French studies of heads.

By the bye, all these ages I have a photograph, inscribed with your name, of that *Mary Magdalene*.

The Hogarth will not be open after the end of March.

C 36.

This note refers to some black-ballings at the Hogarth Club, of which I was a member, as well as my brother.

14 CHATHAM PLACE, BLACKFRIARS.
[4 *April* 1859.]

DEAR WILLIAM,

I certainly did not black-ball ——. In each case after these ballots I have the same thing told me—viz., that the exclusions are owing to me—and have serious thoughts of resigning in consequence, as it is very annoying and very absurd.

The ballot in this way becomes a mere farce. Those I voted against I really objected to, and it is childish in such a case to say anything more about the matter. I should like you to show this note to any one who has expressed to you the opinions you mention.

C 37.

Seddon, here named, is Mr. John P. Seddon, the architect concerned in the restoration of Llandaff Cathedral, brother of the late Thomas Seddon. The head that my brother had now been painting for his old and constant friend Mr. G. P. Boyce, the water-colour painter, must have been the one named *Bocca Baciata*.

[14 CHATHAM PLACE.
13 *November* 1859.]

MY DEAR WILLIAM,

I am afraid the going to Scott's is impracticable for me, much as I should like it, with the amount of work I ought to be doing. I should not feel comfortable. As you said you were *en cas* to pay my journey, would you mind sparing me a few pounds for home use instead? I am setting to

work on the Llandaff centrepiece, and am expecting £50
from Seddon in about a week or ten days, but till then am
run quite dry, and do not know how to get on.   If you can
do this, I would come either to Somerset House or Albany
Street for it before you leave.

Leathart of Newcastle has written me this morning, settling
a commission which he has now given me for the *Found*, at
350 guineas ; so my business motive for going is done away
with.   You know he also has my *Christmas Carol* and *Sir
Galahad*.

Your affectionate Brother,

D. G. R.

If you could come here yourself, I would show you the
head I have painted for Boyce.

B. 22.

12 EAST PARADE, HASTINGS.
Friday [13 *April* 1860].

MY DEAR MOTHER,

I write you this word to say that Lizzy and I are
going to be married at last, in as few days as possible.   I
may be in town again first, but am not certain.   If so, I shall
be sure to see you ; but write this as I should be sorry that
the news should reach you first from any other quarter.

Like all the important things I ever meant to do—to fulfil
duty or secure happiness—this one has been deferred almost
beyond possibility.   I have hardly deserved that Lizzy should
still consent to it, but she has done so, and I trust I may still
have time to prove my thankfulness to her.   The constantly
failing state of her health is a terrible anxiety indeed ; but
I must still hope for the best, and am at any rate at this
moment in a better position to take the step, as regards
money prospects, than I have ever been before.   I shall either
see you or write again soon, and meanwhile and ever am

Your most affectionate Son,

D. G. ROSSETTI.

C. 38.

12 East Parade, Hastings.
Tuesday [17 *April* 1860].

My dear William,

Many sincere thanks for your brotherly letter. I assure you I never felt more in need of such affection as yours has always been than I do now. You will be grieved to hear that poor dear Lizzy's health has been in such a broken and failing state for the last few days as to render me more miserable than I can possibly say. The spectacle of her fits of illness when they come on would be heartrending to a stranger even.

There seems to-day to be a slight rally; but till yesterday she had not been able to keep anything—even a glass of soda-water—on her stomach for five minutes, and this has been the case more or less for a long while. She gets no nourishment, and what can be reasonably hoped when this is added to her dreadful state of health in other respects? If I were to lose her now, I do not know what effect it might have on my mind, added to the responsibility of much work, commissioned and already paid for, which still has to be done,—and how to do it in such a case? I am sorry to write you such a miserable letter, but really it does me some good to have one person to whom I can write it, as I could not bear doing to any other than you.

I must still hope for the best; indeed, she has been as bad before in many respects, but hardly all at once as now. Yesterday, owing no doubt to the improvement in the weather, she has taken some slight things—such as beef-tea and jelly —without as yet bringing them up again. I have been enquiring as to a special license, as there seems little prospect of her being able as yet to enter the cold church with safety; but I find this promises so much delay and expense as to be hardly possible. The ordinary license we already have, and I still trust to God we may be enabled to use it. If not, I should have so much to grieve for, and (what is worse) so much to reproach myself with, that I do not know how it might end for me.

I shall have to be in London for a few hours to-day, but really have not the heart to see you just now, though it is some relief to write this. I have to come up to fetch money (which I left at home, expecting to have fetched her back, when I came here), of which at least, thank Heaven, I am not short at present, though I only have it as an advance on work to do. I shall come back the first thing to-morrow morning at latest. You need not talk much about the state of her health, as it is so wretched a subject, at such a moment especially, but I thought I would tell you.

C. 23.

HASTINGS.
Wednesday [23 May 1860].

MY DEAR MOTHER,

Lizzie and I are just back from church. We are going to Folkestone to-day, hoping to get on to Paris if possible ; but you will be grieved to hear her health is no better as yet. Love to all.

C 39.

My brother and his wife did not become tenants of the château near Boulogne here spoken of ; nor did they give up the Chambers in London, 14 Chatham Place, Blackfriars Bridge, which he had rented for some years.

"Top" was a nickname applied to Mr. Morris. Gillum (Colonel Gillum) is a gentleman whom my brother had seen a good deal of late, and who purchased some of his drawings.

128 RUE DE RIVOLI, PARIS.
Saturday [9 June 1860].

MY DEAR WILLIAM,

On the last page hereof is a paragraph which I wish you would get put in the *Times*. Some one told me our marriage had appeared there ; but it must be a mistake, no doubt, unless you have put it in. If the governor's birthplace is wrong at all, please alter. Would you also send Crouch, 19 Clarence Gardens, whom Mamma knows, with the enclosed order, to get it cashed? . . .

On our way here we stayed several days at Boulogne, and saw a great deal of the Maenzas, who quite fascinated my wife—*i.e.*, Mr. Maenza chiefly. He is far from well, poor old fellow—indeed, has been very ill—but greatly excited of course about the Garibaldi business. After seven years they have at last had accidental news of their son in Australia, who at any rate seemed in good health then, and not starving, but no doubt he is leading a vagabond sort of life. Near Boulogne we saw a very ancient château, with a wonderful garden and lots of paintable things. It might be rented cheap, I believe, and I have some thoughts of taking it for the summer months, in case at the end of that time we found it advisable (if possible) to push further south. One might paint some very paying backgrounds for small pictures, and it is lovely beyond all description. My wife has been in very fluctuating health, and still is so, but on the whole has had fewer violent fits of illness since I saw you than before. Still I need not say what an anxious and disturbed life mine is while she remains in this state. And this is increased by the absolute necessity of setting soon to work again, while in fact her health at times demands my constant care.

I shall be giving up my rooms in London, whether I settle there or at Boulogne for the present; and even in the latter case shall have to come to London to settle things and fetch my work. So no doubt I shall see you before long, whatever happens. We do not propose to stay here much more than a week longer, and were expecting Jones and his wife as soon as they are married; but it seems he has been very ill lately, poor fellow, and on the whole I am not sure it may not prove wiser for him to stay at home. So we are not sure of having them now.

We have been staying a week at the Hôtel Meurice, which is very dear, and have only lately got into these rather cheaper lodgings. I have not got about quite so much as I should, were Lizzy better ; but have had several good looks at the great Paul Veronese, the greatest picture in the world beyond a doubt.

I hope Brown is better than when I last heard of him. Will you give him my news if you see him, and say how glad I should be to hear from him, if he will pardon my not having written yet except once since our marriage? My best address would be—

    Chez Mme. Houston
        (as above) :

the said Mme. is English and very obliging.

I hope they will not charge you extra postage for this, but I have not had the energy yet to buy foreign paper. Give my love to all at home. My wife joins in kind remembrances. Love to Top, Gillum, Woolner, and all friends.

Your affectionate Brother,
D. G. ROSSETTI.

    *   *   *   *   *   *

Ruskin is off, I suppose—I wrote to him.

On the 23rd. ult. at St. Clement's Church, Hastings, by the Rev. T. Nightingale, Dante Gabriel, eldest son of the late Gabriel Rossetti, of Vasto degli Abruzzi, Kingdom of Naples, to Elizabeth Eleanor, daughter of the late Charles Siddal, of Sheffield.

C 40.

The picture which is here spoken of as " going on " appears to be the one entitled *Found*.

PARIS.
Tuesday [19 June 1860].

DEAR WILLIAM,

We shall most likely leave here on Thursday, but I cannot say precisely on what day we shall reach London. Thanks for your letter. I think we shall bring two dogs— a big one and a little one. Lizzy continues rather better on the whole.   Paris certainly agrees with her, as it always does and I only trust she will not get worse again in London. I shall try to see Dr. Crellin about her.

We have given up the Boulogne scheme, I believe. You know of course that Jones has been very ill, but I trust from what you say he is better.

My love to Scott. . . . The picture is going on, and will soon make great advances. . . .

C 41.

The strong term " the Union fools " is applied to the Committee or other authorities of the Union Debating Club in Oxford. Some steps were taken for completing anyhow the pictures there left unfinished by my brother and his colleagues.

[14 CHATHAM PLACE.
18 *August* 1860.]

DEAR WILLIAM,

I am much annoyed at my stupid forgetfulness in not having tried before to get you here one evening. In fact, the few who have been have been asked through my meeting them accidentally, and somehow I have not turned you up lately. Pray pardon. I will write fixing a day next week, I trust, if you are able to come. Just now I am so busy morning and evening with work I am doing here that I had better put it off a few days.

Thanks about Maenza. I have no doubt we mean the same thing, and can do nothing till I see you, as I want to concoct a circular with your help. . . .

I am not on good terms with the Union fools, and had rather no one were sent in our name.

B 24.

[SPRING COTTAGE, DOWNSHIRE HILL, HAMPSTEAD.
1860.]

DEAR MAMMA,

I had Dr. Crellin to see Lizzie yesterday, as she was very ill ; but, while I was gone for him, another doctor had been sent for; who being near at hand, and she I trust improving, I shall continue to see him at present. I did not give Dr. C[rellin] his fee yesterday, having only notes in the house. . . . I believe you have by you a second £20 of mine, as I asked William to send Croucher for it. If so, would you kindly send Croucher with whatever sum is right enclosed to Dr. C[rellin]? . . . Do not send less than two guineas.

A 22.

Lady Bath, I am satisfied, did *not* buy *The Blue Closet*. My brother failed in his endeavours to get a house (other than lodgings) at Hampstead.

BLACKFRIARS.
Thursday [1860].

MY DEAR AUNT,

You are to use your discretion about the subject of this note.

I am under the impression that you told me once that Lady Bath was desirous of possessing a water-colour drawing of mine which was at that little exhibition in Russell Place some years ago. The drawing was not then for sale, but has lately become my property again through an exchange. Its subject is some people playing music, and it is called *The Blue Closet*.

If you think there is any probability of Lady Bath being still in the same mind, you might mention the matter to her, *but not if you feel the slightest awkwardness* in renewing the subject. It occurred to me as possible she might still wish to have it; and, as (like others) I find married life increases one's expenses, I thought I would not leave this stone unturned. But you will judge best about it. I may mention that the price is 50 guineas.

I left at last at Albany Street that photograph which has long lain here inscribed to you.

I wish I could give you the best news of my wife, but I must hope for the best, and meanwhile be content if it goes

a little better with her, as I think it does just now. She has
been at the seaside, but returns to-night, I trust.

I am doing so many things in the way of work, and am in
such a perpetual moil about them, that I really do not know
which to tell you of; but some day you will come and see
them.

I have been trying to get a house at Hampstead, but find
there is nothing so difficult as to get suited in this respect;
so have not yet got rid of these rooms, which, with the
lodging we have at Hampstead (necessary to my wife's
health), comes expensive, you may be sure.

Believe me ever

Your affectionate Nephew,

D. G. ROSSETTI.

B 25.

Thursday evening
[1 November 1860].

MY DEAR MOTHER,

Lizzie is so unsettled just now by constant moving
about that I think we had better put off the plan of her
coming to Albany Street, though I am most anxious it
should be so. We have only just got out of that lodging at
Hampstead, and so cut off an expense; taking instead for the
winter the second floor in the next house to this, additionally
to this one. We take it unfurnished, and must manage to
fill it somehow. I hope then, if not before, we may manage
to have your company in our new rooms. Nothing would
give me greater pleasure, as nothing pains me more than the
idea of our being in any way divided—which would indeed be
a bad return for all I owe to my dear good Mother. But I
trust you feel sure how much I suffer from this idea, and how
wholly I hope to see it set right. My only reason for not
giving Lizzie your letter just now is the one I have named;
and, if I see her stronger and more settled to-morrow or next
day, I shall still give it her. Love to all.

C 42.

[14 CHATHAM PLACE.
18 *January* 1861.]

DEAR WILLIAM,

I am pushing on at last with my *Italian Poets* at the printer's. Could you help me at all, do you think, in collating my *Vita Nuova* with the original, and amending inaccuracies, of which I am sure there are some? I have so much to do that I am tempted to bore you with it if you can and will. If you will answer *yes*, I will send it you by book-post. It ought to be done immediately.

Will you tell me how Mamma is? Lizzy is so-so.

Your affectionate
GABRIEL.

I asked Ruskin whether he would say a good word for something of Christina's to the *Cornhill*, and he promised to do so if she liked. If so, would she send me by book-post the book containing the Poem about the two Girls and the Goblins?

C 43.

Saffi, here mentioned, was Aurelio Saffi, one of the noblest of men, who had been a Triumvir of Rome in 1849, along with Mazzini and Armellini : for some while he held in Oxford University a chair for instruction in Italian. The prose " Tale " by my sister must be the *Folio Q* referred to later on.

[14 CHATHAM PLACE.
19 *January* 1861.]

DEAR WILLIAM,

Many thanks. What I want is that you should correct my translation throughout, removing inaccuracies and mannerisms. And, if you have time, it would be a great service to translate the analyses of the poems (which I omitted). This, however, if you think it desirable to include them. I did not at the time (on ground of readableness), but since think they may be desirable, only have become so unfamiliar with the book that I have no distinct opinion. I enclose in the MS. some notes by Saffi, which may prove useful.

I mentioned to Ruskin Christina's *Goblins*, as one having a subject. But we must see. But has she not a tale too? If so, would she send it me? Will you tell her we are very thankful for her paper-box, which is very useful?

I want to get my own poems out at the same time as the translations, but am not sure yet.

Love to Mamma and all. I am glad indeed to hear she is getting over her illness.

F 4.

This letter opens by referring to the (now celebrated) verses by Christina named *Up-hill*: they were first published in *Macmillan's Magazine* in 1860. Whether the "lively little Song of the Tomb" is the same thing or not I cannot now say. Professor Masson, the Queen's Historiographer for Scotland, was then the Editor of that Magazine, and was well known and deservedly esteemed by us all. "The poem Ruskin has" was, I apprehend, *Goblin Market*; it did not go into the *Cornhill Magazine*. *Folio Q* must have been a prose story which our sister wrote somewhere about the time here in question. It dealt with some supernatural matter—I think, a man whose doom it was not to get reflected in a looking-glass (a sort of alternative form, so far, of *Peter Schlemihl*). I preserve a faint but very favourable recollection of it, as perhaps the best tale Christina ever wrote in prose; but unfortunately it turned out to raise—or to *seem* as if it were meant to raise—some dangerous moral question; and, on having her attention directed to this, my sister, who had been all unconscious of any such matter, destroyed the MS on the spot. A pity now.

My "Preface to Dante" was the preface to a translation of the *Inferno*, which got published eventually, but only in 1865.

[*January* 1861.]

DEAR CHRISTINA,

I saw Macmillan last night, who has been congratulated by some of his contributors on having got a poet at last in your person, and read aloud your lively little Song of the Tomb with great satisfaction. He is anxious to see something else of yours, and is a man able to judge for himself; so I think you might probably do at least as well with him as with Masson. I told him of the poem Ruskin has, and he would like to see it if it does not go into *Cornhill.* He would also specially like to see *Folio Q*; can you get it or make another copy? or have you got anything else available? He asked whether you had much ready in MS., and I told him there was a good deal of poetry. I wish you would make a collected copy in printing-form of all the most available, and allow me to give an opinion beforehand as to which should be included. I believe they would have a chance with Macmillan, or might with others, if they existed in an available form. I would come down one evening for the purpose; or rather, if you would send me the books as soon as you could, I would read them through, and consult with you afterwards. It seems to me that the only plan— so large a section of your poems being devotional—would be to divide the volume into two distinct sections. What do you think?

The *Vita Nuova* will not be long now.

Your affectionate Brother,
D. G. ROSSETTI.

I want very much to hear William's Preface to Dante. Would he be able to take tea here any evening, and read it me?

F 5.

"Thanks about the 'ye.'" It may be inferred that Christina, on reading the MS. of the translated *Vita Nuova*, or other translation, had pointed out to Gabriel that he sometimes used the nominative case 'ye' where it ought to be the objective 'you.' Stokes is Mr. Whitley Stokes, the pre-eminent Celtic scholar, then a young legal man.

Monday [*January* 1861].

DEAR CHRISTINA,

Many and many thanks for your fair copy just received
—which *is so* fair it almost seems a pity to print it.

Thanks about the "ye," but I'm afraid I don't think it
matters much. I've not yet looked into W[illiam]'s notes,
but see they'll be useful.

Last night I read some of your poems to Stokes—a very
good judge and conversant with publishers—who thought
them so unusually excellent that there could be little doubt
ever of their finding a publisher, not to speak of a public.
Really they must come out somehow. I should have come
to Albany Street last night, had not Stokes come in, but shall
probably do so to-morrow evening. Every one seems to have
been struck (on own hooks) by *Up-hill.* The best of all
your things, I think, is " When I was dead my spirit turned."
Might it not be called *At Home ?* I shall give it at once
to Macmillan.

C 44.

Not having any direct authority for publishing the letter from Mr.
Ruskin here referred to, I omit it ; but I may say in general terms
that it objected to the execution of my sister's poems, on the ground
of licenses (real or supposed) in versification.

14 CHATHAM PLACE.
[25 *January* 1861.]

DEAR WILLIAM,

Many and many thanks for a most essential service
most thoroughly performed. I have not yet verified the
whole of the notes, but I see they are just what I needed,
and will save me a vast amount of trouble. I should very
much wish that the translation were more literal, but cannot
do it all again.

My notes, which you have taken the trouble of revising,
are of course quite paltry and useless. What 1 think I shall
do is to write a sort of essay, as short as I can make it, in
front of the second part of my book (called *Dante and his*

Circle), embodying what little has to be said about Dante and Guido Cavalcanti, and indeed various poems of The Canzoniere.

Will you thank Mamma very much for her help?

It is with very great regret and disgust that I enclose a note from Ruskin about Christina's poems—most senseless, I think. I have told him something of the sort in my answer. He has not yet returned the volume I sent him (with the *Goblins*), but I suppose will soon. I have some idea (with Christina's approval) of sending the *Goblins* to Mrs. Gaskell, who is good-natured and appreciative, and might get it into the *Cornhill* or elsewhere. Would she like this done? Or perhaps Allingham might help.

With love to all,

Your affectionate Brother,

GABRIEL.

B 26.

Thursday [2 *May* 1861].

MY DEAR MOTHER,

Lizzie has just been delivered of a dead child. She is doing pretty well, I trust.

Do not encourage any one to come just now—I mean, of course, except yourselves.

B 27.

"Christina's book," for which my brother had designed the binding, was her first published volume, *Goblin Market and other Poems*. The frontispiece was cut on the wood by Mr. Morris, being his first essay in that line, or nearly so, and certainly a most spirited if not conventionally nitid piece of execution.

[14 CHATHAM PLACE.
(?) 1861.]

MY DEAR MAMMA,

We have got some stuff which we want to make up for hangings for our sitting-room, and want some one who

would come here and make it up on the spot under Lizzie's
direction. Do you know any one—competent and not ninety
years of age? If so, would you kindly send such able and
not aged person?

I have designed a binding for Christina's book. I think
both woodcuts are sure to be done engraving before the end
of this month.

C 45.

The principal picture which Mr. Plint had contracted for may
probably have been *The Magdalene at the door of Simon the Pharisee.*
Mr. Leathart, who had now undertaken to buy *Found*, was an owner
of lead-works settled at Gateshead-on-Tyne. He formed an excellent collection of pictures, several of them by my brother and his
associates. My brother entertained, and had every reason for
entertaining, a cordial esteem of Mr. Leathart, and valued his
discernment in questions of art, more especially his true sense of
colour. (I regret to use the word "was" of this most honourable
and friendly gentleman : he died on 9 August 1895, just as these
pages were passing through the press.)

14 CHATHAM PLACE.
[16 *August* 1861.]

MY DEAR WILLIAM,

I think from the tone of your note that Gambart, in
addition to his statement (which may be all or only half or
less true), must have abused me so much as to have left you
with the impression that I was acting wilfully wrong. This
is not so in any degree. I am really quite as anxious to do
justice to the relatives of so excellent a man as Plint as I am
to get myself out of the most difficult fix I was ever in. The
unfortunate thing is that, owing chiefly to Plint's habit of
pressing money on one for work in progress (of which I
naturally availed myself, being always hard up), I am in debt
to the estate for three pictures to the amount of 680 guineas.
These three pictures are in hand, but, especially the principal
one, little advanced. The other two, though needing a good
deal, would be soon finished.

You see, things being thus, it is impossible for me to combine justice to the estate (*i.e.*, to the value of the pictures) with hurry in their completion ; and, besides, must do other work to live by while I paint them. Unhappily, I am even prevented from setting to work at once on the pictures (in which case I might probably get them done somehow by April), but am under promise to finish Leathart's *Found* at once, and do other things, besides the Llandaff picture, on which I am now hard at work, and which has to be sent off in two or three weeks at furthest.

With Gambart I will have nothing further to do (indeed I may say nothing simply, as I have shut him out hitherto)— that is, if I can help it, his letters being very offensive, and attempting intimidation with talk of law, etc. Since answering his last, I have written direct to the trustees, making a proposal that I should give them other finished works to the amount of the money paid, which I could do before April, I doubt not.

They seem to think this feasible (and in no case to contemplate law), but are going to refer the proposal to Gambart, so I do not know what it may come to.

I have been suggesting to them to transact through Ruskin on my behalf; but now it seems unfortunately that it was Ruskin who advised them originally to employ a dealer, and they went to Gambart.

Ruskin, who has been away, is just back, and I shall see him to-day, so perhaps some suggestion may turn up.

In any case, I should be quite as unhappy at adding to the difficulties of Mrs. Plint as at any misfortune to myself personally, and you may be sure I am altogether in a most anxious state. But Gambart cannot be stood at any price.

Your

D. G. R.

I hope Christina got her poems safe.

C 46.

DEAR WILLIAM,

I think the letter is calculated to rile Gambart a little, if not to do him good, which it also may; so would be obliged to you to send it; but would you mind re-writing it for the sake of a slight alteration I have made? as it is well not to seem decidedly to put *everything* else I am doing before these pictures.

*   *   *   *   *   *

B 28.

The portrait here mentioned is a half-length lifesized oil-portrait of our Father which my brother painted in 1848—his first picture after the *Girlhood of Mary Virgin*. It was painted for his god-father Mr. Charles Lyell; and had now been borrowed from his son Sir Charles Lyell, with a view to its being used to illustrate a volume of selections from our Father's poems which I had put together with some pains, and which an Italian publisher, Rossi, had undertaken to publish. Rossi, whether from deficient means or whatever other cause, never fulfilled his engagement; and consequently no use was made of the portrait by way of engraving. My brother's suggestion that I should attempt to make the engraving on wood was hardly of a practical sort, as I had (and have) never made any experiment in that line. Not each of us is a William Morris.

[14 CHATHAM PLACE.]
Tuesday [? 1861].

DEAR MAMMA,

The portrait came last night. It is a funny piece of painting, but no doubt considerably though not perfectly like. The question is now what to do with it. I would willingly make a drawing—perhaps on wood would be best—and get it cut here and sent over. The cutting might be some slight expense to Rossi, though I am not sure whether I could not get it done for nothing.

Would you take the trouble of writing to him, asking the

shape of the edition and when it will be out, and telling him what I say about the portrait? You need not hold out the chance of gratis engraving, but say it could be engraved at a trifling expense here. By the bye, if William liked he might essay wood-engraving on it, as it would be very simple.

*   *   *   *   *   *

B 29.

My brother had gone to the house of Mr. J. Aldam Heaton in Yorkshire, to paint a portrait of Mrs. Heaton (this family is not related to the Miss Heaton of Leeds whose name occurs elsewhere in my pages). The portrait is one out of two or three heads by Rossetti, bearing the title *Regina Cordium*—no undue tribute to Mrs. Heaton.

WOODBANK [MR. J. A. HEATON'S, NEAR BINGLEY, YORKS].
                                        31 *October* [1861].

MY DEAR MAMMA,

I am out here painting a portrait, and left Lizzie staying with the Morrises. Now she writes me that she has left them in a hurry, making me very uneasy, as I know there was not a halfpenny of money at Chatham Place. If at all possible, would you go there, and take her some few pounds, which I shall be able to repay you on my return immediately, and will punctually do so? It was impossible to bring her here with me, both from her very delicate state and from the very reason that what money we had hardly sufficed for my own journey. On my return I shall have earned 50 guineas, and shall certainly be back in a week from to-day. If not convenient to call, you might send the tin by post. I would not trouble you, but know William is away. At present, of course, it makes me very uneasy.

C 47.

Mr. Linton (who had been mentioned in an earlier letter) is Mr. W. J. Linton, the wood-engraver. An offer had been made to the National Portrait Gallery of a portrait of David Scott, painted by himself. The portrait of Wright of Derby, a painter of last century, was one which I myself had erewhile presented to the same gallery. I did not write the proposed letter to the *Athenæum* —being dissuaded by Mr. W. B. Scott—though I quite sympathized in my brother's feeling on the subject.

[14 CHATHAM PLACE.]
Tuesday [4 *February* 1862].

MY DEAR WILLIAM,

I meant to have said before, and have just been incited by Linton to say, that I think reálly you, as a man whose name is known in that way, ought to write a letter to the *Athenæum* on the shameful rejection of David Scott's portrait by the National Portrait Gallery.

He says he has no doubt they would print it, and you might surely instance as a strong comparative case the acceptance of Wright of Derby.

Your

D. G. R.

Linton wants to meet you. Could you appoint to come here one evening? and I'd ask just one or two men besides.

B 30.

My brother (having after his wife's death left Chatham Place for Lincoln's Inn Fields) was now projecting a further move to Cheyne Walk, and furnishing-requisites became a topic for consideration. Our Mother offered him the spacious and well-looking bedstead which had witnessed the birth of all us four. He eventually accepted it, and constantly used it until he left Cheyne Walk to die at Birchington. After his death it ought to have been retained in the family; but (owing to a muddle, for which I was not exactly responsible, at the sale of his effects) it passed out of my ken. Mr. J. Anderson Rose was the solicitor who saw to my brother's interest as to the lease for the Cheyne Walk house.

59 LINCOLN'S INN FIELDS.
Wednesday [1862].

DEAR MAMMA,

*   *   *   *   *   *

Many thanks also about the bedstead. I shall cer- tainly have no absolute neçessity for it: nevertheless should be glad to have it, of course, if you do not prefer selling it. . . . It is by no means improbable that the one you offer me might prove of great use sooner or later, and it is interesting as a family recollection. . . .

I believe we shall be able to conclude the business about the house to-morrow, as Rose has managed to secure our safety in the matter.

*   *   *   *   *   *

F 6.

With this scrap of a note Gabriel sent to his sister transcripts of two passages from reviews of her poems—from *The British Quarterly* and *The National Review*. The former contained the "puff" of Gabriel, *i.e.*, of his designs to the volume. I will quote one of its sentences about the poems : "All of these are marked by beauty and tenderness : they are frequently quaint, and sometimes a little capricious." Condensed as it is, this verdict has stood the test of time.

SIMPSON'S DIVAN.
[*July* 1862].

DEAR CHRISTINA,

Here are the two notices. I forgot that one puffs me too ; so, if you want to show them to any one, I would be obliged if you would copy them, and not show them in my writing.

*   *   *   *   *   *

C 48.

"I have written to Meredith about his share." This relates to the fact that, when first my brother settled at 16 Cheyne Walk, Mr. George Meredith the novelist, and also Mr. Swinburne and myself, occupied certain rooms in the house as sub-tenants. This letter was written from Newcastle-on-Tyne, where my brother was painting a portrait of Mrs. Leathart.

[NEWCASTLE.]
Tuesday morning [30 *December* 1862].

DEAR WILLIAM,

I have just got yours from Somerset House, which shows me that you are well again after the attack of cold of

which I heard. This is well. As to the rent business etc.
I never meant to have reckoned on you for *any* expenses at
present in your own person, as I think you have done more
than enough . . . but certainly whatever you can do without
inconvenience to yourself will be very opportune as regards
me, I being naturally even more pressed than usual this
Christmas.

*   *   *   *   *   *

I have written to Meredith about his share, and am likely,
I find, to see him at Chelsea on my return. I trust I shall be
able to suffice to all by end of January, having that month
clear before me ; but meanwhile the rent is a heavy item, and
endless debts besides which *ought* to be paid, and a few which
must.

You will know when I leave (it will be to-morrow at 1.30
I suppose) by receiving an insurance-ticket from the railway,
as I suppose you did when I came.

B 31.

Baker, here named, was, along with his wife, my brother's servant.
They came from the Muntham neighbourhood, and went back
thither : see A 23. " My *Helen* " means a small oil-picture, *Helen
of Troy*. As the address, " 16 Cheyne Walk, Chelsea," continued
to be my brother's ordinary address up to the close of his life, I
shall for the most part omit this henceforward, and only introduce it
if it should be subject to some interruption, preceding or ensuing.

[16 CHEYNE WALK, CHELSEA.]
Friday night [1863].

DEAR MAMMA,
    Would you give Baker the photograph of *Old Cairo*
which hangs in your parlour; and, if there are any stereo-
scopic pictures, either in the instrument or elsewhere, which
represent general views of cities, would you send them too, or
anything of a fleet of ships ? I want to use them in painting
Troy at the back of my *Helen*, and will return them soon.

C 49.

Pope was my brother's servant. Chapman was George F. Chapman, a painter of considerable ability, more especially in inventive composition. He was much with my brother about this time, sometimes staying in the house for awhile. He died towards 1880.

Saturday [*23 April* 1864].

DEAR W——,

I have seen the owner of the Zebu, and undertaken to buy him for £20,—£5 payable on Monday, and the rest within a fortnight. I shall then have plenty, but just now have none. Could you pay your £5 as the first instalment? If so, I will send Pope to you at Somerset House on Monday morning, and then on to him with the tin. If *not*, however, please let me know by return of post in answer to this, as I must then raise it somehow.

Pope has been in the beast's pen, and says he is quite tame. The owner says he would cost about 2*s*. 6*d*. a week for keep; but, even if rather understated, it would most likely be no great expense. He would need a shed of some sort in winter, but none in summer. Trusting to hear that you can do the needful on Monday,

I am ever your

GABRIEL.

Chapman is coming up to-night (Saturday), if you like to come too. I have let the peacocks out in the garden.

B 32.

"My *David*" is David as Shepherd, one of the wing-pictures in the Triptych for Llandaff Cathedral.

14 June 1864.

MY DEAR MAMMA,

Pray do come Friday evening, or rather as early as you all can in the day, as I shall have no model. I should like you to see my *David*, which will be going on Monday, I suppose.

Thanks for proposed hour-glass. . . .

A 23.

My brother often thought of holding an exhibition of his collected pictures, but never did so. The picture of *The Girlhood of Mary Virgin* had been presented by Lady Bath to her daughter Lady Louisa Feilding.

"I trust shortly to begin a very large work, on commission." I am not sure which this was. The most probable appears to be *The Boat of Love* (from a sonnet by Dante): of this my brother made an oil-monochrome (now in the Public Gallery at Birmingham), but never painted a complete picture. There was also *Cassandra* (pen-and-ink design), not painted.

[25 *June* 1864.]

MY DEAR AUNT,

I am glad you wrote to me, as there is a mixture now, much preferable to milk and water, for setting chalk or pencil drawings. It is a French invention, and can be procured (at 1*s.* 6*d.* a bottle, I think) from Lechertier Barbe, Artists' Colourman, 60 Regent Street. The benefit of it is that it is passed over the *back* of the drawing, not the front, and penetrates the paper.

I wish you had asked your various questions, as nothing would have given me greater pleasure than to answer as many as you pleased. In default of the questions, however, I do not know what the answers should be, and the unvaried tenor of my working-life is not suggestive of spontaneous narrative. The other day I finished and sent off to Llandaff the picture of *David as Shepherd*, completing the Triptych which I have painted as the altarpiece of the Cathedral, and which altogether is entitled *The Seed of David*. It is intended to show Christ sprung from high and low in the person of David, who was both Shepherd and King, and worshipped by high and low—a King and a Shepherd—at his nativity. Accordingly in the centre-piece (which I forget whether you saw at all, but certainly not finished) an Angel is represented leading the Shepherd and King to worship in the stable at the feet of Christ, who is in his mother's arms. She holds his hand for the Shepherd, and his foot for the King, to kiss—so showing the superiority of poverty over riches in the eyes of Christ ; while the one lays his crook, the other his crown, at the Saviour's feet.   There is an opening all round the stable, through which Angels are looking in, while other Angels are playing on musical instruments in a loft above. This is the centre-piece.

The two side-pieces represent, on one side, David as Shepherd with the sling, walking forward and taking aim at Goliath, while the Israelite army watches the throw behind an entrenchment.   The other side-piece is David as King playing on the harp.

The three pictures are in a stone framework in the Cathedral, which I fear, being white, must injure their effect much ; but before long I shall go down there, and give directions for such decoration of the framework as seems best.   Some day I must get them lent me for exhibition in London, whenever I collect my works together for that purpose—as I mean to do at some date, I hope not very distant, but probably not for a year or two as yet.   I have been thinking of some concise mottoes to inscribe on the stone-work round the pictures, and so suggest their purport, and have hit on the following :—

(1) Christ sprang from David Shepherd, and even so
(2) From David King, being born of high and low.
(3) The Shepherd lays his crook, the King his crown,
(4) Here at Christ's feet, and high and low bow down.

Do you not think this will help the spectator?

By the bye, I believe I bothered you once before to enquire who ought to be written to relative to my old picture of *The Girlhood of Mary Virgin*, bought originally by Lady Bath, and which I understood once its present possessor (to whom I believe it was a gift from her) proposed varnishing or doing something to.   This was told me by Hunt.   I did not write to him at the time (though I fancy you kindly gave me some information), but have always meant to do so, and should like to do so still, in case the picture needs my revision in any way.

I have quantities of commissions now, and never was nearly so prosperous before. I trust shortly to begin a very large work, on commission, and henceforward to do almost exclusively large works in oil. Small things and water-colours I never should have done at all, except for the long continuance of a necessity for "pot-boilers."

I am very glad the Bakers are doing rather better. They are worthy souls, but odd.

Will you present my regards to Lady Bath? and believe me

Your most affectionate Nephew,
D. G. ROSSETTI.

C 50.

The flowers which my brother was painting when he wrote this note were the foreground of roses in his *Venus Verticordia*. As to the "large commission," see the note to the preceding letter. The P.S. refers to a little pencil sketch, purposely jejune, of a palm-tree and a setting sun.

Thursday [11 *August* 1864].

DEAR W——,

Can you *conveniently* contribute £10 to house expenses? I, . . . being obliged to stick to painting these flowers, cannot knock off before then to earn the money otherwise. It would have been all right if I had got the remittance I expected on the large commission, and the promise of which has made me over-confident of meeting expenses in time. It does not come, and I cannot keep up the sickening job of writing to the people for ever.

If you can manage £10, I dare say I can get the rest in time somehow.

Your
D. G. R.

P.S.—I have been too busy to send Pope for the chameleons so will expect them when you come. The above is Ned Jones's cartoon of the Eastern style.

B 33.

When this letter was written, our mother was (I think) at Hastings, along with our elder sister, and our cousin Henrietta Polydore, who was a consumptive invalid.

16 CHEYNE WALK.
16 *August* 1864.

MY DEAREST MOTHER,

I received your good old letter, and am very glad to hear of Henrietta's decided improvement. Will you give her my love, as well as to Maggie? I hope the three of you will be even better at arrival of this than at departure of yours. As for me, I have no chance of getting away just now, as I am tied down to my canvas till all the flower part of it is finished. I have done many more roses, and have established an arrangement with a nursery-gardener at Cheshunt, whereby they reach me every two days at 2s. 6d. for a couple of dozen each time, which is better than paying a shilling apiece at Cov[ent] Garden. Also honeysuckles I have succeeded in getting at the Crystal Palace, and have painted a lot already in my foreground, and hope for more. All these achievements were made only with infinite labour on my part, and the loss of nearly a whole week in searching. But the picture gets on well now.

The peahen has hatched two out of her four eggs, and now stalks about with two little whining queernesses at her heels— no bigger or brighter than ordinary chicks, but perhaps a little steadier on their pins.

Chapman is at Malvern doing the cold-water business. He lodges at a house called the Berry, and is improving but slowly. . . .

The other day I sent Christina this month's *Fraser*, which contains a review of her in conjunction with Miss Ingelow, Mrs. Browning, and Miss Procter. The palm among living poetesses is given to Christina on the whole. But probably she will be sending it on to you. I do not know who is the writer, though I have some idea it may be a man of the

name of Skelton whom I met on one occasion. The article
is . . . intelligent in criticism.

*   *   *   *   *   *

I have not yet seen William's chameleons, but shall, I
believe, to-morrow, as he is coming here and proposes to
bring them. I have been so busy that I have not been anywhere except where my picture took me to look for flowers.
I got three different parcels of honeysuckles from three
different friends in three different parts of England, none of
which were of any use, being broken and faded. Then I got
some from a nursery at Waltham Cross which were not much
good either, and lastly from the Crystal Palace. All with
much delay and bother. So you see I have had a time of it.

A friend of Mr. Mitchell, who is to have the *Venus*, called
from Yorkshire to see it the other day, and was much
delighted. I hope it may do me good when it gets there.

Write again when you can, and I will give you such news
as there is in return. The best news I can have is that you
are all well.

C 51.

"I enquired at Delacroix" means "I enquired at the Gallery
where an exhibition of Delacroix's works is now being held." I had
not an opportunity of joining my brother, as suggested, in his brief
Parisian trip. Fantin's Delacroix picture was a work painted by
Fantin Latour, and named (I think) *Hommage à Eugène Delacroix*:
it consisted of a group of portraits—Baudelaire, Fantin himself, etc.,
crowning a bust of Delacroix (or some such incident). I cannot
now recollect whether or not I wrote anything about the picture;
though I appreciated its fine qualities at the very least as highly as
my brother did.

PARIS.
Tuesday [8 *November* 1864]

My DEAR W—,

I have left the Grand Hôtel, and am now at Hôtel de
Dunkerque, 32 Rue Laffitte. I do not know how many days
I may stay now. I enquired at Delacroix when it shuts, and
they said it would be open in all probability to the end of
the month.

I should be very glad to hear you were coming.

Fantin is anxious to see anything you may have written about his Delacroix picture. Is there anything, and where? I saw the picture, and think it has a great deal of very able painting in parts; but it is a great slovenly scrawl after all, like the rest of this incredible new French school—people painted with two eyes in one socket through merely being too lazy to efface the first, and what not. Fantin took me to see a man named Manet who has painted things of the same kind. I also went with him to Courbet's studio. Courbet was away, but I saw various works of his—by far the best an early portrait of himself about twenty-three or twenty-four, resting his head on one hand. It is rather hard and colourless, but has many of the fine qualities of a Leonardo. His other works have great merit in parts, and are all most faulty. Both he and Delacroix are geniuses much akin in style to David Scott, an exhibition of whose works would, I should think, make a great sensation here.

Will you let me know if you have written anything on Fantin? . . .

It is splendid weather, but cold.

B 34.

My brother, being in Paris, went to a certain well-known Japanese shop in the Rue de Rivoli, often visited about this time by Mr. Whistler, and sometimes by myself. The jocular allusion to Mr. Whistler, and to my brother's collection of blue china (which had made some progress in 1864, and had become a noticeable thing by the time when the great majority of it was sold off in 1872), will be understood as marking the friendly rivalry of zealous collectorship in which they indulged about this period.

HÔTEL DE DUNKERQUE,
32 RUE LAFFITTE, PARIS.
12 *November* 1864.

MY DEAR MAMMA,

I am extremely sorry to hear how unwell both you and Christina have been; but both, I learn from William, are better now—I trust definitively so.

I fancy most probably I shall not stay here more than a week longer now. The weather has been splendid hitherto, though rather cold. In fact, I could not have been more fortunate. But to-day is wet for the first time. It does not, however, look like a hopeless case of wet. I have done no work at all as yet, but shall probably do a little if I stay a week longer. I took, according to my habit, enough work to last me for three months in case anything detained me.

Paris is very much altered since I was last here, but I keep in so narrow a circle that I see little of the change. I have bought very little—only four Japanese books, and some photographs from the early Italian masters which William will be much interested in. I went to his Japanese shop, but found that all the costumes were being snapped up by a French artist, Tissot, who it seems is doing three Japanese pictures, which the mistress of the shop described to me as the three wonders of the world, evidently in her opinion quite throwing Whistler into the shade. She told me, with a great deal of laughing, about Whistler's consternation at my collection of china. This, however, will interest William more than you.

It is well worth while for English painters to try and do something now, as the new French school is simple putrescence and decomposition. There is a man named Manet (to whose studio I was taken by Fantin), whose pictures are for the most part mere scrawls, and who seems to be one of the lights of the school. Courbet, the head of it, is not much better.

I shall bring the dear old Ancient a little tortoise-shell purse, and a fan for Christina, and a dress for Maggie, which I hope will not be an abomination to her. It is a sort of brown Coburg, with some embroidery on it, simpler and in better taste than most such things I have seen.

I have changed my address, as you will see, and am now in a house which is one of those curious mechanical contrivances peculiar to this country. My two rooms have seven doors in them, which, according as you open or shut

By D. G. Rossetti

HENRY F POLYDORE

1855.

them, offer you a choice of sounds and sensations, varying between the apex of a windmill, the interior of a paddle-box, and the circular whirl of a maelström.

B 35.

"Brown's Exhibition" is the exhibition, which Mr. Madox Brown opened in Piccadilly, of the majority of his pictures and designs of past years, including especially the painting, then recently finished, named *Work*. This is now in the Public Gallery of Manchester.

16 CHEYNE WALK, CHELSEA.
9 *March* 1865.

MY DEAR MOTHER,

I am very sorry indeed to have missed your visit and that of my aunts to-day. I was gone to Brown's exhibition, where he is hard at work preparing for the public, and, finding I could be of use to him, I stayed late. Thanks for the necklace and sketches. I hope you made yourselves comfortable, and saw what there was to see. I wish you would all name an early day to come and see me again.

G 1.

A very few letters addressed by my brother to our Uncle Henry F. Polydore (resident in Gloucester, or sometimes in Cheltenham) have been preserved. This is the first of them. It shows that our uncle had advanced some amount of money to my brother—I should suppose from £100 to £200. The story about the very large price obtained by Mr. Gambart for a picture, *The Blue Bower*, was, I know, denied by Mr. Gambart: I am unable to clear up the details with any precision. The reference to "problems or enigmas in the Latin tongue" must indicate that our uncle had proposed to consult my brother as to some Latin passage of more or less difficulty.

15 *November* 1865.

MY DEAR UNCLE,

Your last letter is very considerate, but I almost fancy you ought to have some security in the shape of note of

hand for the payment of the capital. Do you not think so?
As to the 5 per cent interest, I have already said I myself
consider, as the payment of the capital is so long deferred,
that the interest might reasonably be higher. However, I
returned to this tariff, from my own proposal of 10 per cent,
on account of your having yourself, since that, proposed 3½
per cent. I was therefore bent on getting you to accept at
least the medium scale, at which it now stands.

My prospects promise to improve very much just now,
through the high prices which some of my pictures have
fetched in the market. Gambart, the great dealer, to whom
I sold a recent picture of mine (*The Blue Bower*), has re-
sold it to a Mr. Mendel of Manchester, as I understand,
for 1,500 guineas! This, as it was not a large picture,
and had been painted in two months, is about the highest
price proportionately that I ever heard of a picture fetching.
Nor is this the only similar instance lately. I need hardly
tell you that the price I received for the above picture,
as for others, is very small, compared to the enormous
rate at which it has been re-sold; but such facts cannot fail
to tell very shortly on my own prices in a very marked
manner, though in themselves mere market-meteors, the
lucky hits of a dealer's ingenuity. I may thus after all
perhaps (who knows?) be in a position to re-pay you my
debt sooner than I looked to do so. Already I am getting
commissions and effecting sales to greater advantage than
hitherto, and such advantage cannot but continue on the increase for the present. Should you mention this phenomenal
market-transaction to any one, it would be better not to
dwell on the fact that the dealer has made an enormous
profit on the price paid to me. It is of course my interest
to help him in getting the highest prices he can for my
works, and not express the least discontent at his being the
first to profit to such extent by the market he creates for
them. I will take care my turn comes too.

I do not know whether you may have seen an article in
the *Athenæum* on some of my pictures about a month ago.

There is also something said in last Saturday's number. Though crippled by editorial revision on the Art-critic's original *dicta*, these articles have proved no doubt of service to me.

These matters are all egotistical, but I have reason to know that you take an interest in my affairs, and are glad I should do well.

I am extremely sorry to hear so poor an account of household health with you. I really fare better in this respect than I have any right to look for. Referring to my diary, I find there have been only twelve days during the five months ending with the close of October which have not been spent by me in work at my easel. I have completely missed all exercise and change of air this year, yet have no reason to complain as regards health.

What success I may have with any problems or enigmas in the Latin tongue I view as being in itself quite a doubtful question. It strikes me that a very amusing pastime for some of your leisure hours might be found in such labours connected with the great Philological Society's Dictionary as William has devoted himself to for some time past. If you felt any call in that direction, no doubt he could put you in the way of it, and the editors would be thankful.

With love to Henrietta, I am
Your affectionate Nephew,
D. G. ROSSETTI.

F 7.

Towards the date of this letter Miss Isa Craig (afterwards Mrs. Knox) held a considerable repute as a poetess : I hardly know whether this endures at the present day. She had some small acquaintance with Christina, who seems to have got Gabriel to look into a question of illustrating some poem by Miss Craig.

Two compositions of Christina's own are here referred to. *Hero* is a fairy-tale in prose, published in the *Commonplace* volume, 1870. As to the poem which Sandys was considering for the purpose of illustration, I have not any distinct idea.

5 *January* [1866].

DEAR CHRISTINA,

Miss Isa Craig called on me to-day, and seems nice. I couldn't do it; but, as the poem seemed good for illustration, I sent her on to Sandys, and, failing him, to Hughes. . . . Only I fear they've no idea of Sandys' prices. Hughes perhaps might do it cheap for love of you. You know he's painted a capital picture from your *Birthday*, with the poem at full length on the frame. You ought to call and see it, which would please him.

Your *Hero* is splendid : I don't know if I'd ever read it. You ought to write more such things.

I think I forgot to tell you about that other poem shown to Sandys. He read it, and on reflection said the only thing he could think of was to make a drawing of the woman lying ead, with some women preparing the grave-clothes and baby-clothes at the same time. This seems a fine idea, but requiring to be pointed to in some way in the poem. Would you mind having it called *Grave-clothes and Cradle-clothes*, or something of that sort?

Love to Mamma and all. What in the world has become of William? And is Hunt married? I'm coming down soon.

By the bye, I suppose you know now of one of the saddest things I ever heard—Mrs. Hannay's death on the 29th. I got a circular, and haven't yet had courage to write. When I've done so, I should like to call with William, if he thinks of doing so.

B 36.

Friday night [*February* 1866].

MY DEAR MUMMY,

The Beloved is going away on Tuesday night or Wednesday morning. I should like you to see it, if you can, finished, as I know you nurse my productions in your dear heart. William will be dining on Tuesday, so would you come then, and stay to dinner? Sisters also of course if practicable.

    *   *   *   *   *   *

B 37.

My brother carried into effect his intention of painting a portrait of our Mother—an oil-picture, life-sized and three-quarters length. He did not paint in oil or water-colour, after the date of this letter, any portrait of Christina : nor do I think that Mr. Chapman did so.

Saturday [?1866].

MY DEAR MAMMA,

I am very anxious to paint your portrait. Do tell me what day next week you could come conveniently, sit to me, and dine. Maria and Christina might come too if they could, and enjoy the garden.

Chapman, whom you met here, has been making interest with me to get Christina to sit to him for a portrait. Now I want to do it myself, as soon as I have done yours, so shall remain neutral.

Your affectionate Son,
D. G. ROSSETTI.

You know Chapman is painting a little picture suggested by Christina's sonnet *A Triad.*

B 38.

"The title-page to Christina's book" is the title-page, illustrated by Gabriel, of her volume of poems, *The Prince's Progress*, etc.

Thursday [? 1866].

DEAR MAMMA,

I think we said the 24th for your next sitting, but suppose we say instead, Tuesday of next week. . . .

Your affectionate Son,
GABRIEL.

*　　*　　*　　*　　*　　*

I have a proof of the title-page to Christina's book.

A 24.

Lord Charles Thynne was a brother-in-law of the Marchioness Dowager of Bath. He had been a clergyman of the Church of

England, but had passed over to the Church of Rome. He died in 1894.

[16 CHEYNE WALK.]
5 *June* [1866].

My dear Aunt,

I should be very happy to receive Lord and Lady C. Thynne's visit on the Wednesday of next week, any time between three and five o'clock. I hope this may be convenient to them, and am sorry to be so precise as to time, but am very busy. Of course all the introduction needed will be that they should send in their card when they call, as I shall be expecting them unless I hear to the contrary.

Thanks for your most kind and I know most sincere good wishes. I have been pretty well in health, and any imperfections in this respect I may pretty safely attribute more to a confirmed habit of life and work than to any defect of constitution. My work progresses continually, such as it is, and I should much like to have an early opportunity of showing you all I have in hand.

Uncle Henry was here yesterday for the second time since he has been in town. I am sorry to say he seems to me far from well. Christina, as you probably know, is in Scotland. Her book is just out at last. Perhaps you have a copy. If not, I shall be happy to send you one. I think Mamma is looking very well again. I have made some progress lately with her portrait, which every one says is very like.

My garden is looking nice again now, though left all to itself, and a wilderness in most people's opinions. I prefer to compare it to an Eden. At any rate, it is primitive enough by this time for the simile.

By the bye, I have been intending, as you probably know, to build a studio in this house, either at the top or in the garden, and have only been deterred hitherto from taking up the job by want of time to attend to it. Now, on enquiry, an architect gives it as his opinion that the thing on various accounts is not easy to accomplish. Thus, could I meet with a satisfactory residence elsewhere, possessing already the desired studio, I might perhaps be willing to relinquish this house, supposing I could let it to any decent advantage. I mention this on account of what you say respecting Lord C. Thynne's notion of living in Cheyne Walk—not of course necessarily for immediate repetition to him ; nor should I mention the idea at all at a first interview. If, however, you subsequently found that he *really* had such a wish, the matter might be named or not at your discretion.

By the bye, let me ask a favour. Will you kindly address me as in the signature of this letter ? I have so written my name nearly all my life, and varieties in one's nomenclature are apt to create confusion. Not that the matter is of consequence to any one, not even greatly to

Your affectionate Nephew,
D. G. ROSSETTI.

B 39.

Whether the Rossettis (or possibly I should rather say the Della Guardias) really have any armorial bearings is a matter unknown to me. My father owned (brought, I suppose, from Italy) a largeish seal marked with a crest—a tree having the motto *Frangas non flectas*—and he said this was regarded as his crest. Mr. Knewstub, my brother's art-assistant, who was connected with the Firm of Jenner and Knewstub, got that firm to present to Gabriel a die with the crest and a monogram ; and the latter for some years habitually used note-paper thus stamped. Hence an allusion in the first paragraph of this letter.

The Toilette picture here named is *Lady Lilith* ; the picture with the gold sleeve, *Monna Vanna* ; the *Beatrice, Beata Beatrix*. Colonel Feilding's picture will be understood as being *The Girlhood of Mary Virgin.*

Mr. Clabburn was a Norwich manufacturer, who purchased two or three of my brother's paintings. Mr. Sandys painted a fine portrait of his very stately head and figure.

24 *August* 1866.

GOOD ANTIQUE,

I have been often thinking of you, and meaning to write. . . . The other day an extraordinary apparent German wrote to me from Manchester about an iron cross in a German churchyard bearing the name of Antonio Rossetti, Maître de Chapelle to a German Duke long ago, and asked me whether he had been an ancestor of mine. I answered with my proverbial courtesy, informing him that I didn't know, and also that the tree on this letter-paper was supposed possibly, though not very certainly, to be the arms of our family. He has written a second eccentric epistle, which I enclose in case it should interest you at all. . . .

I have been working chiefly at the Toilette picture, and at the one with the gold sleeve, both of which I think you know. The former will, I think, be my best picture hitherto. I engaged it some time ago to a Mr. Leyland of Liverpool for 450 guineas, and hope to send it him by the end of September. The other one I have not yet sold, so that all the money is to come when I do. And, what between this and the *Beatrice;* (which I have engaged for 300 guineas to Mr. William Cowper), I hope a goodish sum will come in all at once, and enable me for the first time to open a banking account at the end of this year with a goodish sum, especially as, besides these two, I have some other small things in a forward state and still for sale ; nor do I anticipate any difficulty in selling any of them, though I have as yet hardly shown them to any one. I am glad Mr. Cowper (who is Lord Palmerston's stepson, and was Chief Commissioner of the Board of Works in the last Ministry) is to have the *Beatrice*, as he, and his wife particularly, are very appreciative people, and it is pleasanter sending a poetic work where it will be seen by cultivated folks than to a cotton-spinner or a dealer. I could have got considerably more for the picture in some such quarter, I make no doubt, as I had several requests for it ; but, as Mr. Cowper had asked me for a picture, and is not at present a very rich man, I preferred offering it him for 300 guineas. This panic year, strange to say, promises to be much my best as yet.

I have been telling you all this about myself, because I know you are a dear old thing and like to hear it all.

I lately sent back Colonel Feilding's picture, with the offer to paint his wife's portrait in exchange for it if he liked ; but this he declined, as she had recently been sitting for a portrait, and couldn't stand it over again, and moreover did not wish to part with the picture, as her mother had given it to her.

Mr. Clabburn, who gave me both the peacocks, old and new, was here to-day ; and says the present one may be expected with confidence to start a tail next year, as he will then be three years old, which is the proper age. He shows no sign as yet.

* * * * * *

B 40.

The date of this letter must be in *or about* 1866. My brother made a little excursion with the painter Mr. Sandys, with whom towards that time he was particularly intimate. The " box-tree trained in the form of an armchair " was (as this letter indicates) planted by my brother's servant Loader in the garden of 16 Cheyne Walk, just at the end of the narrow promenade leading from the back door of the house to the larger open space. It flourished tolerably well for awhile ; but after two or three years had withered away to a mere nothing, and was removed.

TENTERDEN, KENT.
Friday night [? 1866].

GOOD ANTIQUE,

I left London on Monday, and till to-night have been at Winchelsea, which is a most delightful old place for quietness and old-world character. I have got you a photograph of the old church, which I shall give you on my return. The outside is fine—partly a ruin—and quite imbedded in ivy, and the inside contains some very fine tombs with effigies. I should think yourself, with Maggie or Christina or both, would find Winchelsea a most delight-fully quiet sojourn some time you are leaving town. The charges at the inn were very moderate, and I should think a moderate lodging could be got in a private house. A walk of two miles takes you to a most solitary sea-beach,

and there are many good directions for a walk. Sandys
and I walked a great deal, and also one day went in a dog-
cart to some distance—about twenty miles—seeing several
nice places, chiefly Northiam, where there is an old house
of the most delightful kind with a garden full of walks of
quaintly cut fir-trees, the best thing of the sort I ever saw.
The proprietor politely allowed us to see over it on appli-
cation. The garden at Northiam has perhaps infected the
neighbourhood with a taste for cut shrubs, of which various
specimens may be seen. I have myself secured a very curious
one for my garden—a box-tree trained in the form of an
armchair. It was at the door of a cottage, and had been
trained by the inmates ever since 1833. The poor old woman,
after these thirty-three years' labours, actually sold it me for
£1, and to-day I have sent it to Chelsea, where it is to be at
once planted by Loader. As soon as I am back, you must
come and see it. I am sure you will admire it very much, as
it is in very splendid condition. Of course it cannot be sat
in, but I shall have a light removable wooden framework
placed inside it to make it fit for use, and take out to show
its beauty when not needed. It was taken up with great
care by the roots yesterday, the operation being performed
by our Winchelsea landlord, who performed a journey for the
purpose, and was looked on with a rather evil eye by the
neighbourhood, the chair being a kind of local lion. It was
then very carefully packed with manure round the roots to
keep it safe till planted in my garden, which it has probably
been to-day, as I telegraphed to Loader. When I see it safely
there I shall send another sovereign to the poor old woman,
who would probably not have parted with it in earlier and
better days. Her husband was once a gardener, but is now
blind. She might no doubt have got much more for it, had
she been on the look-out for a customer, as it is quite a
unique and beautiful thing. I shall be able before long to
show you photographs of one or two spots I greatly admired
at Winchelsea, and wished to recollect for pictures. I have
left an order with a local photographer to take pictures of

them for me, and have also ordered some which already exist of Northiam house and garden.

On the day after our arrival at Winchelsea there was a solemn procession to inaugurate the Sessions, which were opened by the Mayor. The procession consisted of about seven persons, including the Mayor in splendid robes of scarlet lined with sables, and three officials in blue robes, one of whom was the parish barber and another the carpenter. These had silver maces—really splendid pieces of design of about the time of Edward II. or III. at latest ; and I also saw the town-seal of the same period, and got an impression of it in gutta-percha—a very fine design. This procession was viewed in the street by a mob of one female child and by ourselves from the inn window. When it had entered the Town-hall, we rushed in in a mob of three, including the landlord. The public was decidedly out-numbered by the officials, who mustered perhaps fifteen in all—including a dog who belonged to one of the constables, and seemed to consider the extension of their staves during the Mayor's address to be pointedly aimed at him. The Sessions consisted of the Mayor being informed that there were no cases, and then severely animadverting on an individual who had once been found drunk in the streets about six months before, and adding that these observations having fallen from the bench would, he hoped, prevent the recurrence of such an evil in the future.

This may give you some idea of the pleasant doziness of the place, which is more to my taste I think than any other I know. Every one is eighty-two if he is not ninety-six.

·I feel very much better, and have come on here to-night, having heard that there are some interesting things in the neighbourhood. We may probably visit Stratford-on-Avon, Kenilworth, and Warwick, and perhaps take some other direction also before our return. I do not, however, expect to be away much more in all than a fortnight, though it *might* possibly be that I remained longer.

I hope your dear old health continues good, and that

W[illiam], M[aria], and C[hristina], are all well. Love to them and all the family. I do not suggest your answering this letter, as I could not tell you with certainty where to address me. Take care of your darling old self,

And believe me

Your most affectionate Son,

GABRIEL,

C 52.

In this letter there is a rather tart tone which speaks for itself. The general subject is the withdrawal from circulation of Mr. Swinburne's *Poems and Ballads*, by their first publishers, Messrs. Moxon & Co. Mr. Woolner had written to me that he had been charged with conducing to the withdrawal, or "suppression," of the volume; and that, the statement being untrue, he wished me to convey his denial to my brother. The "friendly duty [of my brother] towards Swinburne" had consisted, I believe, in calling on the publishers, and endeavouring to accommodate matters.

16 CHEYNE WALK.
27 September 1866.

MY DEAR WILLIAM,

Though withdrawn for the moment, Swinburne's book is not "suppressed," so no one need exonerate himself from having contributed to such a result. I myself jointly with Sandys· devoted one afternoon to what we considered a friendly duty towards Swinburne ; though not certainly, as you know, because we think the genius displayed in his works benefits by its association with certain accessory tendencies. Since then, my own constant occupations have prevented me from meddling further in the matter, or from becoming the reporter, apologist, or antagonist, of those who do or do not.

B 41.

During the little excursion which he made to Lymington and its neighbourhood, my brother was chiefly in the company of the poet Mr. Allingham, whom he had known since 1850 or thereabouts.

LYMINGTON, HANTS.
Thursday [19 *September* 1867].

DEAR GOOD ANTIQUE,

I have been out here about a week or rather more, and walking eight to ten miles a day, which I have enjoyed very much. There is plenty of delightful country all round, and the weather has been splendid. To-day, however, it seems breaking up for a time ; so, as I must choose some moment to come to London and look at copies going on for me, I may probably come now, and you may see me in a day or two, but I shall, I believe, be coming into the country here or elsewhere again for a while. The hedges are still beautiful here, plentifully enriched with honeysuckles, snap-dragons, and other flowers, and loaded with blackberries. Autumn gives the woods a monotony in their tints, but hardly as yet a decided change. I hope to find you well when I see you, and with love to brother and sisters and all relations am

Your most affectionate Son,
GABRIEL.

C 53.

Burnell Payne was a young clergyman (but he ceased from clerical work in the latter part of his brief life), and was also a writer on art, of keen perception and uncommon promise.

[16 CHEYNE WALK.
28 April 1868.]

DEAR W——,

Will you address and post this at once? Sandys's picture of Medea has been turned out of the R.A.—a most disgraceful affair. I have written also to Burnell Payne. Can *you* do anything in the way of denunciation?

B 42.

May 12, 1868.

MY DEAREST MOTHER,

The reminder of the solemn fact that I am a man of forty now could hardly come agreeably from any one but yourself. But, considering that the chief blessing of my forty good and bad years has been that not one of them has taken you from me, it is the best of all things to have the same dear love and good wishes still coming to me to-day from your dear hand at a distance as they would have done from your dear mouth had we seen each other. This we shall again soon, I trust.

I meant to have given you for your last dear birthday a sideboard which I have got, but some doing-up which it needed was not finished in time, nor indeed is yet quite done. I hope it may be of use to you, though rather large; but it is a really beautiful thing. It has a great plate-glass back with beautiful carved pillars, and some convenient drawers and receptacles. I forget the exact arrangement, but this gives some notion of it [*Diagram here*]. It strikes me the best place for it would be against the folding doors either in the drawing or dining room. The pillars are carved in the "Chippendale" style, and are really beautiful.

Will you give my love to Christina? I am writing to Uncle Henry with this. I hope you are benefiting by the change, and am ever

Your most affectionate Son,
D. GABRIEL ROSSETTI.

C 54.

I had travelled from London to Venice, stopping at Verona in an interval between trains; and, on arriving in Venice, I found that all my money for the trip, except the trivial sum which I had in my pocket, had been stolen at Verona out of my luggage. I had therefore had to telegraph to my brother to supply my present need: the following was his answer. Blumenthal & Co. are bankers in Venice, whom I had consulted on the subject.

17 *June* 1868.

DEAR W——,

I have paid a cheque, £30, into the Union Bank for you, and they have written to-day to Blumenthal & Co., 3945 Traghetto Sto. Benedetto, to pay you that sum. I

wanted the bank here to telegraph to Blumenthal to pay
you the money; but they said this was quite against the
rules, as frauds might be practised. I am much annoyed at
this delay, and do not even know whether you will get this
letter. I telegraphed to you last night in answer to your
telegram, and sent the message to Blumenthal's, as you
gave me no address in yours.

I am sending this to Euston Square in case they know
your address there, but otherwise can only send it to the
Poste Restante in hopes you may call for it. I greatly
regret that your trip should have been baulked by this
hitherto unexplained accident. I would have sent more
money if you had told me; as it is, I send 30 instead of
20; but I presumed, from your only naming that sum, that
it was all you needed. In great haste in middle of a sitting,
                              Your
                              D. GABRIEL ROSSETTI.

                    C 55.

                              16 CHEYNE WALK,
                              22 *June* |1868].

DEAR WILLIAM,
        It is extremely vexatious to think of the inconvenience
to which you have been put. However, I judge by the
telegram received at Euston Square that you got my first
telegram sent immediately on receipt of your first; and I
suppose another which I sent on seeing the one to Christina
has reached you too. I hope to-day you will have got the
money—£30—which I sent through the bank to Blumenthal
on the morning following your first telegram, and that you
will not find it necessary to cut your trip short. I will
show your letter to Mamma to-night, but probably she has
one too.

I wish I had come with you to Italy, but did not see the
great desirableness of it till just after you started. I suppose
from what you say that your pockets or luggage were rifled

without your knowing it, and trust you have not lost your watch also.

Of course I hope to hear of your getting the money, as this will ease my mind about your position.

Your affectionate Brother,

GABRIEL.

P.S.—I wished of course that the bank here should telegraph to Blumenthal to pay you the money; but this they would not do, as they said frauds would follow such a practice.

C 56.

This note was written from the ancient Scottish castle, the seat of our friend Miss Boyd; W. B. Scott was there along with my brother. "The Antique" was a designation of familiar affection which Gabriel (as some preceding letters have witnessed) applied to our Mother. This note is interesting as showing that the terrible affliction of sleeplessness, which was the origin of all the breaking-up of my brother's health, had already been going on some while before the autumn of 1868.

PENKILL CASTLE, GIRVAN, AYRSHIRE.
Saturday [26 *September* 1868].

DEAR W——,

Here I am after toils worthy of Æneas. I shall write before long to the Antique.

This is to ask you to send Scott any *Notes and Queries* that contain articles about the Fairford windows attributed to A. Durer.

I spent a couple of hours in the Exhibition at Leeds, where there are a good many things worth seeing: a most glorious Sandro Botticelli (Nativity), a very fine Carpaccio (*called* Landing of Queen Cornaro in Cyprus), and splendid heads by Titian, Morone, Bellini, and Velasquez.

This is a delightful place, and I slept better last night than I have done for a long time.

Your friends here send regards.

B 43.

PENKILL CASTLE, GIRVAN, AYRSHIRE.
October 2, 1868.

MY DEAREST MOTHER,

l have been meaning to write to you, but was in hopes of being able to give better news of my eyesight, which I am sorry to say is not the case yet. My sleep has improved extremely.

The glen belonging to the house here is a perfect paradise —one of the most beautiful spots I ever was in—and much of the scenery around is interesting. I take good walks and have a good appetite, and in most respects am perfectly well. The weather is in the main fine, and everything favourable ; Miss Boyd's kindness being extreme, and Scotus a good companion, though not over fond of locomotion. Visitors are fortunately most rare, only one party having as yet turned up. Of this party one member was Lady Waterford, who again spoke of the illustrations she had been making, in conjunction with Mrs. Boyle, to Christina's *Maiden Song*, and told me that Mr. Gladstone had repeated the poem to them by heart.

I do not yet know how long I may be staying, but I fear I should find work so little possible, were I to return to London at present, that I have no temptation to do so. However, I may perhaps soon find that I am inconveniencing Miss Boyd in her movements by staying here so late in the year, and that may bring me back.

With love to all at home, including Uncle Henry,
I am
Your most affectionate Son,
GABRIEL.

B 44.

The P.S. of this letter refers to the pictures from *The King's Quair*, by James I. of Scotland, which Mr. Scott painted in Penkill Castle. No doubt these pictures, by calling my brother's attention to the royal poet and his works, conduced to his writing, after an interval of several years, the ballad of *The King's Tragedy.*

GOOD ANTIQUE,

I'm afraid I didn't write very hopefully to you last time, so I had better enclose you a letter just received from Bader, the oculist of Guy's Hospital, who was the first I consulted. I have not seen him for some little time; but, since being here, received a note from him, and wrote in reply respecting some additional troublesome symptoms which had supervened since my seeing him. His favourable view seems, as you see, to be unaltered, however, if that is worth much. I thought at any rate you would like to see the note.

I have just got your dear letter, and one from Willia n. In yours I think I detect a funny old intention of writin ; large for the benefit of my sight. This would be quite in the Antique spirit.

The kindness of Miss Boyd is unbounded, and I suppose I shall not be returning to London at present. The weather here continues almost entirely fine in the daytime; indeed, more splendid walking weather could not well be imagined.

*   *   *   *   *   *

I get up very late here, to give myself the utmost benefit of sleep, which continues in a vastly improved condition. I then simmer gradually to walking-heat, and walk accordingly. In the evening, after dinner, we read aloud, and sometimes play whist. There is an aunt of Miss Boyd's, an old maiden lady named Miss Losh, a year younger than your funny old self, who is staying here, and is a nice, cheerful, intelligent old thing. I read a vast amount of Christina aloud the other evening, which was much enjoyed, though every one knew it already. The 2nd vol. only is here. A passage occurs in *L. E. L.* (Christina's poem) which says

"And rabbit thins his fur."

Miss Losh surmised this to refer to the habit of rabbits

female, which, when they expect a brood, pull off some of their own fur to make a soft bed. This indeed I witnessed in one of my own rabbits just before leaving Chelsea. Was this Christina's intention? In such case *his* should be changed to *its*, as *her* would not come in well.

With love to all,

Your most affectionate Son,

GABRIEL.

P.S.—I did not mention in my last that Scotus's pictures are now quite finished, and look very fine. There is a hedgehog together with other beasts, in the last one, which would delight Christina.

C 57.

The "plan" here referred to was that of the series of publications named *Moxon's Popular Poets*, which I had been invited to edit. Mr. J. Bertrand Payne was the acting partner in the Moxon firm. A volume of selections, not much unlike what my brother suggested, was compiled by me, but finally set aside by the publishers : my brother did not co-operate in it.

James Smetham was the artist who did the delicate little head and tail pieces to the earlier volumes of the series, of landscape-glimpses, foliage, etc. : he did not do any of the regular illustrations. Mr. Madox Brown and his son Oliver (here and elsewhere termed Nolly) did those for the Byron volume. Mr. Scott was not engaged.

[16 CHEYNE WALK.]
Thursday [4 *February* 1869].

DEAR W——,

I like the plan you tell me of. If I were you, I would certainly try and get Payne to conclude with (or include in the series) a volume of selected Minor Poets, comprising many good unknown things, such as Ebenezer Jones, etc. I would lighten your labours by assisting you in this. I don't understand if *old* poets are to be put into the series.

As to the etchings, Smetham is an available man certainly ; but do you propose having all the volumes done by one man?

It seems to me after all that Scott would not be so ineligible, besides that he seems to me under the circumstances almost unavoidable with pleasantness. However, I would mention it first of all to Brown, as I know he is particularly short of work just now, and it is just possible he might like to do it, perhaps with help from Nolly, or with Nolly's name and his own revision. Shields I think unlikely, as I have a decided impression he told me he would do no more book-illustrations. If you wish to try him, his address is

> F. J. S.
> Cornbrook House
> Cornbrook Park
> Manchester.

The only other man I can think of is Nettleship (unless Halliday might be also eligible). Nettleship would do well for Shelley or anything of that sort.

Of course I should be very glad if Smetham were selected, and he has the advantage of being quite as good at landscape as figures.

      *   *   *   *   *   *

I shall see you to-night at Scott's, but write in case talk be difficult there.

B 45.

The sonnets here described in so deadly-lively a style must be those which at this time had just been published in the *Fortnightly Review*, including the quartett named *Willow-wood*. The others were *Winged Hours*, *Sleepless Dreams*, *Broken Music*, *Inclusiveness*, *Known in Vain*, *The Landmark*, *Lost Days*, *Lost on both Sides*, *The Vase of Life*, *A Superscription*, and *Newborn Death*.

March 1, 1869.

DEAR DARLING,

    I send you my sonnets, which are such a lively band of bogies that they may join with the skeletons of Christina's various closets, and entertain you by a ballet. Their shanks

are rather ghastly, it is true, but they will keep their shrouds
down tolerably close, and creak enough themselves to render
a piano unnecessary. As their own vacated graves serve
them to dance on, there is no danger of their disturbing the
lodgers beneath ; and, if any one overhead objects, you may
say that it amuses them perhaps and will be soon over, and
that, as their hats were probably not buried with them, these
will not be sent round at the close of the performance.

It is to be feared indeed that they have left a growing
family who may be trained to the same line of business ; but
in the long run the cock crows, or the turnip-head falls
off the broomstick, or the price of phosphorus becomes an
obstacle, or the police turn up if necessary.

B 46.

The allusion to Christina at the close of this note indicates that
she was then away on a visit at Penkill Castle.

16 CHEYNE WALK.
14 *July* 1869.

GOOD ANTIQUE,

I have not been to see you for whole ages, and am
really most sorry to be so long without your dear company.
The last time I came you were gone to bed, and ever since
I have had an extraordinary number of engagements. I have
taken to going out more than before to dinner-parties etc.,
in the hope of shaking off *ennui*; and, as soon as one
begins that sort of thing, one gets involved to an extent
quite unforeseen. I shall certainly see you in an evening
or two, you dear old thing. And, if you can come up to
my place, the tent and weather together make the garden
charming at present. However, I may possibly be out one
day before the end of this week, so will not ask you to come
without appointment.

I hope you continue to have good news of Christina. I
shall turn up at Penkill myself some time before very long,
I dare say.

B 47.

PENKILL CASTLE, GIRVAN, AYRSHIRE.
Saturday [*August* 21, 1869].

GOOD ANTIQUE,

Here I am since Thursday afternoon, as I know you will be glad to hear in your maternal solicitude. I left London on Tuesday, and spent two nights and a day at old Miss Losh's house near Carlisle, where, as you may be sure, she made me very comfortable. I saw in the neighbourhood some most remarkable architectural works by a former Miss Losh, who was the head of the family about the year 1830. She must have been really a great genius, and should be better known. She built a church in the Byzantine style, which is full of beauty and imaginative detail, though extremely severe and simple. Also a mausoleum to her sister—a curious kind of Egyptian pile of stones with a statue of the lady in the centre, and opposite a Saxon cross—a sort of obelisk, reproduced from an old one, but with restorations by the lady herself. Also a Pompeian house for the schoolmaster, a parsonage, and a most interesting cemetery-chapel attached to a cemetery which she presented to the parish before such things were instituted by law. The chapel is an exact reproduction of one which was found buried in the sands in Cornwall, and excited a good deal of controversy at the time under the name of "The Lost Church." She also built a large addition to the family mansion at Woodside in the Tudor style. All these things are real works of genius, but especially the church at Wreay, a most beautiful thing. She was entirely without systematic study as an architect, but her practical as well as inventive powers were extraordinary. I am sure the whole of this group of her works would interest you extremely, and I should suggest your paying a visit to the neighbourhood on one of your holidays. There is also most lovely scenery, and some amiable Loshes besides the Miss Losh you wot of, whose house is called Ravenside (five miles from Carlisle), where I am sure she would be delighted to welcome you and yours if she heard you were likely to come her way. I suppose you would not be able to go this year, or it is possible I may be in the neighbourhood again on my way back to London. However, my movements are rather uncertain at present as to time, as I am not sure how long I may be able to remain here, from various causes.

Everything here is as pleasant as ever, and Miss Boyd sends you and Maggie her love, as does Scotus also. I have brought no work down, as I felt need of rest and was uncertain as to time.

I hope you are benefiting at Folkestone, and shall be delighted to hear so from yourself. What a good piece of news William's promotion was !

There is some prospect of Brown coming down here. Miss Losh seems very uncertain.

I am printing some old and new poems—chiefly old—for private circulation ; and shall send them you of course when the proofs are complete. To-day I am calling-in William's valuable aid for revision. My object is to keep them by me as stock to be added to for a possible future volume ; but in any case I thought it necessary to print them, as I found blundered transcripts of some of my old things were flying about, and would at some time have got into print perhaps,— a thing afflictive to one's bogie.

With love to Maggie,

Your most affectionate Son,

GABRIEL.

P.S.—I should have said that just before I left town I at last got possession of my stables, and shall very probably be turning them at once into a fine big studio, but must first see about getting leave to build and an extension of lease.

P.P.S.—I suppose I told you of my seeing Bowman before I left London, and that, instead of taking a guinea fee (which he refused), he proposes to pay me 150 for a little water-colour which is fortunately just upon finished, so that the tin will come in conveniently on my return to town without much additional trouble. Scott and Miss Boyd both desire to be most kindly remembered to you.

C 58.

The early lyric *To Mary in Summer*, and the sonnet *The French Liberation of Italy*, were cut out, as here proposed, from my brother's published volume, and they remain unpublished. The sonnet *The Bullfinch* appears printed as *Beauty and the Bird*.

[PENKILL CASTLE, AYRSHIRE.]
Saturday [21 *August* 1869].

DEAR WILLIAM,

After much bother with the proofs, and constantly finding new blunders, I have bethought myself to bother you with them, so send them with this by book-post. Would you read them through, and, if you find anything obviously wrong, correct it? In punctuation I have my own ideas, which may not be yours, so I will ask you generally to leave this alone ; but, if anything seems like a printer's error, will you notify it to me, and I will tell you whether to alter it? Also I should wish much to know of anything you disliked in any poem, as it is still time to alter.

I believe I am likely to cut out *Mary in Summer*, *The Choice* (three sonnets), and *The Bullfinch* (sonnet) ; but am not yet quite certain. I hesitated much to print *Ave*, because of the subject ; but thought it well done, and so included it. Do you think the foot-note is sufficient as a protest? The question I asked about "wert" and "wast" refers chiefly to a line in the first paragraph of this—"Thou hast been sister, etc.,"—which if admissible I should make, "Thou once wert sister," etc. So, if you think this will do, put it.

   *   *   *   *   *

Sonnet, *French Liberation of Italy*, I have removed from the second section, and shall not replace.

When you have realized all your ideas on the proofs, I wish you would write me *at once*. You need not send them back to me, as I have another set. But I will write you when to send them on to the printer. Love to Christina.

C 59.

"The Italian poem" is the one beginning "La bella donna" introduced into *A Last Confession*. I had informed my brother that

I considered some of the lines lax in metre, according to Italian prosody. The lyric *A Song and Music* was eventually omitted from his volume of 1870, but it appears in the *Ballads and Sonnets*, 1881. "The article in Tinsley" was one of the series of articles in *Tinsley's Magazine* on *Our Living Poets*, written by Mr. H. B. Forman—the one which related to my brother.

[PENKILL CASTLE, AYRSHIRE.]
Thursday [26 *August* 1869].

DEAR W——,

Thanks for your valuable letter. I am attending to it, and will do so further when I get your concluding admonitions. I have sent the Italian poem to Maggie to see if she makes the same remarks, and should like to show it to Teodorico. You know, I think there is no doubt that metre of this kind abounds in the *early* poets.

*   *   *   *   *   *

I think I shall omit the *Song and Music*, page 67.

*   *   *   *   *   *

I remember I had made additions (now lost) at points which I thought abrupt in *Stratton Water* and *Staff and Scrip*. In *Stratton Water* some stanzas were inserted after "The nags were in the stall" (page 48), to give the gradual impression of his recognizing the girl whom he thought dead. Do you think it is necessary to write something of the sort again?

In *Staff and Scrip* there was something added where the damsel gives her the relics, to develop this incident and help the transition. Does this seem necessary? Or is there any other point in any of the poems which seems to want working out?

I have added a first stanza to *Sister Helen*, as Scott said the impression of what was going on was not perfectly distinct.

Would the title of the Sonnet at page 93 run better *On the Refusal of Aid to Hungary*, 1849, *to Poland*, 1861, *to Crete*, 1867, or is it better in the simpler form?

The article in *Tinsley* is gratifying. . . . I suppose, from your not being recurred to, there will certainly be a third on you. The raking up of *My Sister's Sleep* will I fancy render it necessary for me to include that rather spoony affair in my reprint, as, now attention is attracted a little to it, it may go on till the thing gets into print again without the correction it ought to have. What think you? I don't remember it clearly, and would be obliged if you or Christina would take the trouble of copying it from the *Germ*, and sending it here by return of post. If Christina would read my things, and give any hints that occur to her, I would be thankful. Tell her this with my love.

B 48.

PENKILL.
26 August 1869.

MY DEAREST MOTHER,

I was very glad to hear from you again, and know that you have been enjoying your trip. The weather here is splendid, though so warm for walking that I generally change my shirt on coming in!

I am doing no work except a little in the way of revising proofs, at which William is now affording me his usual most valuable help. He has fallen very foul of a little Italian poem of mine in which he finds various errors of metre and even of grammar. I would like Maria's opinion, and so enclose it without mentioning the weak points found by William. Will she at her leisure give me *her* verdict? Of course it is meant to be a very irregular sort of antiquated Italian, and I am pretty sure quite as bad slips are continual among the earliest poets.

I have seen *Tinsley*, which is so far satisfactory that, after twenty years, one stranger has discovered one's existence. The . . . opinions supremely correct for the most part, *as far as they go*! ! From what was said in the former article about William, and from the absence of all recurrence to him in this one, I have no doubt he will furnish matter for a third.

I believe I have yet nine years of my lease at Cheyne Walk to run. Thus my plan will be to apply for an extension of lease before building ; but, if this is refused, or a very considerable immediate increase of rent made the condition of it, I shall then, I think, build irrespective of contingencies, as nine years is a long time ; indeed, Time may be no longer for one, for anything one knows.

With love to Maggie,

Your most affectionate Son,

D. GABRIEL R.

P.S.—It is pleasant to know that poor Henrietta is suffering somewhat less.

I believe the author of the *Tinsley* articles is probably a man named Forman, unknown to me.

C 60.

The reader who takes sufficient interest in the minutiæ of my brother's poems should look up the volume of 1870, and follow out in it the points here mooted. I should soon get tedious if I adventured to explain them in detail. I will only say that pages 16 and 14 belong (in the original form of printing not for publication) to *The Burden of Nineveh* ; 25 and 22 to *Ave* ; 5 and 1 to *The Blessed Damozel* ; 10 and 8 to *Love's Nocturn* ; 65 to *Plighted Promise* ; 147 to *The Choice* ; 157 to *Retro me Sathana* ; 167 to *Our Lady of the Rocks* ; 169 to *A Venetian Pastoral* ; 177 to *Venus*. The concluding reference to San Rocco relates to the prose story of *Hand and Soul*. I had pointed out to my brother that San Rocco lived at a date subsequent to the supposed date of this narrative, and that consequently a church dedicated to him could not then have existed.

PENKILL.
Friday 27 August 1869.

DEAR W——,

Your second to hand to-day. I'll now go over some of your ground—neglecting such things as I quite agree in, and ignoring others here and there, where they involve corrections I must attend to.

Page 16. *Mummies.*—This I had thought of already, and it troubled me. I can alter it as follows :—

> "A traveller. Nay, but were not some
> Of these even then antiquity?"

Or "thine own antiquity?" Which is the best?

The word *traveller* I do not quite like. I meant no more by *pilgrim.* Do you think the change desirable?

* * * * * *

Page 25. I don't like to shorten the last line. It used to stand "*Saint* Mary Virgin," etc. Is this better? There is a point in this poem I am going to change, either less or more thus (the present simile trivial for the sea) :—

Page 22.

> "the sea
> Sighed further off eternally,
> human ⎫
> As heavy ⎬ sorrow sighs in sleep."
> ancient ⎭

or,

> "Like ancient sorrow or sad sleep."

The first would require to change *eyes* in next line to *gaze.* However, I am not sure whether I do not wish to omit the whole five lines beginning " Within " and ending " through," and substitute one comprehensive line of some sort rhyming to *sleep.* What say you? In last page of *Ave,* I remember I had changed *arrayed* into some word more of the same latinized value as *conjoint,* but cannot remember what. Can you suggest a word?

Page 5. A question I wish to ask on my own hook is whether *trembling* or *tremulous* would be best in the last line in italics. The first is objectionable because of *stepping* above, but does not the second trip awkwardly? "Circlewise": would this be better, "They sit in circle"? I dare say you agree with the removal of *lapse* for "flight" in last stanza but one.

Page 1. "And her hair lying down her back." Is the sound awkward? Is "And her hair laid upon" etc. better?

Page 10. Does the last stanza of this page seem awkwardly interpolated? and does it seem that a more distinct speech for the spirit is necessary to introduce the next stanza?

Page 8. Third stanza—last line sounds shortish, but is not. What do you say? Suggest anything.

Page 65. Hecate wouldn't do, as it reminds the general world of *Macbeth.* I see no objection to Luna, but none either to Cynthia except that people know it less as meaning the moon. Dian would answer best of all for the meaning of the passage, but I didn't like the sound so well as Luna. I like the long lines myself.

*   *   *   *   *   *

Page 14. It occurs to me to go back and ask your opinion on a point here. The stanza "On London stones" is combined from what was once two stanzas. The change was made when I printed the poem first.

"On London stones. . . .

. . . . the old earth and sea.
How much Heaven's thunder—how much else
Man's puny roar?—what cry of shells
Cleft amid leaguered citadels—
How many lordships loud with bells
Heardst thou in secret Nineveh?

Oh when upon each sculptured court
Where even the wind might not resort—
O'er which Time passed, of like import
With the wild Arab boys at sport—
A living face looked in to see,—
Oh seemed it not," etc. . . . .

I hardly know why I made the omission, except for the great end of condensation. Is there anything lost by it, and does the present form seem at all abrupt? However, Scott, to whom I have just read what I am writing for *his* opinion, thinks the second half of the first stanza rather extraneous, but the first half of the second a great gain. I have some idea that Brown once suggested difficulties about the shells, bells, etc.—could they be heard under the earth? were there any to be heard? etc.   If you think first half second stanza *very* desirable, and the previous omitted lines objectionable, try and suggest some point of idea to fill the gap.

Page 147. "Care, gold, and care," can be altered to "Vain gold, vain lore," which meets your views.   There is a very vexatious point connected with this sonnet which was one reason for my thinking of omitting the three.   The idea, "They die not, never having lived," is identical with one at the close of Browning's *In a Gondola*.   I know that I had never then read that poem, and that on first reading it this annoying fact struck me at once; but then this is not known to the world.   The point is just what is wanted, and not possible to alter.   There is a similar case in the *Nocturn* (page 8)—"Lamps of an *auspicious* soul" stood in my last correction (made long ago) "pellucid," which is much finer. But lately in the *Ring and Book* I came on *pellucid soul* applied to Caponsacchi, and the inevitable charge of plagiarism struck me at once as impending whenever my poem should be printed.

There is also in the *Ring and Book* "Pale frail wife," which interferes in the same way with the "*pale frail mist*" of my *New Year's Burden*, also of course written long before. But this I left.

Page 157. "Many years," etc., is a favourite line of mine. It used to stand *A few years*, etc., which of course was one of the impossible intonations of that early epoch.

Page 167. I also object to *difficult* rhyming with *vault* of course most absolutely.   But, the distance from rhyme to rhyme being considerable, and alteration difficult, I have left it.   I suppose I did not notice it at the moment of writing the sonnet (in front of the picture in British Institution many years ago), though I know I did just afterwards.

Page 169. "Life touching lips," etc.   I remember you expressed a preference once before for the old line, which seems to me quite bad.   "Solemn poetry" belongs to the class of phras absolutely forbidden, I think, *in* poetry.   It is intellectually incestuous,—poetry seeking to beget its emotional offspring on its own identity. Whereas I see nothing too " ideal " in the present line. It gives only the momentary contact with the immortal which results from sensuous culmination, and is always a half-conscious element of it.

   *   *   *   *   *   *

Page 177. " Venus Verticordia." I knew the passage in Lemprière—*since* writing the sonnet, or rather christening the picture. It is awkward. I'll cut the " Verticordia " out here, I think.

Pages 202, 207. " San Rocco." Please suggest a new saint.

On reflection, I think the best plan will be for you to post your set of proofs to me *at once* on getting this letter, as I have other changes to make in them before sending back to the printer, and can more shortly do them myself than explain them to you.

Please answer questions here asked as soon as possible. I will probably apply again for Christina's views with the *next* revise.

C 61.

Leys, mentioned in the P.S. of this letter, was Baron Leys, the famous Belgian painter. The inspiration and excellence of his works were such as could not fail to secure my brother's hearty admiration.

PENKILL.
Tuesday [31 *August* 1869].

DEAR W——,

Thanks for your note to-day. I think I shall most likely omit the Italian poem. At the same time I get Christina's copy of *Sister's Sleep*, which I return tattooed to you for consultation. The thing is very distasteful to me as it stands, and I have quite determined on all changes made in pen and ink. In pencil I indicate a very radical change in the omission of two more stanzas which would eliminate the religious element altogether. Scott thinks the poem in

this most rarified form is simplest and best, and I incline to
that view myself.   However, I feel by no means quite sure,
and have annotated the MS. explaining my conflicting views.
Will you give them your best attention, and let me know
your views on all the points?   I should not care to reprint
this thing at all, were it not for the likelihood of its reappearing some day otherwise without even the changes
absolutely necessary.

      *   *   *   *   *   *

In *Love-Lily* do you like best

> " Ah let not life be still distraught,"

(as it stands) or

> " Ah let not *hope*" etc. ?

In this poem it has crossed my mind to change the title, and
merely use a proper name, as *Dorothy*.   What is the meaning
of that name?   I forget.   But I do not think I shall really
do this.   What say you?   " Whose speech *truth* knows not "
etc. is better than *faith*, is it not?

But perhaps, as it occurs to me the proof will probably
have left you before you get this, I had better put off further
questions till I can send you them again in a revised state.

Your
D. G. R.

I don't think dating throughout would do.

I had not heard of Leys's death.   It is indeed a sad and
premature event.   He called on me the year before last, or
beginning of last, looking perfectly well.

P.P.S.—What do you think of the proposed note to *Sister's
Sleep*?   The curse of *In Memoriam* would be thus avoided.
I remember too there is some Christmas Eve business in
In Memoriam, but what I cannot remember.   Of course the
note is strictly true.   This *In Memoriam* question was one
great reason for my burking it.

Will you thank Christina much, with my love ?

C 62.

The only passage in this letter which requires elucidation is the paragraph " About Miching Mallecho." I had been struck with a couplet in Longfellow's *Hiawatha* about an American-Indian mythologic personage—

> " Mitche Manito the mighty,
> He the dreadful Spirit of Evil "—

and had queried whether this possibly might throw light on the much-debated phrase in *Hamlet* " Miching Mallecho." I soon afterwards wrote on the subject to *Notes and Queries*. I think the point was never followed up by other correspondents ; nor perhaps did it deserve to be.

PENKILL.
Thursday [2 *September* 1869].

DEAR W——,

To-day I have sent my proofs to the printers, and told them to forward you a corrected set, as well as one to me. This I suppose will be before many days. I benefited much by your labours, as you will see. Your last line to the Satan sonnet I adopted with a slight change, but am rather uncertain whether I may not change back again. What you said of the foggy opening of *Nocturn* induced me to restore a second stanza which I had cut out in printing it, in case this might make things any clearer. I have also added three new stanzas towards the close of this poem, to develop the sudden flight of the bogie on finding another bogie by the girl's bed, which seemed funkyish, though of course the right thing if she was already in love. I have also added three stanzas at the point I referred to in *Stratton Water*, and made the proposed restoration (with addition) to the *Nineveh*. Also added a further useful stanza in the middle of *Sister Helen*.

    *   *   *   *   *   *

I have cut out *Mary in Summer, Song and Music*, and

the Italian thing, about which I am sorry you should have taken certainly more trouble than it deserved.

I await your opinion about *Sister's Sleep*. I have sent to be inserted one new sonnet, two more old ones revised, and an old poem, *The Card Dealer*, which I have divested of trivialities.

About "Miching Mallecho," I must say Keightley's explanation seems to me final, unless he has really quite made some mull of the language. Have you reason to think so? Certainly the coincidence you have been struck by is very singular, and, failing Keightley, well worth following up. I suppose the name is not Longfellow's invention?

    *   *   *   *   *   *

Have you heard of the death of poor little Burnell Payne after a few days' illness?

Love from all here.

C 63.

My brother thought much from time to time about his proposed poem *The Orchard Pit* (or, as he generally called it, *The Orchard Pits*). His prose synopsis of the subject, and a few verses which were to have formed part of the poem, are printed in his *Collected Works*. The other poem which he had now begun was, I think, *The Stream's Secret*, or possibly *Eden Bower*. The wombat was a specimen of that quaint Australian beast which had arrived at Gabriel's London house during his absence at Penkill Castle.

PENKILL.
Tuesday [14 *September* 1869].

MY DEAR W——,

I suppose ere this you have doubtless got the new proofs of which I received a set yesterday. You will see much that is due to your labours in them. However, I have been at work on them still further now, and have done various things. I have revised the additional verses to *Stratton Water*, which were rather in the rough, and have added one further on about the priest in a funk. In the

additional verses to *Nocturn* I have made the following change
in the third, which now runs :—

> " So a chief who all night lies
>   Ambushed where no help appears—
> 'Mid his comrades' unseen eyes
>   Watching for the growth of spears—
>   Like their ghosts, as morning nears,
>   Sees them rise,
>   Ready without sighs or tears."

I think you will agree with me that this is preferable, as in
the first form the plural pronouns applied to " legion " were
awkward.

However, I have been worrying about what you said of
the obscurity of the opening of this poem, and have now put
it thus :—

> " Master of the murmuring courts
>   Where the shapes of sleep convene !
> Lo ! my spirit here exhorts
>   All the powers of thy demesne
>   For their aid to woo my queen.
>   What reports
>   Yield thy jealous courts unseen ?
>
> " Vaporous, unaccountable,
>   Dreamland lies unknown to light,
> Hollow like a breathing shell.
>   Ah that from all dreams I might
>   Choose one dream and guide its flight !
>   I know well
>   What her sleep should tell to-night."

Surely this makes all plain, does it not ? Dreamland is a
rather hackneyed phrase I don't like, but it is so valuable
for clearing up that I adopted it.

Now there is another question. The first conception of
this poem was of a man not yet in love who dreams vaguely
of a woman who he thinks must exist for him. This is not
very plainly expressed, and not I think very valuable, and
it might be better to refer the love to a known woman whom
he wishes to approach. There is only one stanza I think
that stands in the way of this interpretation,—the one be-

ginning " As since man waxed deathly wise"; and I want
your opinion as to whether it would not be better to cut
this stanza out. It is a good one, but is rather objectionable
as resembling in its rhymes the penultimate preceding one.
I think it should go. Another slight point. The fourth
stanza used to say :—

> " Youth's warm fancies all are there :
>   There the elf-girls flood with wings
>   Valleys full of plaintive air," etc.

This perhaps flows better, and I have just noticed that in
the present version there is " whisperings " rhyming with
" rings," which is bad. But on the other hand I like the new
meaning best. What is your view?

You will have noticed another new stanza in *Sister Helen*
—" But he calls for ever on your name," etc. This is
valuable for elucidation. However, I have improved both
this and stanza 1.

*   *   *   *   *   *

In *Penumbra* I have altered in last stanza " rasp the sands "
to " chafe." The other seemed violent and inexact. In
sonnet *A Dark Day*—" sowed hunger *once*,"—I believe this
used to stand *since*. Which is better?

In *Mary's Girlhood*—" This is," etc. Could one say as well
—" '*Tis of* that blessed " etc.? In *Palmifera* sonnet there is
" *This is* that Lady Beauty"; and I think the same form
is elsewhere.

Venus sonnet has—" She hath the apple in" etc. Now
" apple " is here placed awkwardly between two vowels, which
makes the prosody dubious. Does any change suggest itself?

In the new sonnet, *Parted Love*, the last line is declared by
Scott to be too violent. Do you think so? It occurs to me
to say, "And thy feet stir not, and thy body endures." Do
you like this better? It conveys the sense of impotent reten-
tion, which is wanted, but that is already conveyed in line
seven. You will observe that I have now included two old
sonnets, *Autumn Idleness* and *A Match with the Moon*. The

first as now revised I like well. The second I like too, but do you think it lays itself open to ridicule?

The Card Dealer you will find improved, I doubt not.

I am now sending the printer seven new sonnets, of which four are for designs of mine—viz., two for *Cassandra*, one for *Passover*, and one for *Magdalene*. I think this may help me in defending the subjects against plagiarists. I think all are very good. I have also begun two new poems. One, called *The Orchard Pit*, will be my best thing; but I have not yet got much beyond a careful synopsis in prose, which I consider a very good plan of action. I shall certainly go on and finish it as soon as may be, as I feel great confidence in it. The other I have done rather more to. I find this place most favourable to writing, and should soon get into very regular habits of production.

However, I had determined to leave here next Thursday, but find so much more benefit within the last few days than before that I may perhaps stay on till Tuesday next, on which day I certainly expect to start homeward, but may be detained a day with Miss Losh. I have felt far from well till just now, but am now feeling better.

*　　*　　*　　*　　*　　*

I was nearly forgetting the Italian poem, which I had put pretty well out of my head. I sent it to Teodorico, and enclose you his answer and new version, which no doubt you will think with me rather modern and loaded. I cannot gather clearly that he objects on grounds of *prosody* other than what may be said to depend on taste. If you see him, you might discuss the point. I must answer his letter. Of course if I print the thing it must be as I wrote it, or nearly so. Should a version resulting from mine and his occur to you, I would be obliged by your sending it me. I am sick of the affair.

With love to all,

Your affectionate
GABRIEL,

Have you seen the wombat?

C 64.

"The sea must remain at Nazareth." This refers to a passage in the poem *Ave :* I had pointed out to my brother that Nazareth is far distant from any sea. The passage about Mr. Scott and Durer refers to the proofs, which I was about this time looking over, of our friend's *Life of Durer.* "The Shrine in the Italian taste" which Christina had reared for the wombat consisted of certain verses in the Italian language.

PENKILL.
Wednesday [15 *September* 1869].

DEAR W——,

I may as well answer one or two points in your letter.

Page 24. I fear the sea must remain at Nazareth ; you know an old painter would have made no bones if he wanted it for his background. The lines following this I have altered now.

    °   *   *   *   *   *   *

I have made a change in the *Hill Summit* (page 141) thus :—

"And, now that I have climbed and won this height,
   I must tread downward through the sloping shade,
And travel the bewildered tracks till night.
   Yet for this hour I still may here be stayed," etc.

The symbolism being thus more distinct than before, do you not think this sonnet should properly be transferred to the *House of Life* section?

I am in a rather productive mood, and have written two sonnets since writing to you yesterday. For one of the *Cassandra* ones, I want to know whether Achilles killed Hector with a sword or a spear. Will you look this up? or perhaps you know.

Scott wanted me to tell you that you were to keep back a certain proof of his where a newly-discovered Durer picture should be described, till he hears whether it is genuine or not.

Will you thank Maggie for her most complete information about the Passover? Also Christina for the Shrine in the Italian taste which she has reared for the wombat. I fear his habits tend inveterately to drain-architecture. I wrote for directions about his food to Nettleship, who is always at the Zoo, and he has sent me some. It appears the wombat follows people all over the house!

About the Byron business, I certainly think I have heard —— allude to the connexion with his sister. *I* also thought at first there could be no doubt, but am very uncertain now. It seems to me by no means impossible that Lady Byron laboured under a hallucination on this subject; and that, even if she did rear an illegitimate child of Byron's, this particular attribution of its birth *may* have been her own inveterate fancy. The question of relationship raised in the *Times* is well worth considering also. Did you see a letter by a man named Radclyffe in the *Telegraph* (I think)? He was brought up by Mrs. Leigh, and speaks in the most reverential terms of her,—employing I must say a rather Irish style of phraseology. It has been sent here, and, if you have not seen it, I can look it up for you.

(P.S.—I send it.)

Lastly . . . the vital interest of his poetry is all we have to do with.

Your

GABRIEL.

P.S.—Scott agrees, especially with the last sentiment.

I saw a letter from W. Howitt in one paper about Lady Byron's great obstinacy in fixed ideas.

I still have rather a grudge to the three sonnets called *The Choice.* Do you feel sure they ought to be in? Also to the two on Ingres's picture, which are merely picturesque, and which stupid people are sure to like better than better things.

C 65.

[16 CHEYNE WALK.]
Tuesday [21 *September* 1869].

DEAR WILLIAM,

I came back last night, and shall of course be seeing you immediately ; but write lest you should write again to Penkill.

Your last letter has already been sent back to me here. I wrote some more poetry, and one Ballad, which is my best thing, I think—*Troy Town.*

The Wombat is " A Joy, a Triumph, a Delight, a Madness."

I have got *Tinsley* to-day. They treat you very respectfully, but are obtuse about *Mrs. Holmes Grey,* which they discuss at great length. Perhaps you will have it.

Your affectionate

GABRIEL.

I have seen no one yet.

C 66.

Sunday [3 *October* 1869].

DEAR W——,

Will you dine here Thursday ? I hope so. Nettleship and Brown are coming—also Tebbs. . . . I hope you will manage to come.

I suppose you have the proofs. I have improved a good many lines in the *Eden* since seeing it in print. Also done other things to the proofs.

*   *   *   *   *   *

C 67.

13 *October* 1869.

MY DEAR WILLIAM,

I wished last night to speak to you on a subject which however I find it necessary to put in writing. I am very anxious to know your view of it, and to remind you beforehand that no mistrust or unbrotherly feeling could possibly have caused my silence till now.

Various friends have long hinted from time to time at the possibility of recovering my lost MSS., and when I was in Scotland last year Scott particularly referred to it. Some months ago Howell of his own accord entered on the matter, and offered to take all the execution of it on himself. This for some time I still hung back from accepting ; but eventually I yielded, and the thing was done, after some obstacles. on Wednesday or Thursday last, 1 forget which. An order had first to be obtained from the Home Secretary, who strangely enough is an old and rather intimate acquaintance of my own—H. A. Bruce. . . . All in the coffin was found quite perfect ; but the book, though not in any way destroyed, is soaked through and through, and had to be still further saturated with disinfectants. It is now in the hands of the medical man who was associated with Howell in the disinterment, and who is carefully drying it leaf by leaf. There seems reason to fear that some minor portion is obliterated, but I most hope this may not prove to be the most important part. 1 shall not, I believe, be able to see it for at least a week yet.

I trust you will not—but I know you cannot—think that I showed any want of confidence in not breaking this painful matter to you before its issue. It was a service I could not ask you to perform for me, nor do I know any one except Howell who could well have been entrusted with such a trying task. It was necessary, as we found, that a lawyer should be employed in the matter, to speak to the real nature of the MSS., as difficulties were raised to the last by the Cemetery Authorities as to their possibly being papers the removal of which involved a fraud.

*   *   *   *   *   *

C 68.

Friday [16 *October* 1869].

DEAR WILLIAM,

I am glad to hear you are getting better, and very glad you view the matter on which I wrote as I do.

*   *   *   *   *   *

Yesterday I went to see the book at the Doctor's house. It will take some days yet to dry, and is in a disappointing but not hopeless state.

Your affectionate
GABRIEL.

P.S.—You know I always meant to dedicate the book to you. This I shall of course still do.

*   *   *   *   *   *

C 69.

Wednesday [20 October 1869].

DEAR W——,

Could you dine here Sunday? One or two fellows are coming, and I would esteem it a boon if you could come. I hope you are better. I got the MSS. to-day.

C 70.

The binding here referred to was to have been for the edition of Shelley, two volumes, which I brought out through the Moxon Firm at the beginning of 1870. The design was regarded by the Firm as involving over-much cost in execution, and nothing came of it. I have quite forgotten now what it was like.

[16 CHEYNE WALK.]
Wednesday [1 December 1869].

DEAR WILLIAM,

In setting Dunn to work at your binding to-day, I find I need the exact size. If you will send it me by return of post, I dare say I shall be able to let you have the thing on Saturday, or Monday at latest. The colour could not be better than that apple-green roan ; but, if they won't take the trouble of staining the cloth to this, let the binder send me his patterns and I will choose a grey of some sort. I remember to have seen a sort of dull indigo-grey once which is not a bad colour.

*   *   *   *   *   *

B 49.

Commonplace and Other Short Stories, prose, is a volume by Christina, now perhaps not very readily procurable : it was not a success with the public. As yet it was only in MS. The article in the *Pall Mall Gazette* related to my edition of Shelley, with Memoir.—It will be seen from this letter that the idea, hitherto generally put forward, that my brother's poem *The Stream's Secret* was written wholly at Penkill, is far from correct.

[SCALANDS, ROBERTSBRIDGE.]
Tuesday [22 *March* 1870].

MY DEAR MOTHER,

Will you thank Christina for the arrival this morning of *Commonplace*, which I already like the looks of? Also thanks to yourself for the *Pall Mall* article, which I will return shortly. It is of course the best I have yet seen. Among the fault-findings as to points of expression at the end, I rather agree with some, but not with others ; notably not with that about the closing sentence of the Memoir, to which I see no objection—though it certainly belongs, in *legitimate* measure, to the class of expression which the Yankees have vulgarized by hyperbole.

I should, as you may suppose, have written before this in answer to yours, if I had been able to give any very favourable account of myself, but I am not very brilliant. I suppose I may perhaps stay a fortnight longer. Stillman is a very pleasant and kindly companion, never obtrusive and always helpful. . . . His little boy is, I fear, not for this world.

I have written just a sheet of additions to my book since I came here, and it is now printing—to wit, a poem called *The Stream's Secret*, of which I had a few opening stanzas already done, and a few additional sonnets. I shall certainly get the book out before the end of April, as three or four friendly hands are already at work on it for the May periodicals. Swinburne is to do it in the *Fortnightly*. . . . The binding is in progress, and will I hope be a success. . . .

God bless you, dear old darling, is the heartfelt prayer of

Your most affectionate Son,

GABRIEL.

F 8.

Miss Boyd, whatever the reason, did not actually produce any designs engraved as woodcuts in the *Commonplace* volume : there are not any illustrations.

[SCALANDS, ROBERTSBRIDGE.]
Wednesday [23 *March* 1870].

DEAR CHRISTINA,

I have read *Commonplace* (which I return by bookpost), and like it very much. It certainly is not dangerously exciting to the nervous system, but it is far from being dull for all that, and I should think it likely to take. Stillman and I noted one or two trifles on the opposite blank pages for your consideration—mere trifles. He likes it much also.

I return the MS. by bookpost. No doubt Ellis will be very glad to have it as soon as you can let him. I am glad Miss Boyd is to do the woodcuts.

Your affectionate
GABRIEL.

P.S.—Of course I think your proper business is to write poetry, and not *Commonplaces*.

P.P.S.—You will be sorry to learn that I hear from Boulogne to-day that old Maenza is dead, just as he was thinking of making a move towards Italy. His poor old wife is of course in a sad state. If any of you would like to write condolences, the address is 19 Rue Simoneau, Boulogne-sur-Mer. She did not write to me herself, but a certain Neapolitan music-master named Siesto, whom I remember there centuries ago, and whose feelings are expressed in three notes of admiration at a time.

B 50.

" My large picture " is the *Dante's Dream*, now belonging to the Walker Art Gallery in Liverpool. " Janey Morris " is Mrs. William Morris : to her highly distinguished husband the nickname "Top " (oftener " Topsy ") had clung ever since his under-graduate days in

Oxford. "The Nortons" are Professor Charles Eliot Norton, a well-known and much-esteemed American man of letters, and his family.

SCALANDS, ROBERTSBRIDGE. HAWKHURST.
Monday [18 *April* 1870].

MY DEAREST MOTHER,

I have not written to you for an age, but have been meaning to do so, only things did not look promising enough to be worth talking about. However, for the last few days this glorious weather seems to be doing me good in some ways at any rate. It is impossible not to feel a different being when such a change is going on all round one. But indeed I have improved for some time past in one essential respect—*i.e.* that the pains I had constantly in the eyes and head have almost entirely left me,—quite so indeed but for a very slight and occasional twinge. I have been drawing regularly, though not many hours, for several days, and am beginning to feel more cheerful. The air is delicious—the weather very hot just now while the sun lasts, but exquisitely cool in the evenings. I send you specimens of the wild flowers which are all out in immense profusion everywhere ; as to the primroses, the country is already smothered in them. The white violets came in a swarm, and are now almost gone. The blue ones are everywhere now, and the wood-anemones, of which I send a few, are most delightful, as well as the wild daffodils. Lambs have tails, and begin to prance a little. They and their mothers make various toy-noises, only the mothers' are penny noises, and the lambs' halfpenny ones.

I find Mme. B[odichon] will need this place after the 7th, but I may possibly stay on till nearly that time if I can manage it. My book is to be out by the end of next week, and perhaps I shall have to come up then for a day.

Things are not quite idle with me in London, as regards work ; since Dunn is grouping the studies for my large picture together, so that it will be ready for me to begin on the moment I return.

Jancy Morris is here, and benefiting greatly. Top comes from time to time. I have an invitation to go to Florence to the Nortons, and fancy I might be wise to accept it, but time is an anxious matter. Would William go if I did?

With love to all,

Your most affectionate Son,

GABRIEL.

B 51.

SCALANDS, ROBERTSBRIDGE, HAWKHURST.
4 *May* 1870.

DEAR OLD DARLING OF 70,

I ought to have put in the book I sent you that it was a birthday present. I did not forget the dear day (27 April), only forgot the inscription. I hope you liked the binding, which I think very successful ; only the back of the pattern has been made too wide, which renders a ridiculous padding of blank paper necessary inside. This will be remedied in the second edition by having the back part recut. Also the fly-leaves will be printed on a greenish paper. At present they look raw. You will be glad to hear that the first edition is almost exhausted, and that Ellis is going to press with the second thousand copies. There are going to be a few special copies printed on large paper, of which I shall get one for you. I was in town for a few hours only last Tuesday week in order to inscribe copies at the publisher's, but returned here in the afternoon. I expect probably to come back for good, or at any rate for the present, early next week. But I believe nothing would do me so much good, if I could make it convenient, as to bring work down and spend the summer in this neighbourhood, so as to get out in good air whenever I pleased. There is a lovely old mansion near here in which I could rent a set of rooms which would do well to paint in, and I have serious thoughts of it ; but in any case I should have to return to London at present, to start fair with my painting and see what I should be going on with.

I dare say you have seen the reviews of my book in *Pall*

Mall, Fraser, Athenæum, etc., and been duly thunderstruck at Swinburne's miraculous article.

I am wonderfully better within the last month—specially last fortnight, and have no doubt I am really benefited in every way, but London might bring on a relapse for all that.

Janey Morris is much better. Top is coming down again to-day, and we shall make some more excursions probably, as there are various things worth seeing.

My book will have brought me £300 in less than a month, which is not so bad for poetry, particularly if it goes on. Love to all.

A 25.

16 CHEYNE WALK.
24 *May* 1870.

MY DEAR AUNT,

I just hear from Mamma, with a pang of remorse, that you have ordered a copy of my *Poems.* You may be sure I did not fail to think of you when I inscribed copies to friends and relatives; but, to speak frankly, I was deterred from sending it to you by the fact of the book including one poem (*Jenny*) of which I felt uncertain whether you would be pleased with it. I am not ashamed of having written it (indeed I assure you that I would never have written it if I thought it unfit to be read with good results); but I feared it might startle you somewhat, and so put off sending you the book. I now do so by this post, and hope that some if not all of the pieces may be quite to your taste. Indeed, I hope that even *Jenny* may be so, for my mother likes it on the whole the best in the volume, after some consideration.

I dare say you have heard, from that only too partial quarter, of the commercial success of the book. The first thousand sold in little more than a week is not amiss for poetry. The second edition is now out, and I have already received £300 for my share of the profits. Of course it will not go on like this for ever, but perhaps a quiet steady sale may be hoped to go on.   I am now about to re-publish my book of the *Early Italian Poets*, as perhaps a new edition may profit by the luck of the other book.

I hope you are well, and that it may not be long before we meet.

C 71.

I did not review the volume of poems by Dr. Hake here referred to : I think Dr. Francis (or Franz) Hueffer did so.

Thursday [12 *January* 1871].

DEAR WILLIAM,

I'm sending you Hake's book as by his request, and no doubt he would be very glad if you could do something for it.   However, I believe Hueffer is disposed to do it for the *Academy*, if you do not.   Hake, in writing to me, says : " I am almost afraid to ask it, but do you think Miss Rossetti would read *Madeline*?   The impression it made on a lady of acute mind it would be interesting to know. . . ."   I dare say Christina would like to oblige him. . . .   If she liked to look through the book, *Old Souls* would certainly please her, and I think the others in that section, and probably much of the *Epitaph;* and, if she liked to write me her views, I would send to Hake.

B 52.

11 *o'clock Tuesday night.* [24 *January* 1871].

DEAREST DARLING,

I am afraid you must have been expecting me to-night, and I fully meant to come, having indeed put off my usual Tuesday evening appointment with the Scotts for that pur- pose, as I had been to my vexation so long without seeing you.   But quite unintentionally I got fidgeting at a perplex- ing piece of work after dinner, and suddenly found it was too late to reach Euston Square with any good chance of seeing you.   I then took a walk, and returned after all to the Scotts—only to find them gone to you—so the whole thing was a *contretemps*.

I now fear I can't get to you till Thursday, but then hope to come without fail in time to see your dear loving face. My evenings are so much taken up at present that I get to you much less often than I should wish ; but believe, dearest Mother, that you are very often in my mind when I am away from you.   I have been blessed with your love so long that I could imagine no good world, here or elsewhere, without it ; and I blame myself a thousand times for the many days that pass me without my seeing you.

As soon as the weather is better again we must get together our family party here which had to be given up on New Year's Day.   Your presence here seems to bring with it always the peace and rest which are often too long away.

C 72.

The library in Florence which Mr. F. S. Ellis was preparing to buy was that of the Barone Seymour Kirkup—the English artist who recovered the portrait of Dante by Giotto in the Bargello, and from of old an esteemed correspondent of our Father.   It was a rich collection, chiefly of old Italian literature.   This is the same Mr. Ellis who has lately (1894) produced a very spirited verse-rendering of *Reynard the Fox.*

Monday [6 *March* 1871].

DEAR W——,

Ellis is going to Florence in a hurry to see about buying old Kirkup's books, which Kirkup has resolved to sell owing to his changing quarters.   He has already had some correspondence with Kirkup about it through a third person, and Kirkup expects him ; but Ellis would like much to have a note of introduction from you, introducing him as a friend of ours.   He is to take Kirkup my book, which it seems never got sent owing to ignorance of address, though I thought I had given it.

Ellis starts on Wednesday.   Could you send him a note for the purpose by then to 33 King St.? . . . He thinks the books will prove a good affair.

B 53.

MY DEAREST MOTHER,

I did not reflect, when I saw you to-day, that it was your birthday, though I have been thinking of it often before in the course of this month, and promising myself for certain to go and see you then if not before; remembering how this day once provided, for four children yet to be, the dearest and best of mothers. It makes me very unhappy to think that extreme worry with my work for a week or so past has put this intention to flight, and even found me oblivious of the anniversary when I saw your dear face to-day. It was a wretched thing to be prevented from benefiting by your visit, and it leaves a painful impression on my mind to remember that such a thing should have occurred just to-day. I must have seemed very neglectful lately in not coming to see you; but daily I find my work pushes the day on, and leaves me so weary that I am unable to start out anywhere till too late to reach Euston Square before your bedtime. In a day or two now I shall be somewhat less taken up, and then trust to see you without fail, and to try and get you to pay me another visit. I was very sorry also to miss Maria, who is so seldom able to come.

With all truest love and every heartfelt wish for you to-day, my dearest Mother,

I am your most affectionate Son,

GABRIEL.

C 73.

This note replies to one in which I had conveyed to my brother an invitation to contribute to some magazine: it must have been *The Dark Blue*, which ran a brief course. Christina had a long, severe, and often alarming illness, beginning in the spring of 1871, and lasting three or four years: it is referred to in this note, and in some others.

"The design for Maggie's binding' was a design which I had made for the binding of our sister Maria's book, *A Shadow of Dante*.

My brother put the sketch into some presentable shape; and Mr. Dunn made the elegantly executed drawings from which the binders worked.

Friday [12 *May* 1871].

MY DEAR WILLIAM,

I don't care about contributing to magazines. It takes the freshness off one's work when collected.

I'm delighted to hear of Christina's improvement. I fear I may not be able conveniently to get round till Sunday evening ; so, if there is any increased anxiety on her account, pray let me know, that I may look in to-morrow.

The design for Maggie's binding is coming on very nicely, and I shall bring it, I do not doubt, when I come next.

B 54.

"Forman's book" is *Our Living Poets*, by Mr. H. Buxton Forman. The picture upon which my brother was now working was the large *Dante's Dream*. Anthony was the very fine landscape-painter Mark Anthony, an old friend of Gabriel and myself. Christina, with our Mother, did about this time get off to Hampstead to recruit, but not, I think, through Mr. Anthony's agency.

Thursday [29 *June* 1871].

DEAR MAMMA,

I was sorry to take away Forman's book the other night, in case you had not done with it ; but it belonged to Scott, and he wanted it back, to take with him to Penkill. As two of your babes figure in it, perhaps it might be a welcome possession to you ; so I have asked Ellis to get a copy, and send it to you, and, when I am next in Euston Square, I will write your dear name in it.

I cannot say how sorry and vexed I am at never seeing you just now. But the fact is that my work at present is almost always standing-work, as I have to go back constantly to look at the effect ; and I am so tired by dusk that, if I do not wait an hour or two to rest before going out, I am obliged to take a cab, and sacrifice my walk—without which I am done for. Thus I seldom get out till after nine, or sometimes (as this evening) even after ten, and then it is no use coming to see you. However, in the course of an evening or two now I hope to do so without fail. I do not expect to get into the country till after next week at any rate. I do hope to do so then, and that the weather may be settled enough to make it worth while going.

I suppose Christina will get away soon. If you like, I could write to Anthony at Hampstead to try to find lodgings on the Heath, as he knows the place well. I spoke of Dr. Hake at Roehampton to Maria, as I feel sure he would be delighted to receive you and Christina in the rooms he has set apart for me ; but I understand from William that this seems to you to involve some awkwardness.

Goodbye, dear darling. I am going out now for a walk, and then home to bed.

C 74.

Sunday [2 *July* 1871].

Whitley Stokes has come from India, and stays only a very short time in London. He is to dine with me Wednesday at 7. I hope you can come, as I am sure he would like to see you again.

C 75.

My " American Selection " forms a volume in the series *Moxon's Popular Poets*. The writer to whom my brother refers was the actress Adah Isaacs Menken. He did not write the brief notice of her which appears in the volume.

Monday [3 *July* 1871].

DEAR W——,

I forgot till this moment that your American Selection ought certainly, I think, to contain some specimens of poor Menken. I have her book, which is really remarkable. If there is still time to introduce them, I would mark the copy for extract, and write some short notice to precede them, to save you trouble, as I know the book.

I may probably look in to-night, but have been so often prevented that I write this.

C 76.

Purnell, here mentioned, was the well-known writer Thomas Purnell. This note contains the first reference to the country house, the Manor House at Kelmscott, which my brother rented for some years jointly with Mr. Morris. Miss Menken's epitaph was "Thou knowest."

[16 CHEYNE WALK.]
Monday [16 *July* 1871].

DEAR W——,

To my surprise I cannot find my Menken's Poems anywhere. So I send you on a letter and notice received from Purnell, and am writing to him to get a copy sent to you.

My own impression is that much the best piece in the book is one called (I think) *Answer Me*; though I remember finding that some points of it were much better than others, and should have been inclined only to print the good stanzas, which make a fine poem enough by themselves; but I don't know if such plan would suit you. There is also a short rhymed poem which is remarkable, called I think *Ambition*, or something of that sort, but it is defective of a line somewhere—accidental omission, I suppose. These two, I remember, are clearly the best. However, there are one or two others I had marked, but my copy seems nowhere. One of the most characteristic is that about "Angels, sweep the leaves from my door."

I am obliged to hand the matter over to you, in the absence of the book, as I leave town to-morrow afternoon. My country address is

The Manor House
Kelmscott
Lechlade.

Love to all.

Your affectionate
GABRIEL.

Purnell told me that she was buried in a shabby way first at Paris; but that her husband Kerr afterwards sent £200, and that she was reinterred more honourably, and her own epitaph (quite sublime, I think) put over her.

B 55.

Allan and Emma were Gabriel's servants at Cheyne Walk—Allan having previously been in the army.

THE MANOR HOUSE, KELMSCOTT, LECHLADE.
17 *July* 1871.

MY DEAREST MOTHER,

I have been here since last Wednesday, and am already greatly benefiting by the change. This house and its surroundings are the loveliest "haunt of ancient peace" that can well be imagined—the house purely Elizabethan in character, though it may probably not be so old as that; but in this dozy neighbourhood that style of building seems to have obtained for long after changes in fashion had occurred elsewhere. It has a quantity of farm-buildings of the thatched squatted order, which look settled down into a purring state of comfort, but seem (as Janey said the other day) as if, were you to stroke them, they would move. Janey is here with her children, and she is benefiting wonderfully, and takes long walks as easily as I do. The children are dear little things—perfectly natural and intelligent, and able to amuse themselves all day long without needing to be thought about by their elders. The younger one—Mary, or May as she is called—is most lovely; the elder interesting also. I mean to make drawings of both while I remain here. Allan and Emma have both come down, and the children's nurse is here; besides which, there are two "native" servants.

My studio here is a delightful room, all hung round with old tapestry, which I suppose has been here since the date of its making. It gives in grim sequence the history of Samson, and is certainly not the liveliest of company. Indeed, the speculation as to the meaning of incredible passages of drawing and detail becomes after a time so wearisome, and is so unavoidable whatever one's train of thought, that I should cover it all up if I knew how. To take it down would not do, as it might go to pieces or get moth-eaten.

I hope you will see this lovely old place some time when it is got quite into order, and I am sure it will fill you with admiration. The garden is a perfect paradise, and the whole is built on the very banks of the Thames, along which there are beautiful walks for miles, though just at this moment the floods rather interfere with their enjoyment. Other walks all round the neighbourhood are of course plentiful, and the nearest town, Lechlade (three miles off), is a most beautiful old town (no Station) ; but on the whole the flatness of the country, being absolute, renders its aspect rather wanting in variety and interest. As for solitude, it is as complete as even at Penkill.

A lot of furniture and conveniences have been got into the place, and order increases daily. This house has never been inhabited but by the family that built it in old times (named Turner), the last surviving member of which, an old lady, lately gave up residing in it on the death of her husband, which caused it to be let.

While I remain here I am having great alterations made in my studio in London, which I have always contemplated, and which my friend Webb the architect will superintend. By this means I shall henceforth have a quite satisfactory light. Otherwise I should really have been obliged to carry my big picture elsewhere, to do the little that remains to do to it on my return, as I never could get a real view of it in any part of the room ; and this evil would of course have renewed itself with every large work I might paint in the future.

I am having my painting-things sent down here, and shall do some leisurely work while I remain, which will be I suppose for two months at least.

I trust you and Christina are both feeling the advantage of Hampstead air, and that C[hristina] is able by this time

to get about pretty well.   Of course I need not say how glad
I shall be of some news of you in these wilds.

With best love to both,

I am your most affectionate Son,

GABRIEL.

C 77.

A public movement had been started in Italy with a view to
removing to the Florentine Church of Santa Croce from Highgate
Cemetery the remains of our Father, as a national patriotic poet : my
brother was mainly in favour of the project, but not the other
members of the family, and the proposal was not carried out.
Knight is Mr. Joseph Knight the dramatic critic, a hearty friend
of my brother's, now his biographer.   I was intending about this
time to go off on a brief Italian trip.

THE MANOR HOUSE, KELMSCOTT, LECHLADE.

[17 *July* 1871.]

DEAR W——,

I have mislaid a letter of Maria's containing Mamma's
address at Hampstead, so must ask you to send on the
enclosed.   You might write me any news there is, for this
is the abode of silence.   It is wonderfully beautiful as to house
and surroundings, but rather monotonous when further afield.
Did you get Menken from Purnell, and do the notice and
extracts ?

How is the *Shadow of Dante* getting on ?   While I stay
here I am having a radical alteration made in my studio at
Cheyne Walk, which will improve the light enormously.
I expect to be away some two months, but may perhaps be
back for a day or so at the end of the first month, to see what
is doing to my studio, etc.

Looking at the *Athenæum* Gossip to-day, it struck me it
might be to the credit of our Father to record the proposal
to remove his remains to Italy.   Do you like to notify this
to Furnivall ?   Or I or you might do so to Knight,

When do you leave London yourself?

A 26.

MY DEAR AUNT,

I am very sorry to have omitted answering your note the moment I got it, as it somehow since escaped my memory till now. However, I cannot say much to the purpose, as I (like most artists) am quite ignorant about picture-cleaning, further than the obvious plan of removing outside dirt with soap and water. To deal with a picture safely is no easy matter, nor should a work of any value be entrusted to every one. If care is worth while in the case you allude to, a safe person to go to is Mr. Merritt, who works a good deal for the National Gallery. His charges (he lately cleaned an old picture for me) are not low, but not immoderate, and he is really capable. His address is H. Merritt Esq., 54 Devonshire Street, Portland Place.—I am sorry I cannot be of more direct use.

You will see by my address that I have left town, having taken, jointly with the Morrises, a share in this very nice old house—as good and genuine a specimen of old middle-class architecture as could be found anywhere. I suppose its aspect is absolutely Elizabethan in every respect, but it is probably a century later. . . . I have been here over three weeks now, and shall probably stay some six weeks longer.

B 56.

" That Beatrice picture " is the painting which my brother named at first *The Death of Beatrice*, or *The Dying Beatrice*, afterwards *Beata Beatrix* : this is more accurate, as the subject is not strictly the death of Beatrice, but Beatrice in a trance ominous of death. The original picture, in which the head had been painted from Gabriel's wife (chiefly or entirely as a reminiscence after her death), belonged to Lord Mount-Temple, and is now in the National Gallery ; the duplicate had been commissioned by Mr. William Graham, then M.P. for Glasgow. He died in July 1885.

THE MANOR HOUSE, KELMSCOTT, LECHLADE.
11 *August* 1871.

MY DEAREST MOTHER,

You see I have dated this letter, as you told me you liked dates. I am afraid there is no reason for writing in these stagnant surroundings except the somewhat phantasmal one (I trust) of the fear lest you should seem to be out of mind with me if I were silent. The heat here is now excessive—so great indeed that walking even at the close of day is no pleasure, and one is tempted to keep indoors altogether. However, I yesterday evening strolled out after dinner when the sun was quite gone, and found it cool and delightful, so I think I shall time my walks chiefly so at present; only the twilights are very short and there is no moon now, and walking in pitch darkness is not pleasant. I have been painting pretty steadily lately here, and getting through a duplicate of that Beatrice picture—dreary work enough. I am also beginning a little picture of Janey with a river background which will come nicely, I think, and am drawing the children too, who are dear little things, particularly the younger one,—she is destined moreover to be a great beauty beyond question. I have written a few small things, and will copy one out for you, to send with this letter and make up a little for want of news. I hope you and Christina both thrive; of Maria I have no doubt on that score, and am very glad she is with you, as I am sure she needs change. I think her book will make a very good appearance—even the frontispiece looking satisfactory enough at last—and am anxious to have a complete copy in my hands.

I rather expect to stay here even as much as two months longer, as the people who were to alter my studio-windows at Chelsea in my absence (of which I think I told you) are so dilatory that I am not sure whether the work is even yet well begun. Morris is expected here in about a month now, —doubtless with wonderful tales of Iceland; for what is the use of going there if you are not allowed to make people stare well when you come back? An Icelandic paper which he sent reporting his arrival describes him as " Wm. Morris, Skald."

The Browns, as you probably know, went for a month to Lynmouth, but are now returned to Fitzroy Square. With them went Hueffer, and William's favourite Miss Mathilde Blind, who by lucky accident unearthed there some old woman who had known Shelley and his first wife Harriet when they were staying at the place, and had all sorts of funny things to tell about them, all of which Miss Blind has written in a letter to William.

Will you thank Maria for her letter in answer to mine? . . .

Did you see that a Miss Rossetti, "young and beautiful" and apparently Irish, has come out successfully as a concert-singer in London? I wonder who her father may have been. Perhaps however the name is merely assumed, as an Italian one ready to hand.

As I have absolutely no more news, I fear, I will proceed to copy a few verses suggested by the river here instead, and, with love to all, remain

Your most affectionate Son,

GABRIEL.

THE RIVER'S RECORD.

BETWEEN Holmscote and Hurstcote
  The river-reaches wind,
The whispering trees accept the breeze,
  The ripple's cool and kind:
With love low-whispered 'twixt the shores,
  With rippling laughters gay,
With white arms bared to ply the oars,
  On last year's first of May.

Between Holmscote and Hurstcote
  The river's brimmed with rain,
Through close-met banks and parted banks
  Now near, now far again:
With parting tears caressed to smiles,
  With meeting promised soon,
With every sweet vow that beguiles,
  On last year's first of June.

Between Holmscote and Hurstcote
　　The river's flecked with foam,
'Neath shuddering clouds that hang in shrouds
　　And lost winds wild for home:
With infant wailings at the breast,
　　With homeless steps astray,
With wanderings shuddering tow'rds one rest,
　　On this year's first of May.

Between Holmscote and Hurstcote
　　The summer river flows
With doubled flight of moons by night
　　And lilies' deep repose:
With lo beneath the moon's white stare
　　A white face not the moon,
With lilies meshed in tangled hair,
　　On this year's first of June.

Between Holmscote and Hurstcote
　　A troth was given and riven,
From heart's trust grew one life to two,
　　Two lost lives cry to Heaven:
With banks spread calm to meet the sky,
　　With meadows newly mowed,
The harvest-paths of glad July,
　　The sweet school-children's road.

P.S.—I doubt not you will note in the above the intention
to make the first half of each verse, expressing the landscape,
tally with the second expressing the emotion, even to
repetition of phrases.

B 57.

Sing-song is the volume of children's rhymes which our sister
Christina was at this time preparing for publication.

KELMSCOTT.
Friday [18 *August* 1871].

DEAREST DARLING,

　　. . . I have now for some time been taking an acid
medicine prescribed me by Bowman, and which is appeti-
zing if taken before meals, and (by my experience) more
beneficial than anything else I had tried.

I am glad *Sing-song* is going on nicely. Do you see that the *Athenæum* quite gratuitously announces a forthcoming volume of mine? Who these very ultra-omniscient gossips may be I cannot conceive, but they are always at it with one person or another.

Having no news in answer to your letter, I'll send you another little poem done from Nature. I don't know if you ever noticed the habit of starlings referred to, which is constant here at sunsets at this season of the year.

I also have by me several French volumes of Tourguenieff, lent me by Ralston, and which I have been intending to read with much anticipated pleasure, yet have not hitherto done so to much purpose—the only piece I have read being *Le Pain d'Autrui*, which I think quite admirable in its way. We read a vast deal of Shakespear aloud in the evenings here, and I also declaimed Browning's new poem *Balaustion's Adventure* one day on the lawn outside the house from first to last (of course with book)—a process lasting about an hour and a half. . . . Of course it has its beauties ; but it consists chiefly of a translation of Euripides' *Alcestis*, inter-larded with Browningian analysis to an extent beyond all reason or relation to things by any possibility Greek in any way.

I am reading also Walter Scott's *St. Ronan's Well*, which I had never read, but which Morris had often recommended to me as one of his best ; which indeed I think it is so far as I have gone,—quite out of his usual way, more like a simple study of actual life, and with much more individual passion in the hero and heroine than that class of personage generally has with him. I dare say a Folkestone library or railway stall would easily furnish you the book, which I am sure you would like if new to you.

We read Plutarch too, so at any rate our studies are not of an ephemeral order.

I think a very fine play might be made of the Life of Pompey, which Shakespear has somehow left alone, though he seems to have given more perfecting labour to Roman subjects than to any. I suppose the most faultless by far of all his plays is *Julius Cæsar*.

With love to all,
Your most affectionate
GABRIEL.

P.S.—I have not told you what beautiful old churches there are here. A famous one at Lechlade, in the churchyard of which Shelley wrote one of his poems ; but, still more interesting to me, one or two simple ones—the Kelmscott church as good as any—of the most primitive order, with two bells hanging visibly on the roof at one end—looking just as one fancies chapels in the *Mort d'Arthur*, particularly from one side when one sees it above some wild-looking apple-trees. I shall certainly get it into some picture one day if I keep on coming here.

SUNSET WINGS.

To-NIGHT this Sunset spreads two golden wings
    Cleaving the western sky ;
Winged too with wind it is, and winnowings
Of birds ; as if the day's last hour in rings
    Of strenuous flight must die.

Sun-steeped in fire, the homeward pinions sway
    Above the dovecote-tops ;
And clouds of starlings, ere they rest with day,
Sink, clamorous like mill-waters, at wild play
    By turns in every copse.

Each tree heart-deep the wrangling rout receives,—
    Save for the whirr within,
You could not tell the starlings from the leaves ;
Then one great puff of wings, and the swarm heaves
    Away with all its din.

Even thus Hope's hours, in ever-eddying flight,
    To many a refuge tend ;
With the first light she laughed, and the last light
Glows round her still ; who natheless in the night
    At length must make an end.

And now the mustering rooks innumerable
   Together sail and soar,
While for the day's death, like a tolling knell,
Unto the heart they seem to cry, "Farewell,
   No more, farewell, no more!"

Is Hope not plumed, as 'twere a fiery dart?
   Therefore, O dying day,
Even as thou goest must she too depart,
And Sorrow fold such pinions on the heart
   As will not fly away.

G 2.

"The circle at Euston Square" consisted of our Mother our two sisters, and myself: the house, 56 Euston Square, being the same which was afterwards named 5 Endsleigh Gardens.

The Italian verse-proverb quoted in this letter means:—

"Who at twenty knows not
   Never will he know:
Who at thirty does not
   Never will he do:
Who at forty owns not
   Never will he own."

THE MANOR HOUSE, KELMSCOTT, LECHLADE.
27 August 1871.

MY DEAR UNCLE,

What you say of the rarity of our intercourse is but too true. However, you would be astounded to learn (if the facts could be conveyed to you) how little or nothing I see even of the oldest friends among whom I live in London, how seldom I meet the circle at Euston Square, and how absolutely every far-between excursion of mine is regulated by such work as I can do away from home.

For instance, just now I have taken this house, in conjunction with my friend Morris, as a means of establishing some country-quarters for work, where I can leave my belongings, and return to them as opportunity offers. When I came here some weeks ago I knew exactly the task I had to do, and surrounded myself with the means of doing it; and,

when it is done, it will be high time for me to return to other
work in London.   I am thus tedious about my own necessities,
that I may not seem unthankful in saying that it is, to my
regret, impracticable for me to transfer my quarters hence to
Gloucester, near as I suppose I am to that city,—though how
near exactly I do not know.   I expect Morris here too on
his return from travelling ; at present he is far enough away
—in Iceland.   His family are here now, however, and this
renders it impossible for me (through want of accommodation
in these hurriedly furnished quarters) to return your invitation,
and hope to see you here at present ; though I hope this
may happen on some other occasion, since we propose keeping the house on.   It is a most lovely old house. . . . It still
belongs to the family whose ancestors built it, and whose
arms are still on some of the chimney-breasts.   The garden,
and meadows leading to the river-brink, are truly delicious—
indeed the place is perfect ; and the riverside-walks are most
charming in their way, though I must say the flatness of the
country renders it monotonous and uninspiring to me.   However, it is the very essence of all that is peaceful and retired—
the solitude almost absolute.   Kelmscott is a hamlet containing, I am told, 117 people, and these even one may be
said never to see, if one keeps, as I do, the field-paths rather
than the highroad.   I am in Oxfordshire here, it seems,
though Lechlade (2½ miles hence) is in Gloucestershire.   It
is very difficult to get anything one wants in the way of
supplies, Lechlade being but scanty in resources, and the
nearest station-town, Faringdon, being so far off that the
carrier who brings our railway-parcels charges 6s. 6d. for
every journey.   Moreover, tradespeople do not send so far
as this from either town.   Thus a good deal of inconvenience
tempers the attractions of the place.   Morris and I had been
for some little time in search of a place to take jointly in the
country when this one was discovered in a house-agent's
catalogue—the last place one would have expected to furnish
such an out-of-the-world commodity.

I may perhaps have to stay here several weeks longer,

owing firstly to my work and need of change, secondly to Morris's expected coming, and thirdly that my studio at Chelsea is undergoing radical alteration for the improvement of its light while I am away, and of course the proceedings are dilatory.

To your enquiries about my prospects I may reply simply that I make lots of money (for a poor painter), and never have a penny to fly with. My father used to have an Italian proverb (perhaps known to you) which said :—

> Chi a venti non sa
> Mai non saprà.
> Chi a trenta non fa
> Mai non farà.
> Chi a quaranta non ha
> Mai non avrà.

And alas it is all true.

I am extremely sorry to hear that your income has suffered lately—let me hope, not permanently or beyond chance of recovery. I am so far from exempt myself from signs of failing health already that I look with the less wonder on the same in your case. Poor Christina's state has been a sad one lately ; and I was deeply grieved to hear such melancholy accounts of Henrietta—as I need hardly tell you. It is great comfort at any rate that my Mother keeps up well.

An autograph is puzzling. Will the one enclosed do?

C 78.

The poem which my brother sent me was *The Cloud Confines*, published in his *Ballads and Sonnets*, 1881. I give here only the last stanzas which differ somewhat from the printed version. The other poem, which he contributed to the *Dark Blue* magazine, appears under the title *Down Stream* in his volume entitled *Poems*, 1881. It is the same as *The River's Record* (see B 56).

THE MANOR HOUSE, KELMSCOTT, LECHLADE.
[10 *September* 1871.]

DEAR WILLIAM,

I wish you'd write me anything of your doings abroad or other news. I am likely to be back in about a fortnight more, I suppose, but I shouldn't wonder if it stretched to three weeks.

The changes in my studio at Chelsea under Webb's directions, giving me a good light at last, will be completed next week. You might go and take a look at them if you liked.

I have been doing a replica here (of that *Beatrice*)—a beastly job, but lucre was the lure. . . . I have written a few things—notably Part I. (51 five-line stanzas) of a poem called *Rose Mary* (you may remember my using the name long ago for some rubbish destroyed), and which is about a magic crystal, or Beryl as it was called—a story of my own, good, I think, turning of course on the innocence required in the seer. Part II. will be much longer, I think, and should hope to get on with it now, were it not that Top comes here to-night from Iceland. . . .

On one short thing I have done, not meant to be a trifle, I want your advice about the close. I copy it herewith, and the form of the four last lines there given is the one I incline to adopt—thus, you see, leaving the whole question open. But at first I had meant to answer the question in a way, on the theory hardly of annihilation but of absorption. As thus (last five lines)—

> "And what must our birthright be?
> Oh never from thee to sever,
>   Thou Will that shalt be and art,—
> To throb at thy heart for ever,
> Yet never to know thy heart."

As I say, I incline to the lines given in the copy as the safest course. . . .

Does the parrot brought me by Stillman talk?

Ever yours,

D. G. R.

P.S.—I'm Dark-Blued at last, owing to Brown, who was asked to illustrate something of mine for them if I would contribute. It's a little sort of ballad I wrote here—to appear in October.

THE CLOUD CONFINES.

THE day is dark and the night
 etc.   etc.   etc.

The sky leans dumb on the sea
 A-weary with all its wings;
 And oh the song the sea sings
Is dark everlastingly.
  Our past is clean forgot,
  Our present is and is not,
  Our future's a sealed seed-plot,
 And what betwixt them are we?
 What words to say as we go?
  What thoughts to think by the way?
 What truth may there be to know,
 And shall we know it one day?

C 79.

"The poor woodchuck" was one of my brother's favourite
animals—otherwise named a "Canadian Marmot." Mr. Scott did
a portrait of him, which was sold among the contents of No. 16
Cheyne Walk in July 1882. In his *Autobiographical Notes* Mr.
Scott has erroneously termed his four-footed sitter the wombat.

KELMSCOTT.
[20 *September* 1871.]

DEAR WILLIAM,

I am getting towards a finish with my poem, which
will be about 150 stanzas, and makes three parts. I ought
to have asked you (though late now) for any information
you have at hand about magic crystals or mirrors. I
remember in a note to Lane's *One Thousand and One
Nights* there is an account of some such transaction—I think
it is in the volume you have; and the only thing I can
remember about it is that the first thing seen is a figure
sweeping with a broom. This I have used. I have been
unlucky in being out here when I wrote the thing, but don't
know after all whether book-information would have served
me much. If you'd give a look in any likely quarter,

however, and let me know results promptly, I'd be much
obliged still.

Ever yours,
D. G. R.

You will be grieved to hear that the poor woodchuck is
dead.

C 80.

KELMSCOTT
Saturday [23 September 1871].

DEAR WILLIAM,

I meant in last writing to have mentioned the matter
about the proposed memorial to our Father at Florence. I
should like myself to subscribe £50 or £100 ; but should not
think it perhaps advisable to take these steps at once if there
were any danger thereby of stopping subscription in Italy,
as it would be a great pity not to be able to say that the
honour done to his memory was thoroughly a national one.
Will you give me your ideas on this point ? I think it most
likely that I shall be back now about the 1st October. I
have finished *Rose Mary*—3 Parts, 160 stanzas.

C 81.

KELMSCOTT.
[28 September 1871.]

DEAR W——,

Thanks about the memorial-matter. I shall be very
glad to do as you suggest when necessary, but do think it a
great pity if the Vasto people are being (or have been)
stopped in a subscription by the news that more than ample
funds were offered by the family. A pity, I mean, for the
honour's sake. If this has *not* yet been done, and could be
staved off by your writing to Ricciardi or any one your
views on the subject, I would certainly do so.

It strikes me, if a medallion had to be done, the best plan
(if our funds are to be used here) would be to employ
some one—say Tupper—to produce something from such

records as I made of my Father during his life, and I could suggest or even retouch. Else an afflictive grotesque will be the certain result.

C 82.

Here begins the matter of the *Contemporary Review*, and the article by "Thomas Maitland" on *The Fleshly School of Poetry*. I think it as well to print, following my brother's note, the reply which I sent to him, and which, after his death, I found among his papers.

[16 CHEYNE WALK.
17 *October* 1871.]

DEAR W——,

What do you think? —— writes me that Maitland is ——Buchanan !

Do you know Buchanan's prose, and can you judge if it be so? If it be, I'll not deny myself the fun of a printed Letter to the Skunk.

—— says he has it " on very good authority."

C 82A.

EUSTON SQ.
18 *October* [1871].

DEAR GABRIEL,

Buchanan had never occurred to me, but on your mentioning him it seemed to me exceedingly probable. I have now read the article through again. It seems to me that in point of style etc. it might very well be Buchanan's, but still I don't feel *strengthened* in that view by the perusal. Buchanan is himself twice named : page 334 as personating Cornelius (which seems to imply a slight more or less); page 343 as your prototype in *Jenny*. This latter (see also the reference to Buchanan's critics attached to it) does seem very much the sort of self-assumption which Buchanan might be minded (in utter ignorance of dates etc.) to indulge in. Also, page 348, *Ballad on a Wedding*, and *Clever Tom Clinch* : I don't know whether these are Buchanan's, but they rather sound as if they might be. The phrases *weird—solemn league and covenant*—have a Scotch sound ; but Maitland is a Scotch name rather than otherwise, so one can make little of that as suggesting Buchanan.

The observation (344) that you are not to be blamed for selecting the *subject* of *Jenny* looks rather like Buchanan, who has been censured for somewhat similar subjects. Also the reference (336) to Swinburne's illness notified in *Athenæum*. Buchanan, I know, saw that or some similar printed report ; for he thereupon took the good-natured trouble (as I suppose I must have mentioned to you) of urging Dr. Chapman to try to get hold of Swinburne and restore him to health, and Chapman called on me in consequence.

My opinion is that there is not at present sufficient material for pinning Buchanan as the author of that review ; and at all events I have a strong belief that you will find it in the long run more to your comfort and dignity to take no public steps whatever for the scarifying of Mr. Maitland—though of course the temptation is considerable.

Your

W. M. R.

B 58.

URRARD HOUSE, PERTHSHIRE.
21 June 1872.

MY DEAREST MOTHER,

We got here to-day at 11, after 14 or 15 hours' hard travelling, but in a most luxurious way such as I could hardly have imagined. An immense deal has been done by Mr. Graham to smooth away difficulties, and his kindness throughout has been excessive. What to say of Brown's brotherly lovingness to me I do not know—even from him I could hardly have supposed such love and long patience possible. Since we arrived here it has been raining, but this evening we three—including George Hake—did manage to walk out a little about the garden etc. There are many beautiful points which we enjoyed, and there is even a scheme for my painting a picture of one if such a thing can be thought of, but I am quite in the dark as to possibilities as yet. Poor Allan is not very brilliant in health just now, but behaves very well.

How wonderful and happy to hear of Christina's sudden rally! I suppose she is now already at Hampstead, and I trust still further benefiting. I was glad to understand that William had managed to get to business again.

The most striking point about the situation of this house is an immense hill which faces the dining-room window, and has from many points of view much that is imposing and noble. It would of course be the leading point in any picture which dealt with the spot. It seems that the battle of Killiccrankie, at which the Marquis of Dundee was killed, was fought on the site of this house—a former Urrard House having been his residence ; and in the garden a mound marks the spot where he fell by a bullet after reaching his own door.

I thought I would not let a day pass without just putting pen—a very bad one—to paper to let you hear of me ; but in fact I am no correspondent just now, and will not ask you to answer this even, knowing well all that your love would say.

With my own love to all at home, I am

Your most affectionate Son,

GABRIEL.

C 83.

During my brother's absence in Scotland I attended mainly to his correspondence and other affairs, and had found some letters regarding a translation from some poem of his, and a request for permission to include others in a volume of Selections. The translator was a German lady. This is the matter spoken of towards the beginning of the letter.

The best wishes for Cathy and congratulations to Hueffer relate to the approaching marriage of Mr. Madox Brown's second daughter to Dr. Hueffer.

TROWAN, CRIEFF.
[22 *August* 1872.]

DEAR WILLIAM,

I have been meaning to answer your letter, though with no particular material. I rejoice to hear that Christina is getting on so fairly well on the whole.

The matters you dwell on about the translation and Selections are quite unimportant. I have been in the habit of answering such applications as the latter, or not, just as it chanced. The lady perhaps required a word of thanks.

I need not be calling on you for further books at present, I believe, as we have got some from a circulating library at Edinburgh.

Will you give my warmest love to Brown, together with all best wishes for Cathy's welfare and congratulations to Hueffer? We have not heard from Brown for some time, but no doubt all his time has been taken up.

The weather is very uncertain here, but a little less so for the last few days. I manage to go out daily, but my lameness and all else is just the same as ever. The goodness of Dr. Hake and George quite unwearying. We read aloud now in the evenings for two or three hours.

I thought I would write, but, as you see, have nothing to say. With warmest love to yourself, Mamma, and Sisters, I am

Your affectionate
GABRIEL.

C 84.

[TROWAN.]
Thursday [5 *September* 1872].

DEAR WILLIAM,

I dare say you know that Dr. Hake is leaving here, and that Dunn is coming down. I think it is very objectionable for my house to be left with the servants only in it, and . . . I should be glad if you would look down there when you can.

*　　*　　*　　*　　*　　*

For myself, I have been painting a little. Of course there was little I could do here without models. I took up the replica of *Beatrice* which I was doing for Graham, and had abandoned last year as hopeless. Now it seems to be coming round tolerably, and, if fit to deliver, will at any rate relieve me of a debt of 900 guineas, though it brings no present grist to the mill.

My lameness continues the same, and I have little doubt will be permanent. An utter sleeplessness, except some two or three hours about once a fortnight, is the state of things in spite of heavy narcotics.

I get out daily for a six miles or so of walk, unless the weather is very bad, in which case my walk is shorter.

Since I ceased to be Graham's guest, expenses here are of course an anxious matter, but it cannot be helped. I heard some time back of your having made some payments in London, and have just asked Dr. Hake to look up your letter on the subject ; but, though he is sure he kept it, he cannot find it now. I did not look at it when it came, not being in the mood.

*　　*　　*　　*　　*　　*

I suppose Hueffer and Cathy Brown were married yesterday. Will you say everything that ought to be said to the Papa and family from me when you see them? I may or may not be able to write myself.

With love,

Ever yours,

D. G. R.

P.S.—In the matter of Brass the Builder's bill, you did right to refer it to Webb. He (Brass) said at starting that the cost of the alterations in the studio would be about £70 or £80. This Webb thought a low estimate. I don't know what . . . his bill is ; but I paid him £60 at Christmas last, and see no reason to be paying more at present.

*　　*　　*　　*　　*　　*

C 85.

The "*Silence* drawing" is a crayon-drawing of a female half-figure, which had been sold during my brother's absence from London: it has been autotyped. Mr. Murray Marks, then an Art-dealer in Oxford Street, and Mr. J. Aldam Heaton, then of Bradford, were concerned in the matter, which was partly of my own transacting. Mr. Parsons had been a painter and photographer; about this time he was also acting as an Art-dealer.

[TROWAN.]
Friday [6 *September* 1872].

DEAR WILLIAM,

I forgot yesterday to allude to the *Silence* drawing, which George tells me was sold by Marks to Heaton. I ought not to have parted with it—at any rate yet—as it is worth more than I got, and is moreover a thing I mean to paint if I go on working. As it is, a photo of it should at any rate have been taken, and if Heaton retains it he would no doubt allow this to be done. The photo should be about the size of the largest Parsons has done for me. I don't know if it could be borrowed, or if Heaton would get it done at Bradford. I dare say you have already written him about it. His address is

J. A. Heaton
Woodbank
Near Bingley
Yorks.

I am rather desirous to get at *Salammbô*, which I possess and have never read. This is not so easy now that Dunn is away : . . . perhaps you would look it up and send it. It may possibly however be in that cupboard in the back room, first floor.

Ever your affectionate

G.

B 59.

AT MRS. STEWART'S,
TROWAN, CRIEFF, N.B.
12 *September* 1872.

MY DEAREST MOTHER,

I received your affectionate letter, and was glad to find the news of Christina pretty good. . . .

I fear you have derived (I know not how) too favourable an impression about myself from my last letter. This would of course be a gain, were it not for the coming *disinganno* when we meet again. However, one must hope for the best, even if the worst is all one gets by it.

I am beginning to be impatient of staying here, yet am not disposed to return to London if I can help it. I may possibly find my way to Kelmscott ere long, but am undecided as yet. Dr. Hake has, as you probably know, left me, but his son is still here, and Dunn has lately arrived.

There are some fine walks here, one of which has now become, almost without variation, our daily choice. The roads are nearly all very hilly, but so gradual and free from unevenness as not to be toilsome. One's path lies sometimes between wooded coverts on both sides, and sometimes emerges on an unscreened platform commanding wide prospects hemmed in by the hills, then again passes into woodland, and so on ; till at last one finds one has unwittingly reached some eminence which, seen from below, would have seemed a task not to be attempted. Sometimes one attains a moorland covered with the most lovely heather, which stands about a foot high, forming a plump bed like moss, and so stiff that the wet sinks through it, and it remains dry enough to lie down on in almost any weather. The fare here would be wofully monotonous, were it not that Graham, ever since the shooting season began, has constantly kept us supplied with hampers of game,—grouse, hares, partridges, and rabbits, which, as you may suppose, have been a welcome addition to our table. The cooking is far from bad, and the quarters here very comfortable. The place was discovered, on our having to leave Stobhall, by the greatest exercise of energy on the part of Dr. Hake. When the time arrived, George first spent two days on the East coast—a considerable distance—looking for new quarters at St. Andrew's and elsewhere, but his reports of the results were not promising. Accordingly next day his father started off in the same direction, but with no better success. He then bethought him somehow of Crieff, and retraced his steps thither. He called on the local doctor, introducing himself as a brother practitioner, and asked if he knew of any farmhouse or such where lodgings could be had ; and thus, step by step, he arrived at this place, and took it. The journeys of both father and son were performed under heavy and almost continual rain, and certainly gave proof of great faculties for exploration, which indeed both possess in a high degree.

I have been painting here lately, and have finished a copy of that Beatrice picture for Graham. This however is un-luckily already paid for, so brings no grist to the mill, but at any rate frees me from a heavy debt. However, he expressed a great wish for a " predella " to the picture,—that is, a small picture running underneath the larger one, as in old Italian art,—and this I am beginning now, and shall be able to charge for. The interruption to my pursuits has indeed been a heavy evil ; and it still remains to be seen whether I can resume them to full purpose.

With warmest love to both of you, believe me

Your most loving Son,
GABRIEL.

C 86.

"Howell's proposal," mentioned in the P.S., was (I think) a friendly offer to assign a separate part of his own house at Fulham for my brother's use, if deemed convenient.

TROWAN.
[17 September 1872.]

DEAR WILLIAM,

I dare say I am mistaken, but in my somewhat morbid state of mind your last letter received this morning seems to possess a kind of reticence as if I had said something in mine which was more or less displeasing to you, and I cannot help (however unnecessarily) casting about for what it can be. If my declining a sudden and violent move in respect of the Chelsea house should seem ill-advised to you, I must retain my belief that such a move would be very rash. I have erected a studio there at great trouble and expense; the job of moving would be a very heavy one, and absorb much time; and, even as a storehouse for my belongings till I know exactly what I am going to do, the place would be better retained than given up; since, if I continue to work at present, the expense of retaining it would be less than the inevitable loss of time and work which giving it up and changing abode would occasion me. I have at Kelmscott quarters already fitted for my work; and, even if I remained there the whole winter (I always speak, barring casualties to health or life which it is no use trying to calculate), it would be much better to have for the present in reserve the question of returning to my really suitable house at Chelsea than to encounter the difficulties of some place almost certainly unsuitable if looked up in a hurry. Moreover, if I did not readily let the house, I should have to pay that rent as well as a new one.

Were a *suitable* place to be heard of in or near London, the question would then assume a different aspect. I expect to leave this for Kelmscott next Monday. . . .

Within the last week or so I have rather decidedly rallied in some respects as regards health and spirits, and I find that work presents no difficulty of any kind. Wherever I can be at peace, there I shall assuredly work. . . .

My sleep has certainly been better for about a week past; and as for the lameness, that must just be put up with, as it interferes neither with work nor even with necessary exercise to any absolute extent. . . .

I look to finish the predella for Graham this week, and so by its price (150 guineas) to defray (or nearly to do so) my expenses in Scotland.

* * * * * *

I am glad even of the slightly improved account of Christina. My love to her and all. I suppose Mamma did not miss getting a letter I lately wrote her to Glottenham.

Your affectionate

D. G. R.

P.S.—Just as I finish this (in answer to one of yours from *Cheyne Walk*) I receive by mid-day post a second of yours from *Somerset House*, apparently both replying to one letter of mine; the tone of the second, however, entirely removing the impression of the first. I see nothing particular otherwise to say further in answer, except that, were I left alone at Kelmscott (or perhaps in any case), I might be availing myself of your brotherly offer to join me, and that I feel much the friendliness of Howell's proposal, but hardly see my way to accepting it—just now at any rate, if at all.

C 87.

A forgery upon my brother is spoken of at the end of this letter. His suspicions pointed in the right direction; but, as the offender (female) had been known to him in childhood, he would not allow any enquiries to be made, preferring to suffer the loss of the money.

[TROWAN.]

20 September 1872.

DEAR WILLIAM,

We (George and I) have now resolved to leave from Perth at 4 o'clock on Monday, and make for Euston Station, reaching it at 4.30 on Tuesday morning. We should then cab it to Paddington, and catch there the 6.30 train for Faringdon, which reaches there at 8.50. I don't think it would be safe for us to come to your house on the way, as catching trains is ticklish work; but, if not too great a tax on you, we might meet if you would be at Euston Station when the train came in, and so accompany us to Paddington and see us off there. George will be going with me to Kelmscott.

Of course I think it very likely you might not be able to come, with the necessity of rest which your overwork requires. If we happened to miss you on the platform, perhaps you might go on to Paddington and meet us there. If you have anything to say in reply to this, you had better telegraph, as I fear a letter wouldn't reach us now.

Before you get this you will have heard probably through Brown of the unlucky forgery of a cheque in my name for nearly £50, and the odd explanation which at once occurred to me, and which I fear must be correct.

*　　*　　*　　*　　*　　*

C 88.

KELMSCOTT.
Wednesday [25 *September* 1872].

DEAR WILLIAM,

The pleasant peaceful hours at Euston Square yesterday were the first happy ones I have passed for months; and here all is happiness again, and I feel completely myself.

I know well how much you must have suffered on my account; indeed perhaps your suffering may have been more acute than my own dull nerveless state during the past months. Your love, dear William, is not less returned by me than it is sweet to me, and that is saying all.

I was greatly relieved to find all the family at Euston Square—even Christina—better than I had ventured to hope. I am determined now to make every effort not to go under again, and feel at this moment as if such a thing were impossible. However, though I do not mean to hurry about giving up the Chelsea house, I am quite of opinion that, if a desirable and feasible place were to be found a little out of London, it would be much the wisest plan to secure it. George has hit on an advertisement of a twenty-three roomed house at Highgate standing in its own grounds. I don't know whether Highgate is quite far enough away, but should like you or some capable person to look at the house. George is away at Faringdon just now, but, if he returns before post-time, I'll enclose the advertisement.

All the effects of the journey have worn off, and I feel quite right to-day.

*   *   *   *   *   *

George has just come from Faringdon with the case of papers and drawings. It has got a good deal knocked about on the journey, but not seriously. Unfortunately, just the very valuable drawing—that of Janey seated—had by some strange fancy been put with its face against the rough wood inside the case. The wonder is that it is not seriously injured : a few places in the hair had got rubbed, but these I have been able to repair.

*   *   *   *   *   *

Your loving Brother,

D. G. R.

If the Highgate house were looked at, it would of course be necessary to see whether there was a good room for studio with *North* aspect.

P.S.—There is one thing I much want sent on to Kelmscott, and that is a large case to contain large and small greenish papers for chalk-drawing, and I want the following put in it, viz. :—

1. The last drawing I was making of Janey, and which I believe is in the glass case, with drawers underneath and a curtain before the glass, which stands in my studio. The rest of the figure is very slightly sketched in—something as here [a sketch given of the figure on which the picture named *The Day-dream* was based].

2. A large greenish paper which would be somewhere against the wall, either in studio or little front-room, and which contains a head of Mme. Zambaco, and one of Janey, just begun, for *Pandora*.

*   *   *   *   *   *

C 89.

KELMSCOTT.
Thursday [*26 September* 1872].

DEAR WILLIAM,

I am happy to say to-day that, through Mr. Watts's friendly offices, the cheque-business seems in a fair way of being quashed : only I shall have to lose the money. This, however, is the minor evil. He asks very pertinently—How are we to guard against a repetition of the offence ? This you see would almost involve a prosecution inevitably. Do you think it would be possible to see whether any clue to the woman's whereabouts could be got at her former lodgings? If so, one might perhaps warn her by letter that she was discovered, but that the matter would this time be overlooked. I have asked Watts's opinion about this.

My strength seems completely re-established here to-day. The floods are not out as yet, so that walking is feasible, and the weather splendid. The place is a perfect Paradise. You must really come and see it sooner or later. George Hake says he never knew such a place in his life.

* * * * * *

C 90.

KELMSCOTT.
[*Friday 27 September* 1872.]

DEAR WILLIAM,

I am very sorry to hear about Christina. My love to her.

By the bye, when I saw you I thought you showed fearful signs of fagging and overwork, as well you might. I don't think you should for a moment relinquish the heartiest holiday you can get. I am doubtful yet what my own moves may exactly be, but trust to do pretty well, on my own hook chiefly now, especially when Dunn is back in London, as he will be very soon, and can attend to commissions. I am wonderfully well now, and even the lameness seems perhaps on the improving tack.　I think of writing to Marshall about one or two things. . . .

All this past cursed state of things began on my birthday. May the spell be removed now that yours is past ! . . .

C 91.

" The children," mentioned here in connexion with Mr. George Hake, are Mr. and Mrs. Morris's two girls.

[KELMSCOTT.
6 *October* 1872.]

DEAR WILLIAM,

The cheque and book reached quite safely.　I'll hope to see you here as soon as you like, since Morris is not coming till Saturday of next week at soonest, and his room is therefore at your service now.　After that, there is plenty of room still, and another bedroom could be got ready for use in no time.　You know you come to Faringdon Station from Paddington.　The train I generally take is the evening one—6.30 I think—which goes quicker than any other. There are two changes, at Didcot and Uffington.　On reaching Faringdon, you come on by fly to Kelmscott Manor, 7 miles by the road.　The whole affair takes from 3½ to 4 hours.　If you let us know exactly when you are coming, George will meet you with the fly.　Otherwise telegraph from Paddington to the Crown Inn, Faringdon, what time you are getting there, and that they should send fly to meet the train.　All the luggage has got here now, so I expect to be at work in good earnest, in which case Janey will be sitting to me the greater part of the day, and I shall not be very much at liberty during the light hours ; but we should nevertheless see lots of each other, and this place would really take you some time to see.　George would do any amount of boating and punting, etc.　You would more-over have a room all to yourself to write in when you wished.

George sticks on here, but there is plenty of room.　He is very useful in all sorts of ways, since the distances are so great for getting anything wanted.　The weather is changeable now, but not very bad yet on the whole, and there seems a fair prospect of some fine spells yet. I have renewed my tenancy and paid up arrears, so 1 have as good a right to ask you down as any one else. Janey joins warmly, and so would Top if here. George yearns also. He seems as happy here as it is possible to be, and gives the children all kinds of treats on the river, etc.

I certainly think it would be very desirable, if you can manage it, that you should stay in London till Dunn's arrival there, but it is not necessary nevertheless. . . .

I should think you might bring your literary work here without waiting to do it in town.

I am extremely sorry about Christina, particularly as, on the day I saw her, she really seemed to me to have attained some sort of settled health. My love to her and all.

I wrote Howell on the business-matter, but have not yet heard from him. . . .

B 60.

The picture for which my brother wanted to ascertain a Dantesque date must have been the predella to the *Beata Beatrix* commissioned by Mr. Graham.

This address sufficient.   KELMSCOTT, LECHLADE.
                                                        10 *October* 1872.

MY DEAREST MOTHER,

I have been meaning all along to write to you since coming here, but, having several other letters daily to attend to, and thinking you would hear news of me when I wrote to William, I have somehow failed in my intentions ; but must now write to say that William is safely ensconced here, looking on his arrival I thought decidedly better than when I saw him in London ; and to-day, after a good walk, looking still further improved. The weather seems unluckily just to-day to be breaking up, and the rain at this moment is very heavy. Hitherto we have had on the whole fine weather, and I have walked daily. The worst of this place is that a few days of rain fetch the floods out in no time, and the country becomes impassable for pedestrians, or indeed for anything but a boat, while even the roads get completely turned to bogs, so badly constructed are they. I have not got very much to work yet, having been in a lazy mood, but shall very soon make a good start, I dare say. George Hake is a perfect god-send to the two little girls, who have made a complete slave of him for boating, punting, and pony-riding purposes, and they keep up a system of excursionizing to their hearts' content, as George seems never so well pleased as when they are making him escort them about. His good-nature is wonderful, but they are such charming and lovable children that it is really a pleasure to be with them. There is a most comically fat and stolid pony here which Morris brought last year from Iceland. He is more like Sancho's donkey than any-thing equine, and was never seen but twice from the window to do anything but eat in his private field. On two occasions only he was meditating with his back against a tree.

I have been very sorry lately to hear such poor accounts of Christina,—however, the last one is a little better. My love to her, to Maria when you write or see her again, and to my aunts. Also to Uncle Henry and poor Henrietta, of whom I suppose it would be no use hoping for better news. Could Maria evoke from her Dantesque chronology, which I know is very minute, the exact year, month, and day, of Dante's meeting with Beatrice in the Eden towards the end of the *Purgatorio*? Would you ask her this if you write? I want the date for a picture. I dare say it would be found in her book, but I have not got that by me.

I have been perfectly well since coming here, except indeed as regards my slight lameness, which however causes me no great inconvenience.

C 92.

Kelmscott.
3 November 1872.

Dear William,

I have been meaning to write to you since your departure, and received your message through the kids about poor Henrietta. I have since heard from her father, and answered him.

I send you on a letter of Howell's which will put you in some degree *au courant* of my present relations with him. The picture he agrees to buy is the one of Proserpine—price 550 guineas—and I have now told him he had better send cheque for half the price on account at once. . . . If I *do* settle out of London, it will be very important—indeed almost indispensable—to me to have a middle-man or agent, and an intermediate purchaser (alias picture-dealer) is the best kind. . . .

I fancy it may perhaps be the very thing for me, if he proves as able as willing to take work of mine freely. The *Proserpine* I am selling him is a second one I have begun. The first did not quite please me, but will sell as a separate thing by cutting out the head, which is done. The second is very well started, and I fully expect to finish it soon and bag the tin. There has been some delay, owing to a very bad cold of Janey's (I have had one too), and meanwhile I have done a very careful chalk-drawing of May, which will be worth 100 guineas, I doubt not.

Dunn will probably be telling you about moves towards houses out of town, but there seems nothing conclusive as yet. Please return me Howell's letter.

With love at home,
Your affectionate
GABRIEL.

C 93.

KELMSCOTT.
7 November 1872.

DEAR WILLIAM,

I send you an Italian sonnet for you to pick holes in. . . .

I got to-day from Parsons a cheque for one half the purchase-money (550 guineas in all) of the *Proserpine*, which progresses rapidly and well.

PROSERPINA.

Lungi la luce che in su questo muro
　　Mi giunge appena, un breve istante scorta
　　Del mio palazzo alla lontana porta.
Lungi quei fiori d'Enna, o lido oscuro,
Dal frutto tuo fatal per cui snaturo.
　　Lungi quel cielo dal tartareo manto
　　Che qui mi cuopre: e lungi ahi lungi ahi quanto
Le notti che saran dai dì che furo!

Lungi da me mi sento; e ognor sognando
　　Cerco e ricerco, e resto ascoltatrice;
　　E qualche cuore a qualche anima dice,
(Di cui mi giunge il suon di quando in quando,
Continuamente insieme sospirando)—
　　"Oime per te, Proserpina infelice!"

C 94.

"Scotus" is a familiar name which we applied to our friend Mr.
W. B. Scott. "Nolly's good luck" was the acceptance by Messrs.
Smith and Elder of Oliver Brown's highly remarkable tale *The
Black Swan* for publication. He was at this time only seventeen
years of age. The tale appeared under the title of *Gabriel Denver*.

KELMSCOTT.
12 *November* 1872.

Dear W——

I send you on this letter from Scotus, on account of
a passage towards the end which I think you would wish
to see. Thanks for your strictures on my sonnet, which I
perceive to be correct. I am glad to hear so pretty good
an account of Christina. Glad also to hear of Nolly's good
luck. I anticipate a great success for him. . . .

It is late bedtime, so good-bye. I never find time for
writing now in the day, being very regularly at work.

With love to all at home,

Your most affectionate
GABRIEL.

C 95.

"The summons" was a summons for my brother to attend on a
jury. I had offered a satisfactory explanation of his inability to

serve. Some years before this he had been on a grand jury, and insisted on throwing out a bill in some case (I forget what it was) which excited a certain public interest. As usual, he carried his point.

[KELMSCOTT.]
25 *November* 1872.

DEAR WILLIAM,

I am very sorry you should have had all this trouble about the summons. The right thing in such a case is to go at once to one's doctor, get a certificate, and send it in. Hearing you had written to Slowman, the thing flew out of my head, or I should have done this with Marshall, as I did once with Bowman when my eyes were bad.

As it is, I suppose you eventually got the thing from Marshall in time—otherwise I must make up my mind to be fined Heaven knows what, though in fact my being now settled out of town should be sufficient. . . .

With thanks for all trouble,

Ever yours,
D. G. R.

George and I are alone here now for the present.

C 96.

" Mouse's field " was the field wherein the Icelandic pony previously spoken of, named Mouse, was accommodated.

[KELMSCOTT.]
11 *December* 1872.

MY DEAR WILLIAM,

I have been meaning to write often, but it is extraordinary how, every day almost (if not indeed *quite*), some necessity of writing several letters turns up, so that any which are not quite necessary are apt to go to the wall.

Scott, as you know, has been here for several days, and has just left, as well as Dr. Hake. Scott told me you seemed anxious as to my state of funds. I am all right in this respect, though I have made a good many payments lately, some of them rather large sums. To-day I have more than

£550 in the bank, and shall certainly have at least £500 more in the course of January, so there is no cause for alarm. I have kept on paying new debts strictly on the nail, so all that is outstanding is what you already know of. . . .

Will you, when at Chelsea, open all letters that may be there for me, and only send on those I should wish to see? *The week's letters had better lie till you come for your inspection.* Will you mention this to Dunn? It is extraordinary, however, how very few letters seem to come to Chelsea.

I believe Scott reported to you an intention of mine to come up to London for Christmas Day, but I find that several causes combine to render this uncertain, much as I should like to see you all. I must write further on the point.

The floods have been out here now for a long time, but walking is still possible in the higher meadows. The tremendous gale of last Sunday night had some disastrous results, uprooting no less than six important trees—three in the avenue in Mouse's field, and three in the island by the boat-house. Three others—very large elms opposite the front gate—are so shaken that they will be sure to fall in the next gale.

I have had to shift my painting quarters from the tapestry-room to the drawing-room, which is now my studio. The other is insufferably cold in winter, and this was bad enough till I resolutely set about a system of stopping out all draughts with the help of the Lechlade carpenter. I have had a double casement made to the east window, and shut the south one up for the winter, so I have no crosslights, and the room is now (with some trouble) quite comfortable. I get on well with work, though much inconvenienced till Janey's return. I may probably, now that the tapestry-room stands empty, commence radical reforms there also. . . .

You may tell Maggie that I got a letter from Mrs. Cowper-Temple (to whom I had written asking her to help Brown's Cambridge affair if she could) in which she speaks enthusiastically of the *Shadow of Dante.*

We are getting into order that room with the tiled fire-

place, which I want to make into a drawing-room, as the old
one is now my studio.   However, most unluckily the
chimney always smokes.   We are setting about ways and
means to stop it, but I don't know how we shall succeed.

   With love to all,

Your affectionate Brother,

D. G. R.

C 97.

Mrs. Munro was the widow of my brother's old friend the sculptor
Alexander Munro. Lucy was the elder daughter of Mr. Madox
Brown. She became my wife on 31 March 1874 ; a tie cruelly
severed by the stroke of death on 12 April 1894.

[KELMSCOTT.]
Tuesday 17 December 1872.

DEAR WILLIAM,

   I got a mourning-card announcing Mrs. Munro's death.
I wrote to Miss Munro, and enclose her answer, which you
might like to see.

   I now think it most likely that I *shall* be at Euston Square
on Christmas Day, but probably leave London again the
following evening, unless I found that *you* could dispose of
a few days following, in which case I might probably enough
remain—say till about Tuesday.   Could you do this?   Or
must you absolutely be at Somerset House?

   An idea had already struck me of asking Mamma, yourself,
and our sisters (aunts also if willing and room possible to
find), to come and spend a few days here at Christmas,
instead of my coming to town.   It would be interesting, no
doubt, to all concerned, but I felt so dubious whether Mamma
and Christina were fit for the journey that I never mentioned
it.   However, I may as well just do so, and hear what you say.

   I believe it is most probable now that Brown, wife, and
Lucy, will be here for a few days *up to* Christmas Day, but
return to town on Christmas Eve.   If therefore the family-
party from Euston Square found it possible to come by any

chance, it would be safe to do so by any Tuesday train, as beds would be free in the evening. George, as I think I told you, is going up to town for a few days at Christmas.

C 98.

This note refers to two Dealers in Japanese and Oriental wares— Hewitt in Baker Street, and Farmer and Rogers then in Regent Street.

[KELMSCOTT.
18 December 1872.]

DEAR WILLIAM,

If you could look in at Hewitt's one day, would you see what Japanese screens he has, and what he wants for them—notably what *height* they are, and how many leaves? Also let me know the sort of colour. I ask you because Howell tells me he gave Hewitt £33 for a full-sized paper screen lately. I cannot understand this, if the same sort is meant as the one I have at Chelsea: that, I think, cost £2 10s. twelve years ago. I asked Howell a little while back to get me two such screens, and he sent me two which he got at the docks from a cargo of many such (all alike as he said). They are both here, but are too low to be thoroughly useful— not quite as tall as I am—each eight-leaved. The curious thing about them is that, while one is a genuine and fine Japanese product—silver-patterned paper outside and bird-and-foliage picture inside,—the other, though exactly similar at a casual glance, is evidently a most inferior copy; whether Japanese or not I don't know, but have often heard of a manufactory of Oriental goods at Lyons.

I should like you to make the enquiry at Hewitt's when you can, and would buy a screen, if reasonable in price and full-sized. Howell says Hewitt sells those like the one I had from him (Howell) for £10 each, and Farmer and Rogers for £15 each. I gave him £4 each.

*   *   *   *   *   *

Ever yours,
D. G. R.

I have not the least doubt Howell gave what he charged me for the two screens, but should like to see if a *suitable* one could be got reasonably.

B 61.

KELMSCOTT, LECHLADE.
2 January 1873.

MY DEAREST MOTHER,

Thanks for sending on the letter. I greatly enjoyed being present at our usual family-gathering on Christmas Day, and, had I failed to be so, should certainly have preserved the regret of such failure during the whole ensuing year. I wish I could have got down to Euston Square again before leaving town, but indeed found so much to do at Chelsea during the three days I remained there that I had my hands too full for another visit to you. I made an inventory of all drawings and commencements of all kinds which I have there, as there is a mass of work lying idle, which, if taken up at odd moments and made presentable, might probably be worth many hundred pounds, and which would otherwise be mere waste. I allude not to important things commenced, but to studies for other things etc. done for a purpose and then thrown aside, but which might easily be made valuable. I shall have these gradually sent down here to work on when it may be. Thus I should realize a fund for emergency out of things which, if left till the emergency came, would fetch next to nothing, and force me to part hurriedly with other things which I wished to keep.

While I was at Chelsea Graham called on me, and said I looked ten years younger! He himself seemed better in spirits than I had ventured to hope after his son's sad death, and appeared to be again taking interest in his former tastes and plans.

I find the weather here was not so fine during my absence as it was in London. George has brought down an additional dog—a very intelligent black-and-tan terrier which he has had from a pup. So now we have three dogs, what with the sheep-dog I got (named Turvy), the dog sent to George from Scotland, which is a cross between a Scotch deer-hound and a collie, and is named Bess, and the new dog who rejoices in the name of Dizzy after a celebrated politician.

Having been absent on Christmas Day, we were last night serenaded with a carol by the village-children. The weather here is decidedly colder than it was in .London, and to-day is very dismal. Moreover, a dreadful man in the neighbourhood, who has a beetroot-spirit factory, has established a steam-whistle to call his workmen. This goes seven times a day, beginning at 5 A.M., and is the dreariest of super- or sub-human sounds. It is a long way off, but still one hears it here much too distinctly to be pleasant.

Ellis is immediately going to republish my *Italian Poets*, which has been out of print for some time. I have also some thoughts of bringing out a small original volume, but on the whole shall probably wait till I have more new material by me.

I still have an idea of exhibiting the large picture with a few others of my latter things this Spring, but cannot quite make my mind up about it. My being here would not matter, as I could get the exhibition conducted in London without the least need of my assistance.

Hoping that you may have a very happy 74th year and many yet to follow it, I remain, my dearest Mother,

Your most loving Son,
GABRIEL.

99.

KELMSCOTT.
3 *January* 1873.

DEAR WILLIAM,

*   *   *   *   *   *

Can you find at your leisure at Chelsea twelve pages of *Salammbô* which are wanting in my copy which I brought here? I have read the book however (the last pages happening not to be very essential), and certainly you ought to read it. It is a phenomenal book, and could only have emanated from a nation on the brink of a great catastrophe. The line of demarcation between this and *Notre Dame de Paris*, published some thirty years before, is very singular to remark. Hugo's book astounds one with horrors, but they seem called up more for the purpose of evoking the extremes of human pity, and for the author's own luxury in that passion, than for any other aim. Flaubert, on the contrary, is not only destitute of pity, but one could not judge from his book, teeming as it does with inconceivable horrors, that such an element existed or ever had existed in human nature. . . . The only thing that deadens the agony of mutual destruction throughout to the reader is that it is perfectly impossible to feel the least preference for one character over another. Whether the picture of Carthaginian society be a perfectly true one it seems impossible to say ; nor can one conceive on what authority the author describes Carthage and all its details as minutely as he might do with Paris or London.

It seems the work of a nation from which mercy had been cast out, and which was destined soon to find none.

I believe Flaubert has written another book since. Do you know what it is ? Have I still *Madame Bovary* at Chelsea ? If so, I should like to have it and read it again.

C 100.

The " *Humorous Poems* " is a selection which I had made, forming one of the volumes of *Moxon's Popular Poets*.

[KELMSCOTT.]
Tuesday 7 January 1873.

MY DEAR WILLIAM,

Thanks for all trouble. The *Humorous Poems* are to hand, and George thanks you for the book—will do so, I dare say, in writing. I don't understand whether Nolly's wish for a hamster has yet been expressed to the Hakes in Germany or not.

There *are* some loose leaves in *Salammbô*, but still about a dozen pages are missing. . . .

I consider it extremely friendly on Stephens's part to revive the question of my picture, as I really had felt shabby towards him, in case I *do not* open an exhibition of it, as having led him to announce such fact beforehand. I can't feel sure yet what my plans in this respect may be. Howell is very pressing, and offers to undertake it, as did Gambart last year ; but Graham seems a little nervous of results on my account, and says the Agnews are the only people who could really carry it through. (Private, of course.)

If Stephens writes anything now, I should like him to speak also of a few things of mine done lately. I think I shall write him and put him in possession of the subject.

His address I think is 10 Hammersmith Terrace ?

The weather here has been terribly dark and most vexatious for painting. . . .

C 101.

[KELMSCOTT.]
8 January 1873.

Ellis is beginning immediately to reprint the *Early Italian Poets*. Would you mind the proofs' being sent always *first* to you to look through ? I find the job distasteful, and moreover have little daylight. But don't if it bores you or you are short of time.

C 102.

My brother's project of translating and editing the poems o. Michelangelo did not take effect. I hardly think he even made a beginning with it.

[KELMSCOTT.]
Friday 10 *January* 1873.

DEAR WILLIAM,

By some inconceivable mental aberration I did not remember when I wrote that of course the copy of my *Italian Poets* in question is the one I sent to Ellis in a dismembered state to print from. Pardon all nuisance in the matter, and thanks about proofs. . . .

I am writing to Ellis for the most recent and exhaustive edition of Michelangelo's poems etc. (if etc. there be). I mean to translate and edit him at odd times. Have you any edition of him, or Life of him? I am also writing to Ellis for a good Vasari. I think you have not one. . . .

Ever yours,
D. G. R.

P.S.—I am telling Ellis to send you the proofs regularly. Please, as each is done with by you, send it on to me, and I will forward to him.

C 103.

"Brown's *Address*," named in the P.S., was an Address which Mr. Madox Brown had prepared and printed, as a candidate for the Slade Professorship of Art at Cambridge. He did not obtain the appointment—Mr. Sidney Colvin being elected. I do not think Rossetti was correct in objecting to what Brown had written regarding Hogarth. Brown spoke (essentially) of Hogarth's originating power as a dramatic inventor of pungent actualities in art; and in this respect he certainly had not followed any tradition derivable from Watteau and the like painters. His "method" in executive painting may possibly have come from Watteau, but surely not any such series of concentrated scrutiny and momentous meaning as *The Harlot's Progress*, *The Rake's Progress*, and *the Marriage à la Mode*.

[KELMSCOTT.]
Sunday 12 January 1873.

DEAR WILLIAM,

I am going in for the Michelangelo scheme, and I have ordered, from Ellis, Vasari, Grimm's *Life*, and the best Italian edition of the Poems etc. Have you any book of value bearing on the subject, or do you know of any? My own impression is that Michelangelo stands about alone as a good Italian poet after Dante etc., unless we except Poliziano. What opinion have your readings led you to on this point ? I wish you would send me a Poliziano. I also want Cellini's *Life*, of which there ought to be a copy in 3 or 4 thin paper-bound volumes at Chelsea. I also want Torri's *Dugento Poeti* (4 vols., perhaps not all at Chelsea, as I think Hueffer has one or two, but am writing to him to send all my books hither instanter). I want both to see whether it contains any scrap by Michelangelo, and also to look at some things by Orcagna which were in it, as one might glance at other painter-poets. I also want a little book by J. E. Taylor, called *Michelangelo a Poet*, of which I fancy Mamma may have a copy. I don't know if it's worth anything, but would like to look at it.

Ellis takes to the plan, and I shall get about it at leisure when feasible.

Ever yours,

D. G. R.

P.S.—I have read Brown's *Address*, and think it excellent, but it is a great pity you did not see a proof. The punctuation is vile, and many sentences involved, besides wretched blunders, such as *A*rcagna. . . . The notion of the Synopsis of Lectures is rather perverse. Why Hogarth to start with ? Besides, it is nonsense about his reviving painting. His method is carried on direct from Watteau and other French painters. I fear all this will go against Brown.

C 104.

" My Blake " was a double picture, which Mr. Woolner had kindly presented to me, of Edward I. and William Wallace. It is the same design as the two "ghostly heads" which have been engraved in Gilchrist's *Life of Blake ;* but is the actual handiwork, not of Blake, but of Linnell. It is not now in my possession, having unaccountably disappeared.

KELMSCOTT.
Tuesday 14 *January* 1873.

DEAR WILLIAM,

I wish you'd send me the Michelangelo books you have. My own Biagioli would be better than yours, if to the fore, as being by itself. I'll write to Ellis not to get the edition I ordered of Michelangelo if he finds yours is the best. No need to send Vasari.

Perhaps I'll write to Knight. The announcement might as well be made.

Among spare frames of which I took notes at Chelsea, I find note of one with plain black bead outside and gilt flat under glass. Sight (*i.e.*, space for picture), 28½ × 24½ inches. Would this fit your Blake? If so, you can have it. It is somewhere near the back-door of the studio, in the passage, or beyond the midway glass-door there.

If it won't fit, I should think something rather in same style might suit the Blake.

C 105.

The "most splendid old portrait" here mentioned was disposed of in the sale at 16 Cheyne Walk in July 1882. I suppose it to be of the school of Antonio More, rather than by Zucchero or Porbus. Howell saw reason for affirming it to be a portrait of Lord Darnley by More himself: I am sure this is not correct, as to either personage or painter.

KELMSCOTT.
23 *January* 1873.

DEAR WILLIAM,

I have not yet acknowledged the books sent by yourself and Maria, as they only reached me this morning. The people who brought them with other parcels from the Station seem actually to have let this parcel fall out of the trap into the road, and there it was found by a bloke who brought it here this morning. Luckily no injury had occurred to the contents. The Guasti's Michelangelo seems an excellent edition, and must no doubt be the best. There is much more of it than I thought. Thanks to Maggie for her Cellini.

Trucchi (not Torri) was the author I meant. Hueffer has now sent all the books he had of mine (as he says) to Chelsea. One or perhaps two Trucchi vols. would be among them, I think. Dunn tells me some books are coming on.

When are you likely to travel this way again? George and I are once more alone.

Did I tell you I have got a most splendid old portrait sent here? which I bought in London some time ago, but had never got home, as it was being varnished and frame regilt. It is a life-size figure to the knees of a man in stiff buckram clothes—sort of armour, I suppose—leaning on his sword. It is a splendid work in the head and colour, which is as glowing as can be. Zucchero, I should think, or might be elder Porbus. Quite good enough even for Holbein, if the hands were not poor. It is in the most perfect preservation—not a false touch anywhere. I look on it as a most valuable acquisition.

I have got on capitally now with *Proserpine*, which will be my best picture, and am also turning two of the false shots I made at it into separate little head-pictures, so the thing altogether will bring me in £1,050.

With love to all,

Your
GABRIEL.

P.S.—For the future all parcels should be directed just like letters—Kelmscott, Lechlade—as a Station has opened at Lechlade.

C 106.

Mr. Stillman has been already mentioned. My brother always viewed him with much regard and predilection, although he did not at this moment encourage an early visit from him. Gabriel did not go with me to Italy in 1873, nor was he ever there. "The Edwards connexion" refers to Mr. Sutherland Edwards, who was an old and attached friend of the Hannay family.

[KELMSCOTT.]
4 February 1873.

DEAR WILLIAM,

I have the two first volumes of Trucchi here, and I see Michelangelo does appear in the second.

I don't know that it would be much use Stillman's coming here just now. I am fully occupied, and, seeing no one, have nothing to talk about. I should always of course like to see you or Brown, or the two or three with whom I keep up relations.

*　　*　　*　　*　　*　　*

I think Dunn is likely to be coming down almost immediately, and bringing a model with him from whom I want to draw. I also expect Howell on business as soon as I can make it convenient to have him. So, though bearing Stillman's proposal in mind, I fancy it might at any rate be better to defer it.

I wonder if combinations will let it suit me to go with you this year to Italy. I should like it much if feasible.

I was very sorry for Brown's defeat, but expected it from the first, and had hardly had my view altered by the views of others : Colvin was so evidently their man.

I would like to know if friends are joining to do anything for the Hannays. I liked their father, and really respected and admired their mother. If you hear of such plans through the Edwards connexion, let me know.

I have got at last the frame for Graham's *Beatrice* and predella, and have made them look quite satisfactory, I think, by last work. I am glad to say Graham seems taking interest again in his usual pursuits.

With love to all,

Your
D. G. R.

Everything is smothered in snow here.

C 107.

My brother's suggestion of my making a translation of Cellini's Autobiography bore no fruit. The work has of late years been done —and I suppose well done—by Mr. J. A. Symonds.

DEAR WILLIAM,

*   *   *   *   *   *

I'm quite uncertain about plans for Italy, since, were it to happen that your departure was just when this place had most attractions, I suppose I should stay here. . . .

Have you seen old Scotus's wonderful Burns letter? He told me he was giving a party, which I suppose you attended. . . .

I was thinking—suppose you were to make a characteristic translation of Cellini's *Life*. It would be worth doing with carefully preserved peculiarities. I suppose Roscoe's translation (I think he did one) would be a cut-and-dried affair, and perhaps with omissions.

*   *   *   *   *   *

C 108.

The volume of Dr. Hake's poetry reviewed by my brother in the *Fortnightly Review* was the *Parables and Tales*. As to the Michelangelo incident named by Gabriel, I think it *has* been painted by some French artist; certainly (but this may date later than 1873) by an Italian one, who exhibited the work in London. "The statue business at Vasto" was a proposal to erect a statue of our Father in his native place. The project remained for some years after this time in a state of suspended animation, on account partly of some shifting of political parties and interests. Afterwards it was revived, but has not yet been carried out. Signor Alfonso Celano, a local sculptor, was at one time expected to be employed.

DEAR WILLIAM,

I am to-day sending to Morley a notice of Dr. Hake's book for the *Fortnightly*. As it is late in the month, I have asked him to get the proof sent to *you* to save time. Will you kindly correct and return it at once, observing that my *punctuation* is retained (as I suppose they will send you the

MS. with it)? When the number is out, I would be obliged if you would get and send me a copy.

I expect Dunn and Howell down here to-morrow.

I am extremely sorry to hear of the disaster at Bath House, if it really proves to be a total destruction. The noblest thing there was a Leonardo (or most likely Luini) of the young Christ and St. John with a lamb, and a lovely background arrangement of lily-heads on darkness. Lady Ashburton wanted me much to copy this for her, and I am now sorry I did not.

There was also a grand Giorgione (so-called) which was two years ago at the R.A. Old Masters; a Titian, which was most likely the best of Bordones; a noble Velasquez of the Boar-hunt order; a large Rubens, almost the finest I ever saw, a hunting-piece, with some splendid sketches of his; an exquisite De Hooghe; and many other good things, including I rather think some charming Stothards.

What an excellent edition of Michelangelo that is which you sent me! I never knew before that all previous editions were from a garbled reproduction, not from the autographs, so in fact one is only just in time to translate it properly. I haven't set to work yet at all on it, finding an incredible amount of occupation, and being tempted a good deal to read in the evenings when I do not draw. There is a fine subject for a picture in Michelangelo's Life. Condivi tells us that he heard Michelangelo, when quite old, say that he regretted nothing more than that, when he visited Vittoria Colonna on her deathbed, he did not kiss her face but only her hand. This interview would make a noble picture, and I think I ought to paint it as a companion subject to my *Dante's Dream*. I suppose the omnivorous French School must have nobbled it somewhere, but don't remember to have seen it done.

I know (or rather have seen) the Burkmair Petrarch, and always thought Burkmair without a German equal for decorative abundance. I don't think people put him high enough. I hardly remember, however, that this book is better than the Cicero which is at Cheyne Walk. Both are more careful (but certainly not finer I think) than the *Weisse König,* which is after all his greatest work. You know he was Holbein's brother-in-law. . . .

I am extremely sorry to hear of Mamma's ailments and also of Christina's. I must try and get up to town for a few days when I can, chiefly for a family-visit. I feel greatly tempted towards Italy when possible, but fancy May will be just the time when I am most detained here.

Ever yours,
D. G. R.

    *   *   *   *   *   *

Have you heard any more of the statue-business at Vasto? Were I to go to Italy, I should feel much tempted in that direction, but for ovations impending. The best would be to go to the very quietest and most Italian places that could be heard of.

Morley's address is Puttenham, Guildford; but I suppose the proof would have to be returned to the printers, Virtue & Co., City Road. Of this you will no doubt hear.

C 109.

"The Vittoria Colonna portrait" must be one of which I possess a small engraving, from an original attributed to Michelangelo. "The piece of panelling" is a scrap of old wood-carving which I had picked up, representing the Creation of Eve. Mr. Madox Brown painted it later on into the background of his picture *Cromwell, Protector of the Vaudois;* here it had a peculiar appropriateness for the figure of Milton, in whose house the scene is laid.

[KELMSCOTT.]
26 *February* 1873.

DEAR WILLIAM,

Referring to my mems. I find that the frame I offered you for the Blake is 28½ × 24½. The first of these measurements is exactly right for you—the second could easily be reduced to 18 by a frame-maker. I think there is a glass. If you used that, it would have to be cut also.

I only lately (through laziness) sent my Italian sheets to Ellis. I suppose you will begin to receive proofs ere long. I have told him to send you the original sheets for rectification with the proofs, as *I* shall not need them. Morley has had to defer my notice of Hake to April, as it was longer than I had told him to expect. You will then probably get the proof.

I should very much like to see the Vittoria Colonna portrait you speak of. I believe there are several well-known portraits of Vittoria Colonna, notably one by Sebastiano del Piombo.

*   *   *   *   *   *

Thanks about the piece of panelling, which must be an unusually good one ; but I don't know that we'd have any particular use for it here. It is little worth while fitting up places unless we got a better hold on the house.

*   *   *   *   *   *

B 62.

KELMSCOTT, LECHLADE.
7 March 1873.

MY DEAREST MOTHER,

I have been meaning to write to you for ever so long, only news is so scarce in this wilderness. I am always meaning to take the first chance of coming to town, if only for a few days, on purpose to see you ; but day by day I find myself busied with work to a degree which might seem unlikely at this distance from the centre of things. I have a good deal of work in hand, of one kind and another, and have hitherto found no impediment to getting ahead with it. I take walks regularly. The floods are now gone again, but even while they lasted there were the higher fields to walk in, which remained free though not over easy walking. Only during the heavy snow, which occurred at two intervals, I was driven to the roads to walk, which are cheerless and monotonous enough. My health continues better than I am habitually in London, but I have lately been getting terribly fat again, which I fear is the healthy condition with me, but is not desirable. I suppose it is partly attributable to good appetite, as my walk always precedes dinner by an hour or so.

The other day I received from a Mr. Cates the MS. of a short biographical notice of my Father, which he had been drawing up for *Maunder's Treasury*, and wished me to revise it. This I did as best I could. He said he had extracted the facts from the *Biographie Universelle*, and they were pretty accurate and complete on the whole, though in small compass. Your progeny were all named, and I inserted you.

I have lately got the *Biographie Générale* in 46 vols., which Ellis recommended me as the best biographical dictionary,—I finding that such a work is a continual desideratum. I looked for my Father, however, and he was absent; though apparently present in the *Universelle*, which would have given it a preference with me. The *Universelle* I seem to have heard of all my life, and suppose they keep bringing out new editions and supplying deficiencies.

I am bringing out again my *Italian Poets*, as William may have told you; and he will help me in looking over proofs. This time I am calling the book *Dante and his Circle*, to direct attention primarily to its Dantesque relation. Proofs will come in soon, I believe, but as yet have not appeared. I wish you would ask William, when he goes to Chelsea, to look into that very old portfolio of MSS. of mine, and find a Canzone of Dante which I translated, but omitted from the first edition. The portfolio is in the bottom drawer, furthest from the corner wall, of the big bookcase in the studio, and the Canzone is, I think, the one beginning in Italian

"Perchè ti piace, Amore, ch'io ritorni," etc.

I think, now I am bringing the book out again, I may as well insert this, which I omitted formerly as bearing on no special event. It should be sent to me here, to insert wherever seems best in the proofs.

I am thinking of translating Michelangelo's Poems at spare time; but find hitherto much less leisure than might seem likely.

The weather here has been brighter and better for the last few days. When settled towards summer, or *in* summer as most feasible, perhaps you might manage a visit here with Christina, and Maria too if it might be. George will drive you, boat you, and punt you, to any extent. He is inexhaustibly active out of doors; and in consequence sometimes very sleepy indoors. His good-nature is without end. His eyes have been somewhat stronger lately, but any light striking on them in bed the first thing in the morning seems to set them wrong for the day. He is now reading leisurely for his degree at Oxford; but, the break-down with his sight having occurred at the moment when he ought to have tried for honours, he will now be able to take only an ordinary degree.

His father's book seems to be doing well on the whole, as regards criticism and sale; and an article which I have written on it is to appear in the *Fortnightly Review* for April.

No doubt you were sorry to hear of the death of John Marshall's boy. I shall write immediately to him, but my doing so was deferred by Brown's not having told me which son it was he had lost.

* * * * * *

You will be astonished to hear that Howell has been elected as Catholic representative to the School Board, and seems to have made some very remarkable *débuts* at the meetings in the way of speechifying—his style being decided and probably unexpected. He seems to think he has found his true vocation, and that a few years will see him in Parliament.

I have heard from time to time of your being poorly, and the accounts of Christina have been fluctuating, but never very satisfactory. I hope both will benefit by the improvement which I suppose we may fairly expect ere long in the weather.

With love to all, and to yourself endless love and remembrance, I remain

Your most affectionate Son,
GABRIEL.

I suppose your accounts of poor Henrietta continue much
as before.   My love to her and her father when you write.

C 110.

Joaquin, here named, is Mr. Joaquin Miller, the American poet.
He dedicated one of his volumes " To the Rossettis."

[KELMSCOTT.
Friday 22 March 1873.]

DEAR WILLIAM,

Thanks for suggestions.   On getting your proofs, I
sent on *my* proofs B and C to Strangeways the printers,
having embodied your corrections in them.   But the plan
you propose is the shortest, and I will write to Ellis to
adopt it.

I forgot before to say that, my Hake notice having been
deferred from the March number to the April one, and full
time thus obtained, Morley sent *me* the proof to correct
lately, and I returned it.

I suppose you have not a copy of Vittoria Colonna's
own poems.   I have been applying for one to Ellis, but
hitherto he has only found a very expensive one which I
don't care to pay for.

I heard yesterday from . . . Joaquin, with a request that
I would write a verse at the bottom of a photo of myself
(for which there was no room), and join my consent to yours
about a dedication. . . . I had rather not be dedicated to,
if there was any available reason for saying so.   However,
there is none, so it must come out.

*   *   *   *   *   *

Your
D. GABRIEL R.

P.S.—I really should like to try a few days' run to Italy

with you this year if feasible, but hardly think it will prove so.

P.P.S.—When Stephens proposed to write about my picture again, do you think he certainly meant *without* its being exhibited?

*   *   *   *   *   *

Please when next at Chelsea send me by post my copy of the *Shadow of Dante*.

KELMSCOTT, LECHLADE.
27 March 1873.

MY DEAREST MOTHER,

I hear with great anxiety from Maria that you have been suffering from an attack of influenza, and that you are still in bed. I hope Maria will continue to let me know regularly how you are. I trust, however, that the next news may be decidedly favourable.

The weather is very much finer here within some days past, and I suppose the same is probably the case in London, so I heartily trust that this may have a beneficial effect on a complaint like influenza.

I have most unaccountably mislaid Maria's letter ; but believe there was only one question in it, relating to the photograph of my drawing of Mary Magdalene. I believe there must be a few copies at Chelsea, but fear they are not good ones. I am writing to Dunn to look them up, and will let Maria know when I hear. The photo was not taken by Parsons, but long ago by Thurston Thompson, who is since dead. His widow still has the negative, which is my property, and prints from it when necessary. Her address is

Mrs. Thompson
The Residences
South Kensington Museum.

I think the number is 1, but am not certain. I will, however, write myself if there is no available proof at Chelsea.

*   *   *   *   *   *

I am meaning to dedicate to you the new edition of my

Italian Poets. The first was dedicated to poor Lizzy, and I had some thought of retaining the dedication with date ; but, this seeming perhaps rather forced, I shall substitute your dear name in the second edition.

Hoping to hear a better account soon,

I am ever

Your most loving Son,

D. GABRIEL R.

P.S.—I must really tell you about Dizzy, George's dog. Some evenings back he was lying by the fire in my studio, when George, who was going to bed, roused him to accompany him, as he generally does. Dizzy, however, was unwilling to quit the fire, and at last got so nasty and wicked that he bit George in the thumb. He was then locked up for the night in the coldest place that could be found.

In the morning he trotted into the breakfast-room as usual, but was received with shouts of obloquy, upon which he turned tail at once and fled. At dinner the same day he reappeared ; whereupon we tied him to the leg of the piano, and had in another dog who is here, called Turvy. We set a plate just out of Dizzy's reach, and fed Turvy with three successive helps of beef and macaroni, between each of which Dizzy's feelings found vent in " voci alte e fioche." After this Turvy was much caressed, and every now and then left us, to walk leisurely round Dizzy and survey him as an accessory deserving of passing notice. Dizzy has been a convict ever since, and knows it. This morning, on entering the breakfast-room, I found him rolled up on the mat before the fire, and, being occupied with other things, for the moment forgot his position. On my appearance, he raised his head in doubt, but, when I sat down and said nothing, he let his head drop again on the mat with an air of luxurious relief. This served as a reminder, and I shrieked, " What, not Dizzy ! " in such tones that he arose in a moment and fled to the shades with an expression of anguish which cannot be described. I think the ban will soon have to be taken off him now. At present the only relaxation is that he is allowed to accompany us in our walks, but without recognition from us. One only has to show one's thumb to him, and his sins fall back on his head in a moment, and drive him into solitude.

B 64.

KELMSCOTT, LECHLADE.
29 *March* 1873.

MY DEAREST MOTHER,

I am most glad to hear to-day from William that you are progressing favourably. I enclose a carte-de-visite of the baby hippopotamus, who seems to be supremely comic. He is something like Dizzy, of whom I must tell you a further anecdote. We are beginning to rehabilitate him gradually, and the other morning at breakfast I told George to rub some kidney-gravy on the thumb which Dizzy had bitten, and see if he would lick it off. He would not touch it, but hung his head piteously; though, as soon as the end of a finger instead was dipped in the gravy, he licked it up greedily. The same experiment was tried with each of the three or four places in which he had slightly bitten George, but he would not lick the gravy off any one of them.

*   *   *   *   *   *

B 65.

KELMSCOTT, LECHLADE.
6 *April* 1873.

MY DEAREST MOTHER,

I meant to have written before this to say how good a hearing it is to me to learn of your improvement, and, I trust I may say, recovery. But I have been unusually busy, as I have got a model—Miss Wilding—down to paint from. Dunn is here also, and is doing some work for me. I have nearly completed my picture of *Proserpine*, which had been lying by lately; and I believe it is about the best thing I have done.

Dizzy has been reinstated in his public position, but on sanitary accounts has been put chiefly on a diet of dog-biscuit. When served to him, he shows a complete superiority to the subject, and examines every other corner of the room as long as any one is in it, thinking that possibly some other *entrée* may be in reserve ; but, as soon as the last back is turned and the last hope fled, he turns-to instantly like a philosopher, and demolishes the dog-biscuit. No fewer than two more dogs have recently been added to the staff of this mansion. One is Nero, a splendid black retriever, whose colour alone makes the name bearable from an Italian point of view ; but I suppose he wouldn't answer to another, though as yet but a young dog. His action and expression are really splendid, and George finds him very useful when he shoots. The second dog is Jemmy, a funny sort of a rough terrier with long hair, and an apologetic St. Vitus's style of movement which suggests ill-treatment in previous abodes. George is going to make a present of him to some one. The result of these additions to the household is that, wherever George meets poor Dizzy, he bow-wows at his heels in an enquiring tone, as much as to say, "What, more dogs ? Explain ! " To-day all three accompanied George on a fifteen-mile walk. I fear the above caninities exhaust the Kelmscott budget of news, and that I have only left to say (with love to all and thanks for Christina's letter) how much I am always

Your most affectionate Son,
GABRIEL.

C III.

The opening of this letter relates to a detail in Rossetti's book *Dante and his Circle*. I need not enter here into the minutiæ. They are referred to in a note of mine to the *Collected Works* (Vol. II., p. 518). The "Article on Painting in *Quarterly*" was written by Mr. William Davies : I do not remember reading it.

[KELMSCOTT.]
Tuesday [6 *May* 1873].

DEAR WILLIAM,

I don't half like that hitch in my note about *Avolino* and *Aguglino*. I was certainly aware that *aquilino* was the name of a coin, since Cecco Angiolieri uses it; and I could almost swear that I looked for it in that sense (in connexion with this Forese matter) in the dictionary, but could not find it.

*　　*　　*　　*　　*　　*

Ever yours,

D. G. R.

P.S.—I at last to-day send 50 guineas to Marshall, which I ought to have done long ago ; but partly have been always short of tin, and partly Brown thought it would be better, if possible, to paint or draw some family-portrait for him— but this would never come about, now I live here.

Have you seen some article on Painting in *Quarterly* ? It seems I am not more blackguarded than other people !

*　　*　　*　　*　　*　　*

B 66.

Towards the close of this letter a question is raised as to a date, 1847, inscribed on a medal of our Father. This was a medal struck in Italy, the artist being Signor Niccolò Cerbara—a fine piece of work. The true explanation of the date is that the medal was struck soon after the publication, 1846, of our Father's poem *Il Veggente in Solitudine*, which, being a strong manifesto of patriotic feeling, anti-papal and anti-Austrian, excited a great sensation in Italy, where its circulation was of course clandestine, but not the less extensive. My brother must have been mistaken, apparently, in supposing that the portrait of our Father which he painted in 1848 could have guided the artist of the medal. The true date of the oil-picture was 1848— not 1847, as named by my brother.

KELMSCOTT, LECHLADE.
20 *May* 1873.

MY DEAREST MOTHER,

I have only learned to-day the distressing news of Maria's illness, which, however, I trust there is every reason to believe has taken a turn towards assured recovery. Will you give her my love, and say how grieved I am to know that she has been suffering so much ?

I hear you have been back in London since Friday last, and that Christina follows to-day. Would you be disposed ere long for a trip hither, if all be propitious? and how many could come? At present the house is not free, but will be so soon, I believe. The only difficulty then might be the possible necessity of my getting a model down here to paint from—but there might be an interval, and it would give me very great pleasure to see you here when feasible.

The weather gives occasional symptoms of thorough revival, but then falls back again. Last night there was a frost with ice! yet to-day it is sunny and fine, though not very warm. The apple-blossom in our orchard has been in full glory, and is still delicious, and everything is most lovely. I shall try if I can pack you a bouquet safely to Euston Square to-day, including wild flowers—especially the yellow Mary-buds (or marsh-marigolds), which are most splendid in the fields wherever the floods have been most persistent. By the bye, I wrote a Sonnet on *Spring* lately, and will copy it at end of this letter. The *Athenæum* people asked me for some verses the other day, and I didn't like to refuse, so a little piece of mine will be in their next number. It is one I wrote when first I came here, and embodies a habit of the starlings which quite amounts to a local phenomenon, and is most beautiful and interesting daily towards sunset for months together in summer and autumn.

I am glad William is bound for Italy, and really still feel sudden impulses to accompany him, but suppose I cannot well do so. . . . I am glad to hear Lucy is going, though old Scotus seems quite sulky about it. Don't let William tell him I said this, as he is able to hate one now on the slightest provocation. How nice it would have been if William, I, and old Brown, could have gone together!

Your dear birthday passed m
from me (most blameably).
more than once beforehand, a
moment slipped by somehow
write ever since.

Can you in any way account for the date 1847 on that medal of my Father? I am glad to have it, and find that, if one shuts off about a third of the length of the chin, it has something decided in the way of likeness.

By the bye, I know you are a great keeper of family-relics, and the other day found here a little portrait of myself as a child, which you once lent me two years ago, and which ought to have been returned before. Shall I send it? At the same time I would ask you for something else in the same line if you have it. I remember that for the family *Hotch Potch*, long and long ago, I first wrote *The Blessed Damozel*, and also a poem about a portrait. Have you these ancient documents, and could you let me have the same if in my own handwriting? Not, however, if you set store by them. What is the date thereof?

I hope Christina reached London safely ere this, and am, with truest love,

Your affectionate Son,

D. GABRIEL R.

The medal is the more puzzling as I suppose the authority was in great measure the photo from that head I painted, which was one sent there lately. But why 1847?

It suddenly strikes me that, 1847 having been the date of the portrait, this might be a sort of reason, though a very stupid one.

C 112.

KELMSCOTT, LECHLADE.
10 *July* 1873.

MY DEAR WILLIAM,

You will not doubt how heartily I rejoice in your engagement to Lucy. I really believe there is not in the whole of our circle a woman on whose excellence all of us could place such perfect reliance, or of whom we should feel so sure that she would make you happy. Both our Mother and Brown are, I am sure, absolutely delighted with the prospect.   Will you give Lucy my sincere love, and say I wish I were worthier to be her brother and yours?

My mother has been thoroughly enjoying herself here, I am sure ; and it is curious that both she and Christina have happened more than once to speak very strongly in Lucy's praise, and express their love for her very warmly.   I just now told George Hake of the engagement, and he said that yesterday in the boat my Mother was saying to him that she valued Lucy more than any woman she knew.

Christina has plucked up in an extraordinary way out here, and is quite active and natural again.   Even in appearance there is an improvement.

My work goes on well ; and I find I have no difficulty, with Howell's assistance as salesman in London, in disposing of what I do to as much advantage as ever, without the awkwardness of writing to purchasers much myself, which might otherwise be so nauseous as seriously to stand in the way of business.   I have several things in hand, some sold, some not, and shall soon be much better stocked with tin than my wont.

Brown has begun a very fine picture of *Cromwell on his Farm*.   He has begun putting in the material straight from Nature, with great vigour and fine tone, and I would almost say that it promises to be his very best picture.

B 67.

KELMSCOTT.
19 *July* 1873.

TEAKSICUNCULUM,

I was very glad to hear that you reached London in comfort.

It is a privation not to see your dear old self trotting about the gardens, and the time we spent here, with Christina, was a most grateful one to me.   That it may recur before long is one of my warmest wishes.

The accounts of George are good, and I believe there is no doubt that he will be here again on Monday next.   The children, who came yesterday with Janey, will be short of their habitual larks till he appears. Both look much in need of country air. . . . Janey looks wonderfully well, I think, but does not seem over strong. She sends kindest regards.

The window of the little drawing-room, at which I often used to see your darling head from the garden, now shows on inspection a dismantled room, everything having been removed,—the furniture to the large drawing-room, my former studio, and the drawings to my present studio in the tapestry-room, where they go along the whole of one wall, and look better than ever they looked before, with the fine dim tone of the tapestry behind them.

In the drawing-room great effects have been produced. That beautiful cast of Psyche (which I dare say you noticed) has been put on a shelf, with another shelf beneath it containing the Hastings earthenware pig, which may serve as a sort of monogram signature to the statue—*Pyg*malion ! ! ! . . .

The white lily in the garden has grown to a perfect decorative cluster now, and is most divinely lovely. Another white lily is developing also, but the others which excited your curiosity remain as yet unexplained. Janey planted them, and believes them to be tiger-lilies. St. Swithin should be called St. Swindler this year, for he has beneficently cheated us. There has not been a drop of rain since his ominous downfall.

* * * * * *

Love to all, Lucy included.

Take care of your dear funny old self, and believe me

Your most loving Son,

D. GABRIEL R.

C 113.

The " very serious step " of our sister Maria was her entering the All Saints' Sisterhood (Anglican) as a novice, and in due course as a professed member.

[KELMSCOTT.]

6 *September* 1873.

DEAR WILLIAM,

A reduced replica is being scaled out for me at Chelsea from the large *Dante's Dream,* which is now there ; and I have a request from Graham to let him have the replica when done instead of the original, as being more convenient to hang in a room. Thus the original returns to me for second sale, and Howell is seeing about it for me. Have you that article Stephens wrote on the picture in *Athenæum?* Howell wants it much for use. If you have or can get it, please kindly at once send it him. I suppose it must have been somewhere towards end of 1871 or beginning of 1872.

*   *   *   *   *   *

I hear to-day from Maria about her very serious step, and with an intimation of her renewed illness, which seems to make such a step still more serious. I must answer as soon as may be.

In haste,

Your affectionate

D. G. R.

B 68.

The picture mentioned at the beginning of this letter is *La Ghirlandata.*

KELMSCOTT, LECHLADE.

13 *September* 1873.

MY DEAREST MOTHER,

It is long since I have written you, I fear ; chiefly because there is little to tell, and to convey correct notions of that little from a distance is a roundabout proceeding when the only thing one does is one's daily work. I am now putting the last touches to the picture I began from Miss Wilding when you were here. It has turned out about my best, I think, but of course has taken me much longer than I looked for, little else having been accomplished since I saw you. Little May Morris appears twice in the picture, as a couple of angels. She has become a most lovely model, but her health is a constant subject of anxiety.

I judge that since Thursday Maria is no longer an inmate of Euston Square. She will indeed be a great loss, being much the healthiest in mind and cheeriest of us all, except yourself. William comes next, and Christina and I are nowhere. I suppose of course she will appear duly at our Christmas gathering, will she not? I am quite uncertain now whether I am likely to see you again before that date. Work thickens round one, wherever one is; and where one's work is, there one must be. My new picture is to go to my good friend Graham, who wants to have it this month in Scotland if possible, as his house is full of visitors.

I look back often with the keenest pleasure to the time of your stay here. The amount of enjoyment you get out of the simplest things is indeed a rebuke to the younger ones around you. I never told you yet that the tall flowers you felt curious about turned out to be tiger-lilies, and, being pretty numerous, made a fine show when in bloom, as a few of them still are. But the garden is fading fast now,—the most noticeable things at present being some most curious flowers growing on long stems. [Here a sketch of the flowers is given.] They are a bright red at top and a paler flame-colour below, and are here familiarly termed red-hot-pokers, but I have some reason to believe that their real name is Ixia. Do you know them? They are perhaps more like foxes' tails than anything else. We have a nice garden-seat now in the arbour opposite the front door and porch of the yew-hedge. I often regret that it was not there during your visit, but will not doubt your sitting in it yet. The river-growths have continued to develop one after the other. The arrow-head rush put forth eventually a most lovely staff of blossoms just like a little sceptre. [Here follows a sketch.] The way that the white blossom grows triple round the staff is most lovely, and the whole might really be copied exactly in gold for a sceptre.

On Thursday George was at a wedding at Manchester, and during his absence Dizzy returned for a while to his cuneiform stage of aspect and demeanour. He has been very funny in various ways. On one occasion we got a musical instrument—a dulcimer, which lies flat on the ground—and put a bit of sugar on the strings. Then, as Dizzy approached to take it, the strings were immediately struck with the plectrum, and the contest of terror and appetite in Dizzy's bosom was delicious. On one occasion an attempt was made, in his interest, to reduce him to a diet of dog-biscuit. He became gradually more and more dejected, until one morning he ate a stone instead, which, reappearing on the hearthrug, convinced his master that he must not be reduced to despair again. Whenever he wants to be petted, his plan is to eat a bit of crab-apple, or something he obviously would not eat if he could help it. An outcry of compassion is the immediate result, followed by successive courses of kidneys, maccaroni, etc.

I was asking Brown to come down here for a day or so, and shall probably fix a date with him in a post or two. Do you think William and Lucy would come also? The weather is pretty good on the whole just now as a rule, though to-day there was a good deal of rain.

* * * * * *

George desires to be most kindly remembered to you. . . . You probably know that his father has gone to Italy: the last we heard of him was from Genoa, which seems to rouse his British sanitary terrors to no small extent.

I'll enclose you some photographs of little May to look at. Please send them me back, as they may be of use to me in painting.

Your most loving Son,

GABRIEL.

Love to M[aria], W[illiam], and C[hristina].

C 114.

[KELMSCOTT.]
Tuesday [23 *September* 1873].

DEAR WILLIAM,

Thanks for sending on letters. Will you open all Dunn sends you, and see if they should be sent on or not ?

I am very sorry you could not come with Lucy, but I know you have no holiday before the end of the year. I have finished my picture for Graham, and think it is the best I have done so should have liked to show it you. However, I dare say there will be some other chance.

Your affectionate

G.

I don't know if there's anything at Chelsea that would be of service to you in furnishing ; but if so it could probably be spared, and you would be most welcome to it.

C 115.

Two books are mentioned here : *The Shepherd's Garden*, by Mr. William Davies, for some years a very cordial friend of my brother ; and *Gabriel Denver*, by Oliver Madox Brown. The idea that our sister would not be allowed a fire at the All Saints' Home turned out to be erroneous. The stricter rule of the Sisterhood was relaxed in her favour.

[KELMSCOTT.]
Thursday [13 *November* 1873].

DEAR WILLIAM,

There is no Italian word—is there ?—to express the fall of the year, as *Capodanno* expresses the beginning : Cascadanno, or Cadifoglia (both of course absurd), or something of that sort.

* * * * * *

If you find a book sent for me called *The Shepherd's Garden*, please send it on. No doubt you agree with me that Nolly's story is quite miraculous. I should think he would get into a swing of regular income by this sort of work very soon.

Love to all at home. I have really felt very sincerely anxious about Maria since what you tell me of no fires in this blessed place. I simply could not exist on such terms— it would be a noviciate for another world; and I view the matter as most serious for her.

B 69.

KELMSCOTT.
18 *December* 1873.

DARLING TEAKSICUM,

I wrote to my wine-merchant to send Christina two dozen Champagne like mine.

*   *   *   *   *   *

I supposed Christina might not be well enough to be visible in the morning when I left Euston Square, but now fear that I forgot to remit her my love in leaving. Still, as she had it already, perhaps this does not matter. I hope she is no worse since; and trust to see you all again on the 24th, including Sister Maria Francesca. I shall probably sleep at Euston Square on the night of 24th, if suiting you.

It is no use to wear out your loving eyes with a wade through *Dante and his Circle*, as it is just the same as the old edition, except for transpositions of arrangement and for minor revisions. The only addition worth naming is a Canzone by Dante, page 115.

C 116.

Mr. Madox Brown's two Lectures were on *Invention in Art.* He was "on his back" through an attack of gout. "My Blake" is the Aldine Edition of William Blake's Poems, prefaced by a memoir which I had recently written.

[KELMSCOTT.]
15 *January* 1874.

DEAR WILLIAM,

Brown was here the other day, and read me his two Lectures, which are full of excellences. But in minor points they are shaky here and there, delivery especially. . . .

Could you not suggest to Brown an official home-reading for this purpose, and to try his powers of delivery before the actual moment? He seemed to clip his words, and run one sentence into another.

I have no news in particular, and merely just write on this point. I hope things are pretty well at home. By the bye, I am sorry to learn that since Brown got home he is on his back again.

Your affectionate
D. G. R.

When will your Blake be out? Brown was very loud in its praise, and I am anxious to see it.

C 117.

The subscription which my brother forwarded with this letter was (if I remember right) £20.

KELMSCOTT, LECHLADE.
18 January 1874.

MY DEAR WILLIAM,

Ever since I heard of poor Hannay's death, I have been wishing to learn something as to his family. You tell me that the circular you send reaches you through Sutherland Edwards. I should have expected to find him among the foremost of Hannay's old friends at such a need, but hardly to find him the *only* one. What has become of the others? But I suppose of course the subscriptions noted in MS. on the circular are not all that have been yet received.

I enclose a subscription, which please forward. It seems to me, however, that this private effort can hardly hope to provide for the "maintenance and education during a certain number of years" of three children, unless it progresses with unusual success. I am anxious to know whether the children, or their elder brothers and sisters, have any special wishes or views as to the course to be taken, and should be extremely glad to hear anything on this head, and to aid at any time in any way in my power. I see Mr. J. L. Hannay's name in the printed list. Is he not now a Police-magistrate? Surely some influence might be exerted to provide proper *education* at least for these three children or for some of them, without outlay: their father's name should command this.

Of course any help I could render would be always limited enough. But at any rate I have no family of my own to provide for, and am therefore doubly bound to do what I can for an old friend's children.

C 118.

Lord Derby (the Peer deceased in 1892) had known Mr. Hannay in some political matters, especially matters of parliamentary candidateship. Mr. Ormsby, a bright writer on the press, died some years ago. Dr. Steele, a physician, had been intimate with Hannay in Edinburgh : he is now, I think, in Rome. Being brother to the lady then married to our cousin Teodorico Pietrocola-Rossetti, he has a distant family-connexion with us.

[KELMSCOTT.]
18 *January* 1874.

DEAR WILLIAM,

Some time ago I remember hearing . . . of the Mr. Gruneisen who receives subscriptions for the Hannay fund. If you think it best to send enclosed cheque to him, do so. I have accompanied it with a letter which you might, if you thought it advisable, send on to Edwards (in case you sent *him* the subscription), as indeed it seems to me some steps should be taken to get these children into some institution, to be educated. Surely this could be done. Do you know if Lord Derby has been appealed to? Don't of course bother to send the letter to any one, if not convenient to you, but the present subscription appears to me likely to be a very slow process. How is it Ormsby does not appear? and Steele?

C 119.

Mr. Madox Brown had undertaken to deliver in Birmingham the lectures mentioned in C 116. Being at this time much disabled by gout, he was thinking of getting the lectures read out by his son, in his own stead. But eventually, with a severe struggle, he managed for himself. "Jenny fille" is the elder daughter of Mr. Morris.

[KELMSCOTT.]
14 February 1874.

MY DEAR WILLIAM,

Your news of Brown is still of an uncomfortable kind. I suppose the lecture-question must be settled by the time this reaches you. The idea of Nolly's going seems totally impossible. In a lecture the sight of the Lecturer himself is a principal ingredient; and surely Nolly has no habit or faculty of delivery whatever.

The date fixed for your wedding is much about what I expected. I am sure that on this subject it would be quite impossible for you or Lucy to mistake my true feeling ; but I have already said that I should not feel equal to coming, unless the party were strictly confined to old friends without admixture of new acquaintances. Otherwise I would hope for and rely on the more congenial kind of meeting which we might have here if (as I trust will not fail me) you can both come down at an early date.

At present I am going about with a black patch over my nose. Last night Jenny *fille* and I agreed to shriek at the same moment (one "Creepy" and the other "Crawly") in Dizzy's two ears, while May beat a tattoo on the top of his head. The instant result was that he turned round howling, and bit me (fortunately not Jenny) across the nose ; at which I am not surprised.

Your

D. G. R.

Love to all at home.

B 70.

KELMSCOTT.
23 February 1874.

MY DEAREST MOTHER,

I have often and often thought of you since we last met,—always whenever my path in the garden lies by the window of that summer-room at which I used to see your dear beautiful old face last summer, reading or enjoying the garden prospect. That room is out of use now, as one cannot make anything of it in the winter; but I do warmly hope that we may renew this coming summer the very happy days we had here last year, and find that room a cheerful and pleasant resort again. It would make us all happy to see Christina pluck up once more as she did the last time.

To-day the little Morris girls collected all the flowers we could find in the garden, no very choice gleaning—and they were sent on to you, so perhaps you have them ere this reaches you. I know they will be better than nothing to your flower-loving heart. This extremely mild winter causes many things to be very forward already. The children were quite sorry afterwards that they had omitted to send you some branches of the palm-willow, with its furry buds not yet as yellow as they will be. The gum-cistus you planted thrives, but of course is very gradual in growth.

My good friend Graham has had a severe attack of illness, resulting chiefly I suppose from over-work, and has not gone in again for Parliament. His improvement has been slow, but he may now be considered well again at present. He is marrying one of his daughters on the 26th, and George Hake will take up a picture on Wednesday 25th to him, which I have been getting done in time to figure at the wedding. It is one of little Annie, the niece of the Cumleys, whom you may remember; indeed you will perhaps call to mind the beginning of the picture, which I took in hand last Spring, but have only just resumed and finished. It represents a young girl putting a jar containing Mary-buds on a mantelshelf. There is a great deal of accessory work in it now—including a black kitten playing with a ball of thread; and in pictorial qualities I think it is as successful as any of mine. I call it *The Bower Maiden.* Graham is still most affectionate, and seems to take such delight in what I paint that it is a pleasure to work for him. George also takes up

Proserpine to Leyland; this, which you saw but which has since been vastly improved, is, I think, perhaps my best picture. I have various other things in hand—one with three heads of lovely little May Morris; and the *Roman Widow* picture, for which you saw a study, will I hope soon be very forward now.

I have been very sorry to hear of Brown's unsatisfactory health. I don't yet clearly understand what sort of wedding-party it will be on the 31st March. . . . If a crowd of new acquaintances . . . are to be assembled, I have told William that I am not equal to such a gathering, and he has most kindly taken the announcement in good part. If, on the other hand, the matter is limited to old friends, I should hope to be there.

Dizzy has had a green velvet coat made for him, and walked about the dinner-table to-day like dog Toby. Perhaps William told you of his biting me, but it was quite my own fault, as I was teazing him past bearing. The bite is all right now.

Good-bye, dearest darling. I'll enclose a Winter Sonnet written lately.

Your loving

GABRIEL.

Love to dear good Maggie when you see her.

C 120.

My marriage with Miss Madox Brown was now fixed for 31 March; and Brown's arrangement was to bespeak a large evening-party for the 30th, and to invite to the wedding-breakfast the various members of the two families, without any one else. It is to this arrangement that my brother's note refers.

He never found out, I think, who was the donor of the *Resurrection* picture. After a while he gave it (if memory serves me) to our sister Maria, and I presume that it is still the property of the All Saints' Sisterhood.

[KELMSCOTT.]
Friday [13 *March* 1874].

DEAR WILLIAM,

    *   *   *   *   *   *

    I am most grieved to hear that Brown continues disabled and ailing. It is a sore trial for him and his. I am most loth, even to great regret, to be away from the party on the eve of your wedding ; but the fact is that, at such a gathering as you indicate, every bore I know and don't know would swoop down on me after these two years' absence, and I am not equal to it, now that solitude is the habit of my life. I cannot say that a breakfast of unknown relations smiles on me either, any more than on you ; but that is unavoidable, so there's an end. I cannot see what is the object of Brown's getting together all the relations he never sees.

                        Your affectionate Brother,

                                    GABRIEL.

    Did I tell you that some unknown party has sent me a little *Resurrection* on panel by Pietro Laurati ? It is very good in its way, and really fine colour. Quite genuine, no doubt. Who has sent it, or why, I cannot imagine.

C 121.

    Rossetti did not ever produce his proposed picture of Madonna Pietra—who is one of the ladies with whom Dante is (rather dubiously) reputed to have been in love during his exile. My brother made a slight pen-and-ink sketch of the subject—also a nude study for it.

                              [KELMSCOTT.
                              21 *March* 1874.]

    Have you among your photographic slides or other photos any representing rocks and water, chiefly distant— something in the way of the background to Lionardo's *Lady of the Rocks* ? Of course I mean from Nature. If so, could you keep it for me when I see you. Or a circle of hills also ?

    I want these things for background of *Madonna Pietra* from Dante's Sestina.

B 71.

Christina's " little book " is her volume of prayers entitled *Annus Domini.*

MY DEAREST MOTHER,

    *   *   *   *   *   *

I enclose a letter from Lucy in W[illiam]'s hand-writing which Nolly, who is here, had in his pocket. I thought you might like to see it. Nolly has been here a week now. He came down with Hueffer, both walking a considerable part of the way, and then coming on by rail. Hueffer went home in two or three days, and Nolly will now shortly leave, I suppose.

I am glad Maria is with you. My love to her, as well as to Christina, and thanks to the latter for her little book. As far as I have seen the contents, I think them fervent and beautiful. I should judge it possible that the book might prove widely acceptable. . . .

The country is getting genial and pleasant. Many flowers are coming out—abundant daffodils in the garden, Mary-buds all over the fields near the river—and the island by the boat-house is rich in wild periwinkles, a large beautiful blue-purple flower. I must try and send you some gleanings.

I am engaged still in painting the *Roman Widow* subject, which goes on well. . . . Do you happen to have anywhere any tortoise-shell article of that very bright tint, strong dark spots on a light-yellow ground, which one sometimes sees, reminding one a little of a panther's skin? I mean to make the surface of the two harps on which the *Roman Widow* plays of tortoise-shell thus tinted.

B 72.

MY DEAREST MOTHER,

Many thanks for loan of the card-case. It is just about the tint I meant, and no doubt will be very useful. I will take greatest care of it.

Why, WHY, WHY did you not come to Kelmscott, if you had to leave town? The weather is divine here now, and everything lovely. . . .

Your most loving

GABRIEL.

I think the poem in *Annus Domini* most excellent, like all Christina's religious poetry. Nolly took the book up while here, and was struck by the beauty of the prayers.

B 73.

KELMSCOTT.
17 *May* 1874.

MY DEAREST MOTHER,

I return William's letter, and am heartily glad to think how thoroughly he has enjoyed his honeymoon. I do trust that his somewhat monotonous existence hitherto will now assume a brighter and warmer tone for him. No man deserves happiness more, or is better adapted to give and receive it. I must say the recurrence of colds and such-like with Lucy seems to me an anxious matter, and one to be guarded against. I fear her constitution is anything but strong; indeed, she hardly ever seems quite free from something of this sort.

* * * * * *

I do not realize William's raptures about Vesuvius in the absence of any fireworks. I suppose what he so much enjoyed must have been the prospect; but of course, never having been there, I do not realize the situation.

That old white *Annunciation* of mine has passed into the possession of my friend Graham, who bought it of the mighty Agnew, its purchaser in the sale-room.

I should have finished the *Roman Widow* picture ere this, but that I am at a standstill for want of roses. Meanwhile I am getting to other things.

You will be amused to hear that we have got a little tame owl. When caught, he was in a nest with two others. One escaped, and the other two became ours; but, during the very first day of their being here, one was lost through carelessness. The other remains.   He was quite young at first—about two or three weeks old—and so covered with a sort of furry moss that I christened him Mossy.   Now that he is growing up, he does not seem to be a barn-owl, but something more like the lost lamented Bobby, only not so dark, and his eyes, though large and fine, not quite so softly expressive.   We keep him upstairs in an attic, where he begins now to fly about, and George feeds him twice a day.   Sometimes he comes down to meals, and sits on the table.   One can stroke him and handle him, and I suppose he will remain quite tame.

    *   *   *   *   *   *

The *Winter* Sonnet you liked, and the one on *Spring*, I have sent to the *Athenæum*, where they will appear Saturday after next.

With love to yourself and to my Sisters, I am
Ever your most affectionate
GABRIEL.

P.S.—Your birthday seldom escapes my memory, but I am ashamed to say that this year it somehow did.   All warmest wishes now.

C 122.

"Christina's title" applied to the book of prose stories which was published in 1874 under the name of *Speaking Likenesses*: the title previously chosen was *Nowhere*.   The bedroom in the Euston Square house was shortly fitted up for my brother as he wished, but he never occupied it: had he done so from time to time, this would probably have conduced not a little to the comfort and cheerfulness of his closing years.

[KELMSCOTT.]
Wednesday [*May* 1874].

MY DEAR WILLIAM,

I had just been answering a letter received from Brown this morning as to your proposed visit, and answering it (alas by compulsion) negatively.   I think I had better enclose it, and you can hand it to him afterwards. Thus I need not recapitulate what vexes me most extremely, as I am sure you know; but you will see with me that the moment would be of unique inopportuneness in the whole year. I shall nevertheless hope for a rapid run-down here from you and Lucy, when Brown (and I trust our people) may be with me.

Christina's title seems unlucky because of that free-thinking book called *Erewhon*, which is "Nowhere" inverted. The title would seem a little stale; I should change it.

You know we spoke of my retaining as my bedroom at Euston Square, when I can come there, that little room at the top where I used to sleep. For this a comfortable iron bedstead, a bath, and otherwise the simplest accommodations, would be needed. You see, never getting sight of you all now, I should like sometimes, when I *do* come to town, to take this means of being with you awhile, as well as at Chelsea. Could you give me at leisure a notion of what would remain to be got for this purpose (for I think you said that, as to the room, it might be mine)? and I would send the needful, if Lucy would kindly take the small matter in hand.

Your loving
GABRIEL.

Your letter reached me mid-day by hand.

H i.

From this point onwards I include a few letters addressed to my wife. "The little old *Annunciation*" had been received by Gabriel from its then owner Mr. Graham, and he re-worked upon it to some extent, but only a very moderate one. Mr. Brown's "Cardiff portrait" was a portrait (I consider) of a local gentleman, Mr. Riches; it was engraved in 1893. Or possibly it was a portrait of Mr. David Davies, who became M.P., or of Mrs. Davies.

[KELMSCOTT.]
23 May 1874.

MY DEAR LUCY,

How very kind of you to write at such a busy moment about my requirements! I will forward £20 ere long for the purposes of the bedroom, and have no doubt that all your arrangements will be perfection. I prefer a chair-shaped bath if attainable—or should one buy a coal-scuttle shape? Bedstead might be not *quite* so exiguous in width as the Euston-Squarites seem to affect, but still quite cheap and simple. Thanks about curtains and carpet, which I had not thought of; of course drugget or anything will do. The rest, just a washstand of any kind, and a Spartan chair or two, with a ditto table of some sort perhaps; but this hardly needed, if washstand suffices without it.

It will be a great pleasure when I *do* see you both here—I trust, in improved weather. Yesterday I went for a walk rather earlier than usual, and was astounded to find everything changed for warmer and brighter—wind south-west, and swarms of dragon-flies round one's head—to such an extent that to walk under the sun in one's usual clothes was quite a labour. To-day all has receded again to gloom, with addition of rain. I hope William will keep his four outstanding days of holiday for the welcome purpose of a visit here ere long. I want it to be before my *Roman Widow* picture leaves me—also the little old *Annunciation*, which I should like to show you for lack of a press of newer work.

I am glad your Papa has got his Cardiff portrait so well forwarded, and trust you and he can manage to be here together.

With love to William (and my other kith and kin if there) I am

Affectionately yours,

D. G. R.

B 74.

The review which my brother mentions in this note must be a notice of his *Poems* which appeared in an American Roman Catholic paper, named *The Catholic World*. It pleased him much; and he often at a later date expressed a wish that he had at the proper time taken steps for learning who the writer might be. He never ascertained this point distinctly. In the Bibliography which is appended to the *Life of Rossetti*, by Joseph Knight (*Great Writers* series), this article is ascribed to " J. C. Earle." The Bibliography is compiled by Mr. J. C. Anderson, of the British Museum—a gentleman not likely to be in error as to such a point.

[KELMSCOTT.]
Friday [? *June* 1874].

MY DEAREST MOTHER,

I am sending you the review I mentioned, which please kindly return when read. It is a curiosity, and about the best written on the book.

Things are very lovely here, but not quite so redundant as at this time last year, owing, I judge, to the absence of fertilizing floods during the past winter.

I mentioned a little ivory handle which I have somewhere [here comes a sketch], and which belongs to the toilet-glass in W[illiam] and L[ucy's] bedroom. I cannot find it here. . . . It was kindly turned for me by poor Mike Halliday (since dead), to supply the place of one broken off, and was an exact match.

H 2.

This note refers to the portrait of my wife in coloured chalks which my brother had begun in 1874 at Kelmscott, and which he completed after his return to London : the same portrait which appears in the present volume.

[16 CHEYNE WALK.]
Wednesday night [1874—? *August*].

MY DEAR LUCY,

I believe, for one or two reasons, that Sunday would be my best day for the sitting, if suiting you equally with Friday ; and I would hope to see the proposed party—viz., William, yourself, and your papa, in the daytime, if possible to all, and Nolly later, about 6, for dinner at 8. I propose this division lest the room should otherwise be full, as I fancy Leyland is very likely to look in. I suppose his presence would not make any difference to you in sitting,— it would make none to me in drawing. . . . Would you kindly wear the same frill as before?

*   *   *   *   *   *

By D. G. Rossetti.

LUCY M. ROSSETTI.

1874.

B 75.

Thursday [1874—? *August*].

MY DEAREST MOTHER,

I should have written before in answer to Christina's, but that I have been wanting to come round, and constantly prevented. This evening I hope to come round if possible, and we could then fix a day for the pleasure of seeing you here. Also I want to bring round Lucy's portrait at the same time, which is now framed. The day you come I must really begin a similar chalk drawing of you—and you must then give me a second sitting one day the following week. Two sittings are enough.

I hope you got all right the half of a salmon which Graham sent me, and which I sent on to you.

Your loving
GABRIEL.

I was glad to learn that Lucy is downstairs again.

C 123.

Our aunts, the Misses Polidori, had recently taken a part of a house, No. 12 Bloomsbury Square. Our Mother and Sister Christina stayed with them from time to time; hence the phrase "Mamma and the whole Bloomsbury Square party."

Friday [2 *October* 1874].

MY DEAR WILLIAM,

Mamma and the whole Bloomsbury Square party are to be here to spend Monday and dine with me. Could you and Lucy come? I have been extremely sorry to hear of the vicissitudes of her health, but should rejoice to know that she was well enough to come. I never see you now.

With love to her,

Your affectionate
GABRIEL.

I have found the little ivory handle which (as I told you) poor Mike Halliday turned for me, to supply the place of the one broken off your bedroom looking-glass.

C 124.

The paper which my brother sent on to me with the subjoined letter was a fly-sheet printed by Mr. Pickering the publisher, regarding the Aldine Edition of Blake, compiled by myself, and Mr. Pickering's own Edition, compiled by Mr. R. H. Shepherd. The writer erroneously attributed to myself, as well as to my brother, certain emendations or variations of diction in Blake's poems, as published in 1863 in Gilchrist's *Life of Blake*. The reference to Nolly (Oliver Brown) relates to the illness which soon afterwards, on 5 November, terminated his life and all its high promise. No. 37 Fitzroy Square was Mr. Brown's residence.

Thursday [*8 October* 1874].

DEAR WILLIAM,

The enclosed has been sent me—I don't gather whether it has appeared in *Academy* or not. I just send it on to you, to say that you should, if necessary, state that you had nothing whatever to do with the editorship of the Poems in Gilchrist's *Blake*, which was done solely by me.

I know you would not quite have coincided in my method of treatment, nor should I now have adopted it to the same extent. I must add, however, that I shall take no public notice of the question myself in any form, and that, if further circulars or papers bearing on it are sent to me, George will simply throw them in the fire without their reaching me.

I am extremely sorry to hear about Nolly, and sorry also that Lucy, in her weak state, should attempt the duties of a nurse. George said yesterday morning that he purposed calling at Fitzroy Square in the course of the day to enquire, but I did not hear later that he had done so.

*   *   *   *   *   *

C 125.

Friday [*9 October* 1874].

DEAR WILLIAM,

About the Blake Poems, I think it would have been better to state plainly in your note to the *Academy* that the editorship was mine. If still feasible, I think it may as well be stated, though I intend not to take any part whatever in any discussion that may arise.

About the *Auguries of Innocence* etc., it strikes me that a verbatim version of the former, at any rate, appeared in Swinburne's *Blake*—did it not?—and might in that case be reprinted by Bell & Daldy if you wish.

Ever yours,
D. G. R.

I am heartily glad of the improvement in Nolly, whom George saw very ill.

B 76.

My dearest Mother,   *Monday evening* [*November* 1874].

I have been meaning to come and see you so much, but constantly prevented. I trust to be able to do so to-morrow (Tuesday) evening about half-past 7.

What a terrible blow this is of poor Nolly's death! I hope Lucy is stronger now.

C 126.

The Sonnet here mentioned is one which my brother wrote on the death of Oliver Brown, and which was published in the *Athenæum*.

My dear William,   *Thursday* [12 *November* 1874].

I have read that Sonnet to Watts, as an independent judge, and he thinks it should be printed. He and George seem to think the *Athenæum* the readiest and most expeditious medium. I will send it there if Brown approves.

A 27.

My dear Aunt,   13 *November* 1874.

You must indeed have thought me neglectful after not hearing in reply to your note for so many days. I am quite ashamed of it, and have no excuse except that your note somehow got out of sight, and that this sad affair of poor Nolly Brown's death and funeral has tended to put other things out of my head. On this melancholy subject you have probably heard at length from other quarters, so I will not dwell on it. I attended the funeral yesterday at Finchley Cemetery. Poor Lucy's health seems still further seriously affected by her pain of mind and exertions as a nurse.

I have no ideas as to the "housel" china, or as to any china except some Oriental kinds. I should suppose your piece to be French. If Sèvres, it might not improbably be worth at least ten times as much as when given to you ; but of course this is the merest guess-work.

Lady Ashburton has been here twice lately, and to-day asked me if I would do a chalk drawing of her daughter. I assented, and she is coming to sit to-morrow. Lady A[shburton] spoke of you in a friendly, even an affectionate, way. Miss Baring (I suppose—or is she Lady Mary B[aring]? I never heard her called anything but her Christian name)—the daughter—is handsome and winning to a very unusual degree, and it will be a satisfaction to draw her face.

Your affectionate Nephew,
D. Gabriel R.

P.S.—My Mother, or Christina, was suggesting that we might get up another little family-gathering at my house in the Christmas-season. I should like it much.

C 127.

"Merton" (a house in Fair Lawn, Merton) was at this time the residence of the Hueffer family. For a few days following the funeral of Oliver Brown, the bereaved parents, along with my wife and myself, were assembled there.

Monday [16 November 1874].

Dear William,

I am sending the Sonnet to the *Athenæum*, which no doubt will print it, unless they think this week's paragraph bars recurrence to the subject.

I do not see [the objection to "mountains" etc. ; neverthe-less I see no objection either to Hueffer's amendment—so adopt it, as the general vote at Merton seems in its favour.

The last words, I should have thought, would have conveyed at once the impression—" Does he hope, like ourselves, to be re-united ? "—and this seems a just question. However—lest there should be any possibility of its seeming to say, " Does he hope, like ourselves, for a changed state ? "—I will adopt the amendment, " And he ? "

With love to all,
Ever your affectionate
D. G. R.

C 128.

15 December 1874.

DEAR WILLIAM,

I have long been wishing to make a chalk head of our Mother, and it has struck me (being so busy and preoccupied with one thing and another that appointments are difficult) that I might combine this with the Christmas family-party, were the latter to take place <i>here</i>. Would you and Lucy give me the pleasure of joining the usual circle in such case? With love to her,

Your affectionate
GABRIEL.

B 77.

31 August 1875.

MY DEAREST MOTHER,

I got your dear letter from Clifton, and now another of Christina's, for which please thank her. It is by no means impossible that the information she gives may prove valuable, though my present wish is to get to the seaside if I can. Many failures have occurred in finding a suitable place, and, as I have been at work all the time, the necessity of getting on with new work commenced has still further prolonged the delay. But I suppose I <i>shall</i> get away—in winter !

The *Bella Mano* picture is still here, and I have not for-gotten Maria's wish to see it. Could we not ere long make an appointment here in which she might be included, and which might be the occasion of another sitting from you? I propose to look in at Euston Square on a very early evening, and we might then see if such arrangement could be made.

You will be glad to hear that I was lately introduced to a new buyer who has commissioned the *Venus Astarte* (for which you saw a pen-and-ink design and a chalk head) at my price of 2,000 guineas, which Leyland, though much want-ing the picture, had declared himself unable to afford. The same man seems likely to go on buying, and to prove a very valuable connexion.

Good-bye, darling Antique, till I see you very soon.

C 129.

Spartaco is an Italian historical romance by Professor Giovagnoli, who had come over from Italy, and had given my brother a call. It is an able book, and was in after years very warmly admired by Mr. Madox Brown. The "other Italian" was Signor Catalani, then attached to the Italian Embassy in London, who had recently called on me at Somerset House, and had shown a familiar knowledge of my brother's poems and an intense admiration of them. The meeting proposed by my brother never came off. This is, I *suppose*, the same Signor Catalani who died in the summer of 1895, being then Italian Ambassador at Constantinople.

[16 CHEYNE WALK.]
Wednesday [8 *September* 1875].

MY DEAR WILLIAM,

Re *Spartaco*.

I didn't send you the book because I doubted your leisure in the matter. Since then the author has again called here. . . . I have now at last written him, . . . and enclosed a letter of introduction to you addressed Somerset House, as he wants some notion as to the possibility of translating and publishing the book in England. You might give him perhaps some notion on this head. In merit it is of course of the usual Italian type (to judge by the 30 pages or so I have yet read), *i.e.*, quite competent but rather level.

I dare say he is a nice fellow, and you like Italians, so I have the less remorse in sending him to you. I have told him he will find you at Somerset House between 11 and 4 or 5.

Your affectionate
GABRIEL.

P.S.—I really have a sort of wish to see the *other* Italian you named to me. Perhaps we might combine him and this one here on some occasion?

I hope Lucy does well.

B 78.

ALDWICK LODGE, NEAR BOGNOR, SUSSEX.
[21 *October* 1875.]

MY DEAREST MOTHER,

I know you will be glad to see a seaside address at last heading this letter. I got here with George on Monday evening. The weather since has not been for the most part very favourable for walking; still I have got out fairly well. The house and grounds are very agreeable, and particularly sheltered and well suited for winter quarters. It is a large fine house—oldish, but without much character. The sea is only two minutes' walk from the house, but there are no downs.

Would there be a chance of getting you and Christina down here—say for a week or fortnight? Later I expect other visitors, to sit for a picture (*Venus Astarte*, which I now want to begin if possible); but this prospect is, unfortunately, uncertain. Would it be more agreeable for you to come here (if at all practicable) with or without the other household of Euston Square? I should, in any case, object to a nurse being brought, as I think servants are better kept apart; . . . we have two women-servants here, who of course would only

be too proud to nurse the babby. I need not say how much
I should like to have William ; but I cannot, I suppose, have
every one, and *you* come first.

*   *   *   *   *   *

B 79.

" The *D'Arblay* " is the *Diary and Letters of Madame D'Arblay*
(Miss Burney).

[ALDWICK LODGE, BOGNOR.
Wednesday 3 *November* 1875.]

MY DEAREST MOTHER,

The time has come to ask, When may I hope to see
you and Christina here ?   The beginning of next week would
suit me perfectly, as early as you may like, and I suppose
you are then free. Miss Wilding comes down to-day, and
will, I suppose, be likely to stay the whole of next week, but
there will be plenty of room for all, if, as I suppose, you have
no objection to Christina's bed being in one well-sized room
with your own.

Will you, if there is an opportunity, give my best love to
dear Maria, and tell her how much I feel with her in this
great change to which her lifelong tendencies have pointed
from the first ?

I hear nothing of William, but hope he and his are benefiting at Bournemouth.

Your most loving
GABRIEL.

P.S.—Mrs. Morris has, I believe, returned you the *D'Arblay*,
with which she was more delighted than I think I ever knew
her to be with any book. She has now got *Evelina*. . . .
I continue to find this place a healthful and agreeable
sojourn, and I suppose it is very probable I may remain
here till the end of the year. The landlady, who lives near,
is obliging. . . .

B 80.

Under the Rose : this was the original title of a poem by Christina which, in the reissue, was named *The Iniquity of the Fathers upon the Children.*

[ALDWICK LODGE, BOGNOR.]
Tuesday [28 *November* 1875].

MY DEAREST MOTHER,

*   *   *   *   *   *

Reading is very scarce here. I remember you used to have *Horace Walpole's Correspondence*, a book I have often fancied reading, though I never did so yet.

*   *   *   *   *   *

Many thanks to Christina for remembering my wish to re-possess her early *Verses*. Her new volume, in George's copy, is of an agreeable enough though quakerish tint. My own impression is that the frontispiece would have been best by itself, in the way of plates. The others fit in awkwardly. I am going immediately to rummage the book for what is new, but have not yet done so. I think the re-christening of *Under the Rose* an advantage to its purport ; but unluckily the new title is unwieldy, a thing to which I don't think Christina pays enough attention. I fancy, if she had called it " Upon the Children " simply, the whole meaning would have been conveyed, and wieldily.

*   *   *   *   *   *

The other day I found a beautiful fan of flag-seaweed complete, with a long strong stem, and beautiful root attached to a stone. But such things, when a goodish size, are not easy to preserve. I have laid it in a drawer for the present.

C 130.

The P.S. of this letter relates to the sudden death in London of a cousin of my wife, married to an Indian official Mr. Samuel Cooper. " Nolly's book " is the collection, in two volumes, of the Remains of Oliver Brown—*The Dwale Bluth*, and other stories and poems, completed or fragmentary : it had not been published at the date of this letter.

ALDWICK LODGE, NEAR BOGNOR.
30 *November* ['1875].

My dear William,

Would it be at all feasible to choose some convenient moment to send me a few books to read here? I have exhausted my own library, and am much in want of something which could be read aloud—amusing books—*memoirs*, stories, or anything readable.

I see such a store of these on your shelves sometimes that I am tempted to bore you with this request. English books are chiefly wanted. As to their return, I would promise faithfully that they should be safely despatched to Euston Square before I left this place, and never see Chelsea at all, which you probably regard as a " Gulf in the middle of Adan Aran."

Blake's cottage at Felpham, by the bye, is within an easy seaside walk of this, but I have not yet been there ; I mean to do so.

I am well in health, but just gripped by a vile cold, which however is going off. It is getting direly cold here.

I heard that Marston's eldest daughter, Mrs. O'Shaughnessy, was very ill. Do you know anything of this ? I hope she is on the mend.

With love to Lucy, to Brown, and to all,

I am your affectionate

GABRIEL.

I was sorry to hear of poor Mrs. Cooper's death. It must have been a great trial in every way.

Is Nolly's book out yet ?

F 9.

Speaking of Christina's poems, my brother here inclines to think that a piece preceding *No thank you, John*, were better omitted. The piece in question is *The Queen of Hearts*—a slight playful effusion, but to my mind a very pleasant one. The " dreadful story about Shelley " was the allegation of a deathbed confession to the effect that Shelley had come to his death by the misdeed of some Italian fishermen who had plotted to steal a sum of money in his boat. It was, I believe, I who first put the story into print; it had come to the aged Edward John Trelawny in a letter from his daughter, and he asked me (I think rightly) to get it published. He was convinced of the truth of the allegation.

BOGNOR.
3 *December* 1875.

MY DEAR CHRISTINA,

I told George to tell you how very glad I shall be to accept the new volume of your *Poems*, but that there is no need of sending it now, as *his* copy is here. To-day I have been looking through it with the same intense sympathy which your work always excites in me. Some of the matter newly added is most valuable. *Amor Mundi* is one of your choicest masterpieces; the *Venus* Sonnet and the one following, most exquisite; *Confluents*, lovely, and penetrating in its cadence; and the two poems on the Franco-Prussian War very noble—particularly the second, which is, I dare say, the best thing said in verse on the subject ... The first of the two poems seems to me just a little echoish of the Barrett-Browning style—fine as the verses and genuine as the motive must be plainly discerned to be. Here, however, it is only in cadence that I seem to notice something of the kind. A real taint, to some extent, of modern vicious style derived from the same source—what might be called a falsetto muscularity—always seemed to me much too prominent in the long piece called *The Lowest Room*. This I think is now included for the first time, and I am sorry for it. I should also have omitted *No thank you, John* (and perhaps the preceding piece also). The *John* one has the same genesis more or less, and everything in which this tone appears is utterly foreign to your primary impulses. The *Royal Princess* has a good deal of it unluckily, but then that poem is too good to omit. If I were you, I would rigidly keep guard on this matter if you write in the future, and ultimately exclude from your writings everything (or almost everything) so tainted. I am sure you will pardon my speaking so frankly.

Mrs. Morris is delighted with the Walpole book. In fact,

I think the amusement she derives from it is very beneficial in giving her strength for the sittings, which are arduous in her delicate state. However, by easy stages, I am getting on successfully with the *Astarte*, which was an anxious question for me, as the commission is an important one. Mrs. M[orris] sends thanks and kindest regards.

What a dreadful story this is about Shelley! I must say that, considering the fact that it seems to have come primarily through such a credulous man as Kirkup, I think it might have been better to wait a little before putting it in print. Shelley's son must be greatly shocked by it. IF the *confession* itself is a fact, *then* I suppose its purport must be viewed as perfectly true.

George has been most attentive to your feathered tribe since the snow set in ; a style of attention opposite (as I am always pointing out to him) to a favourite one with which he takes notice of them at other times through a cylindrical medium.

An article on Dr. Hake's poems by Watts in *The Examiner* contains some perfect fireworks in your honour. So I'll send it on. W[atts] wanted to " do " you for same paper, but was told you were in the hands of Gosse.

Love to the Teakum and to all from

Your loving Brother,
GABRIEL.

P.S.—I am delighted to hear that some attention is being paid to *temperature* in Mamma's case. Depend upon it that, at her age, much must be governed solely by this question, and that the most serious results might follow neglect, yet be easily avoided by watchfulness. I have seen the working of such requirements, and know them.

B 81.

[BOGNOR.]
Wednesday [15 *December* 1875].

MY DEAREST MOTHER,

I am so glad at the prospect of seeing you here again, with Christina and my Aunts. It is a real drawback that poor Maria cannot come—I do not exactly understand why. Is it because of George, or is she precluded from coming at this season? I grieve to think how lonely she will be on Christmas-day without her family. I do hope she will get some other chance equally desirable of making one in the family-circle; otherwise I should feel quite saddened at being the cause of such a privation to her. She has written me an extremely nice letter, and I shall be answering her without delay.

*   *   *   *   *   *

I believe Dr. Hake and two sons are likely to be here for a day or two, besides George; also probably Watts. But I will take care that the Teak is not hemmed in.

Your loving Son,

GABRIEL.

*   *   *   *   *   *

It has just struck me that you wander about without proper clothing; and George considered your condition in the train pitiable. Therefore you must let me make you a Christmas-box. I write with this to a shop in Regent Street where I buy things sometimes, to send down a sealskin cloak for the Teak, having given them the latitude and longitude, and telling them it must be large enough to cover you all over, and with a good warm collar. So now don't say a word, but let me give it you without demur, as it really may be the means of keeping cold out at some important moment. I have told them to send two or three for choice; but now take care that you choose the *largest, best, and warmest.* It is to have wide sleeves, and to open and close in front, in the usual coat-cloak style.

*   *   *   *   *   *

C 131.

Olivia, here mentioned, is my eldest girl—aged on 15 December 1875 less than three months. "The Necromancer book" is Godwin's *Lives of the Necromancers.*

[ALDWICK LODGE, BOGNOR.]
Wednesday [15 *December* 1875].

MY DEAR WILLIAM,

I have not yet thanked you for kindly sending the books. . . . All shall reach you safely again. I am now once more alone with George here. I asked Mamma and Christina to come down for Christmas ; and, finding they could not come without my Aunts, I have asked them too. . . .

Love to Lucy and to the Browns—not forgetting Olivia, in spite of her present happy unconsciousness of all messages whatsoever. I hope, by the bye, you mean to call her Olive ; I should have named her so for good—it is much prettier.

Of course I tried to get poor Maria down here for Christmas, but it seems she cannot come. It is sad to think of her loneliness, but she tells me she will get some other evening instead to spend in the family-circle.

Your affectionate
D. G. R.

By the bye, about the Necromancer book. I thought I had returned it to you, and certainly do not think it is either at Kelmscott or Chelsea. Whether some Gulf of the borrowing order has swallowed it up seems the next conjecture, though I can't remember any such thing. I'll try and realize.

A 28.

ALDWICK LODGE, NEAR BOGNOR.
New Year's Day 1876.

MY DEAR AUNT,

The chairs are going off to-day—one to Muntham, the other to Bloomsbury Square. I have chosen the two most able-bodied that I could find.

I hope you will be enjoying your New Year's evening, and above all that good Maria will have some family-pleasures for once. Had she been with us during your stay here, I am sure we should all have valued her company equally. I hope all got home without misadventure.

Dizzy has seemed somewhat disconsolate in the absence of

protective draperies. However, yesterday at dinner he made a discovery—that of toasted shrimps—and emitted a shout which the cry of Columbus at first sighting land could alone parallel.

I think I told you that the peacock-screen cost £5 to execute ; but that (I now remember) must have been for the *two* screens which I have—even if indeed the two really amounted to so much. I have no doubt it could be got done much cheaper by the gifted butler you spoke of.

With love to all,

Your affectionate Nephew,
GABRIEL.

B 82.

The first paragraph here relates to the project (previously referred to) of removing our Father's remains from England to Italy. The article in the *Examiner* upon the *Life of Haydon* was not my writing.

BOGNOR.
19 *January* 1876.

MY DEAREST MOTHER,

I got this morning the letter I enclose, and have answered to the effect that I know an objection *does* exist on your part; but I thought the letter might interest you, so I send it on.

I often think of the extremely happy time we passed at Christmas here, and of your good health and good spirits at the time. Your dear face always brightens things when I look at it. I hope you are still thriving, and have got over this very cold weather pretty well. Just now there seems a slight change perhaps towards a milder state of things, but not much as yet. I keep well enough, and have been getting on more satisfactorily with my work lately ; but really there is no news to tell you in this quiet place.

I have been reading a new book of Haydon's Correspondence and Table Talk, edited by his son who is or was in the Navy, but I rather think he is now an Admiralty official. Haydonism of obstinacy and set convictions is as prominent in the son as in the father, I think; but the book in my opinion is on the whole well edited, and a great addition to the records of that time. There is an admirable profile drawing of Keats by Haydon—no doubt the best likeness of him in existence; and there is also a plate described as containing a likeness of Haydon by Keats. It is full of rough sketches from a page of the Journal—the most prominent being a full-face dashed in in a masterly way; and one's first cry is—" Why, Keats, to have done this without teaching, must have had more gift for Art than Haydon !" But on closer examination one finds, half hidden among the rough scrawling, a profile which might be drawn by a child, yet is evidently meant for Haydon: this being of course Keats's real masterpiece, as it cannot possibly be by Haydon. The central full-face to which I referred first is, I judge, probably an idealization of Keats's face by Haydon, and seems to me to have been turned to much later by him as a suggestion for his picture of *Uriel*. The other sketches on the page all show reference to Keats's face, except a monkish-looking character in one corner. I suppose William is not the author of a notice of the book I saw in the *Examiner*, though it seems to me probably an outcome of Brown's set, owing to a mention of Oliver B[rown]. There is one very unfair thing in the article—an assertion that Haydon *begged* from Keats : a reference to the letter quoted showing quite clearly that the noble offer of assistance if needed emanated spontaneously from Keats himself. Here is a fine saying of Keats's in one of the letters :—" I value more the privilege of seeing great things in loneliness than the fame of a prophet." There is also a splendid anecdote of Keats' proposing as a toast at a gathering—" Confusion to the memory of Newton !" and, on Wordsworth's wishing to know *why* before he drank it, the reply was " Because he destroyed the poetry of the rainbow by reducing it to a prism." That is magnificent.

It seems that poor Mary Haydon we used to know was the first to enter the studio and find her father's dead body. The account as given by the son is very terrible. There is a head of Haydon's wife, roughly done but showing a very fine face.

I hope Christina, William, Lucy, and all, are well—also that Maria is not suffering at present. I don't know whether you are back by this time at Euston Square, but, judging that you most probably are so, I address this letter thither.

George's article on Christina's poems has not yet appeared in the *Hour*, but I believe it is to do so.

Your ever loving Son,

GABRIEL.

I could lend you the Haydon book if it would interest you —though possibly I might be keeping it a little longer.

B 83.

[ALDWICK LODGE.
Friday 21 January 1876.]

MY DEAREST MOTHER,

I received your dear letter with great pleasure, and am sincerely glad that I have answered Mr. Hopkins as you would have wished respecting what concerns my dear Father and his countrymen.

I did see my Father's name in one of Haydon's letters to Kirkup, and much regretted that Kirkup's letter to which it was a reply had not been included. What you say of Haydon shows how clear and lucid your mind is at an advanced age, and how well and incisively you can express your just conclusions. I assure you that your first inculcations on many points are still the standard of criticism with me, and that I am often conscious of being influenced correctly by these early-imbibed and still valuable impressions.

Among Kirkup's letters I was greatly struck by his masterly criticism on Michelangelo's roof at the Sistine Chapel, which is more like my own impression derived from the photographs than anything I ever saw on the subject.   However, I must confess myself astounded at Kirkup's unfavourable and Vandalic verdict on Michelangelo's sculpture of the Medici Tombs.   There is something most justly said by Wordsworth at page 44, vol. ii., respecting early Italian Art. It quite surprised me, as I had no idea whatever that he had any such insight into subjects of that kind.   His great facial resemblance to Ruskin seems, as usually in such cases, to have been not without a reason.

A 29.

ALDWICK LODGE. BOGNOR.
[1876.]

MY DEAR AUNT,

I wrote, on getting your letter, to enquire about the chairs, but have only just heard.   They are 26*s.* each, and I suppose they can be got singly if wished, but this is not stated.   They come from Morris & Co., 26 Queen Square, London, W.C.

As to the peacock-feather screens. . . . You see it is necessary to get a sheet of cardboard of the size which would fit in the framework of the screen ; to cover it with deep-red silk on both sides ; and then to arrange the feathers tier over tier as you saw in my screen on one side, and adopt a simpler design needing fewer feathers on the other, which is turned to the fire.   I would send one of my screens to the worker as a pattern, if wished.   There is one here, and one in London.

I have been working on here, having a habit of growing where I happen to drop ; but I shall soon get back to town now for the present.   There have been some fearful gales, and we have filled several bell-glasses with sea-anemones and wonders gathered from the deep.

Little news has been exchanged between this and Euston Square, but I have reason to hope that all goes well there.

B 84.

ALDWICK LODGE, BOGNOR.
29 *April* 1876.

MY DEAREST MOTHER,

I was not unmindful that the 27th was your birthday, and that I had been too long neglectful of your too distant love and tenderness. . . . My health has been variable, but never much more or less so than when you have been with me. If I have stayed here so long, it has chiefly been on account of great uncertainties in connexion with the Chelsea house, and the advisability of returning to it, or foregoing the lease and settling elsewhere. . . . I am greatly desirous of retrenchment ; though certainly, as long as I remain here, I am taking no step in that direction. But I am on the look-out for permanent and moderate country-quarters, and hope to find such. Indeed, one such place (in Surrey) is being seen about now—rent £100 only. If I could manage to settle in such a place, and not keep town-quarters also, I might recover somewhat from my chronic impecuniousness. Would you believe it that my Bank passbook shows my receipts from April '75 to the same month this year to have amounted to £3,725 ? and I believe this is somewhere about my average income. Yet I am always hard up for £50 ! This could hardly be the case if I were settled in cheap country-quarters alone.

I think I must have told you that, besides getting the *Blessed Damozel* picture very forward since I came here, I have twice commenced the *Venus Astarte* subject. The second commencement is, I believe, quite a success for me— my best ; and the heads are now all fully secured. I have lately been working-up as a separate picture the principal head of the first commencement ; which, though I was bent on doing it still better for the picture, is by no means a failure. I am making it into another design of head and hands only, to be called *Memory*, or *La Ricordanza*—which word, I suppose (though it might be rather obsolete), is as admissible Italian as " Rimembranza." This belongs to myself as yet, so will bring in something clear, I hope ; but it is terrible how the proceeds of my main works all get sucked up long before they are done, owing to my own fastidiousness in work. However, I don't want to make you uneasy about my commercial prospects, which are good enough if I can only retrench. I possess also a full-sized replica of the *Proserpine* picture, and a few other things of my own. If I can make these bring full value by proper management, I might perhaps begin at last to lay by some little yearly.

*   *   *   *   *   *

C 132.

This note relates to the effort which was then being made by some admirers of Walt Whitman in this country to benefit him by purchasing copies of his *Leaves of Grass*, and *Two Rivulets*, in a new edition which he had then brought out. His letter to me (or I think it was really addressed to Mr. Moncure Conway) was printed for circulation among persons likely to co-operate.

[ALDWICK LODGE, BOGNOR.]
21 *May* 1876.

MY DEAR WILLIAM,

Whitman's letter to you is very manly and touching. Any future plans I should be glad to join in, according to my power. At present I should at once send £5 for myself and £1 for G. Hake, if it did not happen that I am rather short of money at the moment. I reckon on doing so shortly without fail.

I hope you and Lucy and your joint heiress are doing well, and with love to all and to my Mother and Christina am

Your affectionate
GABRIEL.

Would not a distinct agency established for the books somewhere in London, and backed by Whitman's letter, be likely to attract subscribers ?

B 85.

c/o RT. HON. COWPER TEMPLE,
BROADLANDS, ROMSEY.
Wednesday [2 *August* 1876].

MY DEAREST MOTHER,

You will perceive that I have made the unusual move of accepting the kind invitation of my good friends the Cowper Temples, and coming here for a few days for change of air, before the house fills with their visitors for the country-season. I forget whether I told you of any such possible project, but shall not stay here for many days longer. The heats in London were, as you know, extreme before I left, but here the air is most genial, and everything extremely favourable for walking or strolling about. I have brought some easy-going work for occupation.

I thought I would give you thus much news of myself, but there is little to say in detail of so uneventful a trip. Of course the house is a most splendid place, but I confine myself almost entirely to a very quiet corner of it. The estate is extremely large, and includes features of every kind of beauty—indeed the view of the whole from an eminence overlooking it is perfectly surprising. The Isle of Wight is quite visible in the extreme distance on a clear day ; having the aspect of a cloud—the Isle—floating above a halo of light —the sea.

I trust you are now enjoying Maria's society—and to her and to you both my best love.

B 86.

This letter contains the first reference to the last illness of our sister Maria—an internal tumour, with dropsical complications— which terminated fatally on 24 November 1876. She was then in the fiftieth year of her age. Our Mother's "news of home-plans" related to the separation of domicile which was then impending between the two sections of our family, hitherto under one roof— my Mother and Christina on the one hand, and myself with my wife and daughter on the other.

BROADLANDS, ROMSEY.
24 *August* 1876.

MY DEAREST MOTHER,

I have been meaning to write again earlier. I also am on the point of a move this evening to London, after unexpectedly spending a whole month here with these most excellent and devoted friends. Of their goodness to me and plans for my benefit I can never sufficiently speak to you. Mrs. Temple is simply an angel on earth, and, though her husband is less radiantly such, he is no less so in fact. There has been a religious " Conference " held here (chiefly in the open air) during my stay. Many clergy and others have attended it under the auspices of the Temples. I have been confined to my own rooms, and hardly conscious of anything outside them except in going for my daily walks with George. I must tell you that my bodily state is a very suffering one, and that my nights are something of which it would be difficult to convey to you an idea for utter unrest and frequent severe pain of the limbs. Various notions of medical advice and remedies are on foot. Mrs. Temple, who is the Providence of the neighbourhood in all helpful matters, has been herself able to suggest various ideas towards battling the evil. But what may come of it I cannot yet tell. Unfortunately my energies for work are much prostrated, and my power of sitting at the easel greatly restricted by my extreme weakness and bodily pains.

My excellent old friend Miss Munro (sister of the sculptor) lives here as governess to a child adopted by the Temples. She therefore has increased the conversational circle for me ; and a beautiful and excellent Mrs. Sumner (wife of the Royal Master of Hounds) is here also, and a great boon for cheerfulness, intelligence, and no less for willingness to sit. She is one of the most beautiful women I ever saw, though now past her youngest, and of the noblest antique Roman type—a perfect Agrippina or Cornelia. I hope to be able to paint something good from her. A few others have completed *my* circle here, though during our stay I suppose at least 50 or 60 visitors have stayed and gone without my ever seeing them. Christina's Poems have been a great resource in the evenings at times, and I have read many aloud to the sympathizers, the Temples, Mrs. Sumner, and a few others—all true enthusiasts for their beauty. My spirits have gained much through the intercourse with these most sympathetic people, but my physical weakness has of course been a great disadvantage. At some time (I trust not remote) both you and Christina must really know the Temples, and I hope the excellent Mrs. Sumner too. They would glory in the knowledge of both ; and you would simply adore, as all must, the noble beauty of Mrs. Temple's Christ-like character, while all three would sympathize with you on religious as much as on other grounds.

I have made a chalk drawing of Mrs. Temple's head here, which I meant as a present, but which Mr. T[emple] generously insists on viewing as a commission. I have long wished to draw her most noble face, but am only half satisfied with this first result. I shall try again. I have also painted a many-winged baby-head into the *Blessed Damozel* picture—a lovely baby being found for the purpose here.

George has been much—indeed very highly—appreciated, and has done a deal of boating for the ladies. He has quite made himself valued here.

Your news of poor dear Maria should not have been the last thing replied to. I deeply regret to learn how ill she has been for so long, and could never have guessed it from the spirited tone of her letter, which I showed to Mrs. Temple, and which she read with the greatest interest. Her *Shadow of Dante* is greatly appreciated here, and Christina's *Poems* formed on the 22nd a birthday present from Mrs. Temple to Mrs. Sumner. I must soon write to Maria. Your news of home-plans is very interesting—I hope may prove a success. I trust to see you soon in London. I am much advised in some quarters to go to Malvern and try the cold-water cure, but I don't know what my immediate plans may be. At any rate a move to London will, I believe, occur for certain to-night.

With love to Christina, and Maria if still available, of course
with William and Lucy if this reaches you at Euston Square,
Your most loving Son,
GABRIEL.

B 87.

[16 CHEYNE WALK.
Friday, August 1876.]

MY DEAREST MOTHER,
      I have been seeing Sir W. Jenner to-day in consultation
with John Marshall, and they have prescribed me the awful
ordeal of two nights entirely without chloral! This will be
utter sleeplessness; and my only resource will be to try and
read in bed—a thing I generally detest. Something amusing
I need for this purpose, and am very deficient in such pro-
vender. Could you again "loan" your D'Arblay vols.? I
have long meant to go through them. . . .
      I should be extremely glad of another visit from yourself
and Christina, as William told me you possibly proposed; but
perhaps a day or two had better pass over now, since what
sort of a bogie I may be under the new night-system I can't
tell.
                    Your affectionate Son,
                              GABRIEL.

P.S.—The remaining Walpole vols. will shortly return
perfectly safe to your keeping.

B 88.

Thursday [September 1876].

MY DEAREST MOTHER,
      I am so pressed for time this morning that I can only
write a word to say how thankful I feel to know that dear
Maria is experiencing some relief. Thanks for the pre-
scription. I am sending to Maria to-day a series of photos
from the miniatures of a celebrated *Livre d'Heures*, which I

am sure will interest her greatly. They are quite exceptionally fine of their kind.

My own nights have been much improved lately. I have no pains in the limbs at present for some time past, the mesmerism seeming certainly to have carried them off, and I take only about half the chloral I used to take, or hardly so much as half.

Your affectionate Son,
GABRIEL.

Love to Christina. I have been very sorry to hear of her cold, and rejoice she is better.

B 89.

MY DEAREST MOTHER,   *Friday night* [*October* 1876].

* * * * * *

I have been feeling more out of sorts again to some extent, but have no apprehension of getting worse; only this sometimes keeps me in when I would otherwise come out. My work goes on well, and the big picture I am about (the one for Fry) progresses successfully.

Poor sweet Maria! I think of her continually, and hope I may have another chance of talking with her a little before long. I suppose a previous appointment is necessary.

F 10.

MY DEAR CHRISTINA,   *Sunday night* [19 *November* 1876].

I saw dear Maria this morning, as you probably know. I was terribly struck by the absolute change in her appearance, too evidently a final one. I hope to see her again when she expresses such a wish. She conversed clearly and with deep feeling; but all the former tendency to playfulness had left her, though even when I saw her on the previous occasion she was still then bright to a great extent But I am

telling you what you know but too well.   I hope to see our
Mother and yourself very shortly.

With love to her,

Your affectionate

GABRIEL.

B 90.

Tuesday night [21 November 1876].

MY DEAREST MOTHER,

I was wishing to get down to you this evening, but one
thing and another made it get later till too late.   Now I may
not be able to come before two or three nights hence.   Will
you tell Christina that I need not trouble her to write daily
as to dear Maria, but only if something special has to be
said?   Her state is evidently one from which nothing is to
be hoped.   It is terrible indeed to think of that bright
mind and those ardently acquired stores of knowledge now
prisoned in so frail and perishing a frame.   How sweet and
true a life, and how pure a death, hopeful and confiding in
every last instant!   Her expressions to me as to the relation she now felt herself to bear to her Lord, and her certainty of seeing him in person, were things hardly to be
counted as intercourse with a soul still on earth.

I am busied with my picture of *Astarte*, and, whenever
there is any opportunity, shall have great satisfaction in your
seeing it.   It has relieved my mind a good deal to make progress with it at last, and I now see that it will soon be ready
for delivery, a matter about which I was very anxious at the
time when the pains in my limbs made it so difficult to work.

With love to all,

Your affectionate

GABRIEL.

B 91.

Friday [30 November 1876].

MY DEAREST MOTHER,

I had hoped to get down this evening to you, but
find myself prevented.   The scene we went through together

yesterday has been present ever since to my mind. Much crowds on the mind in connexion with such a subject which it is better not to write, as the expression of sorrow, though mutually helpful up to a certain point, should there cease to be habitual. . . .

Shields (whom I saw in the Cemetery) called on me yesterday evening, and sat till late talking. He is a true friend, and was deeply affected by yesterday's scene : the more so that he has a brother buried in the same Cemetery.

*   *   *   *   *   *

H 3.

The first paragraph of this note will be understood as relating to a ticket, sent to my brother, for a stall at some theatre. His disclaimer of being "a convener of conferences" refers to a newspaper-paragraph in which some conference or other was mooted (I forget the details), and his name, along with others, was appended to the notice. The allusion to a possible "conference of creditors" is only to be regarded as jocular.

12 December 1876.

MY DEAR LUCY,

*   *   *   *   *   *

I believe the stall duly arrived, and George will take care it does not remain vacant, though I am no play-goer.

Another thing I certainly am not is a convener of conferences ; though, from my well-scumbled background, I would subscribe my mite towards any good cause, and, supposing this to be one, shall not so far fail it. How my name could have got into the paper I cannot guess.

Your affectionate
D. GABRIEL R.

P.S.—I must modify this statement so far as a conference *of creditors* might be compulsorily convened.

G 3.

Our Uncle was at this time translating an Epistle written by Boccaccio (to Pino de' Rossi, on his exile), and he wished to offer the translation to some periodical. He was then living at Cheltenham.

31 January 1877.

MY DEAR UNCLE,

I was much pleased to hear from you—shocked as I was at the revelation of my own badness as a correspondent, which was so little wilful that I really was not at all aware how long it was since I had written to you.

The Epistle of Boccaccio of which you speak is not known to me, though I have no doubt it would be so, were I versed in his work. I should like to ascertain whether it exists in any work of his or Italian collection I possess; but my frequent moves of late years have caused my books to get into such hopeless confusion that the task would be a more intricate one than I could hastily undertake. Not knowing the Epistle, I of course am unaware whether it has ever been translated; but I should think probably not, unless a translation of Boccaccio's collected writings other than the *Decameron* exists in English. Magazines nowadays consist mainly of such ephemeral writing that I hardly know one which would be likely to find place for such a translation; otherwise I should advise you to continue your task with a view to such issue. That you could translate it excellently I cannot doubt; but you do not tell me what the subject-matter of it is, nor whether likely to interest any reasonable number of modern readers.

I am interested in what you tell me of your occupation in teaching Latin to a young friend, and the possibility of your teaching others also. It seems to me that on the whole, as far as I am able to judge, your present surroundings and habits are of a much more cheerful kind than was the case latterly at Gloucester.

You ask me about myself. I lead a life at least as isolated

as your own—perhaps more so. I keep up with some regularity the practice of evening visits to my Mother, and now find her and Christina always quite cheerful, and thoroughly recovered from the shock of their loss. I hope in a few days to get them to dine with me here; but have latterly been very unsettled as to servants, which made an invitation of the kind difficult. Now I am better suited.

I spent the evening of Christmas-day at Euston Square, and that of the 2nd January at Torrington Square. William I hardly ever see. On the Christmas occasion I saw his fine baby, which I believe is likely almost immediately to have a brother or sister.

My professional success gives me no cause for complaint as yet, though I am beginning to perceive that I (as well as others) am likely soon to experience the great falling-off in the demand for artistic work which the past year has most alarmingly proved. For about a dozen years past certain dealers had kept up a feverish and exaggerated market for the works of living English artists, which brought large profit chiefly to the dealer, but necessarily also to the producer; but now, what between natural reaction, alarm of war, and other causes, the excitement has greatly subsided, and the dealers themselves are beginning to cry out. What then must the artists expect? However, as I say, I have no distinct cause to complain as yet. Old commissions remain to me to work out, and others may yet come in. I have just finished one commissioned picture of a good size (entitled *Astarte Syriaca*, and representing the Syrian Venus with ministering spirits), and it brings me a higher price than any work I have yet done. My health is neither very good nor very bad, but not lately subject to the kind of bodily pains from which I suffered so severely in the summer.

I am apprehensive that your verdict on my letter will be that I have little to tell you. One troublesome item which I may add is that my lease is so rapidly running out as to force me to look without further delay for fresh quarters; since, even were I to renew this lease at a higher rent, the landlord would not forego building over the garden—which would half destroy the convenience of the place. Where I shall next settle down I cannot yet tell.

Your affectionate Nephew,

D. GABRIEL ROSSETTI.

I certainly think that a line to *Notes and Queries* would elicit what you wish to ascertain.

G 4.

7 *March* 1877.

MY DEAR UNCLE,

I proceed to do my best for your queries; but, now that poor Maria is gone, I fancy William remains the best referee, Christina next, and myself the very worst.

(1) The Island of Gàde presents to me no geographical identity.

(2) I should think the translation of the name might pass as *Hypsicrathea*, but she to me is a stranger.

(3) " By these riches of our chief magistrates [*Priori* here is no doubt in that sense] Bishops have recently [nuovamente] begun to be endowed ; nor do I doubt that, were we to look well into the past, the wearers of mitres were then much more numerous in our court." This seems to me the *probable* sense.

(4) The words underlined (*Se Dio* etc.) cannot, I feel certain, be understood by any human being. There must probably be a lacuna somewhere.

(5) Cicilia *is* Sicily.

As regards other matters, I have lately been attempting, with the assistance of a very active and intelligent personal agent, to find myself a new whereabouts. My eye is chiefly on Fulham and that neighbourhood, as large old-fashioned houses with really enormous gardens—sometimes 3 or 4 acres —are to be had there frequently, and not seldom at a moderate rent. My researches have proved this amply, and I cannot conceive why my Mother and those living with her should remain in a house where no garden is to be had. Houses with a garden as large as mine here occur not unfrequently in the neighbourhood I speak of at less than £100 a year, sometimes *much* less ; while the rent they pay at Torrington Square, 100 guineas, always seemed to me exorbitant for such a house. However, my own requirements, as regards painting-light, freedom from noise, etc., are so special that, though places of the most tempting nature in many respects have been found, I cannot say that I am yet suited. But I have a year before me, my lease of this house not expiring till Lady-day 1878. My reason for looking out so early is that, however near I might come to the mark in finding a place, there is little doubt that it would need some adaptation for my purposes before I get into it.

Thanks for your enquiries as to my health, which is pretty well on the whole. I hope yours is the same. I think I told you that I had recently completed a large picture. The owner (to whom I had not shown it before) came and saw it the other day, and was thoroughly delighted with it—which is a relief to me, as the price is 2,000 guineas, and not to have pleased him would have seemed like robbery.

B 92.

16 CHEYNE WALK.
Monday [28 *May* 1877].

MY DEAREST MOTHER,

*   *   *   *   *   *

I have not been very well, but without illness of a decided kind. My indisposition was increased for some time through want of steady work after turning several late pictures out of hand. I have now taken up the reduced replica of the large Dante picture, which is not very amusing but must be done, and at any rate goes steadily on.

It is wonderful how redundantly green the garden is now, yet the weather still frequently so chilly and stormy. I have failed as yet in getting a house for certain, and am beginning to feel desperate on the subject.

*   *   *   *   *   *

B 93.

MY DEAREST MOTHER,

I have now been here for some days. Yesterday for the first time I found myself able to take an hour's walk in the early part of the day, and half an hour's walk later. This is some improvement, but my hand remains wofully unsteady, and I have had a restless bad night. I believe we are ready now for you and Christina to come down as soon as convenient to you. When you come I do hope to begin making an attempt at your portrait, and to that end the materials must at once be sent for.

At present the absolute want of occupation is rotting my life away hour by hour. Brown is the sweetest and kindliest of companions, but such a life is almost unbearable. The nurse is excellent and most efficient.

With love to William,

Your most affectionate
GABRIEL.

C 133.

"The thing I began from Mrs. Stillman " must be the *Vision of Fiammetta*.

MY DEAR WILLIAM,

I have been intending to write you a line, but have not done much caligraphy, or cacography either, since coming here. I am now a little more in the way of it, and might almost say that I am writing this letter without any positive shaking of the hand, though my hand feels weak. This is, however, very fluctuating, as sometimes my hand is little better than before ; but there is on the whole very decided improvement.

I suppose it cannot now be very long before I return to town, and attempt to resume work. I rather project painting a picture without reference to Nature, from some one of the careful drawings which hang in the drawing-room. This, I have always thought, would be perfectly feasible ; and just at present I should find the use of models somewhat onerous, as it interferes with resting when one feels tired. However, I should like to go on also when possible with the thing I began from Mrs. Stillman.

The weather here has been almost uniformly fine, and no doubt I have benefited much by walking and driving daily. I made one attempt at drawing, which was not absolutely discouraging ; and, since I have improved since then in steadiness of hand, I fancy I might be able to get on somehow at the easel. I might have tried again here, but the day is cut up with necessary exercise, and moreover the sun, when out, floods the only room I could paint in.

I hope Lucy and the children benefited by their stay at Gorlestone, and that all are well now. My love to them and to you.

C 134.

The " drawing of Mamma's head " must be one which, including a head of Christina, is now in the National Portrait Gallery. My brother was well entitled to term it " successful."

[HUNTER'S FORESTALL]
Friday [28 *September* 1877].

MY DEAR WILLIAM,

    *   *   *   *   *   *

You will be glad to hear that I have commenced a successful drawing of Mamma's head, quite up to my mark, and that I have no longer any doubts as to my being able to work much as heretofore. I am not quite without inconvenience ; but the result is not apparent in this last attempt, and I must suppose now that it will quite wear off in time.

C 135.

[HUNTER'S FORESTALL.]
Thursday [11 *October* 1877].

MY DEAR WILLIAM,

I am very sorry to hear to-day from Mamma that you are again suffering from toothache. I suppose it is still dependent on the split tooth you told me of. In any case, Gregson and his gas-apparatus would painlessly help you to its extraction, and I urgently advise you not to suffer from it for another day.

I am writing chiefly to fill up the time, and because it is long since I wrote to you. I dare say you will perceive increased steadiness of hand in this letter. Last night I slept rather better than my wont, which now makes the principal remaining difference as to the state of my hand. Thus, when at work again, I must take means to procure a continuance of proper sleep, or work will go to the wall altogether.

I have pretty nearly finished a drawing of my Mother's head, but am not certain whether, in increasing the finish, I may not have diminished the likeness. However, all serious anxiety as to my continued fitness for work may no doubt be considered at an end.

Brown may have told you that he considers a house which he viewed for me at Fulham to be eligible on the whole. Whether it will be attainable, or whether anything better may still be found, I know not.

I was much troubled to hear of Brown's suffering from an abscess; but happily it seems to have got much better, or well by this time. Shields, curiously enough, has had something of the same kind.

The slight attack of shingles (as Marshall surmised it to be, and prescribed accordingly with success), which bothered me very much, is now almost gone.

Will you give my love to all yours? and believe me

Ever your affectionate

D. GABRIEL R,

C 136.

[HUNTER'S FORESTALL.]
Sunday [14 *October* 1877].

MY DEAR WILLIAM,

We have pretty much exhausted our reading-resources here. Have you anything decidedly readable—biography especially, but not about the French Revolution—which you could send us? Not novels, I think. In haste.

Your
D. G. R.

B 94.

[16 CHEYNE WALK.]
4 *December* 1877.

MY DEAREST MOTHER,

On reflecting further as to the Christmas matter, I find it would be a serious incubus to me to have the prospect of dining without you on that day, for the first time these many years : . . . Lucy . . . being of course well aware that I should object to so extended a party. . . . My proposal is that you and Christina should come and dine with *me* at Christmas : I would send a comfortable conveyance to fetch you.

    *   *   *   *   *   *

Pardon my troubling you with these fresh views ; but you know that I am almost always alone ; and that I should be so even on Christmas-day is what you would not view with more pleasure than I should. . . . The matter, I confess, weighs somewhat on my mind ; and, if we were apart this Christmas, I should view it as a bad omen for the coming year.

    *   *   *   *   *   *

B 95.

Friday [14 *December* 1877].

MY DEAREST MOTHER,

You know my anxiety lately as to sale of works ; so I will not delay (knowing how much you shared in it) the information that I have succeeded during the past hour in selling the *Proserpine*, *Fiammetta*, and the little Kelmscott picture, to a Mr. Turner, a new buyer from Manchester. Some deduction on my original price was necessary in these bad times, on his taking several works together: but still 1,500 guineas is a round sum, and will set me on my legs for the present, besides securing him, I trust, for future purchases. It will be better not to mention the *sum* paid. The *Fiammetta* is simple in its materials, and will not take me great trouble to finish.

Mr. Turner saw and much appreciated the drawings of yourself and Christina, of whose poems he is a reader. The drawing which it is proposed to publish in autotype is the last made of her at Herne Bay. I think I told you that it appears an autotype of the old drawing of her which *you* have is current; how I cannot tell, but suspect Howell must have got it done from the original photograph.

*　　　*　　　*　　　*　　　*　　　*

C 137.

Our old friend Frederic George Stephens was alarmingly, almost desperately, ill at this time. Mr. Marshall saved his life. "The Shelley" is the second form, in three volumes, of the edition of Shelley which I brought out, then recently published by Messrs. Ward, Lock, & Co.

Thursday [14 *March* 1878].

MY DEAR WILLIAM,

I saw my Mother to-night, and am very anxious to know what news you have of good old Stephens. Please write me a line.

Thanks for the Shelley. I am sorry to see that the edition is no handsomer than the former one.

C 138.

"The *Poets*" is my book entitled *Lives of Famous Poets.*—As to Mr. Smetham, see the Memoir, p. 351.—The phrase "the Whitman failure" does not mean that my brother paid *nothing* to the Whitman Fund, but he paid, I think, less than he had at first intended.

Monday [25 *March* 1878].

MY DEAR WILLIAM,

Thanks for the *Poets*, which I am beginning to read, and like much—Butler and Dryden both very good ; I have begun at that point.

It has occurred to me as possible that this kind of book might be helpful to Smetham, if he could begin to be roused into any interest in reading. He has been seen to take up a paper lately, though only for a few minutes. Suppose you were to send a copy to Mrs. Smetham, Belle Vue House, Kew Green—and charge it to me. I would pay, in spite of the Whitman failure. By the bye, I am sorry to see that name winding up a summary of great poets : he is really out of court in comparison with any one who writes what is not sublimated Tupper ; though you know that I am not without appreciation of his fine qualities.

C 139.

This note refers briefly to the brutal (and I believe still un-explained) street-murder in Edinburgh of the very promising young Scottish painter Mr. G. Paul Chalmers.

Friday [29 *March* 1878].

MY DEAR WILLIAM,

I send on a letter and enclosure which I opened before I perceived the address was to you. I can't make out how this Chalmers came to be killed.

I dare say you have sent the *Poets* to Mrs. Smetham. She professed to be glad of the prospect when I told her, as S[metham] will now listen to reading, and she is short of suitable books.

*   *   *   *   *   *

B 96.

Wednesday [? *April* 1878].

MY DEAREST MOTHER,

I need not say how glad I shall be to see you here. . . .

I have had my knocker taken off the door; so a good pull at the visitors' bell at the outer gate is necessary; though indeed a bell is to be placed at the doorpost, but may not be up by Saturday perhaps.

You must have thought me very tardy in not coming to T[orrington] Square for so long; but the days have lengthened much, and I always find myself so hampered with work to the last daylight that I never can find the day when I am able to dine earlier than 8-30, as I am obliged to do if I come out to you afterwards. . . .

B 97.

26 *April* 1878.

MY DEAREST MOTHER,

As I shall be prevented, I find, from looking in on you to-morrow, which is your birthday (unless indeed it be to-day, but I think to-morrow), I write a line to show you that you are not out of my mind. Your 78th year was one in which you brought me as much consolatory tending during a time of sickness as at any period of my earlier life; and, if I have since been better, it is in a great measure owing to the months of rest which were only rendered tolerable by your and Christina's help. I view the approach of summer with some apprehension, as, for several years past, it has been my worst season, but must hope for the best.

*   *   *   *   *   *

I dare say you will be surprised to hear that I have been taking up the old large picture of *Dante's Dream* again, to make some alterations in one or two figures; these I have now completed.

The other day I received a visit from a lady, . . . who however appeared to want Christina, in order to get her to write her name in a volume of C[hristina]'s *Poems* which she had with her, apparently just purchased. I gave the address, and suppose she came on to you: but I did not escape writing my own name in the book, on the strength of the illustrations! The good lady reminded me somewhat in

appearance of Miss Heaton ; which would surely be physi-
ognomically probable, as the visit and request were just what
might have been expected from the Muse of Leeds.

*   *   *   *   *   *

B 98.

MY DEAREST MOTHER,   1 *September* 1878.

*   *   *   *   *   *

A piece of news I have for you is that I have re-
entered on possession of the large *Dante's Dream*, and hope
to make it a source of profit.   Mr. Valpy, who had fully
paid up its price, now finds himself in uncertain health and
compelled to reside in the country, where he will not have
room to hang so large a work.   Accordingly he offers me
the return of it on very advantageous terms of exchange ;
consisting in my foregoing the remainder payments on a
small picture for him (which is finished, and therefore gives
me no further trouble), and furnishing him with full-size
replicas of two half-figure pictures, and a half-size replica of
one other.   These will not be troublesome to accomplish ;
and the bargain amounts pretty much to a fresh commission
for 2,000 guineas, as I shall certainly try not to let the large
picture go lower than that.   There is £600 still to pay on
Fiammetta, which is all but finished, and I have £500 now in
the Bank, with other prospects : so at last things look a little
better than usual.   I am particular as to these commercial
details, since I know how anxious you are as to my prospects.

I wrote at last to Signor Gamberale (my translator), and
transmitted all our regards to him.

*   *   *   *   *   *

B 99.

MY DEAREST MOTHER,   27 *April* 1879.

I must not let this anniversary pass without showing
by at least a word that I keep it in remembrance ; though
blessing comes better from you to me than from me to you.

*   *   *   *   *   *

I have been working on three pictures, viz. : a new version of *The Blessed Damozel* ; a *Lady of the Window* (*Vita Nuova*) ; and a *Mnemosyne* (ci-devant *Hero* !) for Leyland —but this alas paid up. Times are very bad, but I must hope the other two will somehow bring grist to the mill. However, I have remnant commissions leaving a considerable aggregate amount to receive—from Graham and Leyland ; but the health of the former has been so long uncertain that he can hardly yet be troubled. However, I am in every way glad to hear that he is now decidedly mending at Algiers—indeed, I am told nearly well again.

*   *   *   *   *   *

B 100.

It may be readily surmised that the Lecture mentioned in this note was the one written by Mr. Hall Caine.

29 July 1879.

MY DEAREST MOTHER,

I know you always love all friendliness towards me and my work ; so I enclose a letter I got, and will send the Lecture alluded to in a day or two. I shall try to know the writer, who has done his work well, and in the spirit I most wish. I had heard of him already as delivering such a lecture, I believe more than once, but do not otherwise know anything of him.

*   *   *   *   *   *

Poor Smetham came home ; but has had to go back again, being no better.

*   *   *   *   *   *

B 101.

As to Brown's "two years' slumbers," see the Memoir, page 564. Mrs. Laura Valentine was (or is) the compiler of a volume entitled *Gems of National Poetry*. A "gem" of mine—written in or about 1848, and published at the time in the *Athenæum*— appeared in her book.

MY DEAREST MOTHER,   *Sunday* [17 *August* 1879].

*   *   *   *   *   *

Old Brown seems to have awakened from his two years' slumbers, and wants to come and dine to-morrow. I told him that he was as welcome as he would have been all along. He must be dreadfully full of news, and needs to pour it even into me. You know he has finished his first picture at the Townhall, Manchester, and it is a great success. The pay (between ourselves) is most wretched— £270 a picture ; and each must take him at least six months of such hard work as I never knew him do before.

*   *   *   *   *   *

By the bye, who is Laura Valentine—does Christina know ?—who wrote me lately that C[hristina] and William (!) had consented that some of *their* "lovely" poetry should appear in a collection of hers, and asked me for a very trifling thing of mine, which I declined to contribute as too slight. What are C[hristina] and W[illiam] sending? However, all this is not to bother you or her for an answer, but merely to fill paper.

*   *   *   *   *   *

I am getting on rapidly with Graham's predellas, and hear he is to be in England by end of October.

*   *   *   *   *   *

F 11.

The book by Christina here mentioned is her devotional volume named *Seek and Find*. Mrs. Stillman was sitting for the *Vision of Fiammetta*.

MY DEAR CHRISTINA,   *Wednesday* [8 *October* 1879].

Many thanks for your book, which I see is full of eloquent beauties. I am sorry to notice that—in my own view—it is most seriously damaged, for almost all if not for all readers, by the confusion of references with the text, which they completely smother. Surely these should all have been marginal, and not nearly so numerous. Shields, who was of course much interested in seeing the book, took quite the same view in this.

Mrs. Stillman has begun her sittings to-day, which last for five hours at a stretch (necessarily), and leave me rather wearied in my somewhat weak state. She is graciousness itself, and received with cordial return the remembrances you sent.

C 140.

My brother got very ill in October 1879, owing to a more than commonly excessive dose of chloral. This note, following a visit of mine on the preceding day, was written soon after the attack began ; and from this time onwards I made a point of seeing him regularly every Monday. The severity of the attack was over in a week or so; and on the whole, between October 1879 and September 1881, when he went to Cumberland for fresh air and change of scene, he was, I think, about as well in health and spirits as he had been at any ordinary time since the summer of 1874.

[19 *October*. 1879.]

My dear William,

I am so low and lonely that it would be a great boon if you could come up for an hour or two this evening. I know it is a tax on you, but tell Lucy, with my love, that I hope she will not mind.

C 141.

Sunday [2 *November*. 1879].

My dear William,

Would there be a chance of you to dinner on Wednesday? Monday and Tuesday I have other visitors, and find it best if possible to bespeak visits separately, so as to avoid solitary evenings as much as possible.

Your

D. G. R.

Love to Lucy, who I trust does well.

B 102.

Our Sister's poem of *Goblin Market* was set to music as a cantata by Mr. Aguilar—and with much success, if I may venture to express an opinion on a musical subject.

My dearest Mother,   29 *November*. [1879].

I have been thinking for some time of writing a line though indeed I felt sure you must get tidings of me through William, who has been here several times. I am very much better—indeed, pretty much in my usual state now, were it not for a bad cold these last few days, which however will of course pass off. I have finished the replica of the large picture for Graham, all but the figure of Beatrice in which I mean to make an alteration. The two predella-subjects are also finished.

Dunn has just returned from Truro, but will have to go back there for awhile in connexion with the portrait he has been painting. Scott has often spent the evening with me, and is always intellectual and interesting. Miss Boyd returns to London to-day.

I hear there is a decided improvement in trade. Even cotton at Manchester, which seemed the most hopeless, is looking up decidedly and rather rapidly. Iron, copper, and coal mines, also on the mend. You may perhaps think this report not much in my line, but I view it as vitally wound up with the picture-market.

I was glad to hear of some venturous mortal having set *Goblin Market* to music, though I cannot exactly see the aim and end of the act unless he has a public performance in view and at command. It would hardly do for a 5 or 10 minutes' brilliant trifling at the evening piano.

I hardly dare hope that Aunt Eliza is seriously improving. Will you give my love to her as well as to Christina?

C 142.

When this note was written I had gone to Birmingham, to deliver a lecture (one of two) on *The Wives of Poets*.

Tuesday [17 *February* 1880].

DEAR WILLIAM,

I have been reading with vast amusement Cottle's *Coleridge* which you lent me; but I can only find vol. i., and have hunted in vain over the whole house for vol. ii. If you've got it, I do wish you'd send it by post, for few things are so funny. I suppose you will be home by to-morrow.

Give my love to Lucy, of whom I heard a much better account from Brown, who looked in yesterday evening, and was as genial as he always is. I hope you had an appreciative audience at Birmingham, and shall be curious to hear about this. I dare say I shall see you one day next week. Wednesday would suit me well, as I almost think we agreed it should be.

C 143.

Sunday [22 *February* 1880].

MY DEAR WILLIAM,

*　　*　　*　　*　　*　　*

I hope you may be able to give me a favourable report of your second lecture also, when I see you. Love to Lucy. I have been much enjoying Donne, who is full of excellences, and not brimming but rather spilling with quaintnesses.

*　　*　　*　　*　　*　　*

H 4.

Tuesday [? *March* 1880].

MY DEAR LUCY,

*　　*　　*　　*　　*　　*

I will hope to see you and show you the picture on Friday if that suits best, or else on Monday.

I must seem as bad an uncle as the one in *The Children in the Wood* almost; only your two are fortunately better cared for, to say nothing of the third. But I have been so far from well lately that I will not be proposing to try and render myself tolerable as a new " object " to Olive just now ; though heartily believe me that I love her and your others, and look forward to their future with as true an interest as any one.

Ever, dear Lucy,

Affectionately yours,

D. GABRIEL R.

C 144.

MY DEAR WILLIAM, *Tuesday* [13 *April* 1880].

When next you come, would you bring any book that gives a good account of the *White Ship* matter, if you have one ? After you went away I wrote some more verses of it ; but am rather at a loss for *some* of the particulars, though some I know. I should like to read all Henry I., but don't possess an English history ! !

Your affectionate

D. G. R.

What you told me about little Olive is most interesting. Will you give my love to Lucy?

B 103.

This letter relates partly to my brother's sonnet on *The Sonnet*, and to the design which he had made in illustration of it (engraved in Mr. William Sharp's book). He had presented them as a birthday gift to our Mother, inserted into a copy of Mr. Main's book on English Sonnet-Literature. The picture here named *Vanna Primavera* is the same which is now known as *The Daydream*.

MY DEAREST MOTHER, *27 April* 1880.

It was sweet indeed to me to receive this day, and written in so firm a hand, the reassurance of what was the first thing I learned to know in this world—my Mother's love. I wish the little offering had been worthier of such a shrine.

I like Christina's sonnet extremely; it is lovely in its heartfelt affection.

I have no doubt that your discerning eyes plucked out the heart of the mystery in the little design. In it the Soul is instituting the " memorial to one dead deathless hour," a ceremony easily effected by placing a winged hour-glass in a rose-bush, at the same time that she touches the fourteen-stringed harp of the Sonnet, hanging round her neck. On the rose-branches trailing over in the opposite corner is seen hanging the Coin, which is the second symbol used for the Sonnet. Its "face" bears the Soul, expressed in the butterfly; its " converse," the Serpent of Eternity enclosing the Alpha and Omega. All this I doubt not you had seen for yourself.

I shall soon be letting you have the ballad of the *White Ship*, which William on Monday pronounced one of my very best things. I hope you will think so too.

I have made great progress with the *Vanna Primavera* picture since you saw it. The figure is now full-length, and looks very well.

B 104.

The "sycamore-tree" appears in the picture of *The Daydream*. The sonnet which my brother wrote for that picture dwells on this matter of early Spring buds and later leaves.

Thursday [*7 May* 1880].

MY DEAREST MOTHER,

I hope to be seeing you soon. Meanwhile I send you (at last) the ballad of *The White Ship*, which I hope will please you. Only three—William, Watts, and Shields—have heard it, and all express great approval. Every incident, including that of the boy at the end, is given in one or other account of the event. You must not be at the exertion, *on any account*, of writing to acknowledge this.

I am painting the sycamore-tree in my picture. Everything is so backward that I can still get the early Spring buds, when I want them, as well as larger leaves.

I hope you found enjoyment in the Sonnet-book : I did much. It is full of excellent examples, and the Notes have much information. There is a Sonneteer quoted among the living ones, in the Notes, of the name of William Watson. He sent me the other day a volume of poems, the chief one in which is called *The Prince's Quest.* Did he send it to Christina, I wonder? I shall hear when I see you. You may suppose I thought of C[hristina's] *Prince's Progress,* and did not fail to say so in acknowledgment. But it is good, and on the opposite tack to Christina's, ending happily; on a somewhat similar scheme as far as the Sleeping Beauty sort of origin is concerned.

I don't know that there is anything else in particular to say in the way of news.

C 145.

The drawings by Blake here mentioned are a set belonging to a member of the Varley family, which had been left with Mr. W. B. Scott, and by him shown to my brother. My Catalogue is the list of Blake's works compiled by me for Gilchrist's *Life of Blake* : I was then revising and enlarging it with a view to the forthcoming new edition of that work.

Friday [7 May 1880].

MY DEAR WILLIAM,

I have here some twenty drawings by Blake, of which you may like to take notes, for your Catalogue, on Monday. One of them seems to me the same head as one (I think a female born under sign Cancer) in Varley's *Zodiacal Physiognomy.* Could you make a tracing of that to compare? I am almost sure that this head is said in some part of the text to·be by Blake.

These drawings are all visionary heads : among them one of Saul—probably that to which you allude as untraceable, in your Catalogue.

Your

D. G. R.

I suspect this head to be Mrs. Blake.

C 146.

My brother was about this time particularly interested in all that related to Thomas Chatterton. I therefore sent him a slight scribble from a portrait, nominally Chatterton, preserved in the Museum at the Peel Park, Manchester, which I had lately visited.

4 *July* 1880.

MY DEAR WILLIAM,

Thanks for the sketch of the Chatterton portrait (so called), for which Chatterton never sat, and which Hogarth never painted. Chatterton's portrait was never done by any one in his life-time, and Hogarth died when Chatterton was 12 or 13 at Bristol. I know this portrait, having bought a photo of it when exhibited at Kensington.

It is a singular fact that this and a still younger-looking portrait (a life-sized oil head in the possession of Sir H. Taylor, and of which I have seen an engraving) seem certainly to represent the same individual, as does also a rougher old engraving I have seen, not in same position as either. The only possible theory I can see is this. One of Chatterton's poems is addressed to a certain Alcock, a Bristol miniature-painter whom he seems to have known personally. Now, if Alcock had painted him *in his lifetime*, the fact would have turned up with all others in the very rapid celebrity which followed his death. But it would be almost strange if Alcock (supposing him to be then still alive) had not been asked to make a *reminiscent* sketch of Chatterton; and from such a source these portraits may possibly be derived. They seem to acquire additional attraction from a certain resemblance in them to the type of Keats.

*   *   *   *   *   *

B 105.

" Nearly as bald as I am now." My brother was *partially* bald— say from the year 1874 or so; but to the last he was not bald in any marked degree.

My dearest Mother,

13 *July* [1880].

* * * * * *

Ned Jones was here yesterday evening, and told me he had met you and Christina in the Academy. He lately, in a friendly way, expressed a wish to come and see me more regularly, so I shall perhaps be seeing more of him. He is nearly as bald as I am now, though six years younger. His boy Phil has just completed his first term at Oxford.

* * * * * *

Perhaps you have read of Tom Taylor's death. I knew him well some years ago. He seems lately to have had some sort of stroke, but wrote to the papers to say it was an attack of gout (in denial of their statement). However, he has corroborated them by dying, poor man! He was not always an unprejudiced critic, I think; but he was a man of many private charities, which will miss him sorely.

* * * * * *

I am always
Your most loving
GABRIEL.

As you have developed the Sonnet taste, I'll copy one on Blake on the other side.

[Here follows the Sonnet " This is the place " etc.]

F 12.

Thomas Dixon, here mentioned, had retired from the business of Cork-cutter in Sunderland : he was the " Working Man " to whom Ruskin addressed his letters published under the title *Time and Tide by Wear and Tyne.* The article in *The Pen* was written, as my brother afterwards ascertained, by Mrs. Meynell.

My dear Christina,

Friday [16 *July* 1880].

I am very glad to hear such thriving news of you both. I may as well write a line in return while I have the pen in my hand.

I think I told you of a visit I had a few weeks ago from Thomas Dixon of Sunderland (whom you must have long heard of, since Newcastle days with Scotus), and Joseph Skipsey the northern collier-poet, a man of real genius. The other day I was shocked to get a letter from Skipsey announcing poor Dixon's death. Having overdone exertion in London, he succumbed to chronic asthma on his return. He was a worthy man ; indeed, I never knew of any one individual in any walk of life—even a much higher one than his—who was so entirely devoted to promoting intellectual good among those within his reach.

I remembered afterwards that *Temple Bar* was not the paper containing an *article* on that great subject, but a paper called *The Pen* which seems since to have died. Whether it " let itself be snuffed out by that article " I don't know. I may perhaps have a copy sent me yet by a friend, but have not seen it.

As our Mother and you liked the Sonnet on Blake, I'll put one on Chatterton overpage, but I'm afraid you don't know much about him.

Your affectionate
GABRIEL.

[Here follows the Sonnet " With Shakespear's manhood " etc.]

Are you within reach of Pevensey Castle—a beautiful ruin ?

B 106.

The picture out of which my brother was now taking the painted head, and painting in another, is *The Daydream*. The friend who proposed to give him a seal was Mr. Bates, a Picture-dealer in Leeds—a thoughtful discerning man whom Rossetti saw several times towards this date.

[July 1880.]

MY DEAREST MOTHER,

I dare say you would like to see *The Pen*, which I send. The beneficent article on myself seems to have killed off the paper, for it appeared no more! I don't think the rest of the family are dwelt upon sufficiently, and they *might* have presented a portrait of the Teak gratis.

Will you let me have the paper again when done with?

I forget if I told you that I was doing the dire deed of taking out the head in my picture, which I never thought quite equal to the cartoon. I have now got it fairly advanced in a new form, and more to my satisfaction.

I heard from Scotus in much sorrow at poor Dixon's death. I enclose a cutting respecting D[ixon]. Also an impression of a seal which a friend proposes to give me. It is of bronze, and was dug up in Pontefract Castle—is supposed "on good authority" to have been the signet ring of Richard II. It does look rather like, but then why not make it to order? It seems to me the original would have been in gold.

C 147.

The Sonnet here spoken of is one written by me, *Shelley's Heart*; which had been published some years before, and was now to be republished in a volume of Selections. My brother proposed some verbal changes in it—of which I adopted (if I remember right) all but one. The *Life of Poe*, mentioned at the close of his note, is that written by Mr. Ingram. I had lent the book to my brother.

Wednesday [25 *August* 1880].

DEAR WILLIAM,

Pray include *all* the changes. With them, the Sonnet is quite exceptionally fine;—*without*, pardon my saying that it reads somewhat obscurely as regards construction of nouns and adjectives, and somewhat cumbrously, in spite of the main beauties' being all there. I have made a MS. copy in case needed.

* * * * * *

The *Life of Poe* is most interesting.

* * * * * *

C 148.

This note refers to Philip Bourke Marston, the blind poet, who could not well get on now without some personal attendance. The plan proposed was carried out ; Miss Robinson (Madame Darmesteter) kindly undertaking the small business arrangements involved.

The last paragraph indicates (apparently) some illness affecting W. B. Scott.

Wednesday night [15 *December* 1880].

MY DEAR WILLIAM,

I forgot to mention to you that Scott told me of a plan started (but as yet to be kept rather quiet till a few can combine) to subscribe, by a guinea apiece, a year's 55 guineas for Philip Marston, to enable him to charter a lad for help of all kinds. Scott thought *you* the best man to do the little organizing necessary, and I said I would speak to you. Watts says he will subscribe a guinea yearly—so will Scott—so will I.

To-day I got enclosed from Miss Boyd and Scotus combined. You will regret the tidings, but his pencilled note looks firm.

With love to Lucy,

Your affectionate

D. G. R.

B 107.

Dr. Olivieri was an estimable and cultivated Italian, much afflicted by ill-health and other troubles. I question whether my brother ever met him personally, but he was known, more or less, to other members of the family. He died some years ago.

23 December 1880.

MY DEAREST MOTHER,

This letter is not written with the least idea of troubling you to answer ; and indeed I would not write if I thought that.

*   *   *   *   *   *

Yesterday I had a note from poor Dr. Olivieri, enclosing

a little book of Italian stories for schools, with a dedicatory MS. Sonnet to myself. Poor man! I felt what this must mean at Christmas-time, and responded as best I could. I have no doubt he deserves sympathy. He spoke with much gratitude of your anonymous donation.

I saw Mr. Graham yesterday, who is most affectionate and friendly to me, but alas no longer a picture-buyer. His state of health is melancholy, and curious in a man surrounded by an exceptionally loving and gracious family. *Tædium vitæ* appears to be the main evil.

I saw Waddington's Sonnet-book, with a good many of mine and Christina's in it. I have not a copy, but Watts brought one in. I will subjoin, for your favourable notice, a Sonnet I have done on *Michelangelo's Holy Family* in the National Gallery. In this picture the Virgin is withdrawing from the Child the book which contains the prophecy of his sufferings—I suppose that of Isaiah. The idea is a most beautiful one ; and behind this group are Angels perusing a scroll. Shields was helpful to me in the interpretation of this. I possess another photograph, having the same intention in the actions of the Virgin and Child, by Sandro Botticelli ; but whether the *motif* was a usual one I do not further know.

I have finished the picture of *La Pia*, which now really looks very fine and perfect.

*   *   *   *   *   *

[Here follows the Sonnet "Turn not the Prophet's page" etc.]

B 108.

Monday night [27 December 1880].

MY DEAREST MOTHER,

Thanks most truly for your loving and firmly-written note. It has been a great privation to me to see nothing of you, but I am often unfit to see any one. My bodily health is fair enough.

I fully expected till quite late to spend Christmas alone,

but of course was glad to see William and Lucy, who brightened me up somewhat, though I was not at all brilliant when they arrived.

William has been here again this evening, and is the truest of true brothers.

I was grieved to hear that Aunt Charlotte's visit to London is delayed, though not through ill-health of her own.

With love to dear Christina and to my Aunt, I am

Your loving Son,

D. G. ROSSETTI.

H 5.

Mr. Madox Brown was now staying (though not as yet permanently settled) in Manchester, busily occupied with his pictures for the Townhall there. I don't remember who was the " Bard " sojourning for a while in his house : perhaps some local semi-celebrity. The " old poem " by my brother was, I think, the one entitled *Soothsay.*—" The Michelangelo point " affected the design by this master called *The Archers.*

[? *December* 1880].

MY DEAR LUCY,

It occurs to me to write you a line as to the *White Ship.* I was most happy that it should be sent to your Father, but think it very needful it should not be shown to others. I find the ideas and even phrases of poetry get so soon caught up that a thing shown in MS. is actually liable to charges of plagiarism when it appears, owing to what it has already furnished to others.

I dare say you would of your own accord have avoided showing it ; but I would be obliged if, in writing to your Papa, you would just say a word on the point—though he cannot perhaps avoid showing it at home, where it seems there is now a Bard. I trust he will not, on my account, let it go out of his hands.

Pardon my troubling you on this point. I was very much concerned to hear from William on Monday that you were not free from touches of ill-health or at any rate inconvenience. I trust you did not get any worse by so kindly coming to the rescue of my otherwise solitary Christmas. I enjoyed the evening much, and was much pleased with the favour that old poem found with you and William.

Affectionately yours,

D. GABRIEL R.

On second thoughts I will write a line to your Papa, as I want to speak on the Michelangelo point.

F 13.

MY DEAR CHRISTINA, [*January* 1881.]

Your most welcome note arrived just as I had been seized with a sudden (and unreasonable) panic as to its non-arrival. You know how these things lay hold of one. I am not surprised at the diminished chance of seeing Aunt Charlotte and yourself in this weather. Indeed, I should feel your visit at present as rather a responsibility to my own conscience. But let us hope for something like a thaw.

As you said our dearest Mother was no less than "delighted" with my last Sonnet [*Michelangelo's Holy Family*], I send another just written last night. With me, Sonnets mean Insomnia.

With love to her and all,

Your affectionate

GABRIEL.

The octave is a grim anecdote, but, as you doubtless know, exact.

[Here follows the Sonnet *Cleopatra's Needle in London*.]

B 109.

MY DEAREST MOTHER, *Friday* [1881].

* * * * * *

Nothing could have brought so much pleasure to my solitary room as your entrance. Perhaps a finer day may make it possible yet, or else I do trust to find my way ere long to you. I have sometimes felt myself to be such poor company, when I have come down at long intervals, that this has partly deterred me ; and the discouragements of the year have only increased to its close. I will not despair, however, of improved times ; it would not be the first occasion when something unexpected has brightened matters for me. I am far from meaning to say that worldly fortunes are everything; but I cannot yet afford to give up a house suited to an artist's needs, and so give [up] a chance of improvement by work ; yet it is all beyond present income. Perhaps I ought not to have troubled you by entering on such points, but it seems natural to confide in you.

The picture of *La Pia* looks well, and will not quite yet be leaving me ; so perhaps I may still show it to you—and to Aunt Charlotte also, if coming to town.

*   *   *   *   *   *

Of course, in speaking of bad luck in my own case, I should not forget that the times are bad for all, and that I am no absolute exception.

With love all round,

Your most affectionate
GABRIEL.

C 149.

When this note was written I was about starting for Newcastle and Glasgow, to deliver some lectures : a few days before there had been a formidable " blizzard," still well remembered by Londoners. "The Calf-picture" is the one named *Found*, so often taken up by my brother, yet never quite finished.

Friday [28 *January* 1881].

MY DEAR WILLIAM,

I write a line to say that I will reckon on seeing you next Thursday *week*, as arranged. I hope you will have fair weather for travelling. It has so happened, by a series of accidents, that I have been almost entirely alone lately, and feeling a good deal depressed. However, I am making good way with the Calf-picture.

With love to Lucy,

Your affectionate

GABRIEL.

C 150.

Very shortly before my going off on the lecturing-trip my brother had urged me to try my hand once again at verse-writing; he suggested a series of " Democratic Sonnets," dealing with appropriate events of my own life-time. While on my trip I determined to make the experiment, and produced (with others) a Sonnet on *Garibaldi*—the one he here acknowledges. The *Blessed Damozel* which he had now sold was a second version of the picture previously disposed of to Mr. Graham, but differing considerably from that in detail. It remained on my brother's hands unsold for an unwontedly long time, but had at length been purchased by Mr. Leyland.

Friday [4 *February* 1881].

MY DEAR WILLIAM,

I rejoice to see so fine a sonnet, and shall await the others with great interest. You may be the family bard yet.

I hope to see you on Thursday of next week. You will be glad to hear that I have at last sold *Blessed Damozel* to very fair advantage, and got the tin.

H 6.

Friday [4 *Febru* 1881].

MY DEAR LUCY,

I write a line to say chiefly how pleased I am at the fine sonnet William has sent me on *Garibaldi*. It seems he has already done 5 others ! I hope to see him (and if possible you) Thursday of next week.

You will be glad to hear that I have at last sold the *Blessed Damozel* in a way to ease completely my present position. The *Found* progresses rapidly.

I hope you and the babies are thriving. Love to them from their phantasmal uncle, and to yourself from a less phantasmal brother-in-law.

H 7.

The reference here to the House of Lords arises from the fact that Mr. Madox Brown had been wishful to see some resumption of the scheme of adorning that building with historical pictures, and to undertake some of the work himself. He thought, I believe, more especially of the rooms where Dyce and Maclise had painted. My brother, in Brown's interest, consulted Lord Mount-Temple, who had at an earlier date been Chief Commissioner of Works.

O'Shaughnessy was (I need hardly say) the poet Arthur O'Shaughnessy, well known to my brother. He had married a daughter of Dr. Westland Marston : this lady preceded him to an early grave.

Monday [*7 February* 1881].

MY DEAR LUCY,

*   *   *   •   *   *

Many thanks for copying William's sonnets. They are not so fine as the very fine one on *Garibaldi*, but neither are the subjects equal—except perhaps *Mazzini*, of which I think he will yet make more. These sonnets are pointed and vigorous, but with a certain tendency to the Browningesque in respect of crowded' phraseology. I think he is doing them rather too fast, though I am very pleased to think he means what he is about. I think the finest of those you send is *The Republic.* I do not think the one on Louis Philippe quite fair. I shall be glad of an opportunity of talking them over with him.

I was very sorry to find from Lord Mount-Temple that there is no chance for your father, or indeed for any other painter, in the House of Lords. He seems, however, to be working on strenuously and happily as ever. Manchester must surely revive, and then I count his luck sure.

With warm return of love (sincere, believe me, though vague it be), I am ever

Your affectionate

D. GABRIEL R.

As perhaps you have not heard about O'Shaughnessy, I may tell you. A fortnight back from to-day he went to the Princess's Theatre, and returned to Bayswater on top of an omnibus. Next day he felt a chill, but went to the Museum. After that he stayed in, saw a doctor who made little of it, made little of it himself; but eventually stayed in bed, and had friends to read to him. On the Saturday evening some friend proposed fetching Dr. Marston, but he said there could be no necessity. At 7, on Sunday morning before last, he died. It seems to have been congestion of the lungs affecting the heart. I heard the particulars from Philip Marston, who spent one evening here : they are certainly most melancholy. It seems his Mother has now only £30 a year, and will try to make things fit by living with a sister.

B 110.

The present " *Beatrice* picture" is the one called *The Salutation of Beatrice*. Though not finished, it was very advanced at the date of my brother's death.

Wednesday [3 *March* 1881].

MY DEAREST MOTHER,

I write a line chiefly because I have been so long without writing. I have, however, the news that I have sold a couple of chalk-drawings, amounting to 200 guineas. So things are improving a little. . . . I have not got on much with painting lately, but have the *Beatrice* picture and the *Found* in a very forward state.

I have written at last the long ballad about Catherine Douglas and the murder of James the First of Scotland. Some day you must see it. It is really a success—nearly three times as long as *The White Ship*.

* * * * * *

C 151.

My " Sonnet on the Transvaal" was an expression of disgust at the English annexation of that Dutch territory, and at the military expedition then endeavouring, under orders from the Beaconsfield ministry, to confirm the annexation by force. The righteous and magnanimous policy of the succeeding Gladstone Government in putting a stop to the war made the Sonnet out of date. The latter portion of my brother's letter will be perceived to relate to his poem of *The King's Tragedy*. Professor Nichol of Glasgow had lately been my kind host for a few days in the Scottish city.

Wednesday [9 *March* 1881].

MY DEAR WILLIAM,

I was very glad to hear that you were progressing all right, of which Lucy kindly wrote me full though duly severe particulars. It would of course give me great pleasure if I could see you both on Monday, and even the more if Brown could accompany you. But of course I view it as still rather doubtful whether you could come out so soon.

I think your Sonnet on the Transvaal forcible, fine, and most appropriate. The last line alone—"Butcher of hundreds of intrepid men"—seems rather flat, partly owing to the two *ofs*. But I think an adjective to *butcher* such as *self-constituted* or something equivalent or appropriate, and the omission of *hundreds of*, would much improve the line.

Would you do me a favour by writing to Professor Nichol, and asking him what sufficient authority exists for Gilfillan's statement as follows :—"It [Catherine Douglas's arm] is broken in a moment, and she sinks back, to bear, with her descendants—a family well known in Scotland—the name of Barlass ever since." I can find nothing about Barlass elsewhere; and, as the leading Scottish historians must be accessible to Prof. Nichol, perhaps he would kindly look up the point. J. Hill Burton (the latest) has nothing, and is very superficial altogether on the subject of James I.

I should like also to know, if Mr. Nichol happens to know (but it is not at all an essential point), what was the site of the Charterhouse of Perth.

H 8.

My brother good-naturedly copied out his historical ballad of *The White Ship*, and sent it to my wife—with some inscription, I think, to our children; the eldest then aged five, and the second four. Hence the allusion to "the babes and the ballad."

MY DEAR LUCY, *Wednesday [? March 1881].*

I need hardly say that it will give me great pleasure to see you here in William's company on Monday.

Your account of the babes and the ballad gives me an insight into their young sympathies which is very welcome. No criticism could have pleased me better.

Your affectionate Brother,

D. GABRIEL R.

H 9.

MY DEAR LUCY, *Sunday [? March 1881].*

I was much concerned to hear from William that he had been and still was so seriously laid up. Would he or you let me know how he progresses? . . . I should think sore throat must have resulted in two sonnets instead of one daily on William's part. I hope the ailment does not make his political poetics quite inexorable.

I finished the ballad a day or two after I saw you, and Watts thinks it my best performance. It is more than twice-and-a-half as long as the *White Ship*.

Your affectionate

D. G. ROSSETTI.

I am afraid the bogy-parts of the new ballad would be too much for your babes, to say nothing of the murder.

H 10.

From this letter, and from some which follow, it will be perceived that I had continued writing my *Democratic Sonnets*, and that my brother considered some of them neither proper nor prudent. I might have missed out these letters altogether from my collection, but prefer to insert them, along with a few words of explanation on my own part. He particularly instances a Sonnet named *Tyrannicide*, and another named *Fenians*. I think he plumped, with kind fraternal nervousness, upon a supposition of what the Sonnets might possibly say, without deliberately attending to what they *do* say. I will be aboveboard with my readers, and insert the Sonnets here ; and I ask any reader to decide two plain questions. Does the Sonnet on *Tyrannicide* say any more than this ? That, whatever may be the theoretical opinion entertained about the act (and it is mere matter of fact that, in all ages and countries, some people have justified it), we are not to pity the actual or attempted tyrant-slayer when he gets put to death, inasmuch as he voluntarily incurred a doom which is and ought to be a capital sentence ? And does not the Sonnet on *Fenians* say that Fenians act with blameable frenzy, consequent though that frenzy is upon a sense of wrongs to their country, which really have been wrongs, and demand redress ?

TYRANNICIDE.

We cannot argue of Tyrannicide.
    An instinct in the world avows it just;
    The laws abhor it, and they will and must.
Pity him not, the man by whom have died
Innocent lives, slain by his act who tried
    And failed to reach the tyrant: if his bust
    Be ranged with Scævola's, his head, august
Or truculent, must pay the debt, and slide
Red to the pannier as the hatchet falls.
    He asks no pity; he who aimed that blow
    Struck hands with Death, and made of Death his scoff.
Pity still less those few—like lurid balls
    Of fire which pierce dim ravening gulfs of woe—
    A Brutus, Chærea, Corday, Elnikoff.

FENIANS.

An Irish patriot we have called a felon:
    No matter; there were always things and names.
    Let's dub a thimblerig the king of games;
Melon termed pumpkin still will taste of melon.
An Irish felon-patriot is a man
    Who loves his country splotched with alien shames,
    And dares a halter. And, if history blames
His frenzy, let us try the manlier plan

To win him back. With kindness? Hardly that—
  Bare justice; for Oppression's dastard heel
    Stamped Ireland's brow, and made our name accurst.
  Murder and confiscation set their seal
Of agelong outrage on her. Bell the cat;
    Strain not the intolerant sinews till they burst.

My wife was not dismayed by my brother's most kindly-intended and in part very sensible letter; neither was I; and for some while ensuing I continued with diligence writing my *Democratic Sonnets.* Eventually I left them off, prompted by two feelings. First and foremost, I have never supposed myself to be authentically a poet. Second, I had contemplated a series of a hundred Sonnets, and less than this would not have made a volume of any tolerable size; but among my hundred subjects I found in practice that several did not inspire me at all, and the result was that, amid some Sonnets more or less admissible, came others which I acknowledged to myself as bad. I have no ambition to swell the densely crowded ranks of the well-meaning in verse who are also the mediocre.

For a moment I will recur to the first of the two Sonnets quoted. It refers, and is intended to refer, only to *Tyrannicide,* and has no bearing upon any such political assassination as that of President Carnot—who was not in any sense a tyrant, but a State-magistrate, lawfully appointed and acting lawfully.

12 April 1881.

MY DEAR LUCY,

I hope you will not think my step a mistaken one when I choose this moment to write you a letter on what I cannot but consider a very serious subject.

Several of William's truest friends, no less than myself, are greatly alarmed at the tone taken in some of his Sonnets respecting "Tyrannicide," Fenianism, and other incendiary subjects. It seems to me and to others that the consequences are absolutely and very perilously uncertain when an official (as William is) of a monarchical government allows himself such unbridled license of public speech. The prosecution against the Editor of the *Freiheit* seems very ominous to us, and perfectly just. The least evil I should apprehend, were

William to persist in including these subjects, would be the certainty of his never attaining the final step of the Secretary-ship in his office which he so well deserves. But very much worse consequences than this seem to all of us but too likely ; and my object in writing this letter is to awaken your mind to the clear possibility of absolute ruin, in such a case, for my dear brother, and his family whom he loves so well. The very title, *Democratic Sonnets*, seems to me most objectionable when coming from one who depends on the Government for his bread. It may be objected that I myself suggested his writing this series. So I did ; but I thought only of the *events of his time*, and my mind was not sufficiently aroused to the purposes he would make such a theme subserve.

It is extremely painful to me to trouble you on this subject, while in your present delicate state ; but I really can keep silence no longer, the series being so far advanced ; also I do not venture to speak to William direct, lest his first impulse should be to resent it as an encroachment, and so frustrate all attempt to avert what I and others view as a great danger.

I shall await with the greatest anxiety the result of the step I am now taking—remaining, my dear Lucy,

Affectionately yours,
D. G. ROSSETTI.

C 152.

12 *April* 1881.

MY DEAR WILLIAM,

It is with the utmost humility, and only at the absolute call of brotherly love, that I have ventured to write a letter to Lucy, which she will doubtless show you, on an affair of your own which I have thought much on without speaking to you in any positive way, but with which I believe the gravest consequences may be involved. I have done so from no presumption, but because, in view of your welfare, I felt more and more that I could do no otherwise. That you may consider it seriously, and that it may cause no kind of division between us, are my two fervent hopes.

Your affectionate Brother,

D. G. ROSSETTI.

B III.

Tuesday [12 *April* 1881].

MY DEAREST MOTHER,

* * * * * *

I have enjoyed nothing so much for years as your and Christina's short stay here, and hope it may be renewed ere long.

I have taken, with great anxiety, the step of writing to Lucy this evening on the subject of William's Sonnets. I have written to him also a short propitiatory note.

You will be glad to hear that Leyland, who starts this evening for Venice, came in last night, and bought the *Beatrice* I am painting, for a good price—an event which quite sets me on my legs for some time to come. I can now wait for what may turn up further, without the least anxiety. He has paid me a good sum on account before starting.

C 153.

14 *April* 1881.

MY DEAR WILLIAM,

Thanks for so cordial and brotherly an answer to what I hoped you would admit as a brotherly appeal. Will you pardon my adding that I addressed the fuller remonstrance to Lucy, in spite of seeing objections to such a course, just because I foresaw the difficulty of awaking you to a sense of any grave danger, not to yourself only, but to those you love?

I cannot say that I see force in your arguments. The country—true—is democratic in great measure, as well as monarchical; but one of the democratic allies you cite—the chief one and Prime Minister—is now under a threat of murder from the very class whom some of your sonnets uphold.

I cannot discern that your present course, in making a personal, forcible, and extreme profession of democracy in our own time, even to assassination, has any affinity to casual references to Charles the First, or other similar questions, occurring in books the object of which was quite other than their utterance.

One of the friends I referred to is himself as strong a democrat as you are, except as regards the murder-point; and he sees the danger you are rushing on to be great.

No doubt no one thought it worth while to tackle such slight matters as the allusions in your former writings; but I have the strongest foreboding that it is very possible (though of course not certain) that your expressing prominently these extreme views may lead to your being deprived of the means for providing for your family. Members of Parliament may speak as they please; but, even if their constituencies should unseat them, their families have still the same dinner and the same education. I fully honour your indifference to personal risk of discomfort or aggression, but should be surprised if you were indifferent to this question also. You can exert no such influence by the expression of political views as would in the least balance such a catastrophe.

I have said my say, which I felt to be my duty. I have no intention to "nag" on the subject when we meet again, but shall be glad to discuss it in any way which you may think fit to lead up to, and should wish decidedly to hear the further portions of the series. By the bye, the fine sonnet on Orsini I consider admissible in any case, and this might suffice in my opinion to represent the whole question by its highest example. Of course, much as I should prize the dedication to me of a work of yours, I think now that I will ask you for some other than this one.

B 112.

"William's family has signalized itself." This refers to a birth of twins on 22 April; Mary, who continues to brighten my small household, and Michael, who died in January 1883.

MY DEAREST MOTHER,   *26 April* [1881].

I must not and do not forget the dear date of to-morrow. Near upon it William's family has signalized itself —I hope, hopefully. My effort was made as strongly as I could put it regarding the projected book ; but I can trace no results either in his mind or his wife's. He answered me. I feel, however, more at ease on the point ; and do think that Lucy must, in spite of appearances, be sufficiently aroused to prevent William from running any real risk.

   *   *   *   *   *   *

I am sending to Liverpool, by request of the Town Council, a photograph of the large picture—which (though not satis-factory, as photographs seldom are) gives, to my judgment, an impression of a good picture. I have told them that I *could* re-touch an impression so as to give a complete idea of the work ; but that, as this would take time and trouble, I should need to understand that the Chairman thought the prospect of sale very promising before I did so. I like the Chairman, who came here, and am sure that he and others are well-disposed.

I am getting on with my volume in press, which must soon be ready.

With truest love,

Your affectionate
GABRIEL.

C 154.

"The Ricciardi draft" was a letter in Italian which I had written for my brother's use, to answer a request on a literary subject made to him by our old family-friend Conte Giuseppe Ricciardi : my brother fancying (for it was perhaps only a fancy) that he would be more rusty than myself in the use of the Italian language Miss Asher was at this time his housekeeper at Cheyne Walk.

Tuesday [17 *May* 1881].

MY DEAR WILLIAM,

Many thanks for the Ricciardi draft, which I am about copying.

Some weeks ago I got your consent to look through the proofs of my book. I hope it would not be more onerous now than then ; but Watts thinks I ought on no account to neglect your kind offer, as he says you are sure to find something amiss. Accordingly I shall send Miss Asher to your office to-morrow with the sheaf of proofs. They are not mostly final proofs, and the points which you will see marked by me have all since been rectified.

Could you in some way mark further emendations as clearly *yours* ? I don't know if you ever use red ink or a red wax-chalk pencil.

Your affectionate
D. G. R.

No doubt you would· show the proofs to no one but Lucy at present.

C 155.

This note refers to the proofs of my brother's volume *Ballads and Sonnets*, then passing through the press.

Wednesday [18 *May* 1881].

MY DEAR WILLIAM,

Many thanks. I should not dream of being *impatient* ; but, if I find it impossible for you to get it done in a short time, I must find out whether the book can wait. My own *impression* is that there are *no* errors left. You have found none, though I think the smoothing of that "crouch close" etc. advantageous, if not too late for press. . . . "Wading moon" I think a just and fine expression.

I am writing to Ellis to ask how the book stands as to publication.

C 156.

The references here apply (as perhaps the reader will perceive without my assistance) to the poem of *The King's Tragedy.*

MY DEAR WILLIAM,   [20 *May* 1881.]

I read all your notes with interest, and some with advantage. Thanks. As to the lion, it is the blazon of Scotland, and C[atherine] D[ouglas] must have had a clear idea of it. . . . As to "stamp," it merely means putting the foot down hard, which a lion might well do. However, I shall use "ramp," as you suggest, because it clears away alliteration.

    *   *   *   *   *   *

Yours,

D. G. R.

Love to Lucy.

As to *Christmas*, the Chronicle states distinctly that the King went to hold a solemn ·feast in Perth *at* that season, and that he afterwards stayed on for rejoicing till the date of the murder. The word *Carnival* is not used, nor do I know whether it was then in use. All is indicated in the poem as in the Chronicle.

    *   *   *   *   *   *

B 113.

"Christina's book," which Mr. Hall Caine was about to review in *The Academy*, is the one entitled *A Pageant and Other Poems.* About the "Italian journal" I cannot now speak definitely. I understand it to have contained an article on Gabriel and Christina; and Gabriel raises a comparison between this article and the translations made by the courteous and accomplished Italian, Signor Gamberale. His volume is named *Poeti Inglesi e Tedeschi* (1881), and contains translations from both Gabriel and Christina. Perhaps the prose article also was Gamberale's own.

MY DEAREST MOTHER,   3 *August* 1881.

What a good dear loving and full letter you have written to me! Till I opened it I took the outside for

Christina's writing, so firm it is, nor is the inside much less so.   It shames this caligraphy of mine, which is but so-so.

*   *   *   *   *   *

Dunn has been away since New Year's Day, and I am now parting with him altogether. . . . You may have heard of a young man named Hall Caine, who has shown himself very well disposed towards me.   I am going to try the experiment of having him to live in the house, and so shall have more society. . . . Caine has tastes similar to my own, and is a reading man.   He follows literature.   He is likely to be coming here by next Saturday.   He is going to do Christina's book for *The Academy*.

Thanks for return of the Italian journal.   I think that article decidedly superior to anything in Gamberale's volume. Italian poetry suffers so much, in comparison with English, from amplification.   In his *Gentì* (short, I presume, for Gentile) there are nearly 200 lines more than in my *Jenny*. I gave him my views as to how much this lessened emphasis. But I think Christina's things better done.

*   *   *   *   *   *

C 157.

If the following letter is read by any person expert in Shelleian matters, he will understand the allusion to Hogg and "the *Werther* MS. ": it would perhaps be superfluous for me to enter into it here.

Mr. Brown's "big house" was No. 37 Fitzroy Square, London : his removal to Manchester had made it requisite for him to dispose of the outstanding lease of the London house.

"The Liverpool purchase"—*i.e.*, the proposed purchase of my brother's large picture of *Dante's Dream* for the Walker Art Gallery in Liverpool—did not "collapse"; it soon afterwards became an accomplished fact.

Wednesday [3 *August* 1881].

MY DEAR WILLIAM,

I never answered your note, but shall be very glad to see you again on the 15th.

I read Hogg's *Shelley* with great enjoyment, but could

nowhere find any hint to lead up to your statement as to the *Werther* MS. Who is it that has brought such facts forward as you mentioned ? They would very likely have been made [known] to the family, and caused the withdrawal of material. I can see nothing of the kind in your *Life of Shelley*.

I hope you have all thriven, and are thriving—Lucy foremost. My love to her. I am very glad to hear that Brown is so likely to get his big house off his hands.

You will be sorry to learn that the Liverpool purchase has collapsed. Their views and mine did not finally agree. However, things look likely enough in other quarters, and I will not repine.

Your affectionate

D. G. R.

P.S.—One Gamberale, who translated my *Last Confession* poem, has made a book of translations containing some of Christina's and mine, and sent a copy for each of the family— one for you which I have. He yearns to possess your *Lives of Poets* and *Mrs. Holmes Grey*. Where he heard of the latter I can't guess.

F 14.

The passage here about "Commonplace Cook" may need a word of explanation. Signor Luigi Gamberale had (as shown in the last preceding letter) sent my brother his volume of Italian translations, including a reference to Christina, who was stated to be author of (*inter alia*) a volume named *Commonplace Cook*. The real name of that volume is *Commonplace, and Other Stories*.—Many of my brother's letters refer to projects of getting some house as a sub- stitute for the one in Cheyne Walk; towards 1881 he thought all the more about this, as the great majority of his large garden was taken away from him for building purposes; the so-called "Rossetti Mansions" now occupy its site. The picture with mag- nolias was never finished by Rossetti. It was a *Lady of Pity*, or *Donna della Finestra* (*Vita Nuova*). Mr. Madox Brown ultimately completed it, and it was sold by Messrs. Foster in July 1894, as

forming part of my wife's estate ; for I had presented to her all
the unfinished works by my brother which remained in my hands
after his death.

Saturday [6 *August* 1881].

MY DEAR CHRISTINA,

Thanks for your sisterly missives. It makes life less
bleak as it advances to find the old care and love still prompt
to hand. I do hope we may be able to arrange another stay
here like the one last April which gave me so much pleasure.
You will not, I am sure, think that it implies indifference
when I say that I have put off to a less harassed moment the
full acquaintance with your *Pageant* volume. The *Pageant*
itself seems to me full of beauties, and well adapted to be
taken up by children for private acting—a paying qualifica-
tion. . . . Watts is sure to do you justice. I have finally
resolved on dedicating my book to him, as I found (quite
unexpectedly) that he had done me the honour to set his
heart rather on my doing so.

   *   *   *   *   *   *

What Gamberale could mean by " Commonplace Cook "
was a puzzle indeed. The mind revolving round it, I judged
it possible that some professed English adept, seeing the title
put correctly in his MS., may have told him that it ought
evidently to read *Commonplace book*, this being a current
English phrase, and he evidently not possessing the volume.
The *c* for *b* might be his error or the printer's. But this is
all mere mental drama. . . . He has now corrected (on my
showing) many errors in *Last Confession*, but there are
many in *Jenny* which I may or may not be at pains to point
out.

I think the little house you mention seems very attractive ;
and the rent just suits me, as well as the date you name, for
I don't expect in any case to get away earlier.

Caine is at this moment in Liverpool, but will be here in a
day or two, if not sooner. The Liverpool Committee are still
yearning after the picture, but I cannot feel sure to what
extent certainty of purchase is intended, and till that is

quite ensured the picture budges not. I am painting into a new picture some beautiful magnolias sent by Lady Mount-Temple.

Sir Noel Paton (always a generous friend to my work) was here lately and most enthusiastic about the large picture. He and Lady P[aton] with one of their sons had a few months ago a most narrow escape from drowning. They had gone in a small sailing-boat to a Highland loch to visit the grave of a lost child on the further shore. In returning, the boat was upset, and they all had to swim a long distance (with sadly failing strength) before, with the greatest difficulty, they struggled to the beach, and instantly all fainted away, being so found and conveyed to a fisherman's cottage.

With dearest love to our Mother and affection all round, I am

Your loving Brother,
GABRIEL.

B 114.

Sunday [4 September 1881].

MY DEAREST MOTHER,

You will be glad to know that the purchase at Liverpool is after all complete. The picture was bought by the Town Council yesterday for 1,500 guineas, on the private-view day of their Exhibition. This I knew (between ourselves) would happen, or I should not have sent it. But they have no power to buy except *from* the Exhibition, so I was necessitated to send it first. This will also cause my not getting paid till the receipts of the Exhibition are realized in November, but then the money will come. The picture hangs "starred" in the gallery as sold. I know you rejoice in my welfare, so hasten to tell you of this stroke of good luck.

*   *   *   *   *   *

I wish C[hristina] would write me a line in answer to this (*not* taxing yourself), and say how she liked Caine's little

VOL. II.   25

notice in *The Academy.* I thought it good and feeling. I find him good company. He is now gone to Liverpool for a day or two (returning to-morrow afternoon), which he did to see that there was no hitch at the gallery.

*   *   *   *   *   *

I think her *Pageant* most lovely, as does Watts also, and we are both deeply impressed by the beauty of the *Monna Innominata* series. I think the *Ballad of Boding* grimmish on the whole; and *Behold, a Shaking,* may chance to keep youngsters awake. She had a poem in her first volume very like the *Boding,* but simpler.

F 15.

Wednesday [7 September 1881].

MY DEAR CHRISTINA,

*   *   *   *   *   *

The poem I meant *is Sleep at Sea;* and I must say the essential *motif* seems to me one with that of the *Ballad of Boding,* though of course each has its varied beauties.

*   *   *   *   *   *

You may like to hear that Swinburne's delight with the *Pageant* amounted to . . . ecstasy.

*   *   *   *   *   *

B 115.

Thursday [15 September 1881].

MY DEAREST MOTHER,

*   *   *   *   *   *

I wish you would read in my book the three Sonnets called *True Woman,* as I am sure you would like these. They are written quite lately.

The sight of you yesterday was very dear to me, and I will not hide from you how painfully conscious I am of the many neglected opportunities of seeing you. But I have lately been much more than usually out of sorts, and will hope, if

I return from the country somewhat improved, to see you more frequently, and also to get you and Christina to stay here again. I will write to you as soon as I am settled.

C 158.

The only interest of this scrap is to mark the date when my brother left London for a holiday in the Vale of St. John, near Keswick, Cumberland. He soon fell ill there—more, I think, through misuse of chloral than any other cause—and was never quite himself again afterwards.

[16 CHEYNE WALK.]
Sunday [18 *September* 1881].

MY DEAR WILLIAM,

I need not be troubling you for a visit to-morrow (Monday), as I am likely to be off to the country. I will write when there.

With love to Lucy,

Your affectionate

D. G. R.

B 116.

FISHER PLACE, FISHER GHYLL,
VALE OF ST. JOHN, NEAR KESWICK.
[22 *September* 1881.]

MY DEAREST MOTHER,

We reached here very comfortably yesterday morning, and are housed in the most comfortable quarters possible. The house, which is an infinitely better one than that at Herne Bay, only costs the same rent—£2 10*s.* It is so clean as to seem as if no one had ever inhabited it before, and the beds and attendance are most excellent. The fare also is unexceptionable. I am already beginning to feel the benefit of country walks, though as yet under rain. This, however, does not keep me in.

The scenery is grand in the extreme—mountains rising on all hands—though the rain has as yet prevented my entering on any explorations. I have said several times to Caine how much you would enjoy this place.   The quiet is more absolute than I have ever met with elsewhere.

The Ghyll (a waterfall) at the back of our house falls within sight between 500 and 600 feet, though several thousand feet in reality.   The rains now will soon swell it, though it was but a thread when we arrived.

Christina will be interested to hear that, as I was leaning over a bridge to-day, an old snail came up out of his shell and submitted to be stroked, after which he retired.

I cannot do better for your maternal delectation than enclose a letter from a friend who quotes one from my generous old friend Sir Noel Paton, relating to my Liverpool picture.   When writing, he did not know my reason for sending it thither—viz. : the purchase.

With love to all,

Your most affectionate
GABRIEL.

C 159.

[VALE OF ST. JOHN, KESWICK.]
Thursday [22 *September* 1881].

MY DEAR WILLIAM,

I find I have left behind a book which Caine much needs for his index of sonnet-forms,—viz., *Rime di Fra Guittone d'Arezzo* in two paper-bound octavo vols.   I fancy it is on the shelf near the sofa in studio, or on the sofa itself, or in some promiscuous position.   It seems really too bad to bore you, but there is no one else at all I can ask.   Could you go down as soon as at all convenient, and forward the vols. ?   Address

Fisher Place
Fisher Ghyll
Vale of St. John
Near Keswick.

Landscape-letters are things to me impossible ; but I

dare say you know this country, which is very beautiful and an absolute solitude.

With love to Lucy,

Your affectionate

GABRIEL.

You would add greatly to the obligation if you could send *Cino da Pistoia*—Ciampi's edition. The book is I believe among a sadly dismembered set which are discoverable in the cupboard *on the floor*, underneath the china-closet in the dining-room which was once the receptacle of your books.

B 117.

FISHER PLACE, VALE OF ST. JOHN, KESWICK.

[*29 September 1881.*]

MY DEAREST MOTHER,

I write a line merely to say how I am getting on. I cannot say that at present I feel very well, but I hope for improvement. The surroundings are most beautiful, and the house very comfortable, with obliging people. You will be glad to hear that I am making an effort to reduce the drug.

One day (but perhaps I told you this before) I climbed the Great Hough, which is a mountain 1,200 feet high. I am painting a little picture here—a replica of my *Proserpine* —which is one of those I have to do for Mr. Valpy in exchange for his return of the large picture. Certainly I have the best of that bargain, but he pleased himself.

It seems my book is out, or at any rate in the hands of the reviewers. I trust Watts's article may be out next Saturday.

Caine is making a most interesting Sonnet-book, which I am sure will afford you much pleasant reading. I was so glad you liked those three Sonnets, and should rejoice to hear of anything else that has pleased you.

With love to all,

Your affectionate

GABRIEL.

B 118.

FISHER PLACE, VALE OF ST. JOHN, KESWICK.
[10 *October* 1881.]

MY DEAREST MOTHER,

I wish this letter could be a longer one, but I am not very well, and there is no news of any kind except that my book is out. There is a fine critique by Watts in *Athenæum*. All you said gave me great pleasure, and your letter was absolutely firm throughout—the best I have long seen.

I have sought for loneliness, but here the solitude and silence are absolute—a magic spell. Still, Caine is good company, and I expect Watts for a few days; but I think I shall return at end of week, as I cannot perceive that I am benefiting as I ought to do.

I have done a little work here in carrying on a replica I brought from London. I have very gratifying accounts on all sides of the Liverpool matter. I regret to say I have climbed no more hills, but contented myself with level walking.

Caine is excessively attentive and friendly, and is really quite an abnegator of self. He went the other day and delivered a lecture at Liverpool (on Richardson) with immense success. It is one of a series of twelve on English literature.

With love to all,

Your most affectionate
D. GABRIEL R.

C 160.

FISHER PLACE, VALE OF ST. JOHN, KESWICK.
[10 *October* 1881.]

MY DEAR WILLIAM,

I had a few copies of my book sent here, and have exhausted them in necessary quarters, and now at last remember that I have actually not sent one to you and Lucy. I must tell Ellis to send one, and inscribe it when I see you again. I hope all goes well with both. I cannot say my visit here has been a success. I don't think the air agrees with me. I doubt not I shall be returning by the end of the week. I will have a second copy sent you for Brown.

B 119.

16 Cheyne Walk.
10 *November* [1881].

My dearest Mother,

I am sending you a copy of the re-printed *Poems*. Twelve hundred of the *Ballads and Sonnets* are already sold—this is a great success. The picture at Liverpool seems to be equally successful.

I will not write much, as I am not well—though my writing will show you that I am somewhat improved. I hear of you favourably from William.

B 120.

Tuesday [31 *January* 1882].

My dearest Mother,

I send you . . . two books. One of them is Caine's Sonnet-volume. I will inscribe it some time that I am with you, but it seemed a pity to undo it.

There is a not very civil article on me in *Macmillan;* also one on me and Christina in *Atlantic Monthly*—C[hristina] pronounced the *original* bard.

Your loving
Gabriel.

I may probably be going to the neighbourhood of Margate, where a friend offers to lend me a commodious house. It has really struck me whether you and C[hristina] could come, as there is lots of room. Think about it, but no need to write.

F 16.

[16 CHEYNE WALK.
Friday 3 *February* 1882.]

MY DEAR CHRISTINA,

Thanks for your letter received to-day. The previous one contained a sore disappointment for me; as I had really hoped that Mamma and you would go with us to Birchington. As it is, we go to-morrow. Caine's little sister has joined us, and is a very nice attractive little girl.

I cannot form any decided idea of how long I shall stay at the seaside. It will much depend on whether I can get to work to even moderate advantage.

With love to our Mother,

Your affectionate

GABRIEL.

F 17.

The "French notice" here spoken of was an article written by Mr. Joseph Knight upon my brother's *Ballads and Sonnets*, and published in *Le Livre*. The long letter named directly afterwards came from M. Ernest Chesneau; who, in preparation for his valuable book *La Peinture Anglaise*, was seeking from my brother, and also from Mr. Madox Brown, numerous details of information regarding their works and the Præraphaelite movement in general.

WEST CLIFF BUNGALOW, BIRCHINGTON-ON-SEA.
[*February* 1882.]

MY DEAR CHRISTINA,

I wish I could report any change as to my health and strength. Need I say that at *any* moment Mamma and you will be more than welcome? The weather here is fine and quite free from fog, but cold.

There is a large garden belonging to the house, which is in all respects commodious. The journey by 3-15 train is very easy—2 hours to Westgate, and a quarter of an hour by chaise to come on here.

Thanks for the French notice, which is a good one enough.
I will send it back soon.   At same time I got a long French
letter, which I enclose in case Mamma might care to read it.
I don't much see my way to do as asked.

With best love to both,

Your Brother,
GABRIEL.

I cannot myself doubt that Mamma would benefit here.
Caine could meet you.

C 161.

Here follows the last letter which my brother ever wrote me.
"The desired sketch" was to have been a sketch of our Father,
giving his characteristic daily aspect : it was wanted with a view to
the monument to him commissioned by the authorities of Vasto,
and the request had been conveyed to me by our cousin Teodorico
Pietrocola-Rossetti, and by me to my brother.   Although Gabriel
did not feel equal to undertaking this work in a definite way, he did
after a while make two or three slight sketches, which I found at
Birchington after his death : mournful and precious reminiscences,
though too unimportant to be of practical service.   "The portrait"
to which his P.S. refers is the oil-painting that he finished (as
heretofore noticed) in 1848—a life-sized head-and-shoulders likeness
of our Father.   "The photos" are photographs taken several years
ago from that same portrait.

"The Stillman report" was a newspaper report—happily baseless
—of the assassination of our friend Mr. Stillman in Turkish territory.

[BIRCHINGTON.
17 February 1882.]

DEAR WILLIAM,

I am sorry to say that in my state I could not make
the desired sketch.   This is a real grief to me, and I wish
you would explain that it is impossible.   I cannot be writing
myself.   My state is lately decidedly worse.

I hear now that our Mother and Sister will not be able to

come. I was obliged to put them off once, owing in reality to my bad state.

I heard of the Stillman report and its contradiction.

Your affectionate

D. G. R.

The portrait could be sent—the photos are bad ; only it might be as well not to *lose* the portrait.

F 18.

[BIRCHINGTON-ON-SEA.]
Monday [20 *February* 1882].

MY DEAR CHRISTINA,

It is fearfully cold to-day here, and I don't know what to say as to possible visits.. Sometimes we have most brilliant weather, but frequent storms of wind and rain.

I am sending you a *Saturday Review*, which please return. The rather ill-natured notice of Caine's book contains a rather good-natured word on yourself. I think there is every reason to suppose the article written by Mr. ——, whose own Sonnet strikes him as particularly good. He will find himself exceptionally so stricken.

  ❋   ❋   ❋   ❋   ❋   ❋

F 19.

The phrase "I have done a little painting" relates to the duplicates, both for Mr. Valpy, of the *Proserpine* and of *Joan of Arc.*

[WEST CLIFF BUNGALOW, BIRCHINGTON-ON-SEA.
received 27 *February* 1882.]

MY DEAR CHRISTINA,

There is a general impression here that the weather is fine enough for Mamma to venture down if she likes. I do not press it, but leave it entirely to her judgment. When I expected her before, I sent for a chair which is the twin of the one she sits in at home, and which is here still.

I have no particular news. I tried galvanism, but just at that time my arm seemed to get worse, so I gave it up again.

I have done a little painting, but, for want of sufficient to work on, have been reduced to reading Miss Braddon—who, however, has risen in my estimation.

There are two articles on Caine's book to-day in *Athenæum* and *Academy*, by Watts and Dowden. Both mention you— the latter very flatteringly.

F 20.

[WEST CLIFF BUNGALOW, BIRCHINGTON-ON-SEA.
Tuesday 28 *February* 1882.]

MY DEAR CHRISTINA,

I will fully expect both of you on Thursday. No doubt you got telegram.

My state is faint and feeble to a degree ; full of pains, and unable to walk to any purpose. But, as you must find this out some time, why not now ?

The weather here might be called, I suppose, fairly mild at ordinary times ; though since I wrote we had an intolerable noise of wind day and night. It is quieter now.

Your affectionate

D. G. R.

INDEX.

397

LETTERS FROM—

LaVergne, TN USA
23 February 2010
173901LV00003BA/21/A